Abortion Bibliography for 1984

Abortion Bibliography

for 1984

Compiled by
Polly T. Goode

The Whitston Publishing Company
Troy, New York
1986

TABLE OF CONTENTS

PREFACE

Abortion Bibliography for 1984 is the fifteenth annual list of books and articles surrounding the subject of abortion in the preceding year. It appears serially each fall as a contribution toward documenting in one place as comprehensively as possible the literature of one of our central social issues. It is an attempt at a comprehensive world bibliography.

Searches in compiling this material have covered the following sources: *Abstracts on Criminology & Penology; Abstracts on Police Science; Access; Air University Library Index to Military Periodicals; America: History and Life; American Humanities Index; American Reference Books Annual; Applied Science & Technology Index; Bibliographic Index; Biological Abstracts; Biological & Agricultural Index; British Humanities Index; Business Periodicals Index; Canadian Education Index; Canadian Periodicals Index; Catholic Periodical & Literature Index; Communication Abstracts; College Student Personnel Abstracts; Criminal Justice Abstracts; Criminal Justice Periodical Index; Cumulated Index Medicus; Cumulative Book Index; Cumulative Index to Nursing and Allied Health Literature; Current Index to Journals in Education; Dissertation Abstracts International: A. Humanities and Social Sciences. Dissertation Abstracts International: B. The Sciences and Engineering; Education Index; Environment Abstracts; Environment Index; Essay & General Literature Index; General Science Index; Hospital Literature Index; Human Resources Abstracts; Humanities Index; Index to Jewish Periodicals; Index to Legal Periodicals; International Nursing Index; Media Review Digest; Music Index; PAIS; PAIS Foreign Language Index; Philosopher's Index; Popular Periodical Index; Psychological Abstracts; Readers Guide to Periodical Literature; Religion Index One: Periodicals (from: Index to Religious Periodical Literature); Religious and Theological Abstracts; Sage Family Studies Abstracts; Sage Urban Studies Abstracts; Social Sciences Index; Social Work Research & Abstracts; Sociological Abstracts; Studies on Women's Abstracts; and Women's Studies Abstracts.*

The Bibliography is divided into two sections: a title section in alphabetical order; and a subject section. Thus, if the researcher does not wish to observe the subject heads of the compiler, he can use the title section exclusively. The subject heads have been issued from the nature of the material indexed rather than being imposed from Library of Congress subject heads or other standard lists.

The Subject Head Index includes page numbers.

Polly T. Goode
Troy, New York

LIST OF JOURNALS CITED

AFER: African Ecclesial Review
AJR: American Journal of Roentgenology
AMB: Revista da Associacao Medica Brasileira
AUAA J: Journal of the American Urological Association Allied
Acta Anthropogenetica
Acta Cardiologica
Acta Clinica Belgica
Acta Endocrinologica
Acta Europaea Fertilitatis
Acta Geneticae Medicae et Gemellologiae: Twin Research
Acta Medica Jugoslavica
Acta Obstetricia et Gynecologica Scandinavica
Acta Physiologica et Pharmacologica Bulgarica
Acta Psychiatrica Scandinavica
Actas Luso-Espanolas de Neurologia y Psiquiatria
Actas Urologicas Espanolas
Adolescence
Advertising Age
Africa
African Journal of Medicine and Medical Sciences
Against the Current
Agenda
Akron Law Review
Akademiya Nauk Gruzinskoi S. S. R. Soobshcheniya
Akusherstvo i Ginekologiia
Alberta Report
Alcoholism
Alternative Lifestyles
America
American Baptist Quarterly
American Bar Association Journal
American Demographics
American Ethnologist
American Family Physician

American Heart Journal
American Journal of Diseases of Children
American Journal of Epidemiology
American Journal of Gastroenterology
American Journal of Human Genetics
American Journal of Medical Genetics
American Journal of Nursing
American Journal of Obstetrics and Gynecology
American Journal of Orthopsychiatry
American Journal of Public Health
American Journal of Reproductive Immunology
American Journal of Veterinary Research
American Libraries
American Medical News
American Psychologist
Anaesthesia
Analytische Psychologie
Andrologia
Anesteziologiia i Reanimatologiia
Anesthesiology
Annales de Chirurgie
Annales de Dermatologie et de Venereologie
Annales d'Endocrinologie
Annales de Medecine Interne
Annales de Pediatrie
Annales de Radiologie
Annales Francaises d'Anesthesie et de Reanimation
Annales Medico-Psychologiques
Annali di Ostetricia Ginecologia, Medicina Perinatale
Annals of the Entomological Society of America
Annals of Human Genetics
Annals of Nutrition and Metabolism
Archiv fur Geschwulstforschung
Archives Belges
Archives Belges de Medecone Sociale, Hygiene, Medecine du travail
    et Medecine Legale
Archives Internationales de Physiologie et de Biochimie
Archives of Andrology
Archives of Environmental Health
Archives of Gynecology
Archives of Internal Medicine
Archives of Sexual Behavior
Arizona Medicine
Arquivos Brasileiros de Cardiologia
Arquivos de Gastroenterologia
Arquivos de Neuropsiquiatria
Artery

Arzneimittel-Forschung
Asia
Asia-Oceania Journal of Obstetrics and Gynaecology
Asian Survey
Atlantic Insight
Atlantis
Audiology
Australian and New Zealand Journal of Obstetrics and Gynaecology
Australian and New Zealand Journal of Surgery
Australian Family Physician
Australian Journal of Biological Sciences
Australian Paediatric Journal

BS
BC Studies
Bangladesh Medical Research Council Bulletin
Basic and Applied Social Psychology
Behavioral Medicine Update
Behavioral Science
Beijing Review
Biochimica et Biophysica Acta
Biological Research in Pregnancy and Perinatology
Biology of Reproduction
Birth
Biulletin Eksperimentalnoi Biologii i Meditsiny
Body Politic
Boletin-Asociacion Medica de Puerto Rico
Breast Cancer Research and Treatment
Briarpath
Bratislavske Lekarske Listy
British Journal of Cancer
British Journal of Clinical Pharmacology
British Journal of Clinical Psychology
British Journal of Hospital Medicine
British Journal of Industrial Medicine
British Journal of Nutrition
British Journal of Obstetrics and Gynaecology
British Journal of Psychiatry
British Journal of Radiology
British Journal of Venereal Diseases
British Medical Bulletin
British Medical Journal
British Veterinary Journal
Brooklyn Law Review
Broomstick
Business and Society Review

Business Insurance
Business Week

CHAC Review: Catholic Health Association of Canada
Canada's Mental Health
Canadian Dimension
Canadian Journal of Psychiatry
Canadian Journal of Surgery
Canadian Medical Association Journal
Cancer
Cancer Detection and Prevention
Capital University Law Review
Catholic Digest
Catholic University Law Review
Center Magazine
Ceskoslovenska Gynekologie
Ceylon Medical Journal
Changes
Chatelaine
Chicago-Kent Law Review
China Quarterly
Chinese Medical Journal
Christian Century
Christianity and Crisis
Christianity Today
Chung Hsi I Chieh Ho Tsa Chih
Chung Hua Fu Chan Ko Tsa Chih
Chung Hua I Hsueh Tsa Chih
Chung Hua Shen Ching Ching Shen Ko Tsa Chih
Clergy Review
Clinical and Experimental Obstetrics and Gynecology
Clinical Endocrinology
Clinical Genetics
Clinical Perinatology
Clinical Pharmacology and Therapeutics
Clinical Reproduction and Fertility
CoEvolution Quarterly
Cognitive Therapy and Research
Communio
Commonweal
Community Outlook
Comptes Rendus des Seances de l'Academie des Science
Comptes Rendus des Seances de la Societie de Biologie et de ses
    Filiales
Concordia Theological Quarterly
Congressional Quarterly Weekly Report

Connecticut Medicine
Conservative Digest
Contraception
Contraceptive Delivery Systems
Corrections Digest
Crime Victims Digest
Criminal Justice Newsletter
Criminal Law Review

Daily Telegraph
Demography
Deutsche Medizinische Wochenschrift
Developmental Psychology
Diagnostic Medicine
Discover
Dissertation Abstracts International: A. Humanities and Social
    Sciences
Dissertation Abstracts International: B. Sciences and Engineering
Drug Intelligence and Clinical Pharmacy
Drug Metabolism and Disposition
Drug-Nutrient Interactions
Duquesne Law Review

E/SA
East African Medical Journal
East West
Ecologist
Economic and Political Weekly
Economic Development and Cultural Change
The Economist
Editor and Publisher-The Fourth Estate
Emergency Medicine
Endocrinologia Experimentalis
Environment
Equinox
Essence
Eta Evolutiva
European Journal of Clinical Pharmacology
European Journal of Obstetrics, Gynecology and Reproductive
    Biology
European Journal of Radiology
Experimental and Clinical Endocrinology

FDA Consumer

FDA Drug Bulletin
Faith and Reason
Family and Community Health
Family Law Reporter
The Family Law Reporter: Court Opinions
Family Planning Perspectives
Family Relations
Far Eastern Economic Review
Feminist Issues
Fertility and Sterility
Financial Post
Folia Medica
Food and Chemical Toxicology
Forbes
Foreign Affairs
Fortschritte der Medizin
Fortschritte der Neurologie-Psychiatrie
Fortune

GEN
Gallup Report
Gan No Rinsho
Gastrointestinal Radiology
Gay Community
Geburtshilfe und Frauenheilkunde
Genetic Psychology Monographs
Geographical Journal
Georgetown Law Journal
Gerontology and Geriatrics Education
Ginecologia y Obstetricia de Mexico
Ginekologia Polska
Glamour
Glendale Law Review
Guardian
Gynaekologische Rundschau
Gynakologe
Gynecologic and Obstetric Investigation

HHS Report
HNO: Hals-, Nasen-, Ohren-Heilkunde
Harefuah
Harpers
Harvard Women's Law Journal
Hawaii Medical Journal
Health

Health and Social Work
Health Care for Women, International
Health Education
Health Education Quarterly
Health Law Vigil
Health Visitor
Healthright
Hingokika Kiyo
Hofstra Law Review
Hokkaido Igaku Zasshi
Homiletic and Pastoral Review
Horizons
Hormone Research
Hormones and Behavior
Hospital Peer Review
Hospital Progress
Human Ecology
Human Events
Human Genetics
Human Organization
Humanist
Hygie

IPPF Research in Reproduction
IRNFP: International Review of Natural Family Planning
Indian Journal of Clinical Psychology
Indian Journal of Experimental Biology
Indian Journal of Medical Research
Indian Pediatrics
Indiana Law Review
Infection
Infirmiere Canadienne
Infirmiere Francaise
Inquiry
International and Comparative Law Quarterly
International Family Planning Perspectives
International Journal of Andrology
International Journal of Clinical Pharmacology, Therapy and
    Toxicology
International Journal of Epidemiology
International Journal of Fertility
International Journal of Gynaecology and Obstetrics
International Journal of Oral Surgery
International Journal of Women's Studies
International Nursing Review
International Surgery

Israel Journal of Psychiatry and Related Sciences
Italian Journal of Surgical Sciences

JAMA: Journal of the American Medical Association
JNCI: Journal of the National Cancer Institute
JOGN Nursing: Journal of Obstetric, Gynecologic and Neonatal
    Nursing
Jet
Jewish Social Studies
Jordemodern
Josanpu Zasshi
Journal de Gynecologie, Obstetrique et Biologie de la Reproduction
Journal for the Scientific Study of Religion
Journal of Adolescent Health Care
Journal of the American Academy of Dermatology
Journal of American College Health
Journal of the American Medical Women's Association
Journal of the American Veterinary Medical Association
Journal of Andrology
Journal of Animal Science
Journal of Applied Physiology
Journal of Biosocial Science
Journal of Black Psychology
Journal of Chronic Diseases
Journal of Clinical Endocrinology and Metabolism
Journal of Clinical Gastroenterology
Journal of Clinical Investigation
Journal of Comparative Family Studies
Journal of Epidemiology and Community Health
Journal of Ethnopharmacology
Journal of Family Law
Journal of Family Practice
Journal of Family Welfare
Journal of Florida Medical Association
Journal of Foot Surgery
Journal of Health and Social Behavior
Journal of Home Economics
Journal of the Indian Medical Association
Journal of Infectious Diseases
Journal of Juvenile Law
Journal of the Kentucky Medical Association
Journal of Marriage and the Family
Journal of the Medical Association of Georgia
Journal of the Medical Association of Thailand
Journal of Medical Ethics
Journal of Medical Genetics

Journal of Medicinal Chemistry
Journal of Natural Products
Journal of Occupational Medicine
Journal of Pastoral Counseling
Journal of Personality and Social Psychology
The Journal of Psychology
Journal of Public Health Policy
Journal of Religion
Journal of Reproduction and Fertility
Journal of Reproductive Immunology
Journal of Reproductive Medicine
Journal of the Royal College of General Practitioners
Journal of the Royal Society of Medicine
Journal of School Health
Journal of Sex and Marital Therapy
Journal of Social History
Journal of Social Political and Economic Studies
The Journal of Social Welfare Law
Journal of Social Work and Human Sexuality
Journal of Steroid Biochemistry
Journal of Tropical Pediatrics
Journal of Urology
Journal of Virology
Jugoslavenska Ginekologija i Opstetricija
Juvenile and Family Law Digest
Jump Cut
Jurist

Kaku Igaku
Kango Gijutsu
Kangogaku Zasshi
Krankenpfleg Journal

Laboratory Animal Science
Ladies Home Journal
Lakartidningen
Lancet
Lasers in Surgery and Medicine
Liguorian
Linacre Quarterly

MCN: American Journal of Maternal-Child Nursing
MMW: Muenchener Medizinische Wochenschrift
MMWR: Morbidity and Mortality Weekly Report

MS Magazine
Maclean's
Mademoiselle
Malaysian Journal of Pathology
Manitoba Law Journal
Mankind Quarterly
Marketing
Marketing News
Maroc Medical
Max Planck Society Science Newsletter
Medical Journal of Australia
Medical Reference Services Quarterly
Medical World News
Medicina Clinica
Medicina Psicosomatica
Medicine and Law
Mental and Physical Disability Law Reporter
Mercer Law Review
Metabolism
Methods in Enzymology
Methods of Information in Medicine
Microsurgery
Midwife, Health Visitor and Community Nurse
Midwives Chronicle
Militant
Mineral and Electrolyte Metabolism
Minerva Ginecologia
Minerva Psichiatrica
Minnesota Medicine
Missouri Medicine
Mother Jones
Mt. Sinai Journal of Medicine
Mutation Research

NLN Publications: National League for Nursing Publications
Nation
National Catholic Reporter
National Civic Review
National Journal
National Review
National Sheriff
Natural History
Nature
Nederlands Tijdschrift voor Geneeskunde
Nephron
Netherlands Journal of Surgery
New Covenant

New Directions for Women
New England Journal on Criminal and Civil Confinement
New England Journal of Medicine
New Republic
New Scientist
New Women's Times
New York
New York Law School Law Review
New York State Journal of Medicine
New Zealand Medical Journal
Newsweek
Nippon Rinsho
Nippon Sanka Fujinka Gakkai Zasshi
North Carolina Medical Journal
Northern Kentucky Law Review
Northwest Passage
Nuovi Annali D'Igiene e Microbiologia
Nurse Practitioner
Nurses Drug Alert
Nursing
Nursing Journal of India
Nursing Mirror
Nursing Times
Nutrition Reviews

Obstetrical and Gynecological Survey
Obstetrics and Gynecology
Off Our Backs
Ohio State Medical Journal
Oklahoma City University Law Review
Origins
Orvosi Hetilap
L'Osservatore Romano
Our Sunday Visitor

Parents Magazine
Patient Education and Counseling
Patologia Polska
Pediatric Nursing
Pediatrics
People Weekly
Perinatal Press
Personal and Social Psychology Bulletin
Personnel and Guidance Journal
Perspectives in Biology and Medicine
Perspectives in Psychological Researches

Register
Reproduccion
Research in Nursing and Health
Review of Religious Research
Revista Clinica Espanola
Revista de Enfermagen
Revista do Instituto de Medicina Tropical de Sao Paulo
Revista Espanola de las Enfermedades del Aparato Digestivo
Revista Medica de Chile
Revue d'Epidemiologie et de Sante Publique
Revue Francaise de Sociologie
Revue Medicale de Bruzelles
Revue Medicale de Liege
Revue Medicale de la Suisse Romande
Rheumatology International
Rutgers Camden Law Journal

St. Anthony Messenger
Scandinavian Journal of Rheumatology
Scandinavian Journal of Social Medicine
Scandinavian Journal of Work, Environment and Health
Scanning Electron Microscopy
Scholastic Update
Schweizer Archiv fuer Tierheilkunde
Schweizerische Medizinische Wochenschrift
Schweizerische Rundschau fur Medizin Praxis
Science
Science Dimension
Science News
Science, Technology and Human Values
Scientific American
Semaines des Hopitaux de Paris
Seminars in Liver Disease
Seton Hall Law Review
Sex Roles
Sexually Transmitted Diseases
Shikoku Acta Medica
Singapore Medical Journal
Smithsonian
Social Action
Social Biology
Social Problems
Social Science and Medicine
Social Service Review
Social Theory and Practice
Society

US Catholic
US News and World Report
USA Today
Ugeskrift for Laeger
Ultraschall in der Medizin
Union Medicale du Canada
Union Seminary Quarterly Review
University of Baltimore Law Review
University of Toledo Law Review
Upsala Journal of Medical Sciences
Urban Health
Urology
Urology Research
Utah Law Review

Vardfacket
Verhandlungen der Deutschen Gesellschaft fur Pathologie
Veterinary Quarterly
Vital Speeches of the Day

WHO Bulletin
WHO Offset Publication
Wall Street Journal
Washburn Law Journal
Washington Law Review
West Indian Medical Journal
Western Journal of Medicine
Western New England Law Review
Western Political Quarterly
Wiadomosci Lekarskie
William Mitchell Law Review
Women and Health
Women Lawyers Journal
Women's Review of Books
Women's Studies International Forum
Women's Studies Quarterly
World Health
World Health Statistics Quarterly
World Press Review
World Today

Xenobiotica

Yao Hsueh Hsueh Pao

Zeitschrift fur Aerztliche Fortbildung
Zeitschrift fur die Gesamte Innere Medizin
Zeitschrift fur Kinderchirurgie
Zentralblatt fur Bakteriologie, Mikrobiologie und Hygiene
Zentralblatt fur Chirurgie
Zentralblatt fur Gynaekologie

SUBJECT HEAD INDEX

BOOKS, GOVERNMENT PUBLICATIONS, AND MONOGRAPHS

ADOLESCENTS, SEX, AND CONTRACEPTION. Hillsdale, MI: Hillsdale, 1983.

Alauddin, M. POPULATION AND FAMILY PLANNING IN BANGLADESH. Washington, D. C.: World Bank, 1983.

Ali, M. Nawab. POPULATION AND FAMILY PLANNING RESEARCH, BANGLADESH; an annotated bibliography. National Institute of Population Research and Training, 1981.

Bopp, James, Jr., ed. RESTORING THE RIGHT TO LIFE: THE HUMAN LIFE AMENDMENT. Provo, UT: Brigham Young University Press, 1984.

Brennan, W. THE ABORTION HOLOCAUST. Landmark Press, 1983.

Bruce. ABOUT FACE. New York: Putnam, 1984.

BASIC FACTS ON THERAPEUTIC ABORTIONS, CANADA, 1982. Ottawa: Statistics Canada, 1982.

CHILD AND MATERNAL HEALTH SERVICES IN RURAL INDIA. Baltimore: Johns Hopkins University Press, 1983.

Chung, C. S. THE EFFECTS OF INDUCED ABORTION ON SUBSEQUENT REPRODUCTIVE FUNCTION AND PREGNANCY OUTCOME, HAWAII. East-West Center, 1983.

Danda, A. K. FAMILY PLANNING: AN ADAPTIVE STRATEGY. Inter-India Publs., 1984.

DEFINING HUMAN LIFE. Arlington, VA: Association of University Programs in Health Adminstration Press, 1983.

1

Falik, M. IDEOLOGY AND ABORTION POLICY POLITICS. New York: Praeger, 1983.

FAMILY PLANNING PROGRAMS IN THE ORGANIZED SECTOR. New York: Sterling Pubs., 1983.

Field, M. J. THE COMPARATIVE POLITICS OF BIRTH CONTROL. New York: Praeger Pubs., 1983.

Flamery, Austin, ed. ABORTION & LAW. Dominican Pubs., 1983.

Fowler, R. A. THE CHRISTIAN CONFRONTS HIS CULTURE. Chicago: Moody Press, 1983.

Fox, Greer Litton, ed. CHILDSPACING DECISION; FERTILITY ATTI-TUDES AND BEHAVIOR. Beverly Hills: Sage Pubs., 1982.

Francome, Colin. ABORTION FREEDOM: A WORLDWIDE MOVE-MENT. Allen and Unwin, 1984.

Fraser, D. THE PEOPLE PROBLEM. Westport, CT: Greenwood, 1983.

Greer, G. SEX AND DESTINY. New York: Harper & Row, 1984.

Hern, W. M. ABORTION PRACTICE. Philadelphia: Lippincott, 1984.

Hollerbach, Paula E. FERTILITY DECISION-MAKING PROCESSES; a critical essay. New York: Population Council, 1982.

Howe, L. K. MOMENTS ON MAPLE AVENUE. New York: Macmillan, 1984.

International Congress on Maternal and Neonatal Health. PRIMARY MATERNAL AND NEONATAL HEALTH. New York: Plenum Press, 1983.

Kass-Annese, B. THE FERTILITY AWARENESS WORKBOOK. Perigee Bks., 1984.

Katz, P. A. and S. L. Boswell. Sex-role development and the one-child family in THE SINGLE-CHILD FAMILY, ed. by T. Falbo. New York: Guilford, 1984, pp. 63-116.

Kent, M. M. and Ann Larson. FAMILY SIZE PREFERENCES: EVI-DENCE FROM THE WORLD FERTILITY SURVEYS. Washington: Population Reference Bureau, 1982.

Kreeft, P. THE UNABORTED SOCRATES. Downers Grove, IL: Inter-Varsity Press, 1983.

Kruck, William E. LOOKING FOR DR. CONDOM. University: University of Alabama Press, 1981.

Laing, J. DEMOGRAPHIC EVALUATION OF FAMILY PLANNING PROGRAMS. Australian National University Development Studies Centre, 1984.

Luker, K. ABORTION AND THE POLITICS OF MOTHERHOOD. Berkelley: University of California Press, 1984.

McLaren, A. SEXUALITY AND SOCIAL ORDER. New York: Holmes & Meier, 1983.

Milbauer, B. THE LAW GIVETH. New York: McGraw-Hill, 1984.

Musallam, B. SEX AND SOCIETY IN ISLAM. Cambridge, England: Cambridge University Press, 1983.

Ness, G. D. THE LAND IS SHRINKING. Baltimore: Johns Hopkins University Press, 1984.

Pacheco, Mario Victor de Assis. "Planejamento familiar" e libertacao do Brasil. Vozes, 1983.

Petchesky, Rosalind Pollack. ABORTION AND WOMEN'S CHOICE: THE STATE, SEXUALITY AND REPRODUCTIVE FREEDOM. New York: Longman, 1984.

POPULATION POLICY COMPENDIUM: EGYPT. New York: United Nations Department for International Economic and Social Affairs, 1982.

THE POPULATION COUNCIL 1982 ANNUAL REPORT. New York: The Council, 1982.

THE RELIGIOUS CASE FOR ABORTION. Ashville, NC: Madison & Polk, 1983.

Rodman, H. THE SEXUAL RIGHTS OF ADOLESCENTS. New York: Columbia University Press, 1984.

Rogers, Carolyn C. and Martin O'Connell. CHILDSPACING AMONG BIRTH COHORTS OF AMERICAN WOMEN: 1905-1959. Washington: U. S. Bureau of Census, 1984.

3

Rosenblum, Art. NATURAL BIRTH CONTROL BOOK. Grand Rapids: Aquarian Research Foundation, 1982.

Shettles, L. B. RITES OF LIFE. Grand Rapids: Zondervan, 1983.

Smith, Janet S. "Rights-conflict, Pregnancy, and Abortion", in BEYOND DOMINATION by Carol Gould. Totowa Rowman and Allanheld, 1984.

SOURCEBOOK OF SEX THERAPY, COUNSELING, AND FAMILY PLANNING. New York: Van Nostrand Reinhold, 1983.

Stycos, J. Mayone. PUTTING BACK THE K AND A IN KAP; a study of the implications of knowledge and attitudes for fertility in Costa Rica. International Statistic Institute, 1984.

Tietze, C. INDUCED ABORTION, A WORLD REVIEW, 1983. Population Council, 1983.

Topalian, E. MARGARET SANGER. New York: Watts, 1984.

United States. Bureau of the Census. Population Division. CHILD-SPACING AMONG BIRTH COHORTS OF AMERICAN WOMEN: 1905-1959. Washington: GPO, 1984.

United States. House. Committee on Government Operations. Intergovernmental Relations and Human Resources Subcommittee. FDA [FOOD AND DRUG ADMINISTRATION]'S APPROVAL OF THE TODAY CONTRACEPTIVE SPONGE: HEARING, JULY 13, 1983. Washington, GPO, 1984.

United States. House. Committee on Post Office and Civil Service. Subcommittee on Civil Service. STUDY OF EFFORT TO EXCLUDE PLANNED PARENTHOOD FROM PARTICIPATION IN COMBINED FEDERAL CAMPAIGN: REPORT, OCTOBER 28, 1983. Washington: GPO, 1983.

United States. Senate. Committee on the Judiciary. Subcommittee on the Constitution. LEGAL RAMIFICATIONS OF THE HUMAN LIFE AMENDMENT: HEARINGS, FEBRUARY 28 AND MARCH 7, 1983, ON S. J. RES. 3, JOINT RESOLUTION TO AMEND THE CONSTITUTION TO ESTABLISH LEGISLATIVE AUTHORITY IN CONGRESS AND THE STATES WITH RESPECT TO ABORTION. Washington: GPO, 1983.

WHO IS FOR LIFE? Westchester, IL: Crossway Bks., 1984.

THE ZERO PEOPLE. Servant Bks., 1983.

PERIODICAL LITERATURE

TITLE INDEX

ABO incompatiblity and reproductive failure. I. Prenatal selection, by T. Schaap, et al. AMERICAN JOURNAL OF HUMAN GENETICS. 36(1):143-151, January 1984.

A. H. Robins hauls a judge into court [M. W. Lord accused of taking sides in Dalkon Shield liability case]. BUSINESS WEEK. July 16, 1984, p. 27-28.

AID ignores food aid, pays for sterilizations, by J. Palmisano. NATIONAL CATHOLIC REPORTER. 20:4, December 23, 1984.

ARIMA models of seasonal variation in U. S. birth and death rates, by K. C. Land, et al. DEMOGRAPHY. 20:541-568, November 1983.

Abdominal pregnancy following tubal hysterectomy, by V. K. Arora. INTERNATIONAL SURGERY. 68(3):253-255, July-September 1983.

Abortion [letter]. MEDICAL JOURNAL OF AUSTRALIA. 140(11):681, May 26, 1984.

Abortion [letter]. MEDICAL JOURNAL OF AUSTRALIA. 141(2):131-132, July 21, 1984.

Abortion [letter]. NEW ZEALAND MEDICAL JOURNAL. 96(744):987, November 23, 1983.

Abortion [letter], by C. A. Kaufman. JOURNAL OF OBSTETRIC, GYNECOLOGIC AND NEONATAL NURSING. (2):131-132, March-April 1984.

Abortion [letter], by K. McAll. MEDICAL JOURNAL OF AUSTRALIA. 141(1):65-66, July 7, 1984.

Abortion [letter], by J. E. McArthur. NEW ZEALAND MEDICAL JOURNAL. 97(756):341, May 23, 1984.

Abortion activists mark January anniversary, by S. Hyde. GAY COMMUNITY. 11(28):1, February 4, 1984.

Abortion advocates stress access, by J. Irvine. GAY COMMUNITY. 11 (26):3, January 21, 1984.

Abortion and the archbishop [J. J. O'Connor]. by J. Klein. NEW YORK. 17:36-43, October 1, 1984.

Abortion and the body politic: an anthropological analysis of legislative activity in Massachusetts, by K. R. Scharf. DISSERTATION ABSTRACTS INTERNATIONAL:A. 45(3), September 1984.

Abortion and the Christian story, by M. K. Duffey. LINACRE QUARTERLY. 51:60-69, February 1984.

Abortion and contraception: apples and oranges, by H. J. Byrne. AMERICA. 151:272-275, November 3, 1984.

Abortion and contraception in Poland, by M. Okolski. STUDIES IN FAMILY PLANNING. 14(11):263-274, November 1983.

Abortion and dialogue, by D. R. Carlin, Jr. AMERICA. 151:64, August 18-25, 1984.

Abortion and euthanasia of Down's syndrome children— the parent's view, by B. Shepperdson. JOURNAL OF MEDICAL ETHICS. 9(3): 152-157, September 1983.

Abortion and its cost. REGISTER. 60:2, January 29, 1984.

Abortion and the law, by M. M. Cuomo. ORIGINS. 14:301-303, October 25, 1984.

Abortion and the potentiality principle, by D. B. Annis. SOUTHERN JOURNAL OF PHILOSOPHY. 22:155-164, Summer 1984.

Abortion and self-defense, by M. Davis. PHILOSOPHY AND PUBLIC AFFAIRS. 13:175-207, Summer 1984.

Abortion as a medical career choice: entrepreneurs, community physicians, and others, by M. S. Goldstein. JOURNAL OF HEALTH AND SOCIAL BEHAVIOR. 25(2):211-229, June 1984.

Abortion at 10 to 12 weeks using a plastic syringe or electric aspirator, by E. Borko, et al. JUGOSLAVENSKA GINEKOLOGIJA I OPSTETRICIJA. 23(1-2):17-20, January-April 1983.

Abortion ban eased in Labor-HHS money bill, by J. Hook. CONGRESSIONAL QUARTERLY WEEKLY REPORT. 42:2359-2360, September, 29, 1984.

Abortion books— a bumper crop, by D. Andrusko. NATIONAL CATHOLIC REPORTER. 20:9, February 24, 1984.

Abortion by ordeal. FAMILY PLANNING PERSPECTIVES. 15:258, November-December 1983.

Abortion cells model reaction to drugs. NEW SCIENTIST. 103:18, August 30, 1984.

Abortion clause fight kills ERA. NATIONAL CATHOLIC REPORTER. 20:4, November 25, 1983.

Abortion: a clear and constant teaching, by J. R. Quinn. ORIGINS. 14:413-414, December 6, 1984.

Abortion clinic firebombed, by C. Oliver. NEW WOMEN'S TIMES. 10(1):1, January 1984.

Abortion clinics and rights attacked, by E. Bader. GUARDIAN. 36 (40):6, July 25, 1984.

Abortion clinics under fire, by M. Snell. MOTHER JONES. 9:8, November 1984.

Abortion counselling, by A. Broome. NURSING MIRROR. 158(20): 19-20, May 16, 1984.

Abortion: court unmoved. ECONOMIST. 287:32-33, June 25, 1983.

The Abortion decision for Minnesota minors: who decides?. WILLIAM MITCHELL LAW REVIEW. 9:194-215, 1983.

Abortion: the demographic argument [letter], by B. Frazer. CANADIAN MEDICAL ASSOCIATION JOURNAL. 130(4):340, February 15, 1984.

Abortion denied— outcome of mothers and babies, by C. Del Campo. CANADIAN MEDICAL ASSOCIATION JOURNAL. 130(4):361-362, February 15, 1984.

The Abortion Epidemic: America's silent holocaust, by J. C. Laney. BS. 139(556):342-355, 1982.

Abortion: from Roe [Roe v. Wade] to Akron, changing standards of analysis. CATHOLIC UNIVERSITY LAW REVIEW. 33:393-428, Winter 1984.

Abortion group says Church violates tax laws. OUR SUNDAY VISITOR. 73:8, October 14, 1984.

Abortion: identity and loss, by W. Quinn. PHILOSOPHY AND PUBLIC AFFAIRS. 13:3-24, Winter 1984.

Abortion, in England, 1919-1939: Legal theory and Social practice, by B. L. Brookes. DISSERTATION ABSTRACTS INTERNATION-AL: A. 45(1), July 1984.

Abortion in South Korea, by P. Marx. HOSPITAL PEER REVIEW. 85: 46-51, October 1984.

Abortion is not a religious issue, by J. Hart. HEALTH EDUCATION. 44:9, October 13, 1984.

The abortion issue in the 1980 elections, by D. Granberg, et al. FAM-ILY PLANNING PERSPECTIVES. 15:231-238, September-October 1983.

Abortion: it can't be left to personal choice, by J. T. Burtchaell. ST. ANTHONY MESSENGER. 92:16-20, October 1984.

Abortion law on trial/Morgentaler, by G. Rodgerson. BODY POLITIC. 1(2):11, April 1984.

Abortion, limited medical resources, and the meaning of health care, by K. Anderson, et al. JOURNAL OF AMERICAN COLLEGE HEALTH. 32(5):231-232, April 1984.

Abortion money pours into North Carolina to defeat Jesse Helms, by M. Meehan. REGISTER. 60:1+, August 19, 1984.

Abortion 1982 [letter], by J. E. McArthur. NEW ZEALAND MEDICAL JOURNAL. 96(745):1032, December 14, 1983.

Abortion 1983: the controversy continues: II, by J. M. Healey. CONNECTICUT MEDICINE. 48(6):413, June 1984.

Abortion offices bombed, by U. Vaid. GAY COMMUNITY. 12(1):6,

July 14, 1984.

Abortion on demand, by J. J. Rovinsky. MOUNT SINAI JOURNAL OF MEDICINE. 51(1):12-14, January-February 1984.

Abortion, politics, and bishops. COMMONWEAL. 111:163-165, March 23, 1984.

Abortion: predicting the complexity of the decision-making process, by A. Friedlander, et al. WOMEN AND HEALTH. 9:43-54, September 1984.

Abortion: a pro-life view, by R. J. Adamek. USA TODAY. 112:98, May 1984.

Abortion— Provisions of city abortion ordinance requiring hospitalization for all abortions performed after the first trimester of pregnancy, notification and consent of parents before peformance of abortions on unmarried minors, conveyance by attending physician of specific statements to insure informed consent, delay of twenty-four hours between the time a woman signs a consent form and the time an abortion is performed, and disposal of the fetus in a humane and sanitary manner are violations of the constitutional right of privacy. City of Akron v. Akron Center for Reproductive Health, Inc. JOURNAL OF FAMILY LAW. 22:159-167, 1983-1984.

Abortion: quicker, therefore earlier [Britain]. ECONOMIST. 290: 53-54, January 21, 1984.

Abortion referendum in Ireland, by J. Marcus. WORLD TODAY. 39: 413-416, November 1983.

Abortion, related issues are snags in ERA battle, by D. Johnson. REGISTER. 59:1+, December 4, 1983.

Abortion, religion and the law, by D. R. Carlin, Jr. AMERICA. 151: 356-358, December 1, 1984.

Abortion: a religious issue?, by Sister M. M. Mooney. LINACRE QUARTERLY. 51:53-59, February 1984.

Abortion/rights of juvenile mother— Nebrasks. JUVENILE AND FAMILY LAW DIGEST. 16:2, February 1984.

Abortion rights offensive launched, by N. Hoodbhoy. GUARDIAN. 36(15):4, January 18, 1984.

Abortion rights: where do we go from here?, by R. Copelon. MS. 12: 146, October 1983.

Abortion risks for teens as low or lower than risks for older women. FAMILY PLANNING PERSPECTIVES. 15(6):282-283, November-December 1983.

Abortion: the role of public officials; New York bishop's statement. ORIGINS. 13:759-760, April 26, 1984.

Abortion services in the United States, 1981 and 1982, by S. K. Henshaw, et al. FAMILY PLANNING PERSPECTIVES. 16(3):119-127, May-June 1984.

Abortion surveillance, 1979-1980, by P. R. Lang, et al. MMWR. 32(2): 1SS-7SS, May 1983.

Abortion surveillance: preliminary analysis-United States, 1981. MMWR. 33(26):373-375, July 6, 1984.

Abortion: who decides?, by F. Horan, et al. NURSING TIMES. 80(10): 16-17, March 7-13, 1984.

Abortion— the woman in conflict, by L. Bier. FORTSCHRITTE DER MEDIZIN. 102(19):78-79, May 17, 1984.

Abortion's penalty: go to jail, by E. Bader. GUARDIAN. 36(43):2, September 5, 1984.

About postcoital contraception, by E. Trimmer. MIDWIFE, HEALTH VISITOR AND COMMUNITY NURSE. 19(11):434, November 1983.

About TOP risks and about mammography, by E. Trimmer. MIDWIFE, HEALTH VISITOR AND COMMUNITY NURSE. 20(9):322-330, September 1984.

Absence of antibodies to ethinyl estradiol in users of oral contraceptive steroids, by N. H. Huang, et al. FERTILITY AND STERILITY. 41(4):587-592, April 1984.

Absence of coagulation changes in voluntary abortions by aspiration [letter], by M. T. Cousin, et al. ANNALES FRANCAISES D'ANESTHESIE ET DE REANIMATON. 1(4):453, 1982.

Absorption, excretion and tissue residue in feedlot heirers injected with the synthetic prostaglandin, fenprostalene, by R. V. Tomlinson, et al. JOURNAL OF ANIMAL SCIENCE. 59(1):164-169, July 1984.

The acceptability of the copper 7, multiload 250 and copper t 220c intrauterine devices, by H. Hutapea, et al. CONTRACEPTIVE DELIVERY SYSTEMS. 5(1):11-16, 1984.

Acceptability of depo-provera [letter], by S. Basnayake, et al. LANCET. 1(8373):390, February 18, 1984.

The acceptable holocaust?, by V. P. Miceli. HOSPITAL PEER REVIEW. 85:56-62, November 1984.

Actinomyces in the female genital tract, by G. C. Grice, et al. BRITISH JOURNAL OF VENEREAL DISEASES. 59(5):317-319, October 1983.

Action now in family planning: the role of the nurse, by A. K. Malhotra, et al. NURSING JOURNAL OF INDIA. 75(2):27-28, February 1984.

Activity of the adrenergic nervous system in the pathophysiology of pregnancy and labor. I. Dopamine beta-hydroxylase (DBH) activity in the plasma of women with physiological pregnancy, threatened and completed abortion and threatened and completed premature labor, by H. Zrubek, et al. GINEKOLOGIA POLSKA. 55(3):161-170, March 1984.

Acts of terror [eleventh act of terrorism against abortion clinics, when Planned Parenthood of Maryland's Annapolis Center was bombed], by P. Kriegel. NEW DIRECTIONS FOR WOMEN. 13:1+, September-October 1984.

Acute poisoning caused by inhalation of an aerosol spray used for waterproofing, by K. J. Christensen, et al. UGESKRIFT FOR LAEGER. 146(4):274-275, January 23, 1984.

Additional data on spontaneous abortion and facial cleft malformations, by J. C. Bear. CLINICAL GENETICS. 24(6):407-412, December 1983.

Adjunctive use of Laminaria tents for termination of early midtrimester pregnancy with intramuscular 15(S)-15-methyl PGF2 alpha, by N. N. Chowdhury, et al. ASIA-OCEANIA JOURNAL OF OBSTETRICS AND GYNAECOLOGY. 9(2):173-179, June 1983.

Admission of abortion patients, by Enjoubault. INFIRMIERE FRANCAISE. (253):15-16, March 1984.

Adolescent pregnancy program stresses family counseling, educational services, by B. A. McNeil, et al. HOSPITAL PROGRESS. 65(5):12-14; 31, May 1984.

Adolescent use of oral contraceptives, by M. A. Babington. PEDIATRIC NURSING. 10(2):111-114, March-April 1984.

Adolescents' communication styles for learning about birth control from mass media, by R. De Pietro, et al. HEALTH EDUCATION QUARTERLY. 10(2):106-119, Summer 1983.

Adolescents' preference of source to obtain contraceptive information, by B. J. van den Berg, et al. AMERICAN JOURNAL OF OBSTETRICS AND GYNECOLOGY. 147(6):719-721, November 15, 1983.

Advanced abdominal pregnancy with a live fetus, by C. Strehl, et al. GINEKOLOGIA POLSKA. 55(2):147-150, February 1984.

Advertising contraceptives on TV; the push is on, by J. Butler. OUR SUNDAY VISITOR. 73:5, November 25, 1984.

Advertising family planning in the press: direct response results from Bangladesh, by P. D. Harvey. STUDIES IN FAMILY PLANNING. 15(1):40-42, January-February 1984.

Africa faces up to overpopulation, by A. Marshall. NEW SCIENTIST. 101:10-11, February 2, 1984.

Again on postcoital contraception, by F. Havranek. CESKOSLOVENSKA GYNEKOLOGIE. 48(7):498-499, August 1983.

The age incidence of spontaneous abortion, by Y. Shiina, et al. HOKKAIDO IGAKU ZASSHI. 59(1):17-20, January 1984.kl

Age pattern of fertility in the Sudan, by M. A. Khalifa. JOURNAL OF BIOSOCIAL SCIENCE. 15:317-324, July 1983.

Aggressive cervical cerclage [letter], by P. Bergsjo. AMERICAN JOURNAL OF OBSTETRICS AND GYNECOLOGY. 149(2):240-241, May 15, 1984.

Aid to stabilize hinged Strauch clamp during microvasovasostomy, by M. Wosnitzer. UROLOGY. 24(2):168-169, August 1984.

Alive or dead? The eye of the beholder, by C. Del Campo, et al. CANADIAN JOURNAL OF SURGERY. 26(5):394-395, September 1983.

All contraceptives have problems: toxic-shock syndrome and the vaginal contraceptive sponge. NORTH CAROLINA MEDICAL JOURNAL. 45(3):197-198, March 1984.

All in the line of duty? . . . Many nurses feel ambivalent towards abortion, by M. Kenny. NURSING MIRROR. 158(20):22-23, May 16, 1984.

Alpha-fetoprotein assay in patients treated with low-dose oral contraceptives, by S. Dessole, et al. CLINICAL AND EXPERIMENTAL OBSTETRICS AND GYNECOLOGY. 11(3):76-78, 1984.

Alterations in prednisolone disposition as a result of oral contraceptive use and dose, by P. J. Meffin, et al. BRITISH JOURNAL OF CLINICAL PHARMACOLOGY. 17(6):655-664, June 1984.

Alevolitis sicca dolorosa after removal of impacted mandibular third molars, by A. Nordenram, et al. INTERNATIONAL JOURNAL OF ORAL SURGERY. 12(4):226-231, August 1983.

American family building strategies in 1900: Stopping or spacing, by S. E. Tolnay, et al. DEMOGRAPHY. 21(1):9, February 1984.

The Americas: patterns are changing, by J. C. Abcede. WORLD HEALTH. June 1984, pp. 21-23.

An analysis of access to contraceptive care in Western Pennsylvania, by S. E. Milligan. DISSERTATION ABSTRACTS INTERNATIONAL: A. 45(5), November 1984.

An analysis of self-reported sexual behavior in a sample of normal males, by A. E. Reading, et al. ARCHIVES OF SEXUAL BEHAVIOR. 13(1):69-83, February 1984.

An ancient method and a modern scourge: the condom as a barrier against herpes [letter], by L. S. Kish, et al. JOURNAL OF THE AMERICAN ACADEMY OF DERMATOLOGY. 9(5):769-770, November 1983.

And the poor get sterilized, by B. Hartmann, et al. NATION. 238: 798-800, June 30, 1984.

Androgenic action of progestins and possible synandrogenic properties of antiandrogens used in oral contraceptives, by J. Spona. GYNECOLOGIC AND OBSTETRIC INVESTIGATION. 17(2):66-72, 1984.

Androgenisation of female partners of men on medroxyprogesterone acetate/percutaneous testosterone contraception [letter], by D. Delanoe, et al. LANCET. 1(8371):276, February 4, 1984.

Aneuploidy in recurrent spontaneous aborters: the tendency to parental nondisjunction, by F. Hecht, et al. CLINICAL GENETICS. 26(1):43-45, July 1984.

Angiographic indications of vasculitis in four cases of acute cerebro-vascular accidents while taking contraceptives, by C. Mestre, et al. REVISTA CLINICA ESPANOLA. 171(1):27-30, October 15, 1983.

Animal experiments, morphologic and endocrinologic studies following various coagulation technics, by H. H. Riedel, et al. ZENTRALBLATT FUR GYNAKOLOGIE. 105(24):1568-1584, 1983.

Anniversary of legalized abortion, by F. Simon. NORTHWEST PASSAGE. 24(7):6, February 1984.

Another look at the costs and benefits of government expenditures for family planning programs, by J. B. Healy, et al. FAMILY PLANNING PERSPECTIVES. 15(6):299-301, November-December 1983.

Another weary round/abortion debate, by A. Hayford. BRIARPATH. 13(2):14, March 1984.

The antiabortion amendments, by S. Poggi. GAY COMMUNITY. 11 (45):3, June 2, 1984.

Anti sex lobby on the move. SPARE RIB. 1(40):17, March 1984.

The (anti-cancer?) pill, by A. Rowand. SCIENCE NEWS. 125: 404, June 30, 1984.

Anti-choice terrorists strike again [at Annapolis, Maryland, Planned Parenthood clinic and the National Abortion Federation's Washington, D. C., headquarters], by F. Elliott. OFF OUR BACKS. 14:5, August-September 1984.

Antiemetic efficacy of droperidol and metoclopramide, by S. E. Cohen, et al. ANESTHESIOLOGY. 60(1):67-69, January 1984.

Antifertility actions of alpha-chlorohydrin in the male, by A. R. Jones. AUSTRALIAN JOURNAL OF BIOLOGICAL SCIENCES. 36(4):333-350, 1983.

Antifertility and uterine activity of Plumbago rosea in rats, by R. Lal, et al. INDIAN JOURNAL OF MEDICAL RESEARCH. 78: 287-290, August 1983.

Antifertility vaccines [letter], by R. Bronson, et al. FERTILITY AND STERILITY. 41(5):786-787, May 1984.

Anti-lipopolysaccharide immunotherapy in management of septic shock of obstetric and gynaecological origin, by E. Lachman, et al. LANCET. 1(8384):981-983, May 5, 1984.

Anti-Ro antibodies and abortions in women with SLE [letter], by R. G. Hull, et al. LANCET. 2(8359):1138, November 12, 1983.

Antithrombin III in oral contraceptive users and during normotensive pregnancy, by G. H. Weenink, et al. ACTA OBSTETRICIA ET GYNECOLOGICA SCANDINAVICA. 63(1):57-61, 1984.

Apropos of a case for deductions and conclusions in gynecologic practice, by Kh. Durveniashki. AKUSHERSTVO I GINEKOLOGIIA. 23(3):270-271, 1984.

Archbishop: Ferraro misstated abortion teaching. OUR SUNDAY VISITOR. 73:5, September 23, 1984.

Archbishop, governor, and veep [J. J. O'Connor's statement on Catholic principles and abortion, by M. Novak. NATIONAL REVIEW. 36:45, September 21, 1984.

Archbishop John J. O'Connor; interview by J. C. O'Neill. OUR SUNDAY VISITOR. 73:3+, October 14, 1984.

Archbishop John O'Connor's strong stand on abortion makes him a holy terror to Democrats. PEOPLE WEEKLY. 22:47-48, October 1, 1984.

Archbishop Law calls abortion primordial darkness, by B. F. Law. OUR SUNDAY VISITOR. 72:8, April 8, 1984.

Archbishop says politicians must fight abortion laws. OUR SUNDAY VISITOR. 73:8, October 28, 1984.

Are men ready to share the burden?, by F. Lesser. NEW SCIENTIST. 101:37-38, January 5, 1984.

Arizona unborn dumped as waste, by V. Warner. REGISTER. 60:1+, April 1, 1984.

The art of contraceptive counselling, by J. Edwards. HEALTHRIGHT. 3:22-24, August 1984.

Arterial complications of estrogen-progestogen contraception, by J. Jaillard. ANNALES DE MEDECINE INTERNE. 134(5):416-420, 1983.

Asian media's impact on family planning, by K. Bhupal. POPULI. 10(4):30-35, 1983.

Ask a lawyer: I had my fallopian tubes tied for sterilization but I still had a baby afterward. Can I sue the doctor?, by L. S. Dranoff. CHATELAINE. 57:28; 32, June 1984.

Assessing cohort birth expectations data from the current population survey, 1971-1981, by M. O'Connell, et al. DEMOGRAPHY. 20 (3):369, August 1983.

An assessment of pre-operative microbial screening on the prevention of post-abortion pelvic inflammatory disease, by A. M. Mills. BRITISH JOURNAL OF OBSTETRICS AND GYNAECOLOGY. 91(2):182-186, February 1984.

The association between smoking and sexual behavior among teens in U. S. contraceptive clinics, by L. S. Zabin. AMERICAN JOURNAL OF PUBLIC HEALTH. 74(3):261-263, March 1984.

Asymptomatic omental herniation following laparoscopic sterilisation, by D. S. Rajapaksa. CEYLON MEDICAL JOURNAL. 28(1):35-36, March 1983.

At risk for PID . . . the IUD. EMERGENCY MEDICINE. 16(1):107; 110, January 15, 1984.

Attitude and behavior of physicians and medical students toward contraception: results of a study carried out in Modena, by G. C. Di Renzo, et al. ANNALI DI OSTETRICIA GINECOLOGIA, MEDICINA PERINATALE. 105(1):37-63, January-February 1984.

Attitude to abortion, attitude to life and conservatism in Asutralia, by J. J. Ray. SOCIOLOGY AND SOCIAL RESEARCH. 68:236-246, January 1984.

Attitudes and behavioral intentions about abortion, by B. K. Singh, et al. POPULATION AND ENVIRONMENT: BEHAVIORAL AND SOCIAL ISSUES. 6(2):84-95, Summer 1983.

Attitudes of a group of Egyptian medical students towards family
    planning, by T. el-Mehairy. SOCIAL SCIENCE AND MEDICINE.
    19(2):131-134, 1984.

Attitudes to abortion, by J. Kemp. NURSING MIRROR. 158(17):34-35,
    April 25, 1984.

Attitudes to abortion among Catholic Mexican-American women:
    the effects of religiosity and education, by S. Rosenhouse-Persson,
    et al. DEMOGRAPHY. 20:87-98, February 1983.

Attitudes toward abortion and contraception among Nigerian
    secondary school girls, by A. U. Oronsaye, et al. INTERNATIONAL
    JOURNAL OF GYNAECOLOGY AND OBSTETRICS. 21(5):423-426,
    October 1983.

Attitudes toward abortion as a means of sex selection, by R. N. Feil,
    et al. JOURNAL OF PSYCHOLOGY. 116:269-272, March 1984.

Attitudes toward the rhythm method in the Philippines, by C.
    Verzosa, et al. STUDIES IN FAMILY PLANNING. 15(2):74,
    March-April 1984.

Attitudinal and motivational factors in contraception among
    women, by P. Kumar, et al. PERSPECTIVES IN PSYCHOLOGICAL
    RESEARCHES. 6(1):27-31, April 1983.

Autoantibodies to zona pellucida in tubectomized women, by A.
    Mhaskar, et al. CONTRACEPTION. 29(1):75-82, January 1984.

An automatic electronic device (Rite Time) to detect the onset of the
    infertile period by basal body temperature measurements, by J.
    P. Royston, et al. BRITISH JOURNAL OF OBSTETRICS AND
    GYNAECOLOGY. 91(6):565-573, June 1984.

Awareness of the existence of postcoital contraception among stu-
    dents who have had a therapeutic abortion, by L. H. Schilling.
    JOURNAL OF AMERICAN COLLEGE HEALTH. 32(6):244-246,
    June 1984.

Azoospermia induced by 19-nortestosterone [letter], by R. F. Parrott.
    LANCET. 1(8379):731, March 31, 1984.

The baby boom and its explanations, by F. D. Bean. SOCIOLOGICAL
    QUARTERLY. 24:353-366, Summer 1983.

Background factors of defective contraception in abortion-seeking patients, by A. Lalos, et al. LAKARTIDNINGEN. 80(26-27):2646-2648, June 29, 1983.

Balanced translocation as one of the genetic causes of habitual abortion, by J. Szabo, et al. ORVOSI HETILAP. 125(2):67-70, January 8, 1984.

Balancing the risks of the pill [to an increased risk of developing certain cancers]. ECONOMIST. 289:91, October 29 1983.

Bankrolling the pro-choice machine, by M. Meehan. REGISTER. 60:1+, January 29, 1984.

Baptists and freedom: some reminders and remembrances of our past for the sake of our present [abortion: homosexuality], by H. Moody. AMERICAN BAPTIST QUARTERLY. 3(1):4-15, March 1984.

Barren policy, by B. Hartmann, et al. GUARDIAN. April 27, 1984, p. 9.

A barrier to HSV . . . the condom. EMERGENCY MEDICINE. 16(11): 135; 138, June 15, 1984.

Battling 'foeticide' [Alberta] therapeutic committees are under pressure, by S. McCarthy. ALBERTA REPORT. 11:45, May 28, 1984.

Beds for abortion: McMurray's new hospital sparks a pro-mill move, by T. Philip. ALBERTA REPORT. 10:37, October 24, 1983.

Behind the lines, by D. Browning. TEXAS MEDICINE. 12:5+, September 1984.

Benign hepatic adenoma associated with oral contraceptive use mimicking pelvic inflammatory disease. A case report, by J. E. Jenks, et al. JOURNAL OF REPRODUCTIVE MEDICINE. 29(3): 200-203, March 1984.

Benign liver tumors following long-term use of oral contraceptives. I. Results of image-producing diagnostic procedures of incidental intraoperatively discovered tumors, by F. Reichenbach, et al. ZENTRALBLATT FUR CHIRURGIE. 108(15):947-954, 1983.

— . II. Clinical diagnosis and therapy, by F. Reichenbach, et al. ZENTRALBLATT FUR CHIRURGIE. 108(15):955-966, 1983.

Benzalkonium chloride tampons. Local tolerance and effects on cervix mucus, by R. Erny, et al. JOURNAL DE GYNECOLOGIE, OBSTETRIQUE ET BIOLOGIE DE LA REPRODUCTION. 12(7):767-774, 1983.

Bernardin: abortion is a public issue. REGISTER. 60:2, October 14, 1984.

Bernardin on prolife future, by M. Meehan. REGISTER. 59:1+, December 4, 1983.

Bernardin still tailoring his seamless garment ethic of life issues, by J. Bernardin. NATIONAL CATHOLIC REPORTER. 20:1, April 6, 1984.

Beta-adrenoceptor blocker pharmacokinetics and the oral contraceptive pill, by M. J. Kendall, et al. BRITISH JOURNAL OF CLINICAL PHARMACOLOGY. 17(Suppl 1):87S-89S, 1984.

Better advice is needed both before and after abortion, by U. Claesson, et al. LARKARTIDNINGEN. 81(4):220-222, January 25, 1984.

Beyond baby doe [reproductive rights], by M. Lipsyte. NEW DIRECTIONS FOR WOMEN. 13:8, January-February 1984.

Bibliographic sur l'avortment, by F. Fourgeroux. REVUE FRANCAISE DE SOCIOLOGIE. 23:527-535, July-September 1982.

Billings natural family planning method: correlation of subjective signs with cervical mucus quality and ovulation, by J. J. Etchepareborda, et al. CONTRACEPTION. 28(5):475-480, 1983.

Biological properties of 1,2-trans-1-(beta-pyrrolidinoethoxy) penyl)-oxyindane (compound E-1487): a new nonsteroidal post-coital anti-fertility agent, by M. M. Singh, et al. INDIAN JOURNAL OF EXPERIMENTAL BIOLOGY. 21(8):432-434, August 1983.

Biphasic oral contraceptives, by S. C. Sasso. MCN. 9(2):101, March-April 1984.

Birth control centers. Are they a necessary supplement to primary health care?, by T. Bull-Njaa, et al. TIDSSKRIFT FOR DEN NORSKE LAEGEFORENING. 103(26):1798-1802, September 20, 1983.

Birth control coercion on the horizon?, by J. Cavanaugh-O'Keefe.

REGISTER. 60:1+, August 26, 1984.

Birth control/custommade child, by A. Barclay. WOMEN AND HEALTH. 9(1):83, Spring 1984.

Birth control— damages— torts. THE FAMILY LAW REPORTER: COURT OPINIONS. 10(16):1219, February 21, 1984.

Birth control discontinuance as a diffusion process, by E. G. Porter. STUDIES IN FAMILY PLANNING. 15(1):20-29, January-February 1984.

Birth control knowledge, attitudes and practice: a comparison of working and middle class Puerto Rican and white American women, by V. A. Borras. DISSERTATION ABSTRACTS INTERNATIONAL: B. 45(10), April 1985.

Birth control: lucky dip [diagnostic kit by Boots-Celltech Diagnostics]. ECONOMIST. 209:84-85, February 18, 1984.

Birth control manual, by L. Kapplow. EAST WEST. 14(2):86, February 1984.

Birth control [natural family planning], by R. A. Jones. MS. 13:54+, August 1984.

Birth control; new data on women's choices. RN. 47:14, January 1984.

Birth control [ovulation method], by R. A. Jonas. MS. 13:54+, August 1984.

Birth-control reliability, by J. Whitlow. ESSENCE. 14:36+, February 1984.

Birth control socialization: how to avoid discussing the subject, by J. Aldous. POPULATION AND ENVIRONMENT. 6(1):27, Spring 1983.

Birth-control survey: sterilization tops list in U. S., by S. D. Kash. MS. 12:17, January 1984.

Birth of handicapped child after negligent sterilisation, by D. Brahams. LANCET. 2(8403):649, September 15, 1984.

Birth of a new role for men, by P. Thomson. TIMES. September 24, 1984, p. 9.

The bishops and the politics of abortion, by M. Meehan. COMMON-WEAL. 111:169-173, March 23, 1984.

Bishops' ERA position avoids equality issue for abortion statement, by Sister M. Fiedler. NATIONAL CATHOLIC REPORTER. 20:30, June 8, 1984.

Bishops' letter on politics: healthy declaration or exhortation to consider abortion above all?, by R. B. Shaw, et al. NATIONAL CATHOLIC REPORTER. 20:8-9, August 31, 1984.

Bitter pills for Garret the Good, by R. Ford. TIMES. November 15, 1984, p. 16.

Black women in double jeopardy: a perspective on birth control, by K. H. Gould. HEALTH AND SOCIAL WORK. 9(2):96-105, 1984.

Blood hormone levels in Egyptian women on norethisterone oenanthate, by F. M. Saleh, et al. CONTRACEPTION. 28(1):41-51, July 1983.

Blood prolactin levels: influence of age, menstrual cycle and oral contraceptives, by F. Pansini, et al. CONTRACEPTION. 28(3):201-207, September 1983.

Blowing the whistle on the squeal rule [defunct regulation requiring clinics to inform parents if daughters are given contraceptives is still on the books], by D. Gates. NEWSWEEK. 104:18, September 24, 1984.

Brazil tries birth control. WORLD PRESS REVIEW. 31:54, February 1984.

Breaking through the stereotypes, by S. Callahan, et al. COMMON-WEAL. 111:520-523, October 5, 1984.

Breast cancer and oestrogen content of oral contraceptives [letter], by P. Bye. LANCET. 1(8370):223, January 28, 1984.

Breast cancer and oral contraceptive use, by L. Rosenberg, et al. AMERICAN JOURNAL OF EPIDEMIOLOGY. 119(2):167-176, February 1984.

Breast cancer and oral contraceptive use: a case-control study, by D. T. Janerigh, et al. JOURNAL OF CHRONIC DISEASES. 36(9): 639-646, 1983.

Breast cancer and oral contraceptives [letter]. LANCET. 2(8359): 1145-1146, November 12, 1983.

Breast cancer and oral contraceptives: reply to critics [letter], by M. C. Pike, et al. LANCET. 2(8364):1414, December 17, 1983.

Breast cancer in young women and use of oral contraceptives: possible modifying effect of formulation and age at use, by M. C. Pike, et al. LANCET. 2(8356):926-930, October 22, 1983.

Breast-feeding and child spacing, by P. Senanayake. HYGIE. 3(2):29-32, June 1984.

Breast feeding and contraception. The effect of low-dose oral contraceptives on the growth of the infant during breast feeding, by J. Gellen, et al. ORVOSI HETILAP. 125(4):193-196, January 22, 1984.

Breast-feeding and family planning policy, by V. Balasubrahmanya. ECONOMIC AND POLITICAL WEEKLY. 18:2099, December 10, 1983.

Breastfeeding and oral contraceptives: Tasmanian survey, by J. F. Coy, et al. AUSTRALIAN PAEDIATRIC JOURNAL. 19(3):168-171, September 1983.

Breast feeding is contraceptive. NEW SCIENTIST. 102:23, May 3, 1984.

Breast feeding . . . its contraceptive effect is increasingly forgotten in the worldwide trend toward bottle feeding, by R. V. Short. SCIENTIFIC AMERICAN. 250(4):35-41, April 1984.

British pill victims win right to sue in U. S. NEW SCIENTIST. 102:8, May 31, 1984.

Brucella ovis-induced abortion in ewes, by M. C. Libal, et al. JOURNAL OF AMERICAN VETERINARY MEDICAL ASSOCIATION. 1853(5):553-554, September 1, 1983.

Budd-Chiari syndrome following pregnancy, by F. V. Covillo, et al. MISSOURI MEDICINE. 81(7):356-358, July 1984.

Building a family: unplanned events, by J. Bongaarts. STUDIES IN FAMILY PLANNING. 15(1):14-19, January-February 1984.

Button-hole technique of tubectomy, by L. N. Garg. JOURNAL OF

THE INDIAN MEDICAL ASSOCIATION. 81(7-8):128-130, October 1983.

C heterochromatin variation in couples with recurrent early abortions, by A. Maes, et al. JOURNAL OF MEDICAL GENETICS. 20 (5):350-356, October 1983.

CA2 enjoins implementation of government's "squeal rule." THE FAMILY LAW REPORTER: COURT OPINIONS. 10(2):1024-1025, November 8, 1983.

The CMA abortion survey [letter]. CANADIAN MEDICAL ASSOCIATION JOURNAL. 129(12):1259-1260, December 15, 1983.

Calcium oxalate crystal growth in normal urine: role of contraceptive hormones, by R. Tawashi, et al. UROLOGY RESEARCH. 12(1):7-9, 1984.

Campaign against reproductive choice in Manitoba, by P. Mitchell. CANADIAN DIMENSION. 17:4, November 1983.

Campylobacter coli speticaemia associated with septic abortion, by M. Kist, et al. INFECTION. 12(2):88-90, March-April 1984.

Campylobacter enteritis associated with recurrent abortions in agammaglobuliemia, by A. Pines, et al. ACTA OBSTETRICIA ET GYNECOLOGICA SCANDINAVICA. 62(3):279-280, 1983.

Campylobacter septic abortion, by P. M. Jost, et al. SOUTHERN MEDICAL JOURNAL. 77(7):924, July 1984.

Can abortion be legally justified?, by W. Esser. MEDICINE AND THE LAW. 3(3):205-216, 1984.

Can Asia's population bomb be diffused?, by G. Pranay. ASIA. 6(3): 16, September-October 1983.

Can effective birth control be legislated? An analysis of factors that predict birth control utilization, by J. G. Murp[hy, et al. JOURNAL OF PUBLIC HEALTH POLICY. 5(2):198-212, June 1984.

Canadian MD's challenge antiabortion, by M. Jones. MILITANT. 48(15):15, April 27, 1984.

Cancer and the pill [letter]. LANCET. 2(8395):166, July 21, 1984.

Cancer and the pill, by E. Grand. ECOLOGIST. 14(2):68-76, 1983.

Cancer and the pill; the mountain which brought forth a mouse, by L. Offerhaus, et al. NEDERLANDS TIJDSCHRIFT VOOR GENEES-KUNDE. 128(2):78-79, January 14, 1984.

Cancer chemotherapy and contraceptive counseling, by R. H. Parrish, 2nd. DRUG INTELLIGENCE AND CLINICAL PHARMACY. 18(1): 71-72, January 1984.

Cancer of the breast. Influence of hormonal contraception, by A. Gorins. PRESSE MEDICALE. 13(19):1207-1210, May 5, 1984.

The cap that fits, by R. Porter. TIMES LITERARY SUPPLEMENT. March 16, 1984, p. 265.

Carbon dioxide laser in tubal microsurgery [letter], by G. M. Grunert. AMERICAN JOURNAL OF OBSTETRICS AND GYNECOLOGY. 148(1):117-118, January 1, 1984.

Cardiomyopathy with hepatic necrosis after several years of using Norbiogest Spofa, by M. Brozman, et al. BRATISLAVSKE LEKARSKE LISTY. 80(5):603-609, November 1983.

Cardiovascular disease and vasectomy. AMERICAN FAMILY PHYSICIAN. 28:304, October 1984.

Cardiovascular disease and vasectomy: findings from two epidemiologic studies, by M. J. Goldacre, et al. NEW ENGLAND JOURNAL OF MEDICINE. 308:805-808, April 7, 1983.

The career of Margaret Sanger and its impact on the family planning movement, by L. Lampe. ORVOSI HETILAP. 125(4):221-222, January 22, 1984.

Carr resigns from women's pastoral, by C. Hays. REGISTER. 60:1+, October 21, 1984.

Carrier Busk's daughter [forced eugenic sterilization], by S. J. Gould. NATURAL HISTORY. 93:14-18, July 1984.

A case-study of oral contraceptive use and breast cancer, by C. H. Hennekens, et al. JNCI. 72(1):39-42, January 1984.

Case of ectopic pregnancy after postcoital contraception with ethinyloestradiol-levonorgestrel, by A. A. Kubba, et al. BRITISH MEDICAL JOURNAL. 287(6042):1343-1344, November 5, 1983.

A case of multiple thromboses: review of the cardiovascular complications of oral contraceptives, by C. Hanssen, et al. REVUE MEDICALE DE LIEGE. 39(11):495-499, June 1, 1984.

Case of successful treatment of a patient with an extremely severe form of gynecologic tetanus, by V. L. Rabinovich, et al. ANESTEZIOLOGIIA I REANIMATOLOGIIA. (6):58-59, November-December 1983.

Case studies for students: a companion to teaching ethics in nursing, by M. L. Applegate, et al. NLN PUBLICATIONS. (41-1963A):1-36, 1984.

Casting a vote for life, by G. C. Zahn. AMERICA. 151:337-339, November 24, 1984.

Castration for rapists criticized. THE NATIONAL SHERIFF. 36(1): 32, February-March 1984.

The Catholic church's view on population, by A. W. Smith. SCHOLAS-TIC UPDATE. 116:3, March 2, 1984.

Catholic teaching on abortion in a secular society, by D. E. Pilarczyk. OUR SUNDAY VISITOR. 73:6, October 7, 1984.

Catholic theologians clash on abortion, by M. Meehan. REGISTER. 60:1+, July 1, 1984.

A Catholic woman in the White House? COMMONWEAL. 111:419-421, August 10, 1984.

Catholics and abortion; interview with Frances Kissling, by M. Meehan. REGISTER. 60:1+, May 20, 1984.

Cause-effect relation between abortion and herpes infection, by N. D. Kolomiets, et al. AKUSHERSTVO I GINEKOLOGIIA. (3):62-64, March 1984.

Causes of spontaneous abortion, by H. J. Huisjes. NEDERLANDS TIJDSCHRIFT VOOR GENEESKUNDE. 127(49):2241-2246, December 3, 1983.

Cerebral arterial occlusion and intracranial venous thrombosis in a woman taking oral contraceptives, by F. Monton, et al. POST-GRADUATE MEDICAL JOURNAL. 60(704):426-428, June 1984.

The cervical cap: a retrospective study of an alternative contraceptive technique, by J. M. Johnson. AMERICAN JOURNAL OF

OBSTETRICS AND GYNECOLOGY. 148(5):604-608, March 1, 1984.

Cervical cytological screening for users of oral contraceptives [letter],
by R. W. Burslem. LANCET. 2(8356):968, October 22, 1983.

Cervical dilatation using PGF2 alpha gel before voluntary interrup-
tion of pregnancy during the first trimester, by B. Maria, et al.
JOURNAL DE GYNECOLOGIE, OBSTETRIQUE ET BIOLOGIE DE
LA REPRODUCTION. 12(7):789-794, 1983.

Cervical dilatation with 16,16-dimethyl-trans-delta 2-PGE1 methyl
ester (Cervagem) prior to vacuum aspiration. A double-blind,
placebo-controlled randomized study, by N. J. Christense, et al.
CONTRACEPTION. 29(5):457-464, May 1984.

Chaff from the Charter's threshing floor, by M. Shumaitcher.
MANITOBA LAW JOURNAL. 13:435-443, 1983.1

The challenge of the future, by M. O'Connor. POPULI. 10(4):23-29,
1983.

Chance, choice, and the future of reproduction, by W. B. Miller.
AMERICAN PSYCHOLOGIST. 38(11):1198-1205, November 1983.

Changes in blood chorionic gonadotropin, progesterone levels and
estradiol in midterm labor induced by rivanol, by F. Y. Liu.
CHUNG HUA FU CHAN KO TSA CHIH. 19(2):114-115, April 1984.

Changes in estrogen metabolism after chorionic oral contraceptive
adminstration in the rhesus monkey, by W. Slikker, Jr., et al.
DRUG METABOLISM AND DISPOSITION. 12(2):148-153, March-
April 1984.

Changes in lipid peroxidation indices and their correction in women
before artificial interruption of pregnancy, by G. N. Kryzhanovskii, et al. AKUSHERSTVO I GINEKOLOGIIA. (3):34-35, March
1984.

Changes in rates of spontaneous fetal deaths reported in upstate New
York vital records by gestational age, 1968-78, by P. K. Cross.
PUBLIC HEALTH REPORTS. 99(2):212-215, March-April 1984.

Changes in serum apo-lipoprotain AI and sex-hormone-binding
globulin levels after treatment with two different progestins
administered alone and in combination with ethinyl estradiol,
by N. Crona, et al. CONTRACEPTION. 29(3):261-270, March 1984.

Changes in serum lipoproteins in women treated with combined oral contraceptives, by P. Bellod, et al. REVISTA CLINICA ESPANOLA. 170(6):275-278, September 30, 1983.

The changing American family, by A. Thornton, et al. POPULATION BULLETIN. 38(4):2, October 1983.

Characteristics of contraceptive acceptors in an urban Nigerian setting, by O. Ayangade. INTERNATIONAL JOURNAL OF GYNAE-COLOGY AND OBSTETRICS. 22(1):59-66, February 1984.

Characteristics of the course and management of pregnancy and labor in women at risk for abortion, by L. N. Chernomaz, et al. AKUSHERSTVO I GINEKOLOGIIA. (12):34-35, December 1983.

Characteristics of family planning clients in Bangladesh, by I. Swenson, et al. INTERNATIONAL JOURNAL OF FERTILITY. 28(3):149-155, 1983.

Characteristics of first trimester abortion patients at an urban Indian clinic, by S. Bahl Dhall, et al. STUDIES IN FAMILY PLANNING. 15(2):93-97, March-April 1984.

Characteristics of women requesting reversal of sterilization, by W. A. Divers, Jr. FERTILITY AND STERILITY. 41(2):233-236, February 1984.

Characteristics of women who stop using contraceptives, by C. R. Hammerslough. FAMILY PLANNING PERSPECTIVES. 16(1): 14-18, January-February 1984.

Characterizations of anti-oLH beta antibodies acting as contraceptives in rhesus monkeys. II. In vivo neutralizing ability for gonadotropic hormones, by Y. Yamamoto, et al. JOURNAL OF REPRODUCTIVE IMMUNOLOGY. 5(4):195-202, July 1983.

Chemosterilization of male tobacco budworm moths (Lepidoptera: Noctuidae); some effects on reproductive physiology, by M. M. Crystal, et al. ANNALS OF THE ENTOMOLOGICAL SOCIETY OF AMERICA. 75:684-689, November 1982.

Childhood disadvantage and the planning of pregnancy, by D. M. Fergusson, et al. SOCIAL SCIENCE AND MEDICINE. 17(17):1223-1227, 1983.

Children by choice or by change: the perceived effects of parity, by J. Ross, et al. SEX ROLES. 9:69-77, January 1983.

Children: yes or no, a decision-making program for women, by J. C. Daniluk, et al. PERSONNEL AND GUIDANCE JOURNAL. 62:240-242, December 1983.

Child-spacing effects on infant and early child mortality, by J. Hobcraft, et al. POPULATION INDEX. 49:585-618, Winter 1983.l

China's one-child families: girls need not apply, by L. Landman. RF. December 1983, p. 8-10.

China's population. SOCIETY. 21:4, September-October 1984.

China's popuation policy: theory and methods, by X. Qian. STUDIES IN FAMILY PLANNING. 14:295-301, December 1983.

Chinese family problems: Research and trends, by Z. Wei. JOURNAL OF MARRIAGE AND THE FAMILY. 45(4):943-948, November 1983.

Choice advocates, by C. Cracolice. NEW DIRECTIONS FOR WOMEN. 13:8, March-April 1984.

Choice: a divisive issue [Manitoba], by P. Mitchell. CANADIAN DIMENSION. 17:5-6, November 1983.

The choice of oral contraception in 1984: general indications and specific cases, by U. Gaspard. REVUE MEDICALE DE LIEGE. 39(7):261-265, April 1, 1984.l

The choice of sterilization: voluntarily childless couples, mothers of one child by choice, and males seeking reversal of vasectomy, by V. J. Callan, et al. JOURNAL OF BIOSOCIAL SCIENCE. 16(2): 241-248, April 1984.

Choice of termination of pregnancy. The significance of demographic and social factors, by N. K. Rasmussen, et al. UGESKRIFT FOR LAEGER. 145(48):3758-3764, November 28, 1983.

Choicers courting Catholic academics, by J. F. Hitchcock. REGISTER. 60:1+, June 3, 1984.

Cholesterol, triglyceride and apolipoprotein concentrations in the serum and lipoprotein fractions in the first trimester of normal pregnancy and threatened abortion, by L. Marianowski, et al. GINEKOLOGIA POLSKA. 55(3):177-184, March 1984.

Choosing an oral contraceptive, by E. Weisberg. HEALTHRIGHT.

3:12-16, February 1984.

Chorionic biopsy and miscarriage in first trimester [letter]. by B. Gustavii. LANCET. 1(8376):562, March 10, 1984.

Christians and the state policy of family planning: attitudinal change, by L. Dsilva. JOURNAL OF FAMILY WELFARE. 30:21-29, September 1983.

Chromosomal aberrations and chromosomal polymorphism in families with reproductive failure, by G. Vulkova. FOLIA MEDICA. 25(3):11-18, 1983.

Chromosome anomalies in 136 couples with a history of recurrent abortions, by U. Diedrich, et al. HUMAN GENETICS. 65(1):48-52, 1983.

Chronic toxoplasmosis in pregnant women— an epidemiological and social problem, by C. Jezyna, et al. ZENTRALBLATT FUR BAKTERIOLOGIE, MIKROBIOLOGIE UND HYGIENE. 177(1-2):96-102, January 1983.

The church and abortion, perception and reality, by P. Zagano. COMMONWEAL. 111:173-175, March 23, 1984.

Church and Cuomo. COMMONWEAL. 111:517-518, October 5, 1984.

The church-state debate [M. Cuomo vs. Catholic bishops on abortion], by C. Krauthammer. NEW REPUBLIC. 191:15-18, September 17-24, 1984.

Cigarettes, contraceptive drugs and lipidogenesis in the female, by J. Lederer. SEMAINES DES HOPITAUX DE PARIS. 59(49):3413-3416, December 29, 1983.

Civil Liberties, by N. Hentoff. INQUIRY. 7(2):25, January 1984.

The classical roots of the personhood debate, by R. H. Feen. FAITH AND REASON. 9:120-127, Summer 1983.

Clearing carcinogenic contraceptives through the FDA [injectable contraceptive, Depo-Provera], by E. Gollub. BUSINESS AND SOCIETY REVIEW. (46):67-70, Summer 1983.

Clinic arson suspect goes to trial, by D. Mathiason. GUARDIAN. 36(44):4, September 12, 1984.

Clinical and analytic hormone studies of the suitability of estrumate for induction of mummified fetus expulsion in cattle, by D. Ruetschi, et al. SCHWEIZER ARCHIV FUER TIERHEILKUNDE. 126(6):323-329, June 1984.

Clinical and histologic evaluation of laser reanastomosis of the uterine tube, by J. K. Choe, et al. FERTILITY AND STERILITY. 41(5):754-760, May 1984.

Clinical data on the use of current oral contraceptives, by M. L. Krymskaia, et al. AKUSHERSTVO I GINEKOLOGIIA. (11):19-22, November 1983.

Clinical estimation of the duration of pregnancy in legal abortion— are doctors biased by their knowledge of the duration of amenorrhoea?, by T. Gjorup, et al. METHODS OF INFORMATION IN MEDICINE. 23(2):96-98, April 1984.

Clinical evaluation of an improved on injectable microcapsule contraceptive system, by L. R. Beck, et al. AMERICAN JOURNAL OF OBSTETRICS AND GYNECOLOGY. 147(7):815-821, December 1, 1983.

Clinical evaluation of uterine hemorrhage in early pregnancy, by J. Krzysiek. GINEKOLOGIA POLSKA. 55(2):109-114, February 1984.

Clinical experience with a triphasic oral contraceptive, by M. Ulstein, et al. ACTA OBSTETRICIA ET GYNECOLOGICA SCANDINAVICA. 63(3):233-236, 1984.

A clinical study of norethisterone enanthate in rural Mexico, by C. Walhter Meade, et al. STUDIES IN FAMILY PLANNING. 15(3): 143, May-June 1984.

Clinical study of the secondary effects associated with taking a triphasic anti-ovulatory contraceptive, by M. Vekemans. REVUE MEDICALE DE BRUXELLES. 5(1):13-19, January 1984.

Clinicaul use of RU 486: control fo the menstrual cycle and effect of the hypophyseal-adrenal axis, by R. C. Gaillard, et al. ANNALES D'ENDOCRINOLOGIE. 44(5):345-346, 1983.

Clinical use of Rigevidon, Ovidon and Postinor, by V. N. Serov, et al. AKUSHERSTVO I GINEKOLOGIIA. (11):17-19, November 1983.

Clinico-experimental evaluation on the use of sulprostone, new PGE2 derivative. I. Interruption of pregnancy in the first trimester, by

I. Stoppelli, et al. MINERVA GINECOLOGIA. 35(12):819-823, December 1983.

—. II. Interruption of pregnancy in the second trimester, by I. Stoppelli, et al. MINERVA GINECOLOGIA. 35(12):825-828, December 1983.

—. III. Its use in some aspects of obstetric pathology, by I. Stoppelli, et al. MINERVA GINECOLOGIA. 35(12):829-831, December 1983.

Clinico-immunologic studies in threatened abortion, by L. S. Dzoz, et al. AKUSHERSTVO I GINEKOLOGIIA. (12):28-29, December 1983.

Clinico-pathologic study on the action of yuanhuadine in mid-trimester abortion, by Q. W. Wang. CHUNG HUA FU CHANG KO TSA CHIH. 18(3):154-156, July 1983.

Clinco-ultrasonic aspects of the diagnosis of complications after induced abortion in the first trimester, by L. P. Bakuleva, et al. AKUSHERSTVO I GINEKOLOGIIA. (12):53-55, December 1983.

Clostridium welchii infection after amniocentesis, by R. E. Fray, et al. BRITISH MEDICAL JOURNAL. 288(6421):901-902, March 24, 1984.

Club of life, tied to LaRouche, is courting U. S. prolife mainstream, by T. Ackerman. REGISTER. 60:1+, April 1, 1984.

Coagulopathy and induced abortion methods: rates and relative risks, by M. E. Kafrissen, et al. AMERICAN JOURNAL OF OBSTETRICS AND GYNECOLOGY. 147(3):344-345, October 1983.

Coital techniques of fertility control: science or fiction?, by E. Browne. HEALTHRIGHT. 3:27-29, November 1984.

Coitus-related cervical cancer risk factors: trends and differentials in racial and religious groups, by G. E. Hendershot. AMERICAN JOURNAL OF PUBLIC HEALTH. 73:299-301, March 1983.

Colonic Crohn's disease and use of oral contraception, by J. M. Rhodes, et al. BRITISH MEDICAL JOURNAL. 1288(6417):595-596, February 25, 1984.

Colorado bishops endorse Amendment No. 3. ORIGINS. 14:223-224, September 20, 1984.

Commentary on abortion article, by T. J. O'Donnell. LINACRE QUARTERLY. 51:11-13, February 1984.

A common tragedy . . . miscarriage, by J. Moore. COMMUNITY OUTLOOK. June 1984, p. 210.

Community characteristics, women's education, and fertility in Peru, by T. Marta. STUDIES IN FAMILY PLANNING. 15(4):162, July-August 1984.

A comparative evaluation of three intrauterine devices, by P. M. Ditchik, et al. CONTRACEPTIVE DELIVERY SYSTEMS. 5(2):117-122, 1984.

Comparative studies of intrauterine devices in Singapore, by T. McCarthy, et al. CONTRACEPTIVE DELIVERY SYSTEMS. 4(3): 219-226, 1983.

A comparative study of Lippes loop and Delta loop intrauterine devices in early postpartum, by S. Chompotaweep, et al. CONTRACEPTION. 28(5):399-404, 1983.

A comparative study of two estrogen dosages in combined oral contraceptives among Sudanese women, by A. S. Gerais, et al. INTERNATIONAL JOURNAL OF GYNAECOLOGY AND OBSTETRICS. 21(6):459-468, December 1983.

Comparative study of various intracervically administered PG gel preparations for termination of first trimester pregnancies, by W. Rath, et al. CONTRACEPTION. 28(3): 209-222, September 1983.

A comparison of crisis variables among groups of women experiencing induced abortion, by G. C. Polk. DISSERTATION ABSTRACTS INTERNATIONAL: B. 45(3), September 1984.

Comparison of first-time and repeat abortions, by E. Michaels. CHATELAINE. 57:16, October 1984.

Comparison of laparoscopic Falope-Ring and minilaparotomy sterilization, by P. A. Sherman, et al. OBSTETRICS AND GYNECOLOGY. 63(1):71-75, January 1984.

Comparison of the operating microscope and loupe for microsurgical tubal anastomosis: a randomized clinical trial, by J. A. Rock, et al. FERTILITY AND STERILITY. 41(2):229-232, February 1984.

Comparison of rigid and flexible cannulae for early abortion without cervical dilatation, World Health Organization Task Force on Sequelae of Abortion. STUDIES IN FAMILY PLANNING. 15 (2):79-83, March-April 1984.

Comparison of three types of tubal sterilization: the medan experience, by H. Sitompul, et al. CONTRACEPTION. 29(1):55-63, January 1984.

Comparison of two prostaglandins used to terminate mid-trimester pregnancy, by K. S. Gookin, et al. SOUTHERN MEDICAL JOURNAL. 77(6):717-718; 721, June 1984.

Compensation for damages due to failure to interrupt pregnancy. MMW. 126(6):128-131, February 10, 1984.

Complementarity of work and fertility among young American mothers, by F. L. Mott, et al. POPULATION STUDIES. 37(2):239, July 1983.

Complete surgical obliteration of the cervix uteri in the treatment of threatened premature labor, by L. Cesak. CESKOSLOVENSKA GYNEKOLOGIE. 48(3):195-197, April 1983.

Compliance with therapeutic regimens, by S. Jay, et al. JOURNAL OF ADOLESCENT HEALTH CARE. 5(2):124-136, April 1984.

Complications following postpartum sterilization by bilateral tubal ligation, by C. L. Cook, et al. JOURNAL OF THE KENTUCKY MEDICAL ASSOCIATION. 82(4):171-174, April 1984.

Complications in a case of pregnancy interruption by the Aburel method, by S. Grigorov. AKUSHERSTVO I GINEKOLOGIIA. 22(5): 406-408, 1983.

Complications in 8509 laparoscopic Falope ring sterilizations performed under local anaesthesia, by R. C. Pattinson, et al. SOUTH AFRICAN MEDICAL JOURNAL. 64(25):975-976, December 10, 1983.

Complications in pregnancy following abortion induced with PGF2 alpha, by G. Koinzer, et al. ZENTRALBLATT FUR GYNAE-KOLOGIE. 106(2):120-125, 1984.

Complications of female sterilization: immediate and delayed, by G. R. Huggins, et al. FERTILITY AND STERILITY. 41(3):337-355, March 1984.

Complications of induced abortion— personal observations, by J. Krasnodebski, et al. POLSKI TYGODNIK LEKARSKI. 38(41):1271-1273, October 10, 1983.

Complications of tubal sterilization [letter], by S. L. Corson. AMERICAN JOURNAL OF OBSTETRICS AND GYNECOLOGY. 147(6):730-731, November 15, 1983.

Computerized birth control, by S. Katz. CHATELAINE. 56:18, November 1983.

Conception control by vaginal administration or pills containing ethinyl estradiol and dl-norgestrel, by E. M. Coutinho, et al. FERTILITY AND STERILITY. 42(3):478-481, September 1984.

Condom conundrum: a birth control gimmick raises hackles in Calgary. ALBERTA REPORT. 11:13, March 5, 1984.

Conference on Population, by J. L. Buckley. VITAL SPEECHES OF THE DAY. 50:677-679, September 1, 1984.

Confidentiality and the abortion act [letter], by J. Chambers. LANCET. 1(8369):165, January 21, 1984.

Confused Cuomo, angry Safire attack bishop, by W. F. Gavin. HUMAN EVENTS. 44:12+, September 22, 1984.

Congenital abnormalities in legal abortions at 20 weeks' gestation or later, by E. Alberman, et al. LANCET. 1(8388):1226-1228, June 2, 1984.

Congenital uterine malformations as indication for cervical suture (cerclage) in habitual abortion and premature delivery, by H. Abramovici, et al. INTERNATIONAL JOURNAL OF FERTILITY. 28(3):161-164, 1983.

Conscience and politics, by B. G. Mitchell. TABLET. 238:966-968, October 6, 1984.

Consequences of China's new population policy, by S. L. Wong. CHINA QUARTERLY. June 1984, pp. 220-240.

Consequences of chorionic biopsy [letter]. NEW ENGLAND JOURNAL OF MEDICINE. 310(17):1121, April 26, 1984.

Consequences of teenage pregnancy and motherhood, by L. Simkins. ADOLESCENCE. 19:39-54, Spring 1984.

Considerations on the possible immune nature of abortions, by E. Laureti. MINERVA GINECOLOGIA. 36(1-2):15-16, January-February 1984.

Consistent ethic of life: morally correct, tactically necessary, by J. L. Bernardin. ORIGINS. 14:120-122, July 12, 1984.

Constitutional law— the "aborted" evolution of fetal rights after Roe v. Wade. WESTERN NEW ENGLAND LAW REVIEW. 542(6):535-553, 1983.

Constitutional law— fourteenth amendment— right to abortion— regulatory framework— standard of review— the United States Supreme Court has held that the state may not, in its regulation of abortion, deviate from accepted medical practice, and that all pre-viability abortion regulation shall be subject to strict scrutiny under the compelling state interest standard of substantive due process analysis— City of Akron v. Akron Center for Reproductive Health, Inc. DUQUESNE LAW REVIEW. 22:767-785, Spring 1984.

Constitutional law— New Jersey statute prohibiting Medicaid funding for abortions except where medically necessary to preserve the life of the mother violates the equal protection clause of the New Jersey Constitution— Right to Choose v. Byrne. TEMPLE LAW QUARTERLY. 56:983-1011, 1983.

Constitutional law— right to privacy— municipal roadblock to abortion denounced— City of Akron v. Akron Center for Reproductive Health, Inc. SETON HALL LAW REVIEW. 14:658-682, 1984.

Constitutional law— state constitutional law— equal protection— state statute restricting the provision of medicaid funds to abortions medically necessary to preserve the mother's life violates state equal protection standards and therefore must be construed to require funding of all abortions necessary to preserve the mother's life or death. Right to Choose v. Byrne. RUTGERS LAW JOURNAL. 14:217-231, Fall 1982.

Continental war (Roman Catholic church), by L. Cohen, et al. ALBERTA REPORT. 11:34, July 9, 1984.

Continuation of contraception following menstrual regulation— a Bangladesh experience, by H. H. Akhter, et al. JOURNAL OF BIOSOCIAL SCIENCE. 16(1):137-151, January 1984.

Continued pregnancy after failed first-trimester abortion, by W. L.

Fielding, et al. OBSTETRICS AND GYNECOLOGY. 63(3):421-424, March 1984.

Contraception and the rejection of God, by L. Ciccone. L'OSSERVA-TORE ROMANO. (50):9-10, December 12, 1983.

Contraception and sexually transmissible diseases, by J. Porter. HEALTHRIGHT. 3:12-15, August 1984.

Contraception and unwanted pregnancy, by N. E. Adler. BEHAVIOR-AL MEDICINE UPDATE. 5(4):28-34, Winter 1984.

Contraception: answers of wives and husbands compared in a survey of Swiss couples, by F. Hopflinger, et al. JOURNAL OF BIO-SOCIAL SCIENCE. 16(2):259-268, April 1984.

Contraception: antibodies an answer?, by J. Silberner. SCIENCE NEWS. 126:46, July 21, 1984.

The contraception controversy. TABLET. 237:1199-1200, December 10, 1983.

Contraception: fad and fashion, by A, Kessler, et al. WORLD HEALTH. June 1984, p. 24.

Contraception for adolescents, by M. Broome. PRACTITIONER. 228(1391):493-498, May 1984.

Contraception for the older woman, by P. Bowen-Simpkins. BRI-TISH JOURNAL OF OBSTETRICS AND GYNAECOLOGY. 91(6): 513-515, June 1984.

Contraception: helping patients choose, by L. G. Cupit. JOGN NURSING (SUPPL). 13(2):23s-9s, March-April 1984.

Contraception: the hope that failed, by A. Lake. LADIES HOME JOURNAL. 101(8):83-85; 137-138; 142+, August 1984.

Contraception in adolescence: a review. 1. Psychosocial aspects, by A. D. Hofmann. WHO BULLETIN. 62(1):151-162, 1984.

— . 2. Biomedical aspects, by A. D. Hofmann. WHO BULLETIN. 62(2): 331-344, 1984.

Contraception in the dog and cat, by E. K. Jackson. BRITISH VET-ERINARY JOURNAL. 140(2):132-137, March-April 1984.

Contraception in the perimenopausal years, by J. A. Need. CLINICAL REPRODUCTION AND FERTILITY. 1(4):332-335, December 1982.

Contraception in young people, by R. Fabian. CESKOSLOVENSKA GYNEKOLOGIE. 49(3):197-198, April 1984.

Contraception methods. AMERICAN FAMILY PHYSICIAN. 28:381, November 1983.

Contraception? No, but we're careful, by J. Richters. HEALTHRIGHT. 3:30-35, November 1984.

Contraception—sports, by Dutry, et al. ARCHIVES BELGES. 41(11-12):504-510, 1983.

Contraception tomorrow, by C. C. Standley, et al. INTERNATIONAL NURSING REVIEW. 31(3):73-75, May-June 1984.

Contraception with an LHRH agonist: effect on gonadotrophin and steroid secretion patterns, by H. Kuhl, et al. CLINICAL ENDOCRINOLOGY. 21(2):179-188, August 1984.

Contraceptive availability and use in five developing countries [Costa Rica, Thailand, Columbia, Honduras, and Nepal], by R. M. Cornelius, et al. STUDIES IN FAMILY PLANNING. 14:302-317, December 1983.

Contraceptive behavior among unmarried young women: a theoretical framework for research, by C. A. Nathanson, et al. POPULATION AND ENVIRONMENT. 6(1):39, Spring 1983.

The contraceptive context: a model for increasing nursing's involvement in family ;health, by J. M. Swanson, et al. MATERNAL-CHILD NURSING JOURNAL. 12(3):169-183, Fall 1983.

Contraceptive continuation among adolescents attending family planning clinics, by F. F. Furstenberg, et al. FAMILY PLANNING PERSPECTIVES. 15(5):211-214; 216-217, September-October 1983.

Contraceptive could kill. NEW SCIENTIST. 98:437, May 19, 1983.

Contraceptive counseling following pregnancy, by A. G. Rebholz. FORTSCHRITTE DER MEDIZIN. 102(17):462-484, May 3, 1984.

Contraceptive effect of low-dosage ovulation inhibitors containing

various progestagen agents, by ;M. Mall-Haefeli, et al. GEBURT-
SHILFE UND FRAUENHEILKUNDE. 44(3):177-179, March 1984.

Contraceptive effectiveness in Mexico, by H. Garrison. DISSERTA-
TION ABSTRACTS INTERNATIONAL: A. 45(3), September 1984.

The contraceptive habits of women applying for termination of
pregnancy, by K. Sidenius, et al. UGESKRIFT FOR LAEGER. 145
(48):3721-3724, November 28, 1983.

Contraceptive knowledge, contraceptive use, and pregnancy risk
experience among young Manawatu women, by A. D. Trlin, et al.
NEW ZEALAND MEDICAL JOURNAL. 96(746):1055-1058,
December 28, 1983.

Contraceptive methods and epilepsy. Consideration on its physiopathogenesis, by J. G. Speciali, et al. ARQUIVOS DE NEURO-
SPIQUIATRIA. 41(4):332-336, December 1983.

Contraceptive patterns of religious and racial groups in the United
States, 1955-76: convergence and distinctiveness, by W. D.
Mosher, et al. STUDIES IN FAMILY PLANNING. 15:101-111,
May-June 1984.

The contraceptive pill and vascular accidents, by M. Lancet. HARE-
FUAH. 104(3):107-108, February 1, 1983.

Contraceptive pill use, urinary sodium and blood-pressure. A population study in two Belgian towns, by J. Staessen, et al. ACTA
CARDIOLOGICA. 39(1):55-64, 1984.

Contraceptive pills and cancer. MIDWIFE, HEALTH VISITOR AND
COMMUNITY NURSE. 19(11):419, 443, November 1983.

Contraceptive pills and cancer [letter], by O. E. Iversen. TIDSSKRIFT
FOR DEN NORSKE LAEGEFORENING. 104(3):186-187, January
30, 1984.

Contraceptive practices of female runners [letter], by J. M. Lutter.
FERTILITY AND STERILITY. 40(4):551, October 1983.

Contraceptive preparations of plant origin, by V. V. Korkhov, et al.
AKUSHERSTVO I GINEKOLOGIIA. (11):8-10, November 1983.

Contraceptive self-efficacy: a primary prevention strategy, by R. A.
Levinson. JOURNAL OF SOCIAL WORK AND HUMAN SEXUAL-
ITY. 3(1):1-15, 1984.

Contraceptive sponge. AMERICAN FAMILY PHYSICIAN. 28:256, July 1983.

The contraceptive sponge: easy—but is it safe?, by A. B. Eagan. MS. 12:94-95, January 1984.

Contraceptive sponge linked to toxic shock. AMERICAN FAMILY PHYSICIAN. 29:16, February 1984.

Contraceptive sponge selling despite opposition. AMERICAN JOURNAL OF NURSING. 83:1372, October 1983.

Contraceptive use and program development: new information from Indonesia, by J. A. Ross, et al. INTERNATIONAL FAMILY PLANNING PERSPECTIVES. 9:68-77, October 1983.

Contraceptive use by adolescent females in relation to knowledge, and to time and method of contraceptive counseling, by S. A. Marcy, et al. RESEARCH IN NURSING AND HEALTH. 6(4):175-182, December 1983.

Contraceptives and acute salpingitis, by L. Svensson, et al. JAMA. 251(19):2553-2555, May 18, 1984.

Contraceptives: back to the barriers, by R. Serlin. NEW SCIENTIST. 91:281-284, July 30, 1984.

Contragestational effects of DL-alpha-difluoro-methylornithine, an irreversible inhibitor of ornithine decarboxylase, in the hamster, by G. Galliani, et al. CONTRACEPTION. 28(2):159-170, August 1983.

Contra-indications of oral contraceptives, by G. E. Lopez de la Osa. MEDICINA CLINICA. 81(9):404-406, October 1, 1983.

The control of male fertility by 1,2,3-trihydroxypropane (THP; glycerol): rapid arrest of spermatogenesis without altering libido, accessory organs, gonadal steroidogenesis, and serum testosterone, LH and FSH, by J. P. Wiebe, et al. CONTRACEPTION. 29(3):291-302, March 1984.

Coping with contraception: cognitive and behavioral methods with adolescents, by L. D. Gilchrist, et al. COGNITIVE THERAPY AND RESEARCH. 7(5):379-388, October 1983.

Copper intravas device (IVD) and male contraception, by M. M. Kapur, et al. CONTRACEPTION. 29(1):45-54, January 1984.

Copper loss from the Copper-T Model TCu220C, by M. Thiery, et al. CONTRACEPTION. 26(3):295-302, 1982.

Correlation between emotional reaction to loss of an unborn child and lymphocyte response to mitogenic stimulation in women, by S. Naor, et al. ISRAEL JOURNAL OF PSYCHIATRY AND RELATED SCIENCES. 20(3):231-239, 1983.

Correlation between morphological and cytogenetical findings in spontaneous abortions, by H. Muntegering, et al. VERHAND-LUNGEN DER DEUTSCHEN GESELLSCHAFT FUR PATHOLOGIE. 66:372-377, 1982.

Correlation of human chorionic gonadotropin secretion in early pregnancy failure with size of gestational sac and placental histology, by P. Jouppila, et al. OBSTETRICS AND GYNE-COLOGY. 63(4):537-542, April 1984.

Corrosion and weight loss from copper wire in the fincoid intra-uterine device in utero, by S. Kaivola, et al. CONTRACEPTIVE DELIVERY SYSTEMS. 5(2):105-108, 1984.

Cottonseed contraceptive update, by J. Silberner. SCIENCE NEWS. 126:60, July 28, 1984.

Counseling and the abortion issue, by P. J. Riga. JOURNAL OF PASTORAL COUNSELING. 117(2):44-55, 1982.

Counseling the patient for vasectomy, by A. E. Kilgore, Jr. AUAA J. 3(1):26, July-September 1982.

Couples with repeat spontaneous abortions: chromosome abnormal-ities, by F. Hecht, et al. ARIZONA MEDICINE. 41(8):530-532, August 1984.

A course on mothering and the right to abortion. WOMEN'S STUDIES QUARTERLY. 11:32-34, Winter 1983.

Court flips ruling that ERA permits abortion, by J. McManus, et al. NATIONAL CATHOLIC REPORTER. 20:6, October 5, 1984.

Creating and controlling a medical market: abortion in Los Angeles after liberalization, by M. S. Goldstein. SOCIAL PROBLEMS. 31:514-529, June 1984.

Criminal law— murder— intentional killing of viable fetus not murder— Hollis v. Commonwealth. NORTHERN KENTUCKY LAW REVIEW. 11:213-227, 1984.

A critique of two theological papers, by G. G. Grisez. HOMILETIC AND PASTORAL REVIEW. 84:10-15, July 1984.

A crucial new direction for international family planning, by F. D. Hosken. HUMANIST. 44(1):5-8; 45, January-February 1984.

A cultural and historical perspective on pregnancy-related activity among U. S. teenagers, by A. C. Washington. JOURNAL OF BLACK PSYCHOLOGY. 9(1):1-28, August 1982.

Cuomo wants political realism in abortion debate, by M. Scheiber. OUR SUNDAY VISITOR. 73:8, September 30, 1984.

Current legal problems of sterilization, by A. Eser, et al. GYNA-KOLOGE. 15(2):62-71, June 1982.

Current technology affecting Supreme Court abortion jurisprudence, by M. Buckley. NEW YORK LAW SCHOOL LAW REVIEW. 27(4): 1221-1260, 1982.

Current trends in the development of hormonal contraception, by E. M. Vikhliaeva. AKUSHERSTVO I GINEKOLOGIIA. (11):3-5, November 1983.1

Custom cervical cap reentering clinical trials, by K. Prupes. JAMA. 250(15):1946-1947; 1951, October 1983.

Cytogenetic findings in 318 couples with repeated spontaneous abortion: a review of experience in British Columbia, by J. T. Pantzar, et al. AMERICAN JOURNAL OF MEDICAL GENETICS. 17(3):615-620, March 1984.

Cytogenetic observations on 24 couples with spontaneous abortions, by J. F. Xu. CHUNG HUA I HSUEH TSA CHIH. 63(6):365-367, June 1983.

Cytogenetic studies in couples with multiple spontaneous abortions, by W. Schlempp, et al. ACTA ANTHROPOGENETICA. 7(2):113-118, 1983.

Cytogenetic studies in spontaneous abortuses, by T. Andrews, et al. HUMAN GENETICS. 66(1):77-84, 1984.

Cytogenetic study in 50 couples with recurrent abortions, by M. Maraeli, et al. GYNECOLOGIC AND OBSTETRIC INVESTIGATION. 17(2):84-88, 1984.

Cytogenetic study of married couples with recurrent spontaneous abortions, by V. G. Kroshikina, et al. TSITOLPGOUA I GENETIKA. 18(3):229-230, May-June 1984.

Cytogenetic survey in couples with recurrent fetal wastage, by J. P. Fryns, et al. HUMAN GENETICS. 65(4):336-354, 1984.

The Dalkon shield case: a plea for corporate conscience, by M. W. Lord. IRNFP. 8:181-188, Fall 1984.

Dalkon shield removal. AMERICAN FAMILY PHYSICIAN. 28:241, August 1983.

Damages and the 'unwanted child'. BRITISH MEDICAL JOURNAL (CLINICAL RES). 288(6412):244-245, January 21, 1984.

Dan Maguire on Catholic theology and abortion; interview with Daniel Charles Maguire, by M. Meehan. REGISTER. 60:1+, October 21, 1984.

Dateline: Romania: a war on abortions, by S. Masterman. MACLEAN'S. 97:12, April 23, 1984.

Day-case anaesthesia for termination of pregnancy. Evaluation of a total intravenous anaesthetic technique, by T. W. Ogg, et al. ANAESTHESIA. 38(11):1042-1046, November 1983.

A debate over sovereign rights [U. S. cuts off funds to family planning agencies that promote abortion], by L. Lopez. TIME. 124:34, August 20, 1984.

A decade of cementing the mosaic of Roe v. Wade: is the composite a message to leave abortion alone?. UNIVERSITY OF TOLEDO LAW REVIEW. 15:681-753, Winter 1984.

A decade of experience. POPULI. 10(1):36, 1983.

Decision for vasectomy— a case study, by S. R. Grover. JOURNAL OF FAMILY WELFARE. 30:49-55, December 1983.

Decision-making in regard to the use of contraceptives after confinement: a study among urban black women, by G. Erasmus. SUID-

AFRIKAANSE TYDSKRIF VIR SOSIOLOGIE. 15(2):94-97, May 1984.

Declining birth rates and growing populations, by K. Davis. POPULA-TION RESEARCH AND POLICY REVIEW. 3(1):61-75, January 1984.

Decreased plasma phosphate under hormonal contraceptives, by W. Tschope, et al. MINERAL AND ELECTROLYTE METABOLISM. 10(2):88-91, 1984.

Defending the right to abortion, by Reiman, et al. AGAINST THE CURRENT. 2(4):31, Winter 1984.

Demands made on general practice by women before and after an abortion, by D. Berkeley, et al. JOURNAL OF THE ROYAL COLLEGE OF GENERAL PRACTITIONERS. 34(263):310-315, June 1984.

Depo approved, by A. Henry. SPARE RIB. 143:12, June 1984.

Depo Provera being used in Seattle. NORTHWEST PASSAGE. 24(9): 5, April 1984.

Depo-Provera— ethical issues in its testing and distribution, by M. Potts, et al. JOURNAL OF MEDICAL ETHICS. 10(1):9-20, March 1984.

The Depo-Provera public hearing, by F. C. Dening. MIDWIVES CHRONICLE. 96(1146):246, July 1983.

Depo Provera/shot that sterilizes, by J. Slaughter. CHANGES. 6(7): 4, July 1984.

Depth charge in the womb [Dalkon shield controversy]. PROGRES-SIVE. 48:10, May 1984.

Detection of subclinical abortion by assay of pregnancy specific beta 1 glycoprotein, by A. G. Ahmed, et al. BRITISH MEDICAL JOURNAL (CLIN RES). 288(6411):113, January 14, 1984.

Determinants of attitudes towards abortion in the American elec-torate, by J. S. Legge, Jr. WESTERN POLITICAL QUARTERLY. 36:479-490, September 1983.1

Determinants of breastfeeding in developing countries: overview and policy implications, by S. L. Huffman. STUDIES IN FAMILY PLANNING. 15(4):170, July-August 1984.

Determinants of cumulative fertility in Ghana, by E. O. Tawiah. DEMOGRAPHY. 84(21):1-8, February 1984.

Determinants of immunological responsiveness in recurrent spontaneous abortion, by P. M. Johnson, et al. TRANSPLANTATION. 38(3):280-284, September 1984.

Determination of progestational potency: a review, by G. I. Swyer. JOURNAL OF THE ROYAL SOCIETY OF MEDICINE. 77(5):406-409, May 1984.

Developing family planning nurse practitioner protocols, by J. W. Hawkins, et al. JOGN NURSING. 13(3):167-170, May-June 1984.

Development in the number of legal terminations of pregnancy, by L. B. Knudsen. UGESKRIFT FOR LAEGER. 145(48):3753-3758, November 28, 1983.

Development of hormonal contraception in the Hungarian People's Republic, by G. Seregelyi. AKUSHERSTVO I GINEKOLOGIIA. (4):70-72, April 1984.

The development of obstetrics and gynecology: dramatically decreased maternal mortality. Far-seeing points of view in the question of abortion, by K. Hagenfeldt. LAKARTIDNINGEN. 80(45):4299-4302, November 9, 1983.

Development of six new contraceptives among 1989 goals of WHO programme. FAMILY PLANNING PERSPECTIVES. 15:226-227, September-October 1983.

Diagnostic procedures in threatened abortion, by J. B. Herta. OBSTETRICS AND GYNECOLOGY. 64(2):223-229, August 1984.

Diagnostic value of plasma progesterone in nonendocrine incipient abortions in the first trimester, by E. Rachev. AKUSHERSTVO I GINEKOLOGIIA. 22(4):270-273, 1983.

The diaphragm: an accomplice in recurrent urinary tract infections, by L. Gillespie. UROLOGY. 24(1):25-30, July 1984.

Differential effects of isoniazid and oral contraceptive steroids on antipyrine oxidation and acetaminophen conjugation, by H. R.

Ochs, et al. PHARMACOLOGY. 28(4):188-195, 1984.

Differential fertility in rural Erie County, New York, 1855, by M. J. Stern. JOURNAL OF SOCIAL HISTORY. 16:49-64, Summer 1983.

Digestive complications of oral contraceptives: a case of extensive digestive necrosis in a young woman, by E. Carpentier, et al. ANNALES DE CHIRURGIE. 38(4):305-308, May 1984.

Dilated cardiomyopathy and thyrotoxicosis complicated by septic abortion, by G. D. Hankins, et al. AMERICAN JOURNAL OF OBSTETRICS AND GYNECOLOGY. 149(1):85-86, May 1, 1984.

Dinoprostone or sulprostone. Comparison of two analogs of prostaglandin for the interruption of pregnancy in the second trimester, by B. Bourrit, et al. JOURNAL DE GYNECOLOGIE, OBSTETRIQUE ET BIOLOGIE DE LA REPRODUCTION. 13(1):87-90, 1984.

Diocesan-wide NFP program reaches broad population groups. HOSPITAL PROGRESS. 65(4):26; 28; 30, April 1984.

Discontinued use of intrauterine contraceptive device and pregnancy loss, by A. A. Levin, et al. AMERICAN JOURNAL OF OBSTETRICS AND GYNECOLOGY. 149(7):768-771, August 1, 1984.

Dismembering the United Way: Edmonton's BC's battle as an abortion referral agency joins, by T. Philip, et al. ALBERTA REPORT. 11:32; 35-36, July 9, 1984.

Dispute continues over federal help for world population control, by J. Frawley. REGISTER. 60:1+, August 12, 1984.

Dis-united: Catholics divorce the [Edmonton] charity federation, by G. Herchak. ALBERTA REPORT. 11:40, July 16, 1984.

Do hormones cause breast cancer?, by D. B. Thomas. CANCER. 53(3 Suppl):595-604, February 1, 1984.

Do oral contraceptives reduce the incidence of rheumatoid arthritis? A pilot study using the Stockholm County medical information system, by P. Allebeck, et al. SCANDINAVIAN JOURNAL OF RHEUMATOLOGY. 13(2):140-146, 1984.

The doctor couldn't bear to watch, by J. Sobran. CONSERVATIVE DIGEST. 10:38, August 1984.

Doctors dismiss link between the pill and cancer. NEW SCIENTIST. 100:559, November 24, 1983.

Doctors in Canada hauled/antiabortion, by P. Habermann. MILITANT. 48(2):20, January 27, 1984.

Doctors 'inoculate' against miscarriages, by J. Chomet. NEW SCIENTIST. 103:6, August 9, 1984.

Does the aborted baby feel pain?, by P. Kaler. LIGUORIAN. 72:18-22, November 1984.

Does a fetus feel pain?. SCIENCE. 5:8+, May 1984.

Domestic group, status of women and fertility, by T. Patel. SOCIAL ACTION. 32:363-379, October-December 1982.

Dominance and control, by G. Corea. AGENDA. 4(3):20, September 1984.

Dorothy, my sister-in-love [in-law with Down's syndrome], by W. Wangerin. CHRISTIANITY TODAY. 28:66, August 10, 1984.

Down under: contraceptive ad sector is fertile ground for debate, by C. Pritchard. MARKETING. 89:15, September 3, 1984.

Drainage of postabortion hematometra by Foley catheter, by M. Borten, et al. AMERICAN JOURNAL OF OBSTETRICS AND GYNECOLOGY. 149(8):980-990, August 15, 1984.

Drug interactions with oral contraceptives: a review, by F. X. Veray. BOLETIN-ASOCIATION MEDICA DE PUERTO RICO. 75(8):361-362, August 1983.

Dual career, delayed childbearing families: some observations, by B. Schlesinger, et al. CANADA'S MENTAL HEALTH. 32(1):4-6, March 1984.

Duration of induced abortion in the second trimester in relation to placental insertion, by E. Rachev, et al. AKUSHERSTVO I GINEKOLOGIIA. 22(5):349-354, 1983.

ELISA antibodies to cytomegalovirus in pregnant patients: prevalence in and correlation with spontaneous abortion, by M. Luerti, et al. BIOLOGICAL RESEARCH IN PREGNANCY AND PERINATOLOGY. 4(4):181-183, 1983.

ERA, abortion linked, by J. Feuerherd. NATIONAL CATHOLIC RE-
PORTER. 20:8, September 14, 1984.

ERA, abortion linked in future of pro-life struggle, by W. A. Ryan.
OUR SUNDAY VISITOR. 72:3, January 29, 1984.

E. R. A. and abortion: really separate issues?, by D. Johnson, et al.
AMERICA. 150:432-437, June 9, 1984.

ERA and abortion/a legal link, by J. Pasternak. GUARDIAN. 36
(26):2, April 4, 1984.

ERA and abortion: Pennsylvania Court ruling. ORIGINS. 13:699-
704, March 29, 1984.

Early and late complications of induced abortion, by A. A. Radionchenko, et al. SOVETSKAIA MEDITSINA. (7):113-115, 1983.

Early birth controllers of B. C., by M. F. Bishop. BC STUDIES. (61):
64-84, Spring 1984.

The early mother-infant relationship and social competence with
peers and adults at three years, by J. H. Kennedy, et al. JOURNAL
OF PSYCHOLOGY. 116:23-34, January 1984.

Early readmission following elective laparoscopic sterilization: a
brief analysis of a rare event, by I. Chi, et al. AMERICAN JOUR-
NAL OF OBSTETRICS AND GYNECOLOGY. 148(3):322-327,
February 1, 1984.

Early signs of infertility, by B. Berg. MS. 12:68+, May 1984.

Ecological factors predicting adolescent contraceptive use: implications for intervention, by L. S. Kastner. JOURNAL OF ADOLES-
CENT HEALTH CARE. 5(2):79-86, April 1984.

Ectopic pregnancy after sterilization [letter], by F. DeStefano, et al.
JAMA. 251(11):1432, March 16, 1984.

Ectopic pregnancy subsequent to sterilization: histologic evaluation
and clinical implications, by R. J. Stock, et al. FERTILITY AND
STERILITY. 42(2):211-215, August 1984.

Educating peers about human sexuality and birth control in natural
settings: a social comparison perspective, by R. De Pietro.
PATIENT EDUCATION AND COUNSELING. 6(1):39-46, 1984.

Education and family planning in the urban sector, by N. I. Fernandez. HYGIE. 3(2):38-40, June 1984.

Effect of abortion on premature labor, by N. Bogdnavo, et al. AKUSHERSTVO I GINEKOLOGIIA. 22(2):100-104, 1983.

The effect of alpha-chlorohydrin on the oxidation of fructose by rabbit spermatozoa in vitro, by S. A. Ford, et al. CONTRACEPTION. 28(6):565-573, December 1983.

The effect of combined oral contraceptive steroids on the gonadotropin responses to LH-RH in lactating women with regular menstrual cycles resumed, by K. Ryu, et al. CONTRACEPTION. 27 (6):605-617, June 1983.

The effect of cotrimoxazole on oral contraceptive steroids: in women, by S. F. Grimmer, et al. CONTRACEPTION. 28(1):53-59, July 1983.

The effect of different contraceptive treatments on the serum concentration of dehydroepiandrosterone sulfate, by K. L. Klove, et al. CONTRACEPTION. 29(4):319-324, April 1984.

Effect of exercise and oral contraceptive agents on fibrinolytic potential in trained females, by I. A. Huisveld, et al. JOURNAL OF APPLIED PHYSIOLOGY. 56(4):906-913, April 1984.

Effect of hormonal contraceptives on cardiovascular function, by I. A. Manuilova, et al. AKUSHERSTVO I GINEKOLOGIIA. (11): 5-8, November 1983.

Effect of infant mortality on subsequent fertility of women in Jordan: a life table analysis, by C. M. Suchindran, et al. JOURNAL OF BIOSOCIAL SCIENCE. 16:219-230, April 1984.

Effect of laparoscopic sterilization and insertion of multiload copper 250 and Progestasert intrauterine devices on serum ferritin levels, by T. H. Goh, et al. CONTRACEPTION. 28(4):329-336, 1983.

Effect of long-term use of composite steroid contraceptives on serum lipids in women, by Z. X. Li. CHUNG HUA FU CHAN KO TSA CHIH. 18(2):98-100, April 1983.

Effect of oral contraception on serum bile acid, by M. M. Shaaban, et al. INTERNATIONAL JOURNAL OF GYNAECOLOGY AND OBSTETRICS. 22(3):111-115, April 1984.

The effect of low dose oral contraceptives on the initial immune response to infection, by D. A. Baker, et al. CONTRACEPTION. 29(6):519-525, June 1984.

The effect of oral contraceptive therapy and of pregnancy on serum folate levels of rural Sri Lankan women, by N. S. Hettiarachchy, et al. BRITISH JOURNAL OF NUTRITION. 50(3):495-501, November 1983.

Effect of oral contraceptives on the formation of cholesterol crystals in gallbladder bile, by R. Pinero, et al. GEN. 36(4):244-250, October-December 1982.

Effect of oral contraceptives on intestinal folate conjugase activity and folate absorption in rats, by J. Leichter, et al. DRUG-NUTRIENT INTERACTIONS. 2(1):1-6, 1983.

The effect of oral contraceptives on rat platelet membrane glycoproteins, by B. Toor, et al. BIOCHIMICA ET BIOPHYSICA ACTA. 770(2):178-182, March 14, 1984.

The effect of partusisten on uterine motility stimulated by blood serum from pregnant women with certain pathological manifestations, by J. Lukanov, et al. FOLIA MEDICA. 25(3):25-29, 1983.

Effect of peer counselors on adolescent compliance in use of oral contraceptives, by M. S. Jay, et al. PEDIATRICS. 73(2):126-131, February 1984.

Effect of plasma substitute solutions on the immunologic indices of pregnant women with spontaneous abortions, by V. V. Shcherbakova, et al. AKUSHERSTVO I GINEKOLOGIIA. (3):68-71, March 1984.

Effect of (+)-gossypol on fertility in male hamsters, by D. P. Waller, et al. JOURNAL OF ANDROLOGY. 4(4):276-279, July-August 1983.

Effect of polyphloretin phosphate on the contraceptive action of a polyethylene intrauterine device in rats, by M. R. Chaudhury. CONTRACEPTION. 28(2):171-180, 1983.

The effect of post partum sterilization on manifest anxiety, by R. S. Ammal. INDIAN JOURNAL OF CLINICAL PSYCHOLOGY. 10(2):305-307, September 1983.

The effect of post partum sterilization on the personality dimensions of extraversion-introversion and neuroticism-stability, by R. S.

Ammal. INDIAN JOURNAL OF CLINICAL PSYCHOLOGY. 10(2): 308-312, September 1983.

The effect of a progestin-only oral contraceptive on lactation, by M. F. McCann. DISSERTATION ABSTRACTS INTERNATIONAL: B. 45(8), February 1984.

Effect of religiosity on sex attitudes, experience and contraception among university students, by N. Notzer, et al. JOURNAL OF SEX AND MARITAL THERAPY. 10(1):57-62, Spring 1984.

Effect of repeated induced abortions on female reproductive function, by I. B. Frolov. AKUSHERSTVO I GINEKOLOGIIA. (2):44-47, February 1984.

Effect of serum on lymphocyte chromatin properties in threatened abortion, by V. S. Tolmachev. AKUSHERSTVO I GINEKOLOGIIA. (10):51-54, October 1983.

The effect of sex steroids and hormonal contraceptives upon thymus and spleen on intact female rats, by H. Kuhl, et al. CONTRACEPTION. 28(6):587-601, December 1983.

Effect of a single maximal and low multiple doses of testosterone propionate (TP) on male reproductive organs in Long Evans rats, by M. A. Bari, et al. BANGLADESH MEDICAL RESEARCH COUNCIL BULLETIN. (10):17-23, June 1984.

Effect of spontaneous abortion in the first pregnancy on the course of subsequent pregnancy, labor, puerperium and the state of the newborn infant, by S. Lembrych, et al. WIADOMOSCI LEKARSKIE. 37(2):122-127, January 15, 1984.

Effect of various oral contraceptive combinations on dysmenorrhea, by I. Milsom, et al. GYNECOLOGIC AND OBSTETRIC INVESTIGATION. 17(6):284-292, 1984.

Effects and side effects of hormonal contraceptives in the region of the nose, throat, and ear, by J. Bausch. HNO. 31(12):409-414, December 1983.

Effects of abortion on subsequent pregnancies, by B. Adelusi. AFRICAN JOURNAL OF MEDICINE AND MEDICAL SCIENCES. 12(2): 65-69, June 1983.

Effects of alpha-trichosanthin and alpha-momorcharin on the development of peri-implantation mouse embryos, by L. K. Law, et al. JOURNAL OF REPRODUCTION AND FERTILITY. 69(2): 597-604, November 1983.

The effects of an antiprogesterone steroid in women: interruption of the menstrual cycle and of early pregnancy, by W. Herrmann, et al. COMPTES RENDUS DES SEANCES DE L'ACADEMIE DES SCIENCE [III]. 296(13):591, 1983.

Effects of contraceptive vaginal ring treatment of vaginal bacteriology and cytology, by A. Schwan, et al. CONTRACEPTION. 28(4): 341-347, October 1983.

Effects of cyproterone acetate with combination of testosterone enanthate on seminal characteristics, androgenicity and clinical chemistry in langur monkey, by N. K. Lohiya, et al. CONTRACEPTION. 28(6):575-586, December 1983.

The effects of federal funding cuts on family planning services, by A. Torres. FAMILY PLANNING PERSPECTIVES. 16:134-138, May-June 1984.

Effects of laser-puncture therapy in threatened abortion on the hormone content of the blood, by G. G. Dzhvebenava, et al. AKUSHSTVO I GINEKOLOGIIA. (12):32-33, December 1983.

Effects of oral contraceptives and of the ovarian cycle on auditory performance at 4 and 6 khz. Demonstration by functional audiometry, by J. C. Petiot, et al. COMPTES RENDUS DES SEANCE DE LA SOCIETIE DE BIOLOGIE ET DE SES FILIALES. 178(1):105-117, 1984.

Effects of oral contraceptives on diazepam-induced psychomotor impairment, by E. H. Ellinwood, Jr., et al. CLINICAL PHARMACOLOGY AND THERAPEUTICS. 35(3):360-366, March 1984.

Effects of oral contraceptives on lipoprotein lipids: a prospective study, by M. G. Powell, et al. OBSTETRICS AND GYNECOLOGY. 63(6):764-770, June 1984.

Effects of oral contraceptives, or lanosterol, on ADP-induced aggregation and binding of 125I-fibrinogen to rat platelets, by L. McGregor, et al. THROMBOSIS RESEARCH. 33(5):517-522, March 1, 1984.

Effects of ovariectomy, estrogen treatment and C 1-628 on food intake and body weight in female rats treated neonatally with gonadal hormones, by T. P. Donohoe, et al. PHYSIOLOGY AND BEHAVIOR. 31(3):325-329, September 1983.

Effects of prostaglandin E2 analogue suppository on blood loss in suction abortion, by M. S. Sidhu, et al. OBSTETRICS AND GYNECOLOGY. 64(1):128-130, July 1984.

The effects of prostaglandins in colpocytology, by J. Koblikova, et al. CESKOSLOVENSKA GYNEKOLOGIE. 49(1):14-17, February 1984.

Effects of sterilization on menstrual pattern [letter], by K. Kennedy. AMERICAN JOURNAL OF OBSTETRICS AND GYNECOLOGY. 148(6):835, March 15, 1984.

Effects of synethetic steroid contraceptives on biliary lipid composition of normal Mexican women, by G. Etchegoyen, et al. CONTRACEPTION. 27(6):591-603, June 1983.

Effects of tobacco smoking and oral contraceptive use on theopylline disposition, by M. J. Gardner, et al. BRITISH JOURNAL OF CLINICAL PHARMACOLOGY. 16(3):271-280, September 1983.

Effects of two estradiol/norgestrel combinations on the ovulatory pattern and on sex hormone binding globulin capacity in women around forty years of age, by A. Hagstad, et al. ACTA OBSTETRICIA ET GYNECOLOGICA SCANDINAVICA. 63(4):321-324, 1984.

Efficacy and safety of low-dose 15-methyl prostaglandin F2 alpha for cervical ripening in the first trimester of pregnancy, by F. Arias. AMERICAN JOURNAL OF OBSTETRICS AND GYNECOLOGY. 149(1):100-101, May 1, 1984.

Efficacy of the condom as a barrier to the transmission of cytomegalovirus, by S. Katznelson, et al. JOURNAL OF INFECTIOUS DISEASES. 150(1):155-157, July 1984.

The efficacy of religious participation in the national debates over abolitionism and abortion, by M. C. Sernett. JOURNAL OF RELIGION. (64):205-220, April 1984.

Eggs to order, by J. S. Biggs. MEDICAL JOURNAL OF AUSTRALIA. 140(10):572-573, May 12, 1984.

Elections may decide future of abort funds, by M. Meehan. REGISTER. 60:1+, November 4, 1984.

Eleven years later, the struggle still goes on, by M. Meehan. REGISTER. 60:1+, January 22, 1984.

Encare contraceptive breaking ad barriers, by N. Giges. ADVERTIS-ING AGE. 55:3+, March 19, 1984.

End runs around choice, by H. Lessinger. GUARDIAN. 36(22):2, March 7, 1984.

Endocrine findings in rabbits after sterilization with electrocagula-tion, by H. H. Riedel, et al. JOURNAL OF REPRODUCTIVE MEDICINE. 28(10):665-670, October 1983.

Endocrine forms of infertility as a risk factor for the failure to carry a subsequent pregnancy to term, by D. V. Vasadze, et al. AKUSHERSTVO I GINEKOLOGIIA. (2):17-21, February 1984.

Endocrinologic events in early pregnancy failure, by M. O. Aspillage, et al. AMERICAN JOURNAL OF OBSTETRICS AND GYNE-COLOGY. 147(8):903-908, December 15, 1983.

Endometrial ossification associated with repeated abortions, by S. Degani, et al. ACTA OBSTETRICIA ET GYNECOLOGICA SCAND-INAVICA. 62(3):281-282, 1983.

Endometriosis and spontaneous abortion, by M. Groll. FERTILITY AND STERILITY. 41(6):933-935, June 1984.

Epilepsy and oral contraceptives. A therapeutic dilemma, by M. E. Fiol, et al. MINNESOTA MEDICINE. 66(9):551-552, September 1983.

Epithelial changes of the vas deferens after vasectomy and vasovaso-tomy in dogs, by N. Wright, et al. SCANNING ELECTRON MICROSCOPY. 1983(3):1435-1440, 1983.

Epizootics of ovine abortion due to Toxoplasma gondii in north central United States, by J. P. Dubey, et al. JOURNAL OF THE AMERICAN VETERINARY MEDICAL ASSOCIATION. 184(6):657-660, March 15, 1984.

Equal protection of the laws and the 14th amendment: value or humanity?, by P. J. Riga. LINACRE QUARTERLY. 51:176-180, May 1984.

Ernst Grafenberg: the life and work of the specialist of Kiel on the hundredth anniversary of his birth on 26 September 1881, by K. Semm, et al. INTERNATIONAL JOURNAL OF FERTILITY. 28(3): 141-148, 1983.

Erythema nodosum and Campylobacter fetus infection, by F. Garcier, et al. ANNALES DE DERMATOLOGIE ET DE VENEROLOGIE. 110(5):449-453, 1983.

Estimating voluntary and involuntary childlessness in the developing countries, by D. L. Poston, et al. JOURNAL OF BIOSOCIAL SCIENCE. 15(4):441-452, October 1983.

Estimation of blood loss in second-trimester dilatation and extraction, by G. Woodward. OBSTETRICS AND GYNECOLOGY. 63(2): 230-232, February 1984.

Ethanol metabolism in women taking oral contraceptives, by M. K. Jones, et al. ALCOHOLISM. 8(1):24-28, January-February 1984.

The ethical challenge. Is the physician allowed to do what he must do?. MMW. 126(6):132-136, February 10, 1984.

Ethical contradiction of the therapeutic use of aborted fetuses and modern medical interventions [letter]. ORVOSI HETILAP. 125 (15):919-920, April 8, 1984.

The ethics of choice— after my amniocentesis, Mike and I faced the toughest decision of our lives, by R. Rapp. MS. 12:97-100, April 1984.

The ethics of family planning, by M. F. Fathalla. WORLD HEALTH. June 1984, pp. 27-29.

Ethnic fertility differences in Canada, 1926-71: an examination of assimilation hypothesis, by K. G. Basavarajappa, et al. JOURNAL OF BIOSOCIAL SCIENCE. 16:45-54, January 1984.

Ethynyl estradiol content of cervical mucus after administration of oral contraceptive, by J. Morvay, et al. HORMONE RESEARCH. 18(4):221-224, 1983.

Etiologic factors and subsequent reproductive performance in 195 couples with a prior history of habitual abortion, by B. Stray-Pedersen, et al. AMERICAN JOURNAL OF OBSTETRICS AND GYNECOLOGY. 148(2):140-146, January 15, 1984.

Etiological factors in sterility and infertility as risk factors in future pregnancies, by D. Avramovic, et al. JUGOSLAVENSKA GINE-KOLOGIJA I OPSTETRICIJA. 23(3-4):68-71, May-August 1983.

Etiological studies of secondary hypertension. Drug-induced

hypertension, by E. Kato. NIPPON RINSHO. 42(2):390-398, February 1984.

Etiology of infertility in monkeys with endometriosis: luteinized unruptured follicles, luteal phase defects, pelvic adhesions, and spontaneous abortions, by R. S. Schenken, et al. FERTILITY AND STERILITY. 41(1):122-130, January 1984.

Etiology of recurrent pregnancy losses and outcome of subsequent pregnancies, by J. H. Harger, et al. OBSTETRICS AND GYNECOLOGY. 62(5):574-581, November 1983.

Eugenic theory in contemporary mainland China: popularizing the knowledge of eugenics and advocating optimal births vigorously, by S. Dongsheng. MANKIND QUARTERLY. 24:167-184, Winter 1983.

Evaluation and management of habitual abortion, by A. DeCherney, et al. BRITISH JOURNAL OF HOSPITAL MEDICINE. 31(4):261-262, April 1984.

An evaluation of an adolescent family planning program, by N. Ralph, et al. JOURNAL OF ADOLESCENT HEALTH CARE. 4(3): 158-162, September 1983.

Evaluation of the in vivo efficacy of a new vaginal contraceptive agent in stumptailed macaques, by L. J. Zaneveld, et al. FERTILITY AND STERILITY. 41(3):455-459, March 1984.

Evaluation of mentally retarded persons for sterilization: contributions and limits of psychological consultation, by G. B. Melton, et al. PROFESSIONAL PSYCHOLOGY: RESEARCH AND PRACTICE. 15(1):34-48, February 1984.

Evaluation of the Olsen technique for estimating the fertility response to child mortality, by J. Trussell, et al. DEMOGRAPHY. 20(3):391-405, August 1983.

Evaluation of risk factors associated with vascular thrombosis in women on oral contraceptives. Possible role of anti-sex steroid hormone antibodies, by V. Beaumont, et al. ARTERY. 11(5):331-344, 1983.

Evaluation of steroids as contraceptives in men, by M. Foegh. ACTA ENDOCRINOLOGICA [SUPPL]. 260:3-48, 1983.

Evaluation of tubal patency in post-abortal infertile women, by S.

Roopnarinesingh, et al. WEST INDIAN MEDICAL JOURNAL. 32(3):168-171, September 1983.

Evaluative methodology of a family planning service, by G. Benussi, et al. NUOVI ANNALI D'IGIENE E MICROBIOLOGIA. 33(2-3):233-258, March-June 1982.

Everett women's clinic firebombed, by A. Fine. NORTHWEST PASSAGE. 24(6):4, January 1984.

The evolution of tubal sterilization, by J. S. Seiler. OBSTETRICAL AND GYNECOLOGICAL SURVEY. 39(4):177-184, April 1984.

Exactly whose right to life is it?, by J. Pasternak. GUARDIAN. 36(17): 3, February 1, 1984.

Exclusive juvenile jurisdiction to authorize sterilization of incompetent minors. INDIANA LAW REVIEW. 16:835-860, 1983.

Exercise may offset lipid alterations in pill users. PHYSICIAN AND SPORTSMEDICINE. 12:42, June 1984.

Experience with combined statement using hemosorption in the generalized suppurative-septic infection of puerperae and women with septic abortion, by G. I. Gerasimovich, et al. AKUSHERSTVO I GINEKOLOGIIA. (2):60-1, February 1984.

Experience with microsurgical two-layer vasovasostomy, by Y. Hirao, et al. HINYOKIKA KIYO. 29(4):385-393, April 1983.

Experience with specialized office (consultation) for abortion, by N. K. Mironycheva, et al. AKUSHERSTVO I GINEKOLOGIIA. (1):64-66, January 1984.

Experiences with Depo-Provera as a contraceptive agent, by E. Kollstedt, et al. JORDEMODERN. 97(1-2):18-20, January-February 1984.

Experimental gynecological microsurgery, by S. S. Sorensen, et al. UGESKRIFT FOR LAEGER. 145(51):3984-3986, December 19, 1983.

Experimental study on reanastomosis of the ductus deferens, by N. N. Rodrigues, Jr., et al. ACTAS UROLOGICAS ESPANOLAS. 7(2): 155-160, March-April 1983.

Experts hammer away at Roe vs. Wade logic, by A. J. Zwerneman.

REGISTER. 60:1+, April 15, 1984.

Exposure to solvents and outcome of pregnancy in university laboratory employees, by G. Axelsson, et al. BRITISH JOURNAL OF INDUSTRIAL MEDICINE. 41(3):305-312, August 1984.

Extent of vaginal absorption of sulphated polysaccharide from A-gen 53 in the rabbit, by S. G. Wood, et al. CONTRACEPTION. 29(4): 375-383, April 1984.

Extraamniotic infusion of prostaglandin F2 alpha in normal saline for termination of midtrimester missed abortion, by O. E. Jaschevatzky, et al. EUROPEAN JOURNAL OF OBSTETRICS, GYNECOLOGY AND REPRODUCTIVE BIOLOGY. 15(3):185-187, July 1983.

FDA considers Depo-Provera as contraceptive, by M. F. Docksai. TRIAL. 19:16, March 1983.

Facing trial, former police chief has no regrets for his prolife activism, by P. Sheehan. REGISTER. 60:1+, July 15, 1984.

Factor VII in plasma of women taking oral contraceptives. Lack of cold activation under blood bank conditions, by U. Seligsohn, et al. TRANSFUSION. 24(2):171-172, March-April 1984.

Factors affecting fertility control in India: a cross-sectional study, by K. Srinivasan, et al. POPULATION AND DEVELOPMENT REVIEW. 10:273-296, June 1984.

Factors associated with compliance to oral contraceptive use in an adolescent population, by P. W. Scher, et al. JOURNAL OF ADOLESCENT HEALTH CARE. 3(2):120-123, September 1982.

Factors discriminating pregnancy resolution decisions of unmarried adolescents, by M. Eisen, et al. GENETIC PSYCHOLOGY MONO-GRAPHS. 108(1st half):69-95, August 1983.

Factors related to subsequent reproductive outcome in couples with repeated pregnancy loss, by J. FitzSimmons, et al. AMERICAN JOURNAL OF MEDICAL GENETICS. 18(3):407-411, July 1984.

Factors responsible for abortion, by Y. Shimono, et al. KANGO GIJUTSU. 30(3):370-373, February 1984.

Failure of post-coital contraception after insertion of an intrauterine device. Case report, by A. A. Kubba, et al. BRITISH JOURNAL OF OBSTETRICS AND GYNAECOLOGY. 91(6):596-597, June 1984.

Failure to insert an intrauterine device, by I. C. Chi, et al. CONTRA-CEPTIVE DELIVERY SYSTEMS. 4(3):207-212, 1983.

The fallacy of time limits . . . therapeutic abortions, by J. Finch. NURSING MIRROR. 158(20):24-25, May 16, 1984.

Fallopian tube occlusion with silicone: radiographic appearance, by S. J. Dan, et al. RADIOLOGY. 151(3):603-605, June 1984.

Familial case of a balanced chromosomal translocation as a cause of reproductive failure, by V. Georgieva, et al. AKUSHERSTVO I GINEKOLOGIIA. 22(5):409-414, 1983.

Family and community factors associated with infant deaths that might be preventable, by E. M. Taylor, et al. BRITISH MEDICAL JOURNAL. 287:871-874, September 24, 1983.

Family and marriage textbook banned from 28 Philadelphia schools, by M. R. Day. NATIONAL CATHOLIC REPORTER. 20:7, September 28, 1984.

The family and marital consulting agency, by S. I. Markovich, et al. SOVETSKOE ZDRAVOOKHRANENIE. (7):46-48, 1983.

Family communication and teenagers contraceptive use, by F. F. Furstenberg, et al. FAMILY PLANNING PERSPECTIVES. 16(4): 163-170, July-August 1984.

Family planners' accord: urgency, by T. C. Fox. NATIONAL CATHO-LIC REPORTER. 20:1+, August 17, 1984.

Family planning. PUBLIC HEALTH REPORTS. Suppl:16-24, September-October 1983.

Family planning. BEIJING REVIEW. 26:4, August 29, 1984.

Family planning among a group of coloured women, by A. Roux. SOUTH AFRICAN MEDICAL JOURNAL. 65(22):898-901, June 1984.

Family planning among the urban poor: sexual politics and social policy, by M. Cummings, et al. FAMILY RELATIONS. 32:47-58, January 1983.

Family planning and health work at the grassroots: some issues and new concerns in the Indian context, by D. N. Saksens. HYGIE. 2(2):9-14, July 1983.

Family planning and maternal-child health in Mexico, 1970-1980, by B. R. Ordonez. JOURNAL OF TROPICAL PEDIATRICS. 29(5): 271-277, October 1983.

Family planning associations in Australia: key events from 1926 to 1983, by D. Wyndham, et al. HEALTHRIGHT. 3:7-18, November 1983.

Family planning centres, sex therapists and the courts, by I. Freckelton. HEALTHRIGHT. 3:25-28, August 1984.

Family planning in developing nations: a global concern, our concern, by L. Harriman. JOURNAL OF HOME ECONOMICS. 76(1): 8-12, Spring 1984.

Family planning in a healthy, married population: operationalizing the human rights approach in an Israeli health service setting, by D. E. Block, et al. AMERICAN JOURNAL OF PUBLIC HEALTH. 74:830-833, August 1984.

Family planning in Lae urban area of Papua New Guinea 1981, by W. K. Agyei. JOURNAL OF BIOSOCIAL SCIENCE. 16(2):269-275, April 1984.

Family planning. A most effective preventive health measure, by J. Rowley. HYGIE. 3(2):3-4, June 1984.

Family planning needs of adolescents, by C. Lane, et al. JOGN NURSING [SUPPL]. 13(2):61s-65s, March-April 1984.

The family planning nurse: in the family way, part 1, by G. Rands. NURSING TIMES. 80(13):28-30, March 28-April 3, 1984.

—. 2. The present and future role of the nurse in family planning, by A. Cowper. NURSING TIMES. 80(13):31-33, March 28-April 3, 1 1984.

—. 3. A centre of excellence, by P. Holmes. NURSING TIMES. 80(13): 34, March 28-April 3, 1984.

Family planning: a nurse's concern, by S. A. Samuel. NURSING JOURNAL OF INDIA. 75(5):105-106, May 1984.

Family planning: a preventive health measure, by A. Petros-

Barvazian. WORLD HEALTH. June 1984, pp. 4-7.

The family planning program and cuts in federal spending. 1. Impact on state management of family planning funds, by M. T. Orr. FAMILY PLANNING PERSPECTIVES. 15(4):176-184, July-August 1983.

—. 2. Initial effects on the provision of services, by A. Torres. FAMILY PLANNING PERSPECTIVES. 15(4):184-191, July-August 1983.

A family planning risk scoring system for health care providers, by W. N. Spellacy, et al. OBSTETRICS AND GYNECOLOGY. 63(6): 846-849, June 1984.

Family planning services from multiple provider types: an assessment for the United States, by G. E. Hendershot. STUDIES IN FAMILY PLANNING. 14:218-227, August-September 1983.

Family planning top priority for Bengalees [Bangladesh], by E. C. Clift. NEW DIRECTIONS FOR WOMEN. 13:5, July-August 1983.

Fatal hemorrhage from legal abortion in the United States, by D. A. Grimes, et al. SURGERY, GYNECOLOGY AND OBSTETRICS. 157(5):461-466, November 1983.

Fate of subsequent pregnancies in relation to the outcome of previous pregnancies, by F. A. Szczotka, et al. PROBEMY MEDYCYNY WIEKU ROZWOJOWEGO. 8:238-245, 1979.

Federal abortion alternatives cut by Reagan administration, by N. Cohodas. CONGRESSIONAL QUARTERLY WEEKLY REPORT. 42:2949-2955, November 17, 1984.

Feeling like a stranger in my own church, by K. Matthews. IRNFP. 8:121-130, Summer 1984.

Female employment and reproductive behavior in Taiwan 1980, by C. S. Stokes, et al. DEMOGRAPHY. 20(3):313, August 1983.

Female sterilization under laparoscopic observation. Evaluation of two electrosurgical occlusive technics, by L. C. Uribe Ramirez, et al. GINECOLOGIA Y OBSTETRICIA DE MEXICO. 50(306):265-271, October 1982.

Female sterilization with silicone tubal rings, by K. Heldaas, et al.

TIDSSKRIFT FOR DEN NORSKE LAEGEFORENING. 103(31):2110-2112, November 10, 1983.

Female urethral pressure profile; reproducibility, axial variation and effects of low dose oral contraceptives, by J. M. Van Geelen, et al. JOURNAL OF UROLOGY. 131(2):394-398, February 1984.

Ferraro's fuzzy thinking on abortion, by A. T. Mitchell. HUMAN EVENTS. 44:11, August 18, 1984.1

Ferraro's pro-abortion record, by M. Stanton Evans. HUMAN EVENTS. 44:9+, October 6, 1984.

Fertility after discontinuation of oral contraceptives, by E. Weisberg. CLINICAL REPRODUCTION AND FERTILITY. 1(4):261-272, December 1982.

Fertility after induced abortion: a prospective follow-up study, by P. G. Stubblefield, et al. OBSTETRICS AND GYNECOLOGY. 63(2): 186-193, February 1984.

Fertility and family planning in Papua New Guinea, by W. K. Agyei. JOURNAL OF BIOSOCIAL SCIENCE. 16(3):323-334, July 1984.

Fertility and pacification among the Mekranoti of Central Brazil, by D. Werner. HUMAN ECOLOGY. 11(2):227, June 1983.

Fertility and pension programs in LDCs: a model of mutual rein-forcement, by B. Entwisle, et al. ECONOMIC DEVELOPMENT AND CULTURAL CHANGE. 32:331-354, January 1984.

Fertility control in vas occluded rats and the biochemical effects of ascorbic acid feeding, by J. D. Sharma, et al. EXPERIMENTAL AND CLINICAL ENDOCRINOLOGY. 82(3):337-341, November 1983.

Fertility differentials in Nepal, by B. Gubhaju. JOURNAL OF BIO-SOCIAL SCIENCE. 15:325-332, July 1983.

Fertility disorders after taking contraceptives tablets, by G. Godo, et al. ORVOSI HETILAP. 125(6):313-316, February 5, 1984.

Fertility of Indian Tamil concentrations in Sri Lanka, by D. F. S. Fernando. JOURNAL OF BIOSOCIAL SCIENCE. 15:333-338, July 1983.

Fertility status and attitudes in a rural based industrial population in Rajasthan, by A. Narayan, et al. JOURNAL OF FAMILY WELFARE. 30:30-34, September 1983.

Fertility trends among overseas Indian populations, by A. Muthiah, et al. POPULATION STUDIES. 37(2):273, July 1983.

Fertilization and early pregnancy loss in healthy women attempting conception, by Y. C. Smart, et al. CLINICAL REPRODUCTION AND FERTILITY. 1(3):177-184, September 1982.

Fertilising ability of spermatozoa of rats treated with STS 557, by P. K. Warikoo, et al. ARCHIVES OF ANDROLOGY. 11(2):157-159, October 1983.

Fetal loss and work in a waste water treatment plant, by R. W. Morgan, et al. AMERICAN JOURNAL OF PUBLIC HEALTH. 74(5):499-501, May 1984.

The fetus and the law— whose life as it anyway?, by J. Gallagher. MS. 12:62+, September 1984.

Fetus papyraceus— 11 cases, by E. Daw. POSTGRADUATE MEDICAL JOURNAL. 59(695):598-600, September 1983.

The fetus, under criminal law is considered a complete human being from the onset of labor pains. FORTSCHRITTE DER MEDIZIN. 102(10):92, March 15, 1984.

The fetus under Section 1983: still struggling for recognition, by P. T. Czepiga. SYRACUSE LAW REVIEW. 34:1029-1066, August 1983.

Few in Congress vote the seamless garment, by M. Meehan. REGISTER. 60:1+, December 9, 1984.

Few restrictions in natural family planning [letter], by H. P. Dunn. NEW ZEALAND MEDICAL JOURNAL. 97(760):498, July 25, 1984.

First experience with extra-amniotic intrauterine administration of prostaglandin F2 alpha, by L. Rotta. CESKOSLOVENSKA GYNEKOLOGIE. 48(9):643-647, November 1983.

Flowers of Hibiscus rosa-sinensis, a potential sourse of contragestative agent: I. effect of benzene extract on implantation of mouse, by S. N. Kabir, et al. CONTRACEPTION. 29(4):385-397, April 1984.

A flurry about the pill. NEW ZEALAND MEDICAL JOURNAL. 96 (745):1009, December 14, 1983.

Focal nodular hyperplasia of great extent in the liver after taking oral contraceptives, by A. Szecseny, et al. ORVOSI HETILAP. 125(12):687-691, March 18, 1984.

A focused approach to quality of care assessment in family planning, by N. Hirschhorn, et al. AMERICAN JOURNAL OF PUBLIC HEALTH. 74(8):825-829, August 1984.

Foes of abortion start a prolife insurance company. CHRISTIANITY TODAY. 28:43, February 3, 1984.

Foetal cell leak (FCL) studies in spontaneous and induced abortion, by R. R. Kulkarni, et al. INDIAN JOURNAL OF MEDICAL RESEARCH. 78:824-827, December 1983.

Forced sterilization, by K. Safford. JUMP CUT. 29:37, February 1984.

The forced sterilization program under the Indian emergency: results in one settlement, by C. H. Brown. HUMAN ORGANIZATION. 43:49-53, Spring 1984.

Forum assesses abortion rights crisis, J. Irvine. GAY COMMUNITY. 11(45):3, June 2, 1984.

A four-year clinical study of Norplant implants, by I. Sivin, et al. STUDIES IN FAMILY PLANNING. 14(6-7):184, June-July 1983.

Freedom and/or separation: the constitutional dilemma of the First Amendment, by L. Pfeffer. UNION SEMINARY QUARTERLY REVIEW. 38(3-4):337-359, 1984.

Fresh thinking on fertility. POPULI. 10(1):13, 1983.

Funding the abortion pros, by M. Meehan. REGISTER. 60:1+, January 15, 1984.

Further investigations on the cytological effects of some contraceptives, by A. Kabarity, et al. MUTATION RESEARCH. 135(3):181-188, March 1984.

A Gemeprost vaginal suppository for cervical priming prior to termination of first trimester pregnancy, by P. Kajanoja, et al. CONTRACEPTION. 29(3):251-260, March 1984.

Gender and oral contraceptive effects on temporary auditory effects of noise, by J. E. Dengerink, et al. AUDIOLOGY. 23(4):411-425, 1984.

Gender, the judiciary, and U. S. public opinion, by G. S. Swan. JOURNAL OF SOCIAL, POLITICAL AND ECONOMIC STUDIES. 8(3): 323-341, 1983.

Gender roles and premarital contraception, by P. L. MacCorquodale. JOURNAL OF MARRIAGE AND THE FAMILY. 46(1):57-63, February 1984.

Genetic screening, eugenic abortion, and Roe v. Wade: how viable is Roe's viability standard?. BROOKLYN LAW REVIEW. 50:113-142, Fall 1983.

Genetics, amniocentesis, and abortion, by K. Hirschhorn. MT. SINAI JOURNAL OF MEDICINE. 51(1):15-17, January-February 1984.

Genetics and morality, by M. H. Shapiro. CENTER MAGAZINE. 16:9-15, July-August 1983.

Georgia Supreme Court invalidates involuntary sterilization statute, by T. D. Harper. JOURNAL OF THE MEDICAL ASSOCIATION OF GEORGIA. 72(11):795-797, November 1983.

Given a free rein, prolife mustangs gallop into trouble [use of anti-fertility drugs to control herds], by J. W. Turner, Jr. SMITHSONIAN. 14:88+, February 1984.

Goals in reproductive decision making, by B. A. Nardi. AMERICAN ETHNOLOGIST. 10(4):697-714, November 1983.

Good times, bad times: a study of the future path of U. S. fertility, by D. A. Ahlburg. SOCIAL BIOLOGY. 30:17-23, Spring 1983.

Gossypol prospects. LANCET. 1(8386):1108-1109, May 19, 1984.

The governor and the bishops [M. Cuomo at Notre Dame]. NEW REPUBLIC. 191:7-9, October 8, 1984.

Governor Reagan, welfare reform and AFDC fertility, by D. E. Keefe. SOCIAL SERVICE REVIEW. 57:234-253, June 1983.

Grandstand play [U. S. position on family planning aid]. NEW REPUBLIC. 191:9-10, August 27, 1984.

Grieving characteristics after spontaneous abortion: a management approach, by P. C. Leppert, et al. OBSTETRICS AND GYNE-COLOGY. 64(1):119-122, July 1984.

Grim reapers for hire, by R. E. Burns. U. S. CATHOLIC. 49:2, June 1984.

Group working to make Democratic Party pro-life, by P. Sheehan. OUR SUNDAY VISITOR. 73:4, October 21, 1984.

The growth of China's population, 1949-1982, by A. J. Jowett. GEOGRAPHICAL JOURNAL. 150:155-170, July 1984.

Guidelines on vasectomy and oral contraception, by D. Llewellyn-Jones. MEDICAL JOURNAL OF AUSTRALIA. 140(11):640, May 1984.

Guidelines on vasectomy and oral contraceptives, by the Medical Task Force of the Australian Federation of Family Planning Associations. MEDICAL JOURNAL OF AUSTRALIA. 140(11): 669-670, May 26, 1984.

Gynecological services utilization by contraceptive clients: a cost analysis, by J. G. Zapka, et al. JOURNAL OF AMERICAN COLLEGE HEALTH. 32:66-72, October 1983.

H. L. v. Matheson— a minor decision about parental notice. UTAH LAW REVIEW. 1982:949-961, 1982.

Habitual abortion and uterine malformations, by A. J. Audebert, et al. ACTA EUROPAEA FERTILITATIS. 14(4):273-278, July-August 1983.

Habitual abortion: parental sharing of HLA antigens, absense of maternal blocking antibody, and suppression of maternal lymphocytes, by A. M. Unander, et al. AMERICAN JOURNAL OF REPRODUCTIVE IMMUNOLOGY. 4(4):171-178, December 1983.

Hard-line stand [Reagan administration considers cutting aid to governments that sanction abortion]. TIME. 124:21, July 2, 1984.

Having a life versus being alive, by T. Kushner. JOURNAL OF MEDICAL ETHICS. 10(1):5-8, March 1984.

Healing the women who sorrow, by K. Arriage. REGISTER. 60:1+, September 30, 1984.

Health: mass use of injectable contraception, by V. Balasubrhman-yan. ECONOMIC AND POLITICAL WEEKLY. 19:371, March 3, 1984.

Health personnel in the matter of legal abortion: physicians and other personnel should have the right to refuse to perform abortions, by L. Jacobsson, et al. LAKARTIDNINGEN. 80(39): 3541-3545, September 28, 1983.

Healthier mothers and children through family planning. POPULA-TION REPORTS (J). (27):J657-696, May-June 1984.

Hedonism returns, by S. Weatherbe. ALBERTA REPORT. 11:33, July 9, 1984.

Hemolytic-uremic syndrome caused by estrogen-progestagen com-bined oral contraceptives [letter], by A. Otero Gonzalez, et al. MEDICINA CLINICA. 82(18):824, May 12, 1984.

Hepatic adenomas and oral contraceptives, by M. C. Jimenez Garrido, et al. REVISTA ESPANOLA DE LAS ENFERMEDADES DEL APARATO DIGESTIVO. 65(1):71-75, January 1984.

Hepatic cell adenoma and peliosis hepatis in women using oral con-traceptives, by F. C. Schmitt, et al. ARQUIVOS DE GASTRO-ENTEROLOGIA. 20(4):153-155, October-December 1984.

Hepatic clearance of aminopyrine in the evaluation of liver function in hormonal contraception, by H. Sensing, et al. ZEITSCHRIFT FUR DIE GESAMTE INNERE MEDIZIN. 38(23):622-626, Decem-ber 1, 1983.

Hepatic infarction related to oral contraceptive use, by M. B. Jacobs. ARCHIVES OF INTERNAL MEDICINE. 144(3):642-643, March 1984.

Hepatic tumors and oral contraceptives, by J. L. Vaur. INFIRMIERE CANADIENNE. (253):17-18, March 1984.

Hepatic tumors induced by sex steroids, by E. T. Mays, et al. SEMI-NARS IN LIVER DISEASE. 4(2):147-157, May 1984.

Hepatocellular carcinoma and oral contraceptives, by B. E. Henderson, et al. BRITISH JOURNAL OF CANCER. 48(3):437-440, September 1983.

Hereditary uroporphyrinogen decarboxylase deficiency in porphyria cutanea tarda caused by hormonal contraceptives [letter], by M. Doss. DEUTSCHE MEDIZINISCHE WOCHENSCHRIFT. 108(48): 1857-1858, December 2, 1983.

Herpes simplex virus transmission: condom studies, by M. A. Conant, et al. SEXUALLY TRANSMITTED DISEASES. 11(2):94-95, April-June 1984.

Herpsvirus suspect in nearly a third of miscarriages, by G. Morse. SCIENCE NEWS. 125:404, June 30, 1984.

Heterotopic tissue in the uterus, by W. Hanski, et al. PATOLOGIA POLSKA. 34(2):195-203, April-June 1983.

High resolution chromosome studies in couples with multiple spontaneous abortions, by T. L. Yang-Feng. DISSERTATION ABSTRACTS INTERNATIONAL: B. a 45(9), March 1985.

High-risk young mothers: infant mortality and morbidity in four areas in the United States, 1973-1978, by M. C. McCormick, et al. AMERICAN JOURNAL OF PUBLIC HEALTH. 74:18-25, January 1984.

Histocompatibility and recurrent abortion [letter], by J. A. McIntyre, et al. FERTILITY AND STERILITY. 41(4):653-654, April 1984.

The historical dimensions of infanticide and abortion: the experience of classical Greece, by R. H. Feen. LINACRE QUARTERLY. 51:248-254, August 1984.

Historical ways of controlling population: a commentary, by W. J. Kramer. IRNFP. 8:20-33, Spring 1984.

History of contraception and a look to the future, by O. Kaser. GEBURTSHILFE UND FRAUENHEILKUNDE. 43(Suppl 1):2-7, June 1983.

Hormonal consequences of missing the pill during the first two days of three consecutive artificial cycles, by B. M. Landgren, et al. CONTRACEPTION. 29(5):437-446, May 1984.

Hormonal contraception, by G. R. de Lima, et al. AMB. 29(7-8):138-142, July-August 1983.

Hormonal contraception— possiblities and problems, by G. Goretzlehner. ZEITSCHRIFT FUR DIE GESAMTE INNERE MEDIZIN. 38 (22):251-253, November 15, 1983.

Hormonal contraceptives. Past, present, and future, by J. W. Goldzieher. POSTGRADUATE MEDICINE. 75(5):75-77; 80; 83-86, April 1984.

Hormonal implants: the next wave of contraceptives, by M. Klitsch. FAMILY PLANNING PERSPECTIVES. 15:239-250, September-October 1983.

Hormonal treatment of spontaneous abortion, by A. Katsulov. AKUSHERSTVO I GINEKOLOGIIA. 23(1):82-88, 1984.

A hormone for all reasons [luteinizing hormone releasing hormone], by J. Silberner. SCIENCE NEWS. 126:60, July 28, 1984.

The horrors of late abortion. TABLET. 238:99-100, February 4, 1984.

House reauthorizes family planning funds. CONGRESSIONAL QUARTERLY WEEKLY REPORT. 42:1438, June 16, 1984.

Housing aspirations and fertility, by C. F. Hohm. SOCIOLOGY AND SOCIAL RESEARCH. 68:350-363, April 1984.

How can they sleep, by J. J. Timmerman. THE REFORMED JOURNAL. 34(2):2, February 1984.

How Catholic can be abortion be?, by M. Meehan. REGISTER. 60:1+, May 20, 1984.

How dangerous is the pill?, by G. Cannon. NEW SCIENTIST. 100:601-602, November 24, 1983.

How does abortion affect a family's other children, by S. Katz. CHATELAINE. 57:16, March 1984.

How freedom of thought is smothered in America: a pluralistic society demands that Christian values be heard, by C. Horn. CHRISTIANITY TODAY. (28):12-17, April 6, 1984.

How nations govern growth. SCHOLASTIC UPDATE. 116:18-19, March 2, 1984.

Human chorionic gonadotrophim and pregnancy— specific beta-1-glycoprotein in predicting pregnancy outcome and in association with early pregnancy vomiting, by A. Kapupila, et al. GYNE-COLOGIC AND OBSTETRIC INVESTIGATION. 18(1):49-53, 1984.

Human chorionic gonadotropin in maternal plasma after induced abortion, spontaneous abortion, and removed ectopic pregnancy, by J. A. Steier, et al. OBSTETRICS AND GYNECOLOGY. 64(3): 391-394, September 1984.

Human chorionic gonadotropin levels in complete and partial hydatidiform moles and in nonmolar abortuses, by E. B. Smith, et al. AMERICAN JOURNAL OF OBSTETRICS AND GYNE-COLOGY. 149(2):129-132, May 15, 1984.

The Human Life Bill: some issues and answers, by H. J. Hyde. NEW YORK LAW SCHOOL LAW REVIEW. 27(4):1077-1100, 1982.

Human life— its value and sanctity, by W. E. Power. CHAC REVIEW. 11(2):19-20, June 1983.

Human lives, human rights, by J. J. O'Connor. ORIGINS. 14:291-301, October 25, 1984.

Human sterilization: emerging technologies and reemerging social issues, by R. H. Blank. SCIENCE, TECHNOLOGY AND HUMAN VALUES. 9:8-20, Summer 1984.

Humanae Vitae revisited: the argument goes on, by J. M. Dominian. TABLET. 238:1052-1053, October 27, 1984.

Husband has no standing to enjoin wife from having an abortion. THE FAMILY LAW REPORTER: COURT OPINIONS. 10(21):1284, March 27, 1984.

Husband-wife inconsistencies in contraceptive use responses, by M. A. Koenig, et al. POPULATION STUDIES. 38:281-298, July 1984.

Hyde and go seek: a response to Representative Hyde, by H. F. Pilpel. NEW YORK LAW SCHOOL LAW REVIEW. 27(4):1101-1023, 1982.

Hyde: standing up for what's right, by D. De Celles. REGISTER. 60:2, October 7, 1984.

Hysterectomies in one Canadian province: a new look at risks and benefits, by P. R. Noralou. AMERICAN JOURNAL OF PUBLIC HEALTH. 74(1):39, January 1984.

Hysterectomy as treatment for complications of legal abortion, by D. A. Grimes, et al. OBSTETRICS AND GYNECOLOGY. 63(4):457-462, April 1984.

Hysterectomy facilitates proceptive behavior in rats, by H. B. Ahdieh, et al. HORMONES AND BEHAVIOR. 17(1):134-137, March 1983.

Hysteroscopic reversible tubal sterilization, by J. Hamou, et al. ACTA EUROPAEA FERTILITATIS. 15(2):123-129, March-April 1984.

Hysteroscopic tubal occlusion with formed-in-place silicone plugs: a clinical review, by R. M. Houck, et al. OBSTETRICS AND GYNE-COLOGY. 62(5):587-591, November 1983.

IUD-associated hospitalization in less developed countries, by I. C. Chi, et al. AMERICAN JOURNAL OF PUBLIC HEALTH. 74:353-357, April 1984.

IUD risk in lactation. AMERICAN FAMILY PHYSICIAN. 28:359, October 1983.

IUDs and pelvic inflammatory disease. SCIENCE NEWS. 124:127, August 20, 1983.

IUD's and the risks of disease, by S. Katz. CHATELAINE. 57:16, January 1984.

IUDs stimulate interferon release. NEW SCIENTIST. 99:848, September 22, 1983.

I did know how babies come into the world, by C. Esposito, et al. ETA EVOLUTIVA. (14):5-12, February 1983.

Ideology and opposition to abortion: trends in public opinion, 1972-1980, by C. H. Deitch. ALTERNATIVE LIFESTYLES. 6(1):6-26, Fall 1983.

If men got pregnant, abortion-sacrament, by E. Lubetsky. BROOM-STICK. 6(4):29, July 1984.

Ignorance of family planning methods in India: an important constraint on use, by A. M. Basu. STUDIES IN FAMILY PLANNING. 15(3):136-142, May-June 1984.

Ill effects from pill paper, by B. Dixon. NEW SCIENTIST. 101:50, March 15, 1984.

An ill for every pill?, by A. Cotter. NURSING TIMES. 79(46):12-14, November 16-21, 1983.

"Illusory" savings as a result of California's FP copayment system. FAMILY PLANNING PERSPECTIVES. 15:281, November-December 1983.

Imipramine disposition in users of oral contraceptive steroids, by D. R. Abernethy, et al. CLINICAL PHARMACOLOGY AND THERAPEUTICS. 35(6):792-797, June 1984.

Immediate postabortion insertion of an IUD, by H. Lehfeldt. EUROPEAN JOURNAL OF OBSTETRICS, GYNECOLOGY AND REPRODUCTIVE BIOLOGY. 17(2-3):141-147, May 1984.

Immediate sequelae following tubal sterilization. A multi-centre study of the ICMR Task Force on Female Sterilization. CONTRACEPTION. 28(4):369-384, October 1983.

Immune complex and complement levels in spontaneous abortions and normal pregnancy, by S. Saitoh, et al. NIPPON SANKA FUJINKA GAKKAI ZASSHI. 35(11):19;81-1990, November 1983.

Immune factors and recurrent abortion: a review, by C. W. Redman. AMERICAN JOURNAL OF REPRODUCTIVE IMMUNOLOGY. 4(4):179-181, December 1983.

Immunoglobulins and hormonal contraception, by P. Fassati, et al. CESKOSLOVENSKA GYNEKOLOGIE. 48(7):475-479, August 1983.

Immunologic considerations before and after vasovasostomy, by E. F. Fuchs, et al. FERTILITY AND STERILITY. 40(4):497-499, October 1983.

Immunologic indicators in threatened abortion, by V. V. Shcherbakova, et al. AKUSHERSTVO I GINEKOLOGIIA. (12):29-31, December 1983.

Immunological analysis of women with repeated spontaneous abortions, by J. Bousquet, et al. GYNECOLOGIC AND OBSTETRIC INVESTIGATION. 17(3):113-119, 1984.

Immunological aspects of spontaneous and habitual abortion, by W. R. Jones. CLINICAL REPRODUCTION AND FERTILITY. 1(3):244-246, September 1982.

Immunological factors and recurrent fetal loss [letter], by J. S. Scott.

LANCET. 1(8386):1122, May 19, 1984.

Immunization with spermatozoal peptide antigens resulting in immuno-suppression of fertility rates in female rats, by L. Mettler, et al. ANDROLOGIA. 15(6):670-675, November-December 1983.

Immunopathologic factors contributing to recurrent spontaneous abortion in humans, by A. E. Beer. AMERICAN JOURNAL OF REPRODUCTIVE IMMUNOLOGY. 4(4):182-184, December 1983.

Impact of accessibility of contraceptives on contraceptive prevalence in Guatemala, by C. H. Chen, et al. STUDIES IN FAMILY PLANNING. 14(11):275-283, November 1983.

Impact of child mortality and sociodemographic attributes on family size desires: some data from urban India, by D. N. Saksena, et al. JOURNAL OF BIOSOCIAL SCIENCE. 16:119-126, January 1984.

The impact of family planning on neonatal mortality, by J. C. Caceres-Baltazar. DISSERTATION ABSTRACTS INTERNATIONAL: B. 45(6), December 1984.

The impact of U. S. family planning programs on births, abortions and miscarriages, 1970-1979, by J. D. Forrest. SOCIAL SCIENCE AND MEDICINE. 18(6):461-465, 1984.

Impairment of vas sympathetic nervous system and contractility following vasectomy in rats, by K. C. Kanwar, et al. INDIAN JOURNAL OF EXPERIMENTAL BIOLOGY. 21(11):585-586, 1983.

Implants: better than the pill? USA TODAY. 112:13, February 1984.

Implications of future fertility trends for contraceptive practice [developing countries], by J. Bongaarts. POPULATION AND DEVELOPMENT REVIEW. 10:341-352, June 1984.

The importance and technic of postpartum sterilization, by J. Poradovsky, et al. CESKOSLOVENSKA GYNEKOLOGIE. 48(10): 748-751, December 1983.

In God's image: a statement on the sanctity of human life. ORIGINS. 14:151-153, August 9, 1984.

In praise of the one-child family [China], by J. Marshall. TIMES

The in vitro effect of grandiflorenic acid and zoapatle aqueous crude extract upon spontaneous contractility of the rat uterus during oestrus cycle, by E. Bejar, et al. JOURNAL OF ETHNOPHARM-ACOLOGY. 11(1):87-97, June 1984.

Incidence of arterial hypertension in women taking oral hormonal contraceptive agents (femigen), by W. Mikrut. WIADOMOSCI LEKARSKIE. 36(19):1587-1592, October 1983.

The incidence of intrauterine abnormalities found at hysteroscopy in patients undergoing elective hysteroscopic sterilization, by J. M. Cooper, et al. JOURNAL OF REPRODUCTIVE MEDICINE. 28(10):659-661, October 1983.

The incidence of repeat induced abortion in a randomly selected group of women. A retrospective study, by J. F. Heinrich, et al. JOURNAL OF REPRODUCTIVE MEDICINE. 29(4):260-264, April 1984.

Income and other factors influencing fertility in China, by N. Birdsall, et al. POPULATION AND DEVELOPMENT REVIEW. 9(4): 651, December 1983.

Incomplete abortion and hydrometrosis in a squirrel monkey (Saimiri sciureus), by M. M. Swindle, et al. LABORATORY ANIMAL SCIENCE. 34(3):290-292, June 1984.

Incomplete pregnancy, by N. M. Pobedinskii, et al. AKUSHERSTVO I GINEKOLOGIIA. (12):22-25, December 1983.

Increased decidual prostaglandin E concentration in human abortion, by O. E. Jaschevatzky, et al. BRITISH JOURNAL OF OBSTETRICS AND GYNAECOLOGY. 90(10):958-960, October 1983.

Increased risk for cancer of the breast due to previous medication, by R. W. de Levin, et al. ARCHIV FUR GESCHWULSTFORCHUNG. 54(2):153-158, 1984.

Increased risk of abortion after genetic amniocentesis in twin pregnancies, by C. Palle, et al. PRENATAL DIAGNOSIS. 3(2):83-89, April-June 1983.

Increased urinary androgen levels in patients with carcinoma in situ of the breast with onset while taking oral contraceptives, by

G. Secreto, et al. CANCER DETECTION AND PREVENTION. 6 (4-5):439-442, 1983.

Increasing natality in China, by M. Cartier. POPULATION. 38:590-591, May-June 1983.

Incremental program of contraceptive care of women, by H. G. Neumann, et al. ZEITSCHRIFT FUR AERZTLICHE FORT-BILDUNG. 77(20):841-843, 1983.

India's family planning programme— its impace and implications, by K. Srinivasan. JOURNAL OF FAMILY WELFARE. 30:7-25, December 1983.

Indicators of psychological well-being in a sample of employed women: an exploratory study, by M. W. O'Rourke. HEALTH CARE FOR WOMEN, INTERNATIONAL. 5(1-3):163-177, 1984.

Individual levels of plasma alpha 2-antiplasmin and alpha 2-macroglobulin during the normal menstrual cycle and in women on oral contraceptives low in oestrogen, by J. Jespersen, et al. THROMBOSIS AND HAEMOSTASIS. 50(2):581-585, August 30, 1983.

Induced abortion and fertility: a quarter century of experience in Eastern Europe, by T. Frejka. POPULATION AND DEVELOP-MENT REVIEW. 9:494-520, September 1983.

Induced abortion in the early stages of pregnancy. CESKOSLO-VENSKA GYNEKOLOGIE. 48(6):456-457, July 1984.

Induced fertility transition: impact of population planning and socio-economic change in the People's Republic of China, by H. Y. Tien. POPULATION STUDIES. 38:385-400, November 1984.

Inducing the birth of change in Ireland, by R. Ford. TIMES. May 21, 1984, p. 10.

Inevitable abortion, by D. Rutledge. NURSING MIRROR. 158(6):Mid-wifery Forum:v, viii, February 8, 1984.

Infant mortality by socio-economic status for Blacks, Indians and Whites— a longitudinal analysis of North Carolina, 1968-1977, by F. Bertoli, et al. SOCIOLOGY AND SOCIAL RESEARCH. 68:364-377, April 1984.

Infertility, and how it's treated, by R. W. Miller. FDA CONSUMER.

17(5):7, June 1983.

Influence of augmented Hageman factor (Factor XII) titers on the cryoactivation of plasma prorenin in women using oral contraceptive agents, by E. M. Grodon, et al. JOURNAL OF CLINICAL INVESTIGATION. 72(5):1833-1888, Novembre 1983.

The influence of child spacing on child survival, by C. Desweemer. POPULATION STUDIES. 38:47-72, March 1984.

Influence of a levonorgestrel-containing contraceptive vaginal ring on plasma lipids and lipoproteins in cynomolgus monkeys, by M. R. Adams, et al. CONTRACEPTION. 28(3):253-266, September 1983.

Influence of nutritional status on pharmacokinetics of contraceptive progestogens. NUTRITION REVIEWS. 42:182-183, May 1984.

The influence of oral contraceptives on the frequency of acute appendicitis in different phases of the menstrual cycle, by E. Arnbjornsson. SURGERY, GYNECOLOGY AND OBSTETRICS. 158(5):464-466, May 1984.

Influence of oral contraceptives on the incidence of premalignant and malignant lesions of the cervix, by L. Andolsek, et al. CONTRACEPTION. 28(6):505-519, December 1983.

The influence of psychological and situational factors on the contraceptive behavior of single men: a review of the literature, by D. Gold, et al. POPULATION AND ENVIRONMENT: BEHAVIORAL AND SOCIAL ISSUES. 6(2):113-129, Summer 1983.

Influence of psychological factors on adolescent compliance with oral contraceptives, by R. H. Durant, et al. JOURNAL OF ADOLESCENT HEALTH CARE. 5(1):1-6, January 1984.

Influence of STS 557 on the mitotic activity in the endometrium of ovariectomized mice and comparison with the effects of progesterone and levonorgestrel, by M. Koch. EXPERIMENTAL AND CLINICAL ENDOCRINOLOGY. 83(3):310-314, May 1984.

Influence of sex and oral contraceptive steroids on paracetamol metabolism, by J. O. Miners, et al. BRITISH JOURNAL OF CLINICAL PHARMACOLOGY. 16(5):503-509, November 1983.

Inhibin contraception. AMERICAN FAMILY PHYSICIAN. 29:396, May 1984.

Inhibition of rat embryonic development by the intrauterine administration of alpha-difluoromethylornithine, by J. D. Mendez, et al. CONTRACEPTION. 28(1):93-98, July 1983.

Inhibition of 3-beta-hydroxy steroid dehydrogenase activity in first trimester human pregnancy with trilostane and WIN 32729, by Z. M. van der Spuy, et al. CLINICAL ENDOCRINOLOGY. 19(4):521-531, October 1983.

Initiating contraceptive use: how do young women decide?, by J. E. White. PEDIATRIC NURSING. 10(5):347-352, September-October 1984.

Insertion of the laparoscopic Trocar without the use of carbon dioxide gas, by S. Pine, et al. CONTRACEPTION. 28(3):233-239, September 1983.

Insertion of the Multiload Cu 250 IUD immediately after abortion or labor, by L. Morup, et al. UGESKRIFT FOR LAEGER. 146(14): 1045-1048, April 2, 1984.

Instructions on family planning at the ambulatory clinic of Nagasaki University Hospital: the current status of training in pessary use, by H. Hotta, et al. JOSANPU ZASSHI. 37(3):209-211, March 1983.

Instructions on sexual activities and contraception, by A. Ishihama. JOSANPU ZASSHI. 38(2):124-129, February 1984.

Integrated approach to MCH and family planning [letter], by A. K. Sood, et al. INDIAN PEDIATRICS. 20(11):876-877, November 1983.

Integrated child development services: impact on fertility regulation, by M. K. Vasundhra, et al. JOURNAL OF FAMILY WELFARE. 30:3-7, September 1983.

Integrating health services into an MCH-FP program: lessons from Matlab, Bangladesh, by J. F. Phillips, et al. STUDIES IN FAMILY PLANNING. 15(4):153-161, July-August 1984.

Interaction between oral contraceptives and griseofulvin, by C. P. Dijke, et al. BRITISH MEDICAL JOURNAL [CLIN RES]. 288 (6424):1125-1126, April 14, 1984.

Interaction of drugs with steroidal oral contraceptives, by K. Dvorak.

CESKOSLOVENSKA GYNEKOLOGIE. 48(3):222-228, April 1983.

Interception (postcoital contraception), by J. G. Schenker, et al. HAREFUAH. 105(7):176-177, October 2, 1983.

Interruption of early pregnancy in the monkey with mestranol and 5-oxy-17-phenyl-18,19,20-trinor prostaglandin F1 alpha methyl ester, by J. W. Wilks. BIOLOGY OF REPRODUCTION. 30(4):886-893, May 1984.

Interval Falope ring sterilization in the Cape Province: experience with 9175 cases over four years, by A. J. Nieuwoudt, et al. SOUTH AFRICAN MEDICAL JOURNAL. 64(25):972-974, December 10, 1983.

InterVarsity withdraws a book opposed by prolifers, by R. Frame. CHRISTIANITY TODAY. 28:63+, September 21, 1984.

Interview with Ellen Kruger, by E. Kruger. CANADIAN DIMENSION. 17:8-9, November 1983.

Interview with Muriel Smith, by M. Smith. CANADIAN DIMENSION. 17:7-8, November 1983.

Intracervical instillation of PGE2-gel in patients with missed abortion or intrauterine fetal death, by G. Ekman, et al. ARCHIVES OF GYNECOLOGY. 233(4):241-245, 1983.

Intracervical release of ST-1435 for contraception, by H. Kurunmaki, et al. CONTRACEPTION. 29(5):411-421, May 1984.

Intramuscular administration of 15(S) methyl prostaglandins F2 alpha for midtrimester abortion, by G. Sakunthala, et al. ASIA-OCEANIA JOURNAL OF OBSTETRICS AND GYNAECOLOGY. 10(2):191-195, June 1984.

Intrauterine contraceptive device insertion with suture fixation at cesarean section, by B. H. Liu, et al. CHINESE MEDICAL JOURNAL [ENGL ED]. 96(2):141-144, 1983.

Intrauterine device associated hospitalization in less developed countries, by I. C. Chi, et al. AMERICAN JOURNAL OF PUBLIC HEALTH. 74(4):353-357, 1984.

Intrauterine devices. Their role in family planning care. WHO OFF-SET PUBLICATION. (75):1-53, 1983.

Intrauterine incarcerated bowel following uterine perforation during an abortion: a case report, by P. S. Dunner, et al. AMERICAN JOURNAL OF OBSTETRICS AND GYNECOLOGY. 147(8):969-970, December 15, 1983.

Intrauterine small bowel entrapment and obstruction complicating suction abortion, by C. R. McArdle, et al. GASTROINTESTINAL RADIOLOGY. 9(3):239-240, 1984.

An intravaginal contraceptive device for the delivery of an acrosin and hyaluronidase inhibitor, by P. J. Burck, et al. FERTILITY AND STERILITY. 41(2):314-318, February 1984.

Intubation, aspiration prophylaxis in midtrimester abortions? [letter], by D. J. Dehring, et al. ANESTHESIOLOGY. 61(2):223-225, August 1984.

Involuntary sterilizations considered. MENTAL AND PHYSICAL DISABILITY LAW REPORTER. 8(1):27, January-February 1984.

Ionized copper as contraceptives in male rhesus monkey, by S. S. Riar, et al. ANDROLOGIA. 16(2):116-117, March-April 1984.

Ireland: bishops' pawns [constitutional amendment that would bar legalization of abortion]. ECONOMIST. 287:44+, April 9, 1983.

Ireland outlaws abortion, by R. Boyd. SPARE RIB. 1(35):15, October 1983.

Ireland: rights for the unborn. ECONOMIST. 288:39-40, September 3, 1983.

Irish bamboozlement, by P. Kirby. COMMONWEAL. 111:26+, January 13, 1984.

Is wide availability of abortion essential to national population growth control programs? Experiences of 116 countries, by S. D. Mumford, et al. AMERICAN JOURNAL OF OBSTETRICS AND GYNECOLOGY. 149(6):639-645, July 15, 1984.

Issues in fertility control for mentally retarded female adolescents: I. Sexual activity, sexual abuse, and contraception, by A. Chamberlain, et al. PEDIATRICS. 73(4):445-450, April 1984.

— . II. Parental attitudes toward sterilization, by A. Passer, et al. PEDIATRICS. 73(4):451-454, April 1984.

It takes a death, by M. O'Brien. SPARE RIB. (141):9, April 1984.

It's time to move on abortion. REGISTER. 60:2, November 11, 1984.

Jail term over, no regrets, by D. Goldkamp. REGISTER. 60:7, February 5, 1984.

Jesse Jackson changes position on abortion, by M. Meehan. REGISTER. 59:1+, November 20, 1983.

Jewish-Christian feminist dialogue: a wholistic vision, by D. McCauley, et al. UNION SEMINARY QUARTERLY REVIEW. 38(2):147-190, 1983.

John Paul argues forcefully against population planning. REGISTER. 60:3, June 24, 1984.

John Paul II and Humanae Vitae, by S. C. Wroblewski. HOMILETIC AND PASTORAL REVIEW. 85:52-55, October 1984.

Judge tells Dalkon Shield producer to confess, by S. Tarnoff. BUSINESS INSURANCE. 18:66-67, March 12, 1984.

Judging teenagers: how minors fare when they seek court-authorized abortions, by P. Donovan. FAMILY PLANNING PERSPECTIVES. 15(6):259-262; 264-267, November-December 1983.

Judicial decision [Medhurst vs. Medhurst] that takes us back to the pre-barbarian, by T. Byfield. ALBERTA REPORT. 11:52, April 16, 1984.

The kindest month, by M. Richards. CLERGY REVIEW. 68:382, November 1983.

Kinetic studies on prostaglandin concentrations in the amniotic fluid during rivanol-induced abortion, by Z. R. Zhou, et al. YAO HSUEH HSUEH PAO. 18(8):569-571, August 1983.

Knowledge and attitudes toward sexuality and sex education of a select group of older people, by M. M. Smith, et al. GERONTOLOGY AND GERIATRICS EDUCATION. 3(4):259-269, Summer 1983.

Knowledge, attitude and practice of family planning in Hausa women, by N. Rehan. SOCIAL SCIENCE AND MEDICINE. 18(10): 839-844, 1984.

Knowledge, attitudes, and practice regarding vasectomy among residents of Hamilton County, Ohio, 1980, by C. A. Huether, et al. AMERICAN JOURNAL OF PUBLIC HEALTH. 74(1):79-82, January 1984.

Knowledge of contraception and use of contraceptive methods among college students in a major southeastern public university, by N. S. Palmer. DISSERTATION ABSTRACTS INTERNATIONAL: A. 45(3), September 1984.

Krol defends single issue of abortion as a top priority, by M. Meehan. REGISTER. 60:1+, November 25, 1984.

LAPAC announces deadly dozen, by M. Meehan. REGISTER. 60:1+, May 6, 1984.

Lack of association between contraceptive usage and congenital malformations in offspring, by S. Linn, et al. AMERICAN JOURNAL OF OBSTETRICS AND GYNECOLOGY. 147(8):923-928, December 15, 1983.

Lack of correlation between contraceptive pills and Down's syndrome, by A. Ericson, et al. ACTA OBSTETRICIA ET GYNE-COLOGICA SCANDINAVICA. 62(5):511-514, 1983.

Lack of an elevated risk of malignant melanoma in relation to oral contraceptive use, by S. P. Helmrich, et al. JNCI. 72(3):617-620, March 1984.

Lactation and fertility regulation, by V. Hull. HEALTHRIGHT. 3:17-21, August 1984.

Laminaria— a modern cervix dilatation method with more than a 100-year history, by A. Jonasson. JORDEMODERN. 97(6):187-195, June 1984.

Laparoscopic clip sterilization in a free-standing facility: an evaluation of cost and safety, by T. Crist, et al. NORTH CAROLINA MEDICAL JOURNAL. 44(9):546-549, September 1983.

Laparoscopic sterilization during the puerperium employing electro-coagulation. A retrospective study of 76 women, by B. Toft, et al. UGESKRIFT FOR LAEGER. 145(48):3731-3733, November 28, 1983.

Laser-assisted vas anastomosis: a preliminary report, by C. M. Lynne, et al. LASERS IN SURGERY AND MEDICINE. 3(3):261-263, 1983.

Late abortion and prostaglandin, by L. W. Sorbye. SYKEPLEIEN. 71(6):13, March 20, 1984.

Late abortions [letter], by C. Woodroffe, et al. LANCET. 1(8374):454, February 25, 1984.

Late abortions: there is madness in our methods. PRACTITIONER. 228(1389):247; 249, March 1984.

Late complications of laparoscopic clip sterilization, by R. Punnonen, et al. ACTA OBSTETRICIA ET GYNECOLOGICA SCANDINAVICA. 63(2):149-151, 1984.

Late results in fallopian tubes studies on the Bleier clip, by H. Jung, et al. GEBURTSHILFE UND FRAUENHEILKUNDE. 43(Suppl 1): 67-69, June 1983.

Late sequela of legal abortion, by E. B. Obel. UGESKRIFT FOR LAEGER. 145(48):3716-3721, November 28, 1983.

Latest developments in contraception [letter], by E. L. Billings. MEDICAL JOURNAL OF AUSTRALIA. 140(6):381-382, March 17, 1984.

Latest polls show that public support for legal abortion continues. FAMILY PLANNING PERSPECTIVES. 15:279-280, November-December 1983.

Law and family planning, by M. D. Kirby. MEDICAL JOURNAL OF AUSTRALIA. 140(6):356-362, March 17, 1984.

Law: the fallacy of time limits, by J. Finch. NURSING TIMES. 158(20):24-25, May 16, 1984.

Leads from the MMWR. Oral contraceptive use and the risk of breast cancer in young women. JAMA. 252(3):326-327, July 20, 1984.

Leads from the MMWR. Toxic-shock syndrome and the vaginal contraceptive sponge. JAMA. 251(8):1015-1016, February 24, 1984.

Legal abortion and placenta previa, by D. A. Grimes, et al. AMERICAN JOURNAL OF OBSTETRICS AND GYNECOLOGY. 149(5):501-504, July 1, 1984.

Legal abortion in Georgia, 1980, by A. M. Spitz, et al. JOURNAL OF THE MEDICAL ASSOCIATION OF GEORGIA. 73(2):87-91, February 1984.

The legality of abortion by prostaglandin, by G. Wright. THE CRIMINAL LAW REVIEW. June 1984, pp. 347-349.

Legislation and teenage sex. BRITISH MEDICAL JOURNAL [CLIN RES]. 287(6408):1826, December 17, 1983.

Levels of serum lipids during abortion induced by a hypertonic saline solution, by A. S. Sane, et al. JOURNAL DE GYNE-COLOGIE, OBSTETRIQUE ET BIOLOGIE DE LA REPRODUCTION. 12(5):477-480, 1983.

Liability for unsuccessful sterilization?, by O. Gritschneder. GERBURTSHILFE UND FRAUENHEILKUNDE. 43(7):469-471, July 1983.

Liberals shun abortion as single issue, by S. Askin. NATIONAL CATHOLIC REPORTER. 20:10, September 28, 1984.

Life of Mrs. Taki Hanyu, a leader in patient education in the use of pessary application, by K. Nakashige. JOSANPU ZASSHI. 37(3):187-196, March 1983.

The life they saved was yours, by B. Weinhouse. LADIES HOME JOURNAL. 101:30+, January 1984.

Light microscopy and electron microscpy observation in the placenta and viscera of fetus in mid-stage abortion induced by Radix euphorbiae Kansui, by T. W. Yu. CHUNG HSI I CHIEH HO TSA CHIH. 4(4):201-202, April 1984.

Limiting state regulation of reproductive decisions, by L. H. Glantz. AMERICAN JOURNAL OF PUBLIC HEALTH. 74:168-169, February 1984.

Lipid and lipoprotein triglyceride and cholestrol inter-relationships: effects of sex, hormone use, and hyperlipidemia, by P. W. Wahl, et al. METABOLISM. 33(6):502-508, June 1984.

Listeriosis in mother and fetus during the first trimester of preg-nancy. Case report, by R. Pezeshkian, et al. BRITISH JOURNAL OF OBSTETRICS AND GYNAECOLOGY. 91(1):85-86, January 1984.

Lithium and pregnancy. A cohort study on maniac-depressive women, by B. Kallen, et al. ACTA PSYCHIATRICA SCAN-DINAVICA. 68(2):134-139, August 1983.

Local anti-fertility effect of inhibin-enriched preparation (IEP) in female hamsters, by B. V. Bapat, et al. CONTRACEPTION. 29(4): 367-373, April 1984.

Locus of control and decision to abort, by P. N. Dixon, et al. PSYCHOLOGICAL REPORTS. 54(2):547-553, April 1984.

Long-acting contraceptive agents: aliphatic and alicyclic carboxylic esters of levonorgestrel, by A. Shafiee, et al. STEROIDS. 41(3): 349-359, March 1983.

— . Analysis and purification of steroid esters, by S. A. Matlin, et al. STEROIDS. 41(3):361-367, March 1983.

— . Design of the WHO Chemical Synthesis Programme, by P. Crabbe, et al. STEROIDS. 41(3):243-253, March 1983.

— . Levonorgestrel esters of unsaturated acids, by A. S. Wan. STEROIDS. 41(3):339-348, March 1983.

— . Structure activity relationships in a series of norethistcrone and levonorgestrel esters, by G. Bialy, et al. STEROIDS. 41(3):419-439, March 1983.

Long acting injectable hormonal contraceptives, by I. S. Fraser. CLINICAL REPRODUCTION AND FERTILITY. 1(1):67-88, March 1982.

Long-term effect of vasectomy on coronary heart disease, by E. B. Perrin, et al. AMERICAN JOURNAL OF PUBLIC HEALTH. 74:128-132, February 1984.

The long-term effects of vasectomy on sexual behavior, by P. L. Dias. ACTA PSYCHIATRICA SCANDINAVICA. 67(5):333-338, May 1983.

Long-term effects of vasectomy. 1. Biochemical parameters, by Z. Shikary, et al. CONTRACEPTION. 28(5):423-436, 1983.

Long-term follow-up of children whose mothers used oral contraceptives prior to conception, by S. Magidor, et al. CONTRACEPTION. 29(3):203-214, March 1984.

Long-term reversible contraception with levonorgestrel-releasing Silastic rods, by S. Roy, et al. AMERICAN JOURNAL OF OBSTETRICS AND GYNECOLOGY. 148(7):1006-1013 April 1, 1984.

Long-term survival after resection of a hepatocellular carcinoma with lymph node metastasis and discontinuation of oral contraceptives, by O. T. Terpstra, et al. AMERICAN JOURNAL OF GASTROENTEROLOGY. 79(6):474-478, June 1984.

Long-term vasectomy shows no association with coronary heart disease. JAMA. 252:1005, August 24, 1984.

A low-power magnification technique for the re-anastomosis of the vas—further results in a personal series of 125 patients, by D. Urquhart-Hay. AUSTRALIAN AND NEW ZEALAND JOURNAL OF SURGERY. 54(1):73-74, February 1984.

Lucky dip [urine analysis]. ECONOMIST. 290:84-85, February 18, 1984.

The lupus-anticoagulant: clinical and obstetric implications, by W. F. Lubbe, et al. NEW ZEALAND MEDICAL JOURNAL. 97(758): 398-402, June 27, 1984.

Lupus anticoagulant, recurrent abortion, and prostacyclin production by cultured smooth muscle cells [letter], by C. de Castellarnau, et al. LANCET. 2(8359):1137-1138, November 12, 1983.

Lupus nephropathy and pregnancy. A study of 26 pregnancies in patients with systemic lupus erythematosus and nephritis, by E. Imbasciati, et al. NEPHRON. 36(1):46-51, 1984.

Luteal phase inadequacy and a chromosomal anomaly in recurrent abortion, by A. C. Wentz, et al. FERTILITY AND STERILITY. 41 (1):142-143, January 1984.

Luteinizing hormone-releasing hormone (LHRH) and its analogs for contraception in women: a review, by R. B. Thau. CONTRACEPTION. 29(2):143-162, February 1984.

Lymphocyte-reactive antibodies and spontaneous abortion [letter], by P. M. Johnson, et al. LANCET. 2(8362):1304-1305, December 3, 1983.

Maguire urges pluralism, jailed prolifer heartsick, by M. Meehan. REGISTER. 60:1+, September 30, 1984.

The Maguires bring abortion issue to a turbulent boil, by M. Meehan. REGISTER. 60:1+, May 27, 1984.

Major study dispels fears of possible harm in vasectomy, by J. E.

Brody. NEW YORK TIMES. November 15, 1983, p. C1.

Making choices. AMERICAN DEMOGRAPHICS. 6:13-14, February 1984.

Making up her mind: consent, pregnancy and mental handicap, by R. Higgs. JOURNAL OF MEDICAL ETHICS. 9(4):219-226, December 1983.

Male adolescent sexual behavior, the forgotten partner: a review, by M. L. Finkel, et al. JOURNAL OF SCHOOL HEALTH. 53(9):544-547, November 1983.

Male contraception, by A. Demoulin. REVUE MEDICALE DE LIEGE. 39(7):266-272, April 1, 1984.

Male contraceptive. ENVIRONMENT. 25:23-24, October 1983.

Male contraceptive. SCIENCE DIMENSION. 16(1):7, 1984.

Male migration, machismo, and conjugal roles: implications for fertility control in a Mexican municipio, by R. E. Wiest. JOURNAL OF COMPARATIVE FAMILY STUDIES. 14(2):167-181, Summer 1983.

Males and contraception: the relationship between contraception knowledge, attitudes and behavior, by D. A. Foss-Goodman. DISSERTATION ABSTRACTS INTERNATIONAL: B. 45(10), April 1985.

March for life. CHRISTIANITY TODAY. 28:53, March 2, 1984.

Marie Stopes society's good work. NURSING JOURNAL OF INDIA. 75(6):138, June 1984.

Marital fertility at older ages in Nepal, Bangladesh, and Sri Lanka, by J. P. Tan. POPULATION STUDIES. 37:433-444, November 1983.

Marital sexual relationships and birth spacing among two Yoruba sub-groups, by L. A. Adeokun. AFRICA. 52(4):1-14, 1982.

Marketing enables population control group to boost results, by K. Higgins. MARKETING NEWS. 17:12-13, October 14, 1983.

Massive hemoperitoneum from rupture of richly vascularized benign liver tumors in women on oral contraceptives, by B. B. Kroon, et al. NETHERLANDS JOURNAL OF SURGERY. 36(3):85, June 1984.

Maternal age and overdue conceptions, by G. E. Hendershot. AMERICAN JOURNAL OF PUBLIC HEALTH. 74(1):35-38, January 1984.

Maternal blocking antibodies, the fetal allograft, and recurrent abortion. LANCET. 2(8360):1175-1176, November 19, 1983.

Maternal-paternal histocompatibility: lack of association with habitual abortions, by J. R. Oksenberg, et al. FERTILITY AND STERILITY. 42(3):389-395, September 1984.

Maternal plasma estradiol and progesterone levels during therapeutic abortion induced by 16,16 dimethyl PGE2 p-benzaldehyde semicarbazone ester, by K. C. Tan, et al. PROSTAGLANDINS LEUKOTRIENES AND MEDICINE. 14(2):215-224, May 1984.

Matters of conscience: all in the line of duty?, by M. Kenny. NURSING MIRROR. 158(20):22-23, May 16, 1984.

—. The other side of the question, by J. Robinson. NURSING MIRROR. 158(20):20-21, May 16, 1984.

Mayor, neighbors unite against abortion facility. REGISTER. 60:2, January 1, 1984.

Measurement issues involved in examing contraceptive use among young single women, by E. S. Herold. POPULATION AND ENVIRONMENT. 4(2):128-144, Summer 1981.

Mechanisms of fetal demise in pregnant mice immunized to murine alpha-fetoprotein, by G. J. Mizejewski, et al. AMERICAN JOURNAL OF REPRODUCTIVE IMMUNOLOGY. 5(1):32-38, January-February 1984.

The medicaid cutoff and abortion services for the poor, by S. K. Henshaw, et al. FAMILY PLANNING PERSPECTIVES. 16(4):170-172; 177-180, July-August 1984.

Medical counseling and activities of the Specialty Committee—final conclusions drawn from current trends in irreversible contraception, by J. Rothe, et al. ZEITSCHRIFT FUR AERZTLICHE FORTBILDUNG. 78(2):57-60, 1984.

Medical experts affirm that life begins at conception. OUR SUNDAY VISITOR. 73:8, November 4, 1984.

Medical indication of induced abortion and its criticism [letter]. ORVOSI HETILAP. 124(45):2773-2774, November 6, 1983.

Medical intervention, by D. Gould. NEW SCIENTIST. 98:485-486, May 19, 1983.

Medical risks of teenage pregnancy, by J. A. Straton, et al. AUSTRALIAN FAMILY PHYSICIAN. 12(6):474; 477-478; 480, June 1983.

Medical societies vs. nurse practitioners, by P. Donovan. FAMILY PLANNING PERSPECTIVES. 15(4):166-171, July-August 1983.

Medroxyprogesterone acetate. Biochemical and clinical aspects, by A. R. Ayala, et al. GINECOLOGIA Y OBSTETRICIA DE MEXICO. 50(305):253-259, September 1982.

Medroxyprogesterone. And now, propranolol for birth control? RN. 47:107, February 1984.

Melanoma, pregnancy and oral contraception, by G. Veen, et al. NEDERLANDS TIJDSCHRIFT VOOR GENEESKUNDE. 127(41): 1865-1868, October 8, 1983.

Melanoma, pregnancy and oral contraception [letter], by T. A. van der Ploeg-Phaff. NEDERLANDS TIJDSCHRIFT VOOR GENEESKUNDE. 127(48):2210, November 26, 1983.

Men's new role in pregnancy prevention. SCIENCE DIGEST. 92:88, January 1984.

Menstrual changes after tubal sterilization, by F. DeStefano, et al. OBSTETRICS AND GYNECOLOGY. 62(6):673, 681, December 1983.

Menstrual disorder after medical termination of pregnancy, by J. Mitra, et al. JOURNAL OF THE INDIAN MEDICAL ASSOCIATION. 82(1):4-6, January 1984.

Menstrual regulation and contraception in Bangladesh: competing or complementary?, by H. H. Akhter, et al. INTERNATIONAL JOURNAL OF GYNAECOLOGY AND OBSTETRICS. 22(2):137-143, April 1984.

Menstrual regulation versus contraception in Bangladesh: characteristics of the acceptors, by H. H. Akhter, et al. STUDIES IN FAMILY PLANNING. 14(12 Pt 1):318-323, December 1983.

Mental health and female sterilization. Report of a WHO collaborative prospective study. JOURNAL OF BIOSOCIAL SCIENCE. 16 (1):1-21, January 1984.

Mental health law— proposed legislation: involuntary sterilization of the mentally incompetent in Illinois. SOUTHERN ILLINOIS UNIVERSITY LAW JOURNAL. 1983:227-245, 1983.

Mental illness— sterilization— due process. THE FAMILY LAW REPORTER: COURT OPINIONS. 9(49):2742, October 18, 1983.

Mercy or murder? Ethical dilemmas in newborn care, by M. Klitsch. FAMILY PLANNING PERSPECTIVES. 15:143-145, May-June 1983.

Metabolic effects of two triphasic formulations containing ethinyl estradiol and dl-norgestrel, by R. P. Smith, et al. CONTRACEPTION. 28(2):189-199, August 1983.

Metabolic pathways of the contragestational agent, 3-(2-ethyl-phenyl)-5-(3-methoxyphenyl)-1H-1,2,4-triazol (DL 111-IT), in the rat, by A. Assandri, et al. XENOBIOTICA. 14(6):429-443, June 1984.

Method failure pregnancy rates with depro-provera and a local substitute [letter], by E. B. McDaniel, et al. LANCET. 1(8389): 1293, June 9, 1984.

Methodologic considerations in studies on female sterilization— a review for clinicians, by I. C. Chi, et al. CONTRACEPTION. 28(5):437-454, November 1983.

Methods for the study of the experimental interruption of pregnancy by ornithine decarboxylase inhibitors: effects of DL-alpha-difluoromethylornithine, by J. R. Fozard, et al. METHODS IN ENZYMOLOGY. 94:213-216, 1983.1

Methods of terminating pregnancy and acute complications, by L. Heisterberg. UGESKRIFT FOR LAEGER. 145(48):3711-3715, November 28, 1983.

Methods to determine success of attempts to terminate early gestation pregnancies with prostaglandin vaginal suppositories, by P. F. Brenner, et al. CONTRACEPTION. 28(2):111-124, August 1983.

Microsurgery for vasectomy reversal and vasoepididymostomy, by S. J. Silber. UROLOGY. 23(5):505-524, May 1984.

Microsurgical reversal of female sterilization, by J. G. Lauritsen. UGESKRIFT FOR LAEGER. 145(51):3976-3979, December 19, 1983.

Microsurgical tubal anastomosis: a controlled trial in four Asian centers, by J. A. Rock, et al. MICROSURGERY. 5(2):95-97, 1984.

Midtrimester abortion. Intra-amniotic instillation of hyperosmolar urea and prostaglandin F2 alpha v dilatation and evacuation, by M. E. Kafrissen, et al. JAMA. 251(7):916-919, February 17, 1984.

Midtrimester abortion: techniques and complications, by J. J. La-Ferla. CLINICAL PERINATOLOGY. 10(2):305-320, June 1983.

Midtrimester pregnancy termination: a study of the cost effectiveness of dilation and evacuation in a freestanding facility, by T. Crist, et al. NORTH CAROLINA MEDICAL JOURNAL. 44(9):549-551, September 1983.

Migraine and hormonal contraceptives, by W. Grassler, et al. ZEITSCHRIFT FUR AERZTLICHE FORTBILDUNG. 78(6):229-232, 1984.

Mini-abortion, the determination of its effectiveness and the present method of performing it at the Institute for Maternal and Child Care, by F. Havranek, et al. CESKOSLOVENSKA GYNE-KOLOGIE. 49(1):23-26, February 1984.

Mini-abortion— 3 years' experience in the district of Mlada Boleslva, by V. Divekcy, et al. CESKOSLOVENSKA GYNE-KOLOGIE. 48(5):362-363, June 1983.

Minilaparotomy under acupuncture analgesia, by P. L. Dias, et al. JOURNAL OF THE ROYAL SOCIETY OF MEDICINE. 77(4):295-298, April 1984.

Minimizing risk of repeated pregnancy loss, by A. C. Cruz, et al. JOURNAL OF THE FLORIDA MEDICAL ASSOCIATION. 70(9):728-731, September 1983.

Minor's right of privacy: access to contraceptives without parental notification. JOURNAL OF JUVENILE LAW. 7:238-245, 1983.

Miscarriage, by P. A. Hillard. PARENTS MAGAZINE. 59(1):72; 75, January 1984.

Miscarriage: a common tragedy, by J. Moore. COMMUNITY OUT-

LOOK. June 13, 1984, p. 210.

"Miscarriage": a medico-legal analysis, by I. J. Keown. CRIMINAL
LAW REPORTER. October 1984, pp. 604-614.

Missed abortion presenting as a vascular tumour on hysterosal-
pingography, by A. Ho. BRITISH JOURNAL OF RADIOLOGY.
57(673):102-103, January 1984.

Mitotic and apoptotic response of breast tissue to oral contraceptives
[letter], by T. J. Anderson. LANCET. 1(8368):99-100, January
14, 1984.

Mixed feelings on abortion, by S. Egan. SPARE RIB. 1(40):21, March
1984.

Mixed-up message [U. S. changes family planning position]. NA-
TION. 239:4, July 7-14, 1984.

Mixed verdict for family at U. N. population meet, by J. C. O'Neill.
OUR SUNDAY VISITOR. 73:3, September 16, 1984.

Mode of action of dl-norgestrel and ethinylestradiol combination
in postcoital contraception. III. Effect of preovulatory administration following the luteinizing hormone surge on ovarian
steroidogenesis, by W. Y. Ling, et al. FERTILITY AND STERILITY.
40(5):631-636, November 1983.

Modern fertility patterns: contrasts between the United States and
Japan, by S. P. Morgan, et al. POPULATION AND DEVELOP-
MENT REVIEW. 10(1):19, March 1984.

Modification of cycle-dependent changes in the uterus by the intake
of hormonal contraceptives, by W. Bartl, et al. ULTRASCHALL
IN DER MEDIZIN. 5(2):74-76, April 1984.

Monitoring sterilization, by B. Hartmann, et al. NATION. 239:98,
August 18-25, 1984.

Monoclonal antibody to a human germ cell membrane glycoprotein
that inhibits fertilization, by R. K. Naz, et al. SCIENCE. 225:342-
344, July 20, 1984.

Monoclonal sperm antibodies: their potential for investigation of
sperms as target of immunological contraception, by L. Mettler,
et al. AMERICAN JOURNAL OF REPRODUCTIVE IMMUNOLOGY.
5(3):125-128, April-May 1984.

The moral act, by N. J. Rigali. HORIZONS. 10:252-266, Fall 1983.

Moral controversies and the policymaking process: Lowi's framework applied to the abortion issue, by R. Tatalovich, et al. POLICY STUDIES REVIEW. 3(2):207-222, February 1984.

Moral leadership and partisanship, by J. A. Califano. AMERICA. 151:164-165, September 29, 1984.

The moral status of the bodies of persons, by S. A. Ketchum. SOCIAL THEORY AND PRACTICE. 10(1):25-38, 1984.

The moral status of the human embryo: a tradition recalled. JOURNAL OF MEDICAL ETHICS. 10:38-44, March 1984.

Moralizing minority/chastity act, by J. Pasternak. GUARDIAN. 36(32):9, May 16, 1984.

More about natural family planning, by J. Gallagher. AUSTRALIAN FAMILY PHYSICIAN. 12(11):786-792, November 1983.

More cautionary labeling appears on isotretinoin, by C. Marwick. JAMA. 251(24):3208-3209, June 22-29, 1984.

More conflict over abortion, by J. G. Deedy. TABLET. 238:810-811, August 25, 1984.

More debate on abortion, by M. Beck. NEWSWEEK. 104:27, September 24, 1984.

More on reproductive mortality [letter], by R. A. Edgren. FAMILY PLANNING PERSPECTIVES. 15(4):155, July-August 1983.

More worries about the pill. NATURE. 305(5937):749-750, October 27-November 2, 1983.

Morning-after pill. AMERICAN FAMILY PHYSICIAN. 27:250, May 1983.

'Morning-after pill' and antithrombin III, by G. H. Weenink, et al. ACTA OBSTETRICIA ET GYNECOLOGICA SCANDINAVICA. 62(4):359-363, 1983.

Morphologic evidence for vaginal toxicity of Delfen contraceptive cream in the rat, by L. Tryphonas, et al. TOXICOLOGY LETTERS. 20(3):289-295, March 1984.

Mortality among young black women using contraceptives, by H. W. Ory, et al. JAMA. 251(8):1044-1048, February 24, 1984.

Mortality impact of an MCH-FP program in Matlab, Bangladesh, by L. C. Chen, et al. STUDIES IN FAMILY PLANNING. 14(8-9):199-209, August-September 1983.

Mortality in women of reproductive age due to diseases of the circulatory system caused by the use of oral contraceptives in Yugoslavia, by J. Ananijevic-Pandey, et al. ACTA MEDICA JUGO-SLAVIA. 37(3):185-195, 1983.

Mortality levels and family fertility goals, by J. Y. Parlange, et al. DEMOGRAPHY. 20(4):535, November 1983.

Mosher case enters final phase, by M. Sun. SCIENCE. 224:701, May 18, 1984.

Motives for pregnancy, birth and parenthood. Results of an empirical study of females using contraceptives, by O. Mittag, et al. PSYCHOTHERAPIE, PSYCHOSOMATIK, MEDIZINISCHE PSYCHOLOGIE. 34(1):20-24, January 1984.

Motives of deficiency, want and illness in the conception of the godhead within the chasidic mysticism, by J. Mendelsohn. ANALYTISCHE PSYCHOLOGIE. 14(3):165-185, August 1983.

Mrs. Gillick's campaign. LANCET. 2(8363):1346, December 10, 1983.

Multinational comparative clinical trial of long-acting injectable contraceptives: norethisterone enanthate given in two dosage regimens and depot-medroxyprogesterone acetate. Final report. CONTRACEPTION. 28(1):1-20, July 1983.

My interactions with Mrs. Taki Hanyu, by S. Narabayashi. JOSAN-PU ZASSHI. 37(3):197-201, March 1983.

A mysterious drop in the abortion rate. NEWSWEEK. 104:26, July 16, 1984.

Myth of the month. HEALTH. 16:64, March 1984.

NCCB undertakes study of ERA implications. ORIGINS. 13:778, May 3, 1984.

Naral's new way, by V. Rosenquist. SOUTHERN EXPOSURE. 12:26-32, January-February 1984.

Natural childbirth brings back good memories. NEW SCIENTIST. 96:356, November 11, 1982.

Natural family planning, by R. Rodriguez. REVISTA DE ENFER-MAGEN. 6(62):12-19, October 1983.

Natural family planning as reflected in contemporary rabbinic response, by G. Ellinson. JEWISH SOCIAL STUDIES. 46:51-60, Winter 1984.

Natural family planning: a comparison of continuers and discontinuers, by K. J. Daly, et al. POPULATION AND ENVIRONMENT. 6(4):231, Winter 1983.

Natural family planning in the Philippines, by J. E. Laing. STUDIES IN FAMILY PLANNING. 15(2):49, March-April 1984.

Natural family planning; interview with Joseph A. Menezes, by T. O'Donnell. REGISTER. 60:1+, April 1, 1984.

Natural family planning (symptothermal method) and objective ovulation parameters— a pilot study, by G. Freundl, et al. GEBURT-SHILFE UND FRAENHEILKUNDE. 44(6):368-373, June 1984.

Natural family planning: a way of life, a way of love, by M. O'Malley. AFER. 25:356-361, December 1983.

The nature of nursing care of women seeking an abortion, by F. Hebert, et al. INFIRMIERE CANADIENNE. 26(5):25-28, May 1984.

Negative psychological sequelae and psychiatric sequelae of abortion obtained in a hospital: possible application of an evaluation scale, by G. R. Brera, et al. MINERVA PSICHIATRICA. 24(1):19-24, January-March 1983.

Neoplasia of the cervix uteri and contraception: a possible adverse effect of the pill, by M. P. Vessey, et al. LANCET. 2(8356):930-934, October 22, 1983.

A new approach to measuring menstrual pattern change after sterilization, by J. A. Fortney, et al. AMERICAN JOURNAL OF OBSTETRICS AND GYNECOLOGY. 147(7):830-836, December 1, 1983.

New contraceptives for men. What are the prospects?, by M. R. Prasad, et al. INTERNATIONAL JOURNAL OF ANDROLOGY. 6(4):305-309, August 1983.

New data on nuptiality and fertility in China, by J. C. Caldwell, et al. POPULATION AND DEVELOPMENT REVIEW. 10(1):71, March 1984.

New developments in vaginal contraception. POPULATION RE-PORTS [H]. (7):H157-190, January-February 1984.

New importance in the social aspects of the care of the pregnant women, by Z. Stembera. CESKOSLOVENSKA GYNEKOLOGIE. 48(9):633-637, November 1983.

New Jersey court recognizes limited "Wrongful life" action. THE FAMILY LAW REPORTER. 10(44):1603-1604, September 11, 1984.

New life for the doctrine of unconstitutional conditions?-Committee to defend reproductive rights v. Myers. WASHINGTON LAW REVIEW. 58:679-707, July 1983.

A new look at antifertility vaccines, by D. J. Anderson, et al. FERTILITY AND STERILITY. 40(5):557-571, Novembre 1983.

New look at happiness. BEIJING REVIEW. 26:27-28, February 14, 1983.

The new neonatal dilemma: live births from late abortions, by N. K. Rhoden. GEORGETOWN LAW JOURNAL. 72:1451-1509, June 1984.

New products [Ovutest 77 Baby Computer (for natural family planning); PMT-eze (for premenstrual tension and as a nutritional supplement for women using oral contraceptives); Synphasic (oral contraceptives), by L. Wray. HEALTHRIGHT. 3:35-38, May 1984.

New roads to contraception, by J. E. Jirasek. CESKOSLOVENSKA GYNEKOLOGIE. 48(10):764-768, December 1983.

A new strategy for preventing unintended teenage childbearing . . . social and welfare needs of disadvantaged adolescents must be addressed, by J. G. Dryfoos. FAMILY PLANNING PERSPECTIVES. 16(4):193-195, July-August 1984.

A new superagonist of GnRH for inhibition of ovulation in women, by S. J. Nillius, et al. UPSALA JOURNAL OF MEDICAL SCIENCES. 89(2):147-150, 1984.

New sure-death abortion method. REGISTER. 60:2, September 9, 1984.

New techniques in contraception: gossypol, vaccines, and GnRH analogues, by R. J. Aitken. PROCEEDINGS OF THE ANNUAL SYMPOSIUM OF THE EUGENICS SOCIETY. 19:1-18, 1983.

The 1983 Supreme Court abortion decisions: impact on hospitals, a conflict with Baby Doe?, by R. A. Carlson. HEALTH LAW VIGIL. 6(21):2-7, October 14, 1983.

A 1984 perspective of contraceptive technology, by I. S. Fraser. HEALTHRIGHT. 3:7-11, August 1984.

Nitrous oxide and termination of pregnancy [letter], by M. Mikhael, et al. ANAESTHESIA. 38(11):1103-1104, November 1983.

No increased risk of cancer with Depo-Provera contraception. NURSES DRUG ALERT. 7(11):87, November 1983.

No pill-cancer link. FDA CONSUMER. 18:4, May 1984.

No time limit on maintaining "dead" mother to save fetus? MEDICAL WORLD NEWS. 24:20-21, May 9, 1983.

No way for planned parenthood, by A. Singer. ALBERTA REPORT. 11:40, June 25, 1984.

Non-therapeutic sterilization of mentally retarded patients: yes in certain cases, under certain conditions, by A. Cote. UNION MEDICALE DU CANADA. 112(8):737-740, August 1983.

Norethisterone levels in maternal serum and milk after intramuscular injection of norethisterone oenanthate as a contraceptive, by K. Fotherby, et al. CONTRACEPTION. 28(5):405-411, November 1983.

Norplant implants and the Tcu 200 IUD: a comparative study in Equador, by P. Marangoni, et al. STUDIES IN FAMILY PLANNING. 14(6-7):177, June-July 1983.

Not a single-issue Church, bishops say. ORIGINS. 14:217-218, September 20, 1984.

NOW vs. Judge: abortion used as morality test, by V. Quade. AMERICAN BAR ASSOCIATION JOURNAL. 70:40, May 1984.

Nun urges NFP as humane alternative. REGISTER. 60:3, July 8, 1984.

Nurse protests spur hospitals to limit second-trimester abortions.

RN. 46:13, June 1983.

Nurses in conflict. A survey, by B. Jamtback. KRANKENPFLEGE JOURNAL. 21(10):7, October 1, 1983.

Nursing Mirror midwifery forum. Problems in pregnancy: inevitable abortion, by D. Rutledge. NURSING MIRROR. 158(6):v; viii, February 8, 1984.

Nursing of unmarried teenagers undergoing induced abortion— a description of their care in case studies, by K. Hirano, et al. KANGOGAKU ZASSHI. 47(6):648-652, June 1983.

Nursing protocol for diaphragm contraception, by C. J. Pyle. NURSE PRACTITIONER. 9(3):35; 38; 40, March 1984.

Nutritional and medicinal factors in biliary cholesterol lithiasis, by E. Loizeau. REVUE MEDICALE DE LA SUISSE ROMANDE. 104(3):179-184, March 1984.

Nutritional consequences of oral contraceptives, by M. G. Emery, et al. FAMILY AND COMMUNITY HEALTH. 6(3):23-30, November 1983.

OSV/Gallup report: abortion limits favoured, by J. Castelli. OUR SUNDAY VISITOR. 73:8, December 9, 1984.

Observation: contraceptive method use following an abortion, by S. K. Henshaw. FAMILY PLANNING PERSPECTIVES. 16:75-76, March-April 1984.

Obstetric and gynecological care for Third World women, by J. A. Pinotti, et al. INTERNATIONAL JOURNAL OF GYNAECOLOGY AND OBSTETRICS. 21(5):361-369, October 1983.

Obstetric ultrasonography: recent observations in first trimester of pregnancy, by J. F. Pedersen, et al. EUROPEAN JOURNAL OF RADIOLOGY. 4(2):167-168, May 1984.

O'Connor defends obsession of abortion, by D. Ryan. NATIONAL CATHOLIC REPORTER. 21:23, October 26, 1984.

O'Connor says politicos must fight abortion with laws. REGISTER. 60:2, October 28, 1984.

Oestrogen deficiency following tubal ligation [letter], by J. Cattanach.

MEDICAL JOURNAL OF AUSTRALIA. 140(5):309-310, March 3, 1984.

Of many things [speech by H. J. Hyde on Catholic Church and abortion], by G. W. Hunt. AMERICA. 151:inside cover, October 6, 1984.

Off the backstreets. ECONOMIST. 290:51, February 4, 1984.

Omentum presenting at the vulva after a normal labor and delivery. An unusual late complication of induced abortion, by D. E. Marsden. ACTA OBSTETRICIA ET GYNECOLOGICA SCANDINAVICA. 63(3):277-278, 1984.

On an inconsistency in Thomson's abortion argument, by R. Gibson. PHILOSOPHICAL STUDIES. 46:131-139, July 1984.

On this picket line, trouble, by V. Warner. REGISTER. 60:1+, May 13, 1984.

On the treatment of early and late toxicoses in pregnancy and spontaneous abortion, by Y. Lukanov, et al. FOLIA MEDICA. 25(4): 50-53, 1983.

Open forum: preferred method for tubal sterilization. INTERNATIONAL JOURNAL OF FERTILITY. 29(1):10-12, 1984.

Opinion poll: evaluation and analysis. What the Spanish nursing profession thinks about abortion. REVISTA DE ENFERMAGEN. 6(60):12-17; 19-21, July 1983.

Oral contraception and cerebral thrombosis in a Jamaican, by A. Campbell, et al. WEST INDIAN MEDICAL JOURNAL. 32(3):191-193, September 1983.

Oral contraception, the press and the CSM, by V. R. Bloom. JOURNAL OF THE ROYAL SOCIETY OF MEDICINE. 77(5):359, May 1984.

Oral contraceptive agents do not affect serum prolactin in normal women, by J. R. Davis, et al. CLINICAL ENDOCRINOLOGY. 20(4): 427-434, April 1984.

Oral contraceptive use and fibrocystic breast disease among pre- and postmenopausal women, by G. S. Berkowitz, et al. AMERICAN JOURNAL OF EPIDEMIOLOGY. 120(1):87-96, July 1984.

Oral contraceptive use and fibrocystic disease of different histologic classifications, by C. C. Hsieh, et al. JNCI. 72(2):285-290, February 1984.

Oral contraceptive use and the risk of breast cancer in young women. MMWR. 33(25):353-354, June 29, 1984.

Oral contraceptive use and the risk of epithelial ovarian cancer, by C. La Vecchia, et al. BRITISH JOURNAL OF CANCER. 50(1):31-34, July 1984.

Oral contraceptives and acute viral hepatitis [letter], by C. Abadia Dolz. MEDICINA CLINICA. 82(17):782, May 1984.

Oral contraceptives and benign breast disease, by T. G. Hislop, et al. AMERICAN JOURNAL OF EPIDEMIOLOGY. 120(2):273-280, August 1984.

Oral contraceptives and benign breast disease: a case-control study, by S. Franceschi, et al. AMERICAN JOURNAL OF OBSTETRICS AND GYNECOLOGY. 149(6):602-606, July 15, 1984.

Oral contraceptives and benign tumors of the liver, by J. G. Fitz. WESTERN JOURNAL OF MEDICINE. 140(2):260-267, February 1984.

Oral contraceptives and breast cancer. LANCET. 2(8395):145, July 21, 1984.

Oral contraceptives and breast cancer, by A. Kalache, et al. BRITISH JOURNAL OF HOSPITAL MEDICINE. 30(4):278-283, October 1983.

Oral contraceptives and breast cancer [letter]. LANCET. 2(8360):1201-1202, November 19, 1983.

Oral contraceptives and breast cancer [letter], by K. McPherson, et al. LANCET. 2(8364):1414-1415, December 17, 1983.

Oral contraceptives and breast cancer rates [letter], by M. C. Pike, et al. LANCET. 1(8373):389, February 18, 1984.

Oral contraceptives and breast-cancer rates [letter], by R. A. Wiseman. LANCET. 1(8380):791, April 7, 1984.

Oral contraceptives and breast cancer rates [letter], by R. A. Wiseman. LANCET. 2(8364):1415-1416, December 17, 1983.

Oral contraceptives and cancer [letter]. LANCET. 2(8357):1018-1020, October 29, 1983.

Oral contraceptives and cancer [letter]. LANCET. 2(8358):1081, November 5, 1983.

Oral contraceptives and cancer [letter], by A. Pedersen. LANCET. 2(8361):1259, November 26, 1983.

Oral contraceptives and cancer. FDA DRUG BULLETIN. 14(1):2-3, April 1984.

Oral contraceptives and cardiovascular complications, by V. Murad. ARQUIVOS BRASILEIROS DE CARDIOLOGIA. 40(3):215-221, March 1983.

Oral contraceptives and cardiovascular disease— aspects of lipid metabolism, by N. Crona, et al. LAKARTIDNINGEN. 81(6):425-427, February 8, 1984.

Oral contraceptives and cardiovascular mortality, by I. Stucker, et al. REVUE D'EPIDEMIOLOGIE ET DE SANTE PUBLIQUE. 32(1):16-24, 1984.

Oral contraceptives and cervical cancer [letter]. LANCET. 2(8359): 1146-1147, November 12, 1983.

Oral contraceptives and cervical cancer [letter], by L. Andolsek, et al. LANCET. 2(8362):1310, December 3, 1983.

Oral contraceptives and cervical cancer [letter], by M. P. Vessey, et al. LANCET. 2(8363):1358-1359, December 10, 1983.

Oral contraceptives and deep venous thrombosis with pulmonary embolism, by R. T. Bouche, et al. JOURNAL OF FOOT SURGERY. 21(4):297-301, Winter 1982.

Oral contraceptives and endometrial cancer [letter], by E. S. Maxey. JAMA. 250(16):2111, October 28, 1983.

Oral contraceptives and mortality from circulatory system diseases: an epidemiologic study in Taiwan, by L. P. Chow, et al. INTER-NATIONAL JOURNAL OF GYNAECOLOGY AND OBSTETRICS. 21(4):297-304, August 1983.

Oral contraceptives and neoplasia. LANCET. 2(8356):947-948, October 22, 1983.

Oral contraceptives and prolactinomas: which caused what? NURSES DRUG ALERT. 7(9):71-72, September 1983.

Oral contraceptives and the risk of cancer, by K. E. Sapire, et al. SOUTH AFRICAN MEDICAL JOURNAL. 64(25):964-965, December 10, 1983.

Oral contraceptives and stroke, by W. T. Longstreth, Jr., et al. STROKE. 15(4):747-750, July-August 1984.

Oral contraceptives and stroke: findings in a large prospective study, by M. P. Vessey, et al. BRITISH MEDICAL JOURNAL [CLIN RES]. 289(6444):530-531, September 1, 1984.

Oral contraceptives, carbohydrate metabolism and diabetes mellitus, by J. M. Ekoe, et al. SEMAINES DES HOPITAUX DE PARIS. 59(45):3162-3166, December 8, 1983.

Oral contraceptives may promote cancer. SCIENCE NEWS. 124:127, August 20, 1983.

Oral contraceptives, pregnancy, and endogenous oestrogen in gall stone disease— a case-control study, by R. K. Scragg, et al. BRITISH MEDICAL JOURNAL [CLIN RES]. 288(6433):1795-1799, June 16, 1984.

Oral contraceptives, pregnancy, and focal nodular hyperplasia of the liver, by L. D. Scott, et al. JAMA. 251(11):1461-1463, March 16, 1984.

Oral contraceptives: the risks in perspective, by R. G. Kanell. NURSE PRACTITIONER. 9(9):25-26; 28-29; 62, September 1984.

Original sin and the unborn, by A. L. Garcia. CONCORDIA THEO-LOGICAL QUARTERLY. 47:147-152, April 1983.

The other side of the question . . . the adverse affects of abortion, by J. Robinson. NURSING MIRROR. 158(20):20-21, May 16, 1984.

Our experience with the clinical trial of postinor— an oral hormonal preparation for postcoital contraception, by D. Vasilev, et al. AKUSHERSTVO I GINEKOLOGIIA. 22(3):239-242, 1983.

Out-of-wedlock abortion and delivery: the importance of the male partner, by J. M. Robbins. SOCIAL PROBLEMS. 31(3):334-350, February 1984.

Outcome of delivery subsequent to vacuum-aspiration abortion in nulliparous women, by O. Meirik, et al. ACTA OBSTETRICIA ET GYNECOLOGICA SCANDINAVICA. 62(5):499-509, 1983.

Outcome of first delivery after second trimester two-stage induced abortion. A controlled historical cohort study, by O. Meirik, et al. ACTA OBSTETRICA ET GYNECOLOGICA SCANDINAVICA. 63(1):45-50, 1984.

Ovarian function, bleeding control and serum lipoproteins in women using contraceptive vaginal rings releasing five different progestins, by T. Ahren, et al. CONTRACEPTION. 28(4):315-327, October 1983.

Ovarian function is effectively inhibited by a low-dose triphasic oral contraceptive containing ethinylestradiol and levonorgestrel, by U. J. Gaspard, et al. CONTRACEPTION. 29(4):305-318, April 1984.

Oviduct occlusion by intraluminal thread and silver clips, by S. L. Ding. CHINESE MEDICAL JOURNAL. 96(8):604-606, August 1983.

Ovine abortion and neonatal death due to toxoplasmosis in Montana, by J. C. Rhyan, et al. JOURNAL OF THE AMERICAN VETERINARY MEDICAL ASSOCIATION. 184(6):661-664, March 15, 1984.

Ovulatory function after microsurgical reversal of sterilization in the rabbit, by A. Pellicer, et al. CLINICAL AND EXPERIMENTAL OBSTETRICS AND GYNECOLOGY. 11(1-2):6-10, 1984.

Oxytocic drugs and anesthesia. A controlled clinical trial of ergometrine, syntocinon and normal saline during evacuation of the uterus after spontaneous abortion, by D. Beeby, et al. ANAESTHESIA. 39(8):764-767, August 1984.

PID and IUD use. AMERICAN FAMILY PHYSICIAN. 30:272, July 1984.

PW interviews [G. Greer], by W. Smith. PUBLISHERS WEEKLY. 225:61-62, May 25, 1984.

A painful experience, by L. Hardie. NURSING TIMES. 80(18):64, May 2-8, 1984.

A panel tries to judge a judge, by M. S. Serrill. TIME. 124:88, July 23, 1984.

Parental occupation and cytogenetic studies in abortuses, by M. Hatch. PROGRESS IN CLINICAL AND BIOLOGICAL RESEARCH. 160:475-483, 1984.

Parental occupational exposure and spontaneous abortions in Finland, by M. L. Lindbohm, et al. AMERICAN JOURNAL OF EPIDEMIOLOGY. 120(3):370-378, September 1984.

Parental origin of autosomal trisomies, by T. Hassold, et al. ANNALS OF HUMAN GENETICS. 48(Pt 2):129-144, May 1984.

Parents, judges, and a minor's abortion decision: third party participation and the evolution of a judicial alternative, by W. Green. AKRON LAW REVIEW. 17:87-110, Summer 1983.

Passage of child abuse pill applauded by U. S. Senator. CRIME VICTIMS DIGEST. 1(12):5-6, September 1984.

Pastoral teaching links abortion, nuclear threat in call for ethic of life, by J. McManus. NATIONAL CATHOLIC REPORTER. 20:8, May 11, 1984.

Patchy garment [G. Ferraro's stand on abortion], by D. R. Carlin, Jr. COMMONWEAL. 111:422-423, August 10, 1984.

Pathogenesis of in utero infections with abortogenic and non-abortogenic alphaviruses in mice, by A. R. Milner, et al. JOURNAL OF VIROLOGY. 50(1):66-72, April 1984.

Paths to zero population growth, by T. J. Espanshade. FAMILY PLANNING PERSPECTIVES. 15:148-149, May-June 1983.

Paternal child-support tort parallels for the abortion on maternal demand era: the work of Regan Levy and Duncan, by G. S. Swan. GLENDALE LAW REVIEW. 5:151-187, 1981-1982.

Paying a high price for the pill [damages awarded in P. Buchan's suit against Ortho Pharmaceutical Canada], by R. Block. MACLEAN'S. 97:52, April 30, 1984.

Peer counselors. AMERICAN JOURNAL OF NURSING. 84:590, May 1984.

Peers, not RN's, should teach teens oral contraception. RN. 47:14, May 1984.

Pelvic infections and the IUD. AMERICAN JOURNAL OF NURSING.

83:1374, October 1983.

Pelvic venous changes after tubal sterilization, by M. F. El-Minawi, et al. JOURNAL OF REPRODUCTIVE MEDICINE. 28(10):641-648, October 1983.

Pennsylvania court uses ERA to strike down abortion limits, by C. McDonnell. REGISTER. 60:1+, March 25, 1984.

The people problem [U. S. position on birth control aid]. AMERICA. 151:62, August 18-25, 1984.

Perceived availability of contraceptives and family limitation, by J. D. Teachman, et al. HUMAN ORGANIZATION. 42:123-131, Summer 1983.

Perceptions about having children: are daughters different from their mothers?, by V. J. Callan, et al. JOURNAL OF MARRIAGE AND THE FAMILY. 45(3):607-612, August 1983.

Perceptions and acceptability of Norplant implants in Thailand, by S. Satayapan. STUDIES IN FAMILY PLANNING. 14(6-7):170, June-July 1983.

Perceptions of contraceptive methods: a multidimensional scaling analysis, by V. J. Callan, et al. JOURNAL OF BIOSOCIAL SCIENCE. 16:277-286, April 1984.

Performance of multiload intrauterine device models with different copper loads, by M. Thiery, et al. CONTRACEPTIVE DELIVERY SYSTEMS. 4(3):227-230, 1983.

Personal abortion opinions shake political platforms. OUR SUNDAY VISITOR. 73:3, August 19, 1984.

Personal experience with committee family planning at the Institute for Continuing Education of Health Personnel, by V. Kliment, et al. CESKOSLOVENSKA GYNEKOLOGIE. 48(5):388-389, June 1983.

Pharmacodynamics of a contraceptive vaginal ring releasing norethindrone and estradiol: ovarian function, bleeding control and lipoprotein patterns, by A. Victor, et al. UPSALA JOURNAL OF MEDICAL SCIENCES. 89(2):179-188, 1984.

Pharmacokinetic and 'potency' of contraceptive steroids [letter], by

D. J. Back, et al. LANCET. 1(8369):171, January 21, 1984.

Pharmacokinetic interaction of contraceptive steroids with prednisone and prednisolone, by B. M. Frey, et al. EUROPEAN JOURNAL OF CLINICAL PHARMACOLOGY. 26(4):505-511, 1984.

The phasic approach to oral contraception: the triphasic concept and its clinical application, by G. V. Upton. INTERNATIONAL JOURNAL OF FERTILITY. 28(3):121-140, 1983.1

Phenoxybenzamine— an effective male contraceptive pill, by Z. T. Homonnai, et al. CONTRACEPTION. 29(5):479-491, May 1984.

Pill affected older women more. NEW SCIENTIST. 101:21, January 12, 1984.

Pill and cancer. AMERICAN FAMILY PHYSICIAN. 29:383+, January 1984.

The pill and cancer of the breast and cervix uteri, by A. Pedersen. UGESKRIFT FOR LAEGER. 146(14):1063-1066, April 2, 1984.

Pill and tumors. AMERICAN FAMILY PHYSICIAN. 28:372+, November 1983.

The pill, breast and cervical cancer, and the role of progestogens in arterial disease, by R. Lincoln. FAMILY PLANNING PERSPECTIVES. 16(2):55-63, March-April 1984.

Pill— cancer link re-examined, by F. Fraser. NEW SCIENTIST. 100: · 264, October 27, 1983.

The pill for men: available soon?, by W. Frese. MAX PLANCK SOCIETY SCIENCE NEWSLETTER. June 1984, p. 8.

Pill the morning after. SCIENCE NEWS. 125:59, January 28, 1984.

Pill questions that remain unanswered. NEW SCIENTIST. 100:247, October 27, 1983.

Pill research professor in bit to halt inquiry, by G. Maslen. TIMES HIGHER EDUCATION SUPPLEMENT. 621:9, September 28, 1984.

The pill/taking stock of consequences, by A. Hayford. BRIARPATH. 13(6):28, July 1984.

Pill revisited: new cancer link?, by J. Silberner. SCIENCE NEWS. 124:279, October 29, 1983.

Placental hormone for birth control. SCIENCE NEWS. 124:74, July 30, 1983.

Planning the family, by M. E. Rankin. NURSING. 2(19):543, November 1983.

Planning sex: critics suspect the motives at Red Deer's family clinic, by T. Fennell, et al. ALBERTA REPORT. 11:43, March 19, 1984.

Plasma carnitine in women. Effects of the menstrual cycle and of oral contraceptives, by A. C. Bach, et al. ARCHIVES INTERNATIONALES DE PHYSIOLOGIE ET DE BIOCHIMIE. 91(4):333-338, November 1983.

Plasma hormone concentrations in induced abortion with local prostaglandin administration in the first trimester, by W. Rath, et al. ZENTRALBLATT FUR GYNAEKOLOGIE. 105(15):961-971, 1983.

Plasma hormone levels in women receiving new oral contraceptives containing ethinyl plus levonorgestrel or desogestrel, by U. J. Gaspard, et al. CONTRACEPTION. 27(6):577-590, June 1983.

Plasma renin substrate in the prediction of pregnancy outcome in threatened abortion, by A. S. Siimes, et al. BRITISH JOURNAL OF OBSTETRICS AND GYNAECOLOGY. 90(12):1186-1192, December 1983.

Plasma renin substrate, renin activity, and aldosterone levels in a sample of oral contraceptive users from a community survey, by S. Z. Goldhaber, et al. AMERICAN HEART JOURNAL. 107(1):119-122, January 1984.

Playing safe, keeping quiet, by W. Cooper. GUARDIAN. June 29, 1984, p. 11.

A plea for corporate conscience [product liability suit against A. H. Robins in Dalkon Shield case], by M. W. Lord. HARPERS. 268:13-14, June 1984.

Plea to love aborters, by S. Weatherbe. ALBERTA REPORT. 11:31, January 9, 1984.

A political party is born: single-issue advocacy and the New York

State election law, by R. J. Spitzer. NATIONAL CIVIC REVIEW. 73:321-328, July-August 1984.

Politics and abortion, by K. L. Woodward. NEWSWEEK. 104:66-67, August 20, 1984.

The politics of abortion, by J. G. Deedy. TABLET. 238:262-263, August 11, 1984.

"The politics of abortion: trends in Canadian fertility policy", by M. F. Bishop. ATLANTIS. 9:105-117, Fall 1983.

The politics of abortion: trends in Canadian fertility policy, by L. D. Collins, et al. ATLANTIS. 7(2):2-20, 1982.

The politics of contraception, by S. Bell. WOMEN AND HEALTH. 8(4):57, Winter 1983.

The pols and the bishops. NATIONAL REVIEW. 36:18-19, October 5, 1984.

Polybrominated biphenyls and fetal mortality in Michigan, by C. G. Humble, et al. AMERICAN JOURNAL OF PUBLIC HEALTH. 74(10):1130-1132, October 1984.

Pondering direct action: acting out of anger or love?, by P. Sheehan. OUR SUNDAY VISITOR. 73:3, May 13, 1984.

Pope attacks government family methods. OUR SUNDAY VISITOR. 73:8, June 24, 1984.

Pope hits birth control. NATIONAL CATHOLIC REPORTER. 20:4+, August 31, 1984.

Pope reaffirms Humanae Vitae, by T. C. Fox. NATIONAL CATHOLIC REPORTER. 20:1+, July 20, 1984.

Popline: an overview for searchers, by D. R. Farre, et al. MEDICAL REFERENCE SERVICES QUARTERLY. 2(4):1-20, Winter 1983.

Population and health. WORLD HEALTH. June 1984, pp. 2-29.

Population and U. S. policy. NATIONAL REVIEW. 36:13-14, September 7, 1984.

Population explosion predicted. ENVIRONMENT. 26:22-23, July-August 1984.

Population lid: China cajoles families and offers incentives to reduce birth rate; but one-child policy stirs resistance, hasn't ended the preference for sons, by A. Bennett. WALL STREET JOURNAL. 202:1+, July 6, 1983.

The population of China, by N. Keyfitz. SCIENTIFIC AMERICAN. 250(2):38-47, February 1984.

The population question. SCHOLASTIC UPDATE. 116:2-8+, March 2, 1984.

Population: trading places [U. S. restrictions on family planning aid to discourage abortions], by R. Watson. NEWSWEEK. 104:50, August, 20, 1984.

Positive effects of oral contraceptives, by G. Colla, et al. MINERVA GINECOLOGIA. 35(7-8):505-510, July-August 1983.

Possible herpesvirus role in abortion studied, by M. F. Goldsmith. JAMA. 251(23):3067-3068, June 15, 1984.

The possible use of phenoxybenzamine as a male contraceptive drug: studies on male rats, by G. F. Paz, et al. CONTRACEPTION. 29(2): 189-195, February 1984.

Postabortal contraception with norethisterone enanthate injections, by P Lahteenmake, et al. CONTRACEPTION. 27(6):553-562, June 1983.

Post-abortion depression: study of cases and controls, by S. Arturo Roizblatt, et al. ACTAS LUSO-ESPANOLAS DE NEUROLOGIA Y PSIQUIATRIA. 11(5):391-394, September-October 1983.

Post-abortion reconciliation growing, by B. J. Hubbard. NATIONAL CATHOLIC REPORTER. 20:1+, October 19, 1984.

Post-coital contraception, by J. R. Ashton, et al. JOURNAL OF THE ROYAL COLLEGE OF GENERAL PRACTITIONERS. 34(260):175-176, March 1984.

Postcoital contraception, by M. Farkas. AKUSHERSTVO I GINE-KOLOGIIA. (11):31-33, November 1983.

Postcoital contraception, by R. Wyss, et al. SCHWEIZERISCHE RUNDSCHAU FUR MEDIZIN PRAXIS. 73(9):283-286, February 28, 1984.

Postcoital contraception: awareness of the existence of postcoital contraception among students who have had a therapeutic abortion, by L. H. Schilling. JOURNAL OF AMERICAN COLLEGE HEALTH. 32(6):244-246, June 1984.

Postcoital contraception: student choices and effectiveness, by L. H. Schilling. JOURNAL OF AMERICAN COLLEGE HEALTH. 32(6): 239-243, June 1984.

Postcoital contraceptive efficacy and hormonal profile of Lepidium capitatum, by M. M. Singh, et al. PLANTA MEDICA. 50(2):154-157, April 1984.

Postcoital IUD insertion, a review, by M. R. van Santen, et al. GEBURTSHILFE UND FRAUENHEILKUNDE. 44(4):266-272, April 1984.

Postcoital intervention. A family-planning-clinic experience of 213 cases, by G. T. Kovacs, et al. MEDICAL JOURNAL OF AUSTRALIA. 141(7):425-426, September 29, 1984.

Postcoital pregnancy interception, by D. Llewellyn-Jones. MEDICAL JOURNAL OF AUSTRALIA. 141(7):407-408, Septembr 29, 1984.

Postmolar trophoblastic disease in women using hormonal contraception with and without estrogen, by G. L. Eddy, et al. OBSTETRICS AND GYNECOLOGY. 62(6):736-740, December 1983.

Postpartum and postabortion mental health in Denmark [letter], by H. P. David, et al. FAMILY PLANNING PERSPECTIVES. 15(4): 156, July-August 1983.

Postpartum and post-abortion contraception, by A. A. Yuzpe. UNION MEDICALE DU CANADA. 113(3):191-194, March 1984.

Postpartum contraception, by J. H. Meuwissen. NEDERLANDS TIJDSCHRIFT VOOR GENEESKUNDE. 128(12):565-567, March 24, 1984.

Postpartum sterilization and maternal mortality in Paarl Hospital, by V. P. De Villiers. SOUTH AFRICAN MEDICAL JOURNAL. 65(2):49-50, January 14, 1984.

Postpartum sterilization with the Filshie titanium silicon rubber clip, by V. P. De Villiers, et al. SOUTH AFRICAN MEDICAL JOURNAL. 64(25):977-978, December 10, 1983.

Post-TMI miscarriages may show stress. SCIENCE NEWS. 124:92, August 6, 1983.

Potency of estrogen, progestin can affect levels of cholesterol. FAMILY PLANNING PERSPECTIVES. 15:228-229, September-October 1983.

Povidone-iodine (Betadine) as prophylaxis against wound infection in abdominal tubal ligation, by A. Khanna, et al. INDIAN JOURNAL OF MEDICAL SCIENCE. 38(1):1-2, January 1984.

Practical viewpoints of various preventive methods with emphasis on alternative minipills, by A. K. Mansson. JORDEMODERN. 96(6):159-164, June 1983.

The practice of tubal sterilization: review of a departmental practice pattern, by N. Gleicher, et al. MT. SINAI JOURNAL OF MEDICINE. 51(2):157-160, April 1984.

Practice of using castration as sentence being questioned. CRIMINAL JUSTICE NEWSLETTER. 15(4):3-4, February 15, 1984.

Practices in pregnancy and family planning of women in slum and the government housing project of the Din-Daeng community, Bangkok, 1981, by A. Leimsombat, et al. JOURNAL OF THE MEDICAL ASSOCIATION OF THAILAND. 66(Suppl 1):13-19, June 1983.

Preabortion cervical dilatation with a low-dose prostaglandin suppository. A comparison of two analogs, by N. H. Lauersen, et al. JOURNAL OF REPRODUCTIVE MEDICINE. 29(2):133-135, February 1984.

The precious child: family planning in the People's Republic of China, by D. Bulger. PERINATAL PRESS. 8(2):23-27, 1984.

Predicting adolescent sexual and contraceptive behavior: an application and test of the Fishbein model, by S. R. Jorgensen, et al. JOURNAL OF MARRIAGE AND THE FAMILY. 46(1):43-55, February 1984.

Predicting contraceptive behavior from attitudes: a comparison of within- versus across-subjects procedures, by A. R. Davidson, et al. JOURNAL OF PERSONALITY AND SOCIAL PSYCHOLOGY. 45(5):997-1009, November 1983.

Predicting male and female contraceptive behavior: a discriminant analysis of groups high, moderate, and low in contraceptive effectiveness, by B. D. Geis, et al. JOURNAL OF PERSONALITY AND SOCIAL PSYCHOLOGY. 46(3):669-680, March 1984.

Prediction of inflammatory complications in female reproductive organs when using the intrauterine contraceptive device, umbrella, by immunochemical determination of the serum content of individual inflammation protein in female blood, by Z. A. Chiladze, et al. AKADEMIYA NAUK GRUZINSKOI S. S. R. SOOBSHCHENIYA. 107(2):421-424, 1982.

Predictive value of hormone determinations in the first half of pregnancy, by I. Gerhard, et al. EUROPEAN JOURNAL OF OBSTETRICS, GYNECOLOGY AND REPRODUCTIVE BIOLOGY. 17(1):1-17, April 1984.

Pregnancy interruption in the GDR. KRANKENPFLEGE JOURNAL. 21(10):10-11, October 1, 1983.

Pregnancy outcome among women in a Swedish rubber plant, by O. Axelson, et al. SCANDINAVIAN JOURNAL OF WORK, ENVIRONMENT AND HEALTH. 9(Suppl 2):79-83, 1983.

Pregnancy outcome in diabetics with other endocrine disorders [letter], by K. J. Cruickshanke, et al. LANCET. 1(8377):629-630, March 17, 1984.

Pregnancy-resolution decisions. What if abortions were banned?, by J. G. Murphy, et al. JOURNAL OF REPRODUCTIVE MEDICINE. 28(11):789-797, November 1983.

Pregnancy suppression by antibodies to gestation-specific riboflavin carrier protein. NUTRITION REVIEWS. 41:130-132, April 1983.

Prelate uncomfortable with Reagan's approach to issues. REGISTER. 60:2, October 21, 1984.

Preliminary experience with the use of human chorionic gonadotrophin therapy in women with repeated abortion, by J. Svigos. CLINICAL REPRODUCTION AND FERTILITY. 1(2):131-135, June 1982.

Preliminary findings on used cervical caps, by M. Smith, et al. CONTRACEPTION. 29(6):527-533, June 1984.

A preliminary study of the antifertility effect of Vicoa indica in albino rats, by M. Gandhi, et al. INDIAN JOURNAL OF MEDICAL

RESEARCH. 78:724-725, November 1983.

Prenatal diagnosis of fetal disorders: issues and implications. Part 2, by D. Beeson, et al. BIRTH. 10(4):233-241, Winter 1983.

Prenatal exposure to diethylstilbestrol (DES) and the development of sexually dimorphic cognitive abilities and cerebral lateralization, by M. Hines, et al. DEVELOPMENTAL PSYCHOLOGY. 20:81-94, January 1984.

Pre-operation indicators and post-hysterectomy outcome, by M. M. Tsoi, et al. BRITISH JOURNAL OF CLINICAL PSYCHOLOGY. 23(2):151-152, MAY 1984.

Preoperative cervical dilatation in abortion during the first trimester with sulprostone, by B. O. Schulz, et al. GEBURTSHILFE UND FRAUENHEILKUNDE. 44(3):185-187, March 1984.

Preoperative cervical dilatation with a single long-acting prostaglandin analog suppository. An alternative to traumatic mechanical dilatation before surgical evacuation, by D. R. Kent, et al. JOURNAL OF REPRODUCTIVE MEDICINE. 28(11):778-780, November 1983.

A prescription for the prevention of birth defects, by H. C. Slavkin. USA TODAY. 112:87-89, March 1984.

Presence of the Beaumont protein in serum of oral contraceptive users, by D. C. Collins, et al. FERTILITY AND STERILITY. 40(4): 490-496, October 1983.

Pressing the abortion issue; the Catholic view, by E. Magnuson. TIME. 124:18-20, September 24, 1984.

Prevalence of antinuclear antibodies in patients with habitual abortion and in normal and toxemic pregnancies, by I. Garcia-De La Torre, et al. RHEUMATOLOGY INTERNATIONAL. 4(2):87-89, 1984.

Preventing adolescent pregnancy: an interpersonal problem-solving approach, by E. W. Flaherty, et al. PREVENTION IN HUMAN SERVICES. 2(3):49-64, Spring 1983.

Prevention of conception— fate of prevention. The achievements of Ernst Grafenberg and the reaction of gynecology in his time, by H. Ludwig. ZENTRALBLATT FUR GYNEKOLOGIE. 105(18):1197-1205, 1983.

Prevention of habitual abortion and prematurity by early total occlusion of the exernal os uteri, by E. Saling. EUROPEAN JOURNAL OF OBSTETRICS, GYNECOLOGY AND REPRODUCTIVE BIOLOGY. 17(2-3):165-170, May 1984.

Prevention of pregnancy with a low dosage three-stage oral preparation, by R. Gimes, et al. ZENTRALBLATT FUR GYNEKOLOGIE. 105(22):1436-1440, 1983.

The prevention of procreation: contraception, by D. C. Overduin, et al. IRNFP. 8:131-144, Summer 1984.

Prevention of the prothrombotic effects of oral contraceptives with vitamin B6, by J. Koutsky, et al. CESKOSLOVENSKA GYNE-KOLOGIE. 49(2):98-103, March 1984.

Prevention of uterine perforation during curettage abortion, by D. A. Grimes, et al. JAMA. 251(16):2108-2111, April 27, 1984.

Preventive health services: family planning. PUBLIC HEALTH REPORTS. (Suppl):16-24, September-October 1983.

Previous abortions exert favourable effects on the prognosis of breast cancer patients, by M. Yoshimoto, et al. GAN NO RINSHO. 30(7): 777-784, June 1984.

Prince Edward Island: the abortion battle goes on— and on, by K. Jones. ATLANTIC INSIGHT. 6:13, June 1984.

Private physicians and the provision of contraceptives to adolescents, by M. T. Orr. FAMILY PLANNING PERSPECTIVES. 16:83-88, March-April 1984.

Probabilism and abortion, by D. C. Maguire. CHRISTIAN CENTURY. 101:174, February 15, 1984.

Probability of requests for desterilization. Prospective study of 50 cases, by R. Denjean, et al. JOURNAL DE GYNECOLOGIE, OB-STETRIQUE ET BIOLOGIE DE LA REPRODUCTION. 12(4):339-343, 1983.

Problems of contraception in teenage girls, by H. Barth, et al. ZENTRALBLATT FUR GYNAEKOLOGIE. 106(6):389-392, 1984.

Pro-choice perspectives, by D. Andrusko, et al. COMMONWEAL. 111: 183+, March 23, 1984.

Procreation: a choice for the mentally retarded. WASHBURN LAW
JOURNAL. Winter 1984, pp. 359-378.

Progestagen 'potency' and breast cancer [letter], by G. I. Swyer.
LANCET. 2(8364):1416, December 17, 1983.

Progesterone-induced sequential inhibition of copulatory behavior
in hysterectomized rats: relationship to neural cytoplasmic
progestin receptors, by H. B. Ahdieh, et al. PHYSIOLOGY AND
BEHAVIOR. 31(3):361-365, September 1983.

Prognosis for couples who have experienced repeated pregnancy loss,
by D. N. Abuelo, et al. FERTILITY AND STERILITY. 40(6):844-
845, December 1983.

Prognosis of pathological menstrual bleeding caused by the use of
the intrauterine contraceptive Umbrella by immunochemical
determination of some components of the fibrinolytic system,
by Z. A. Chiladez, et al. AKADEMIYA NAUK GRUZINSKOI S. S. R.
SOOBSCHENIYA. 107(3):613-616, 1982.

Prognosis of threatened abortion and serum levels of TBG, by S.
Wanibe, et al. KAKU IGAKU. 21(2):155-163, February 1984.

Prognostic predictions of threatened abortion. A comparison between real-time ultrasound, clinical assessment and urinary
human chorionic gonadotrophin (HCG), by S. K. Ping.
AUSTRALIAN AND NEW ZEALAND JOURNAL OF OBSTET-
RICS AND GYNAECOLOGY. 23(2):99-102, May 1983.

Prognostic value of biochemical tests in the assessment of fetal outcome of threatened abortion, by H. T. Salem, et al. BRITISH
JOURNAL OF OBSTETRICS AND GYNAECOLOGY. 91(4):382-
385, April 1984.

Prognostic value of changes in serum histaminase (DAO) activity
in cases of threatened abortion, by K. Kaminski, et al. PRZEGLAD
LEKARSKI. 41(2):205-207, 1984.

Prognostic value of immunoglobulin determination in women with
threatened abortion, by H. Donat, et al. ZENTRALBLATT FUR
GYNAEKOLOGIE. 106(12):814-826, 1984.

Prolactin plasma levels and oral contraceptives at low dosage, by S.
Milia, et al. CLINICAL AND EXPERIMENTAL OBSTETRICS
AND GYNECOLOGY. 10(4):188-190, 1983.

Prolife activists reject both nukes and abortion, hold national gathering, by M. Meehan. REGISTER. 60:1+, June 17, 1984.

The pro-life amendment to the constitution: one year later; pastoral letter, by K. McNamara. L'OSSERVATORE ROMANO. (43):11, October 22, 1984.

A "Prolife" population delegation?, by C. Holden. SCIENCE. 224: 1321-1322, June 22, 1984.

Prolife social worker facing new jail term, by D. Goldkamp. REGISTER. 60:1+, October 21, 1984.

Prolife update in a year of small successes, by M. Meehan. REGISTER. 59:1+, December 11, 1983.

Prolifers claim they'll make headway in the new Congress, by M. Meehan. REGISTER. 60:1+, November 18, 1984.

Prolifers criticize Ferraro record, by M. Meehan. REGISTER. 60:1+, July 29, 1984.

Prolifers gear up for election-year battles. CHRISTIANITY TODAY. 28:65-66, September 7, 1984.

Prolifers hit Polish paper, by J. Higgins. REGISTER. 60:1+, February 26, 1984.

Pro-lifers protest abortion as subject on TV sitcom. OUR SUNDAY VISITOR. 72:8, February 19, 1984.

Pro-lifers regroup for new battles. AMERICAN JOURNAL OF NURSING. 83:1270, September 1983.

Prolonged elevation of hypothalamic opioid peptide activity in women taking oral contraceptives, by R. F. Casper, et al. JOURNAL OF CLINICAL ENDOCRINOLOGY AND METABOLISM. 58(3):582-584, March 1984.

Pronatalist population policies in some western European countries, by H. J. Heeren. POPULATION RESEARCH AND POLICY REVIEW. 1(2):137-152, May 1982.

Properties of chromatin of peripheral blood lymphocytes in women with threatened abortion, by V. S. Tolmachev, et al. BIULLETIN EKSPERIMENTALNOI BIOLOGII I MEDITSINY. 97(2):181-183, February 1984.

Propranolol as a novel, effective spermicide, by J. Zipper, et al. BRITISH MEDICAL JOURNAL. 287:1245-1246, October 29, 1983.

Propranolol concentrations in plasma after insertion into the vagina, by L. G. Patel, et al. BRITISH MEDICAL JOURNAL. 287:1247-1248, October 29, 1983.

Prospect of gossypol as a contraceptive agent for men, by H. P. Lei. YAO HSUEH HSUEH PAO. 18(5):321-324, May 1983.

A prospective cohort study of oral contraceptives and cancer of the endometrium, by E. J. Trapido. INTERNATIONAL JOURNAL OF EPIDEMIOLOGY. 12(3):297-300, September 1983.

A prospective multicentre trial of the ovulation method of natural family planning. III. Characteristics of the menstrual cycle and of the fertile phase. FERTILITY AND STERILITY. 40(6):773-778, December 1983.

—. IV. The outcome of pregnancy. FERTILITY AND STERILITY. 41(4):593-598, April 1984.

A prospective study of Norplant implants and the TCu 380 Ag IUD in Assiut, Egypt, by M. M. Shaaban, et al. STUDIES IN FAMILY PLANNING. 14(6-7):163, June-July 1983.

Prostaglandin F2 alpha, oxytocin, and uterine activation in hypertonic saline-induced abortions, by A. R. Fuchs, et al. AMERICAN JOURNAL OF OBSTETRICS AND GYNECOLOGY. 150(1):27-32, September 1, 1984.

Prostaglandins in gynecology and obstetrics, by E. Bakali, et al. MAROC MEDICAL. 5(4):285-292, December 1983.

Protection of the mentally retarded individual's right to choose sterilization: the effect of the clear and convincing evidence standard. CAPITAL UNIVERSITY LAW REVIEW. 12:413-438, Fall 1983.

Protective antibodies and spontaneous abortion [letter], by R. W. Beard, et al. LANCET. 2(8358):1090, November 5, 1983.

Providing contraceptive choices for the intellectually handicapped client, by A. Rauch. HEALTHRIGHT. 2:41-43, February 1983.

Proxies for birth control, by D. G. Sloan. SOCIOLOGICAL FOCUS. 17:77-81, January 1984.

Prudence and the pills, by A. Veitch. GUARDIAN. January 18, 1984, p. 11.

Pseudocyesis following sterilization: role of the pseudofather, by W. W. Weddington, Jr., et al. PSYCHOTHERAPY AND PSYCHOSOMATICS. 25(7):563-565, July 1984.

Psychiatric case detection in gynaecological patients, by P. J. Cooper, et al. PSYCHOTHERAPY AND PSYCHOSOMATICS. 40(1-4)-246-256, 1983.

Psychiatric sequelae of induced abortion, by M. Gibbons. JOURNAL OF THE ROYAL COLLEGE OF GENERAL PRACTITIONERS. 34(260):145-150, March 1984.

The psychodynamics of spontaneous abortion, by J. M. Stack. AMERICAN JOURNAL OF ORTHOPSYCHIATRY. 54(1):162-167, January 1984.

Psychological consultations in regard to female sterilization and IUD contraception, by Y. W. Zhao. CHUNG HUA SHEN CHING CHING SHEN KO TSA CHIH. 16(3):136-140, June 1983.

Psychological sequelae of female sterilization. LANCET. 2(8395): 144-145, July 21, 1984.

Psychological sequelae of sterilisation [letter], by E. Lewis, et al. LANCET. 2(8398):347, August 11, 1984.

Psychosexual issues in adolescent contraception, by J. G. Greer. PUBLIC HEALTH REVIEWS. 10(1):27-47, January-March 1982.

Psychosocial aspects of repeat abortions in Singapore— a preliminary report, by W. F. Tsoi, et al. SINGAPORE MEDICAL JOURNAL. 25(2):116-121, April 1984.

The public funding of abortion services: comparative developments in the United States and Australia, by K. A. Petersen. INTERNATIONAL AND COMPARATIVE LAW QUARTERLY. 33:158-180, January 1984.

Public funding of contraceptive, sterilization and abortion services,

1982, by B. Nestor, et al. FAMILY PLANNING PERSPECTIVES. 16(3):128-133, May-June 1984.

The public health effects of legal abortion in the United States, by C. Tietze. FAMILY PLANNING PERSPECTIVES. 16(1):26-28, January-February 1984.

Public remains closely divided on Supreme Court's 1973 abortion ruling; 5-point decline since '81 in percent feeling abortions should be outlawed. GALLUP REPORT. August 1983, pp. 16-18.

Public support for legal abortion continues, although polls show conflicting trends in 1983. FAMILY PLANNING PERSPECTIVES. 15(6):279-281, November-December 1983.

Pulpit politics [Bishop J. W. Malone criticizes pro-choice politicians]. TIME. 124:26, August 20, 1984.

Putting the sex back into contraception, by R. Shapiro. COMMUNITY OUTLOOK. April 11, 1984, pp. 123-131.

Quantitative measurement of blood loss in medical termination of pregnancy, by I. Gupta, et al. INDIAN JOURNAL OF MEDICAL RESEARCH. 78:49-52, July 1983.

Quarterly versus monthly supervision of CBD family planning programs: an experimental study in northeast Brazil, by J. R. Foreit, et al. STUDIES IN FAMILY PLANNING. 15(3):112-120, May-June 1984.

Quick-bibs: abortion, by B. Ott. AMERICAN LIBRARIES. 15:691, November 1984.

A quest for better contraception: the Ford Foundation's contribution to reproductive science and contraceptive development 1959-1983, by R. Hertz. CONTRACEPTION. 29(2):107-142, February 1984.

Quinine toxicity in pregnancy, by M. E. Rivera-Alsina, et al. BOLETIN-ASOCIACION MEDICA DE PUERTO RICO. 76(3):114-115, March 1984.

Rabbinic comment: Abortion, by D. M. Feldman. MT. SINAI JOURNAL OF MEDICINE. 51(1):20-24, January-February 1984.

Radiographic findings in cervix uteri after prostaglandin abortion induction, by P. Kajanoja, et al. ACTA OBSTETRICA ET GYNE-

COLOGICA SCANDINAVICA. 62(3):253-256, 1983.

Randomized comparison of prostaglandin treatment in hospital or at home with vacuum aspiration for termination of early pregnancy, by A. S. Rosen, et al. CONTRACEPTION. 29(5):423-435, May 1984.

Randomized trial of intracervical prostaglandin E2 gel and intra-amniotic prostaglandin F2 alpha for induction of second trimester abortion, by S. Stampe Sorensen, et al. CONTRACEPTION. 29(2):171-179, February 1984.

The rapid fertility decline in Guam natives, by S. L. Tung. JOURNAL OF BIOSOCIAL SCIENCE. 16:231-240, April 1984.

Rapid onset of an increase in caffeine residence time in young women due to oral contraceptive steroids, by E. C. Rietveld, et al. EUROPEAN JOURNAL OF CLINICAL PHARMACOLOGY. 26(3):371-373, 1984.

Rating the press on pro-life questions, by J. J. Higgins. LIGUORIAN. 72:26-31, October 1984.

Ray Flynn and lesbian/gay liberation. GAY COMMUNITY. 12(11):4, September 29, 1984.

Reactions to induced abortion [letter]. UGESKRIFT FOR LAEGER. 145(48):3781-3782, November 28, 1983.

Reagan courts Catholics on abortion, relief aid, by S. Askin, et al. NATIONAL CATHOLIC REPORTER. 20:7, May 18, 1984.

Reagan: no funds to groups that promote abortion, by J. Friedland. NATIONAL CATHOLIC REPORTER. 20:4, August 3, 1984.

Reagan's war on abortion, by M. Kramer. NEW YORK. 17:27+, September 24, 1984.

The reality of abortion, by R. Diamond. NEW DIRECTIONS FOR WOMEN. 13:5, November-December 1984.

Reasons for discontinuing contraception among women in Bangkok, by S. Sunyavivat, et al. WHO BULLETIN. 61(5):861-865, 1983.

Reasons for not using contraceptives: an international comparison, by N. K. Nair, et al. STUDIES IN FAMILY PLANNING. 15:84-92, March-April 1984.

Recent cases: children, by A. Bainham. THE JOURNAL OF SOCIAL WELFARE LAW. September 1984, pp. 287-290.

A recent review on the use of Copper IUDs. IPPF RESEARCH IN REPRODUCTION. 15(3):1, July 1983.

Recognizing DMPA as a contraceptive [letter], by T. F. Britton. AMERICAN JOURNAL OF NURSING. 84(3):306, March 1984.

Recurrence risk of neural tube defects following a miscarriage, by H. S. Cuckle. PRENATAL DIAGNOSIS. 3(4):287-289, October 1983.

Recurrent abortion— a review, by G. M. Stirrat. BRITISH JOURNAL OF OBSTETRICS AND GYNAECOLOGY. 90(10):881-883, October 1983.

Recurrent spontaneous abortion, by B. J. Poland. EUROPEAN JOURNAL OF OBSTETRICS, GYNECOLOGY AND REPRODUCTIVE BIOLOGY. 16(6):369-375, March 1984.

Recurrent spontaneous abortion in human pregnancy: results of immunogenetical, cellular, and humoral studies, by J. A. McIntyre, et al. AMERICAN JOURNAL OF REPRODUCTIVE IMMUNOLOGY. 4(4):165-170, December 1983.

Reduced plasminogen activator content of the endometrium in oral contraceptive users, by B. Casslen, et al. CONTRACEPTION. 28(2):181-188, August 1983.

Reducing misclassification errors through questionnaire design, by C. J. Hogue. PROGRESS IN CLINCIAL AND BIOLOGICAL RE-SEARCH. 160:81-97, 1984.

Reflections on midtrimester pregnancy termination by dilation and evacuation in a free-standing facility, by R. T. Parker. NORTH CAROLINA MEDICAL JOURNAL. 44(9):537, September 1983.

The regrets of sterilised women [letter]. LANCET. 2(8402):578-579, September 8, 1984.

The regulation of American fertility: facts and misconceptions, by C. E. Welch, III. INTERNATIONAL JOURNAL OF WOMEN'S STUDIES. 7:273-281, May-June 1984.

Regulation of fertility and child health: a governmental option, by F. Mardones Restat. REVISTA MEDICA DE CHILE. 111(5):544-548, May 1983.

Rejection of husband's claim to stop wife's abortion, by J. K. Bentil. SOLICITORS' JOURNAL. 128:288-290, April 27, 1984.

Relationship of gross appearance of vas fluid during vasovasostomy to sperm quality, obstructive interval and sperm granuloma, by I. D. Sharlip, et al. JOURNAL OF UROLOGY. 131(4):681-683, April 1984.

Reliability of reporting of spontaneous abortion [letter], by W. H. James. AMERICAN JOURNAL OF OBSTETRICS AND GYNE-COLOGY. 147(4):473, October 15, 1983.

Religion and fertility: a replication, by W. D. Mosher, et al. DEMOG-RAPHY. 21(2):185, May 1984.

Religion and politics: clearing the air. COMMONWEAL. 111:451-452, September 7, 1984.

Religion and politics; interview with David Patrick O'Keefe, by M. Arnold. REGISTER. 60:1+, April 22, 1984.

Religion comes first [M. Cuomo's attack on Catholic position], by J. Sobran. NATIONAL REVIEW. 36:16, September 7, 1984.

Religious belief and public morality, by C. M. Whelan. AMERICA. 151:159-163, September 29, 1984.

Religious influence and congressional voting on abortion, by B. W. Daynes, et al. JOURNAL FOR THE SCIENTIFIC STUDY OF RELIGION. 23(2):197-200, June 1984.

Religious leaders join to back abortion funding [Michigan]. JET. 66:29, April 30, 1984.

Religious preference, religious participation, and sterilization decisions: findings from the National Survey of Family Growth, Cycle 2, by K. W. Eckhardt, et al. REVIEW OF RELIGIOUS RE-SEARCH. 25:232-246, March 1984.

Repeat abortion. AMERICAN FAMILY PHYSICIAN. 30:262, August 1984.

Repeat abortion: is it a problem?, by C. Berger, et al. FAMILY PLAN-NING PERSPECTIVES. 16(2):70-75, March-April 1984.

Repeated pregnancy loss, by J. FitzSimmons, et al. AMERICAN JOUR-NAL OF MEDICAL GENETICS. 16(1):7-13, September 1983.

Repetitive requests for voluntary abortions, by B. Mattauer, et al. ANNALES MEDICO-PSYCHOLOGIQUES. 142(1):151-164, January 1984.

Report of a high pregnancy rate after sterilization with the Bleier clip, by N. C. Lee, et al. SOUTHERN MEDICAL JOURNAL. 77(5): 601-602, May 1984.

Report on the experience with 2829 prescriptions for IUD at Modena family counseling centers, by G. Masellis, et al. MINERVA GINECOLOGIA. 36(3):127-132, March 1984.

Report shows abortion rate declining slightly in U. S. OUR SUNDAY VISITOR. 73:8, July 22, 1984.

Reports conflict on link between hysterectomy, prior tubal sterilization. FAMILY PLANNING PERSPECTIVES. 15:229, September-October 1983.

Reproductive choice [Manitoba]. CANADIAN DIMENSION. 17:3, November 1983.

Reproductive endocrinology: new problems call for new solutions, by J. E. Tyson. DIAGNOSTIC MEDICINE. 7(4):24-31, April 1984.

Reproductive hazards in the workplace. Development of epidemiologic research, by P. J. Landrigan, et al. SCANDINAVIAN JOURNAL OF WORK, ENVIRONMENT AND HEALTH. 9(2 Spec No):83-88, April 1983.

Reproductive health services for men: is there a need?, by P. H. Gordon, et al. FAMILY PLANNING PERSPECTIVES. 16(1):44-46, January-February 1984.

Reproductive health update. HORIZONS. 2(3):18, June 1984.

Reproductive impairments among married couples: United States, by W. D. Mosher, et al. HHS REPORT [PHS] 1983-1987. 23(11), December 1982.

Reproductive performance among DES exposed daughters compared with that of their mothers, by T. G. Kirkhope. OHIO STATE MEDICAL JOURNAL. 79(11):867-869, November 1983.

Reproductive risks for translocation carriers: cytogenetic study and analysis of pregnancy outcome in 58 families, by G. Neri, et al.

AMERICAN JOURNAL OF MEDICAL GENETICS. 16(4):535-561, December 1983.

Request for abortion after the 12th week, by C. W. Schmidt. ZEIT-SCHRIFT FUR AERZTLICHE FORTBILDUNG. 77(23):975-977, 1983.

Request for reversal of tubal sterilization. Survey conducted by the National College of French Gynecologists and Obstetricians, by J. M. Antoine, et al. JOURNAL DE GYNECOLOGIE, OBSTETRIQUE ET BIOLOGIE DE LA REPRODUCTION. 12(6):583-591, 1983.

Research on the effects of hormonal contraceptives on lactation: current findings, methodological considerations and future priorities, by V. J. Hull. WORLD HEALTH STATISTICS QUARTERLY. 36(2):168-200, 1983.

Research on methods of fertility regulation, by E. B. Connell. JOGN NURSING. 13(2 Suppl):50s-56s, March-April 1984.

Respect for life, sexual morality, and opposition to abortion, by T. G. Jelen. REVIEW OF RELIGIOUS RESEARCH. 25:220-231, March 1984.

Response from women to adverse publicity about oral contraceptives, by A. Portnoy. JOURNAL OF THE ROYAL COLLEGE OF GENERAL PRACTITIONERS. 34(263):334-335, June 1984.

A response to Gov. Cuomo, by H. J. Hubbard. ORIGINS. 14:304, October 25, 1984.

Response to termination of pregnancy for genetic reasons, by J. Lloyd, et al. ZEITSCHRIFT FUR KINDERCHIRURGIE. 38 (Suppl 2):98-99, December 1983.

The results of epididymal ablation by sclerosing agents in the non-human primate, by R. W. Lewis, et al. FERTILITY AND STERILITY. 41(3):465-469, March 1984.

Results of establishing medical guidelines for selecting oral contraceptive types in family planning agencies, by P. G. Stumpf. CONTRACEPTION. 29(6):511-517, June 1984.

Retained fetal bones in chronic tubal pregnancy, by D. M. Avery, et al. AMERICAN JOURNAL OF OBSTETRICS AND GYNECOLOGY. 149(7):794-795, August 1984.

Return of fertility after use of the injectable contraceptive Depo Provera: updated data analysis, by T. Pardthaisong. JOURNAL OF BIOSOCIAL SCIENCE. 16:23-34, January 1984.

Return of ovulation and fertility in women using norethisterone oenanthate, by K. Fotherby, et al. CONTRACEPTION. 29(5):447-455, May 1984.

Reversal of female sterilization. Review of 252 microsurgical salpingo-salpingostomies, by E. Owen. MEDICAL JOURNAL OF AUSTRALIA. 141(5):276-280, September 1, 1984.

The reversibility of female sterilization with the use of microsurgery: a report on 102 patients with more than one year of follow-up, by S. R. Henderson. AMERICAN JOURNAL OF OBSTETRICS AND GYNECOLOGY. 149(1):57-65, May 1, 1984.

Reversible azoospermia induced by the anabolic steroid 19-nortestosterone, by T. Schurmeyer, et al. LANCET. 1(8374):417-420, February 25, 1984.

Reversible contraception like activity of embelin in male dogs (Canis indicus Linn), by V. P. Dixit, et al. ANDROLOGIA. 15(5):486-494, September-October 1983.

Reversible inhibition of spermatogenesis by danazol with combination of testosterone enanthate in rabbit, by N. K. Lohiya, et al. ANDROLOGIA. 16(1):72-75, January-February 1984.

A review of the current status in male contraceptive studies, by S. Gombe. EAST AFRICAN MEDICAL JOURNAL. 60(4):203-211, April 1983.

A review of psychiatric aspects for termination of pregnancy, by H. V. Perera. CEYLON MEDICAL JOURNAL. 28(1):42-47, March 1983.

Rheumatoid arthritis and oral contraceptives. AMERICAN FAMILY PHYSICIAN. 28:309-310, November 1983.

Rhythm: 1. Periodic abstinence, by H. Ratner. IRNFP. 8:162-169, Summer 1984.

Riboflavin, self-report, and serum norethindrone. Comparison of their use as indicators of adolescent compliance with oral contraceptives, by S. Jay, et al. AMERICAN JOURNAL OF DISEASES OF

CHILDREN. 138(1):70-73, January 1984.

Rigevidon and Ovidon in the therapy of menstrual cycle disorders, by V. N. Prilepskaia, et al. AKUSHERSTVO I GINEKOLOGIIA. (11):24-27, November 1983.

Rigevidon (clinical trial of the preparation), by V. Kliment, et al. THERAPIA HUNGARICA. 29(2):94-95, 1981.

Right-to-life meeting: destroying stereotypes, by G. Palumbo. NATIONAL CATHOLIC REPORTER. 20:5, September 7, 1984.

Right to life president continues the abortion battle, interview with Jean Eleanor Doyal, by B. Kennedy. OUR SUNDAY VISITOR. 72:4, January 22, 1984.

The right to privacy: Roe v. Wade revisited, by P. A. Smith. JURIST. 43(2):289-317, 1983.

Rightist charged in Washington antiabortion bombing, by L. Hickler. MILITANT. 48(29):24, August 3, 1984.

Ring chromosome 21 in a healthy woman with three spontaneous abortions, by K. Rhomberg. HUMAN GENETICS. 67(1):120, 1984.

Risk factors, by C. Dyer. GUARDIAN. April 6, 1984, p. 12.

Risk of PID 5x greater from Dalkon Shield than from other IUDs. FAMILY PLANNING PERSPECTIVES. 15:225-226, September-October 1983.

Risk of serum hepatitis following laparoscopic sterilisation [letter], by S. M. Athale. JOURNAL OF THE INDIAN MEDICAL ASSOCIATION. 81(7-8):147-148, October 1983.

Risks and costs of illegally induced abortion in Bangladesh, by A. R. Khan, et al. JOURNAL OF BIOSOCIAL SCIENCE. 16:89-98, January 1984.

The risks associated with teenage abortion, by W. Cates, Jr., et al. NEW ENGLAND JOURNAL OF MEDICINE. 309:621-624, September 15, 1983.

Risks of sterilization procedures [letter], by J. L. Pfenninger. JOURNAL OF FAMILY PRACTICE. 18(1):28, January 1984.

Robins to appeal Dalkon award, by B. Densmore. BUSINESS INSUR-
ANCE. 17:2+, December 26, 1983.

Role of alkaline phosphatase in contraception— a review, by P. C.
Das. ACTA PHYSIOLOGICA ET PHARMACOLOGICA BULGARICA.
9(2):74-78, 1983.

The role of the clinician in natural family planning, by H. Klaus.
JOURNAL OF AMERICAN COLLEGE HEALTH. 32(3):114-120,
December 1983.

The role of epidemiology in the regulation of oral contraceptives, by
S. Sobel. PUBLIC HEALTH REPORTS. 99(4):350-354, July-
August 1984.

Role of gestagens in contraception and the treatment of menstruation
disorders in women, by L. Grzeniewski. WIADOMOSCI
LEKARSKIE. 36(21):1779-1787, November 1, 1983.

Role of maternal prolactin in early pregnancy failure, by P. Jouppila,
et al. OBSTETRICS AND GYNECOLOGY. 64(3):373-375, September 1984.

The role of the midwife in family planning, by N. M. Bentley. MID-
WIVES CHRONICLE. 96(1146):254, July 1983.

The Roman Catholic Church and abortion: an historical perspective,
by D. T. De Marco. HOMILETIC AND PASTORAL REVIEW. 84:
59-66, July 1984; 68+, August-September 1984.

Ronald Reagan on abortion. NEWSWEEK. 103:23, April 30, 1984.

Rules for liberals [Catholics opposed to abortion], by D. R. Carlin, Jr.
COMMONWEAL. 111:486-487, September 21, 1984.

Ruptured appendix after elective abortion. A case report, by S. Pine,
et al. JOURNAL OF REPRODUCTIVE MEDICINE. 28(10):691-
693, October 1983.

The rural Chinese fertility transition: a report from Shifang Xian,
Sichuan, by W. R. Lavely. POPULATION STUDIES. 38:365-
384, November 1984.

SHSTF's answer to the Abortion Committee: support patient and
personnel and expand contraceptive counseling, by A. Widen.
VARDFACKET. 8(3):42-45, February 9, 1984.

Safety last at the FDA, by D. St. Clair. GUARDIAN. 36(39):2, July 11, 1984.

The safety of fetoscopy: (II). Effect on maternal plasma levels of 13, 14-dihydro-15-oxo-prostaglandin F2 alpha, by K. H. Nicolaides, et al. PRENATAL DIAGNOSIS. 3(23):97-100, April-June 1983.

Salt Lake City: Baby City, U. S. A., by E. Stansfield. HUMANIST. 44:19+, May-June 1984.

The sanctity of life. RECON. 49:5, February 1984.

Saving the unborn earns a jail cell, by D. Goldkamp. REGISTER. 59:1+, December 11, 1983.

Say, brother, by L. Holder. ESSENCE. 14:22, March 1984.

Scanning electron microscopy and x-ray microanalysis of foreign bodies associated with Silastic implants in humans, by A. H. Tatum, et al. CONTRACEPTION. 28(6):543-552, December 1983.

A school-, hospital- and university-based adolescent pregnancy prevention program. A cooperative design for service and research, by L. S. Zabin, et al. JOURNAL OF REPRODUCTIVE MEDICINE. 29(6):421-426, June 1983.

Scrutiny of Ferraro remarks on abortion only deepens worry, by M. Meehan. REGISTER. 60:1+, September 2, 1984.

Seamless garment issue tied up with controversy. OUR SUNDAY VISITOR. 72:3, April 15, 1984; 3, April 22, 1984.

Seamus Bond to the rescue. ECONOMIST. 288:60-61, September 17-23, 1983.

Search for male contraceptive complicated by adverse effects, by T. Ziporyn. JAMA. 252(9):1101-1103, September 7, 1984.

A second look at the Pomeroy method of tubal sterilization, by J. F. Spitaleri. NEW YORK STATE JOURNAL OF MEDICINE. 84(4): 157-158, April 1984.

Second-trimester abortion by extra-amniotic instillation of Rivanol combined with intravenous administration of oxytocin or prostaglandin F2 alpha, by I. Klinte, et al. ACTA OBSTETRICIA ET GYNECOLOGICA SCANDINAVICA. 62(4):303-306, 1983.

Second-trimester amniocentesis and termination of pregnancy, by A. C. Turnbull, et al. BRITISH MEDICAL BULLETIN. 39(4):315-321, October 1983.

The secretion of human chorionic gonadotropin-like substance in women employing contraceptive measures, by S. C. Huang, et al. JOURNAL OF CLINICAL ENDOCRINOLOGY AND METABOLISM. 58(4):646-653, April 1984.

Seeking the middle ground, prolife quarterly struggles hard to survive, by G. Erlandson. REGISTER. 59:1+, December 18, 1983.

Selected psychosocial characteristics of males: their relationship to contraceptive use and abortion, by D. Andres, et al. PERSONALITY AND SOCIAL PSYCHOLOGY BULLETIN. 9(3):387-396, September 1983.

Selection bias in studies of spontaneous abortion among occupational groups, by G. Axelsson. JOURNAL OF OCCUPATIONAL MEDICINE. 26(7):525-528, July 1984.

Selective reduction in cases of multiple pregnancy, by R. Jeny, et al. ANNALES DE RADIOLOGIE. 26(5):446, June-July 1983.

Self images and contraceptive behavior, by K. McKinney, et al. BASIC AND APPLIED SOCIAL PSYCHOLOGY. 5(1):37-57, March 1984.

Self-induced: a Red Deer woman stabs her own foetus, by R. Lenz, et al. ALBERTA REPORT. 11:22, August 6, 1984.

Self perception of women who elect tubal ligation, by G. Coutu-Wakulezyk. INFIRMIERE CANADIENNE. 26(3):26, March 1984.

The self-sustaining clinic [letter], by L. A. Villadsen. FAMILY PLANNING PERSPECTIVES. 16(2):100, March-April 1984.

Senate panel agrees to relax federal abortion restrictions. CONGRESSIONAL QUARTERLY WEEKLY REPORT. 42:1592, June 29, 1984.

The sentiments of love and aspirations for marriage and their association with teenage sexual activity and pregnancy, by J. W. Scott. ADOLESCENCE. 18:889-898, Winter 1983.

Septic abortion caused by Salmonella heidelberg in a white-handed gibbon, by J. D. Thurman, et al. JOURNAL OF THE AMERICAN VETERINARY MEDICAL ASSOCIATION. 183:1325-1326, December 1, 1983.

Septic abortion: clinical aspects, diagnosis, treatment, by V. A. Kulavskii. AKUSHERSTVO I GINEKOLOGIIA. (2):73-78, February 1984.

Septic abortion in Wellington 1960-1979, by J. M. Shepherd, et al. NEW ZEALAND MEDICAL JOURNAL. 97(756):322-324, May 23, 1984.

Septicemias of obstetrico-gynecological origin: clinical and therapeutical aspects, by H. de la Cuadra, et al. REVISTA MEDICA DE CHILE. 112(1):36-42, January 1984.

Sequelae of therapeutic abortion [letter], by J. F. Cattanach. MEDICAL JOURNAL OF AUSTRALIA. 141(4):316-317, September 1, 1984.

Sequelae of therapeutic abortion, by I. S. Fraser. MEDICAL JOURNAL OF AUSTRALIA. 140(11):639-640, May 26, 1984.

Serial multiple laminaria and adjunctive urea in late outpatient dilatation and evacuation abortion, by W. M. Hern. OBSTETRICS AND GYNECOLOGY. 63(4):543-549, April 1984.

Serologic research of toxoplasmosis, cytomegalovirus infection and listeriosis in women with and without previous abortion, by V. Amato Neto, et al. REVISTA DO INSTITUTO DE MEDICINA TROPICAL DE SAO PAULO. 25(2):62-6, March-April 1983.

Serum AFP concentration in threatened abortion, by J. Woyton, et al. WIADOMOSCI LEKARSKIE. 36(17):1411-1414, September 1, 1983.

Serum complement levels and perinatal outcome in pregnancies complicated by systemic lupus erythematosus, by L. D. Devoe, et al. OBSTETRICS AND GYNECOLOGY. 63(6):796-800, June 1984.

Serum ferritin levels in normal pregnancy and in women in threatened abortion and premature labor, by M. Sirakov, et al. AKUSHERSTVO I GINEKOLOGIIA. 23(1):10-13, 1984.

Serum folate concentrations during pregnancy in women with

epilepsy: relation to antiepileptic drug concentrations, number of seizures, and fetal outcome, by V. K. Hiilesmaa, et al. BRITISH MEDICAL JOURNAL. 287:577-579, August 27, 1983.

Serum lipids and proteins during treatment with a new oral contraceptive combination containing desogestrel, by I. M. Penttila, et al. EUROPEAN JOURNAL OF OBSTETRICS, GYNECOLOGY AND REPRODUCTIVE BIOLOGY. 16(4):275-281, December 1983.

Serum prolactin levels following abortion in normal and molar pregnancy, by O. Shinkawa, et al. NIPPON SANKA FUJINKA GAKKAI ZASSHI. 36(6):911-916, June 1984.

Serum prostaglandin F levels during menstrual cycle in women using oral contraceptives, by S. K. Garg. INTERNATIONAL JOURNAL OF CLINICAL PHARMACOLOGY, THERAPY AND TOXICOLOGY. 21(8):431-432, August 1983.

Serum steroid binding protein concentrations, distribution of progestogens, and bioavailability of testosterone during treatment with contraceptives containing desogestrel or levonorgestrel, by G. L. Hammond, et al. FERTILITY AND STERILITY. 42(1):44-51, July 1984.

Setback for Morgentaler, by R. Block. MACLEAN'S. 97:46, July 30, 1984.

Severe and prolonged oral contraceptive jaundice, by D. A. Lieberman, et al. JOURNAL OF CLINICAL GASTROENTEROLOGY. 6(2):145-148, April 1984.

Severe intrahepatic cholestasis due to the combined intake of oral contraceptives and triacetyloleandomycin, by J. Fevery, et al. ACTA CLINICA BELGICA. 38(4):242-245, 1983.

Sex advice to the rich nations, by J. Leo. TIME. 123:53, April 16, 1984.

'Sex and society': Gotland project. A research project in primary health services, by B. Stokstad, et al. SYKEPLEIEN. 70(17):16-17, October 5, 1983.

Sex, contraception and parenthood: experience and attitudes among urban black young men, by S. D. Clark, Jr., et al. FAMILY PLANNING PERSPECTIVES. 16(2):77-82, March-April 1984.

Sex-hormone-binding globulin (SHBG) in serum in threatened abortion, by J. B. Hertz, et al. ACTA ENDOCRINOLOGICA. 104(3): 381-384, November 1983.

Sex hormone profiles in oligomenorrheic adolescent girls and the effect of oral contraceptives, by R. Siegberg, et al. FERTILITY AND STERILITY. 41(6):888-893, June 1984.

Sex of previous children and intentions for further births in the United States, 1965-1976, by D. M. Sloane, et al. DEMOGRAPHY. 20(3):353, August 1983.

Sex-related differences in clinical drug response: implications for women's health, by J. Hamilton, et al. JOURNAL OF THE AMERICAN MEDICAL WOMEN'S ASSOCIATION. 38(5):126-132, September-October 1983.

Sexual and contraceptive experience among teenagers in Upsala, by E. Weiner, et al. UPSALA JOURNAL OF MEDICAL SCIENCES. 89(2):171-177, 1984.

Sexual behavior and contraceptive practice at Oxford and Aberdeen Universities, by P. Anderson, et al. JOURNAL OF BIOSOCIAL SCIENCE. 16(2):287-290, April 1984.

Sexual information and contraception in adolescence, by M. P. Breton, et al. ANNALES DE PEDIATRIE. 31(3):245-249, March 1984.

Sexuality, contraception and pregnancy in the adolescent girl, by I. R. M. I. Rey-Stocker. GYNAEKOLOGISCHE RUNDSCHAU. 23(2):108-120, 1983.

Sexually transmitted diseases and family planning. Strange or natural bedfellows?, by W. Cates, Jr. JOURNAL OF REPRODUC-TIVE MEDICINE. 29(5):317-322, May 1984.

Shake hands with a prolife peacemaker: interview, by J. Loesch. U. S. CATHOLIC. 49:22-28, May 1984.

The shift from natural to controlled fertility: a cross-sectional analysis of ten Indian states, by S. J. Jejeebhoy. STUDIES IN FAMILY PLANNING. 15(4):191-198, July-August 1984.

The short-term effects of a low-dose contraceptive on glucose meta-bolism, plasma lipids and blood clotting factors, by S. O. Skouby, et al. CONTRACEPTION. 28(5):489-499, November 1983.

Showdown on abortion: polarized views, by J. Bell. NEW DIREC-
TIONS FOR WOMEN. 13(5):15, September 1984.

Sickle cell diseases and hormonal contraception, by H. M. Freie.
ACTA OBSTETRICIA ET GYNECOLOGICA SCANDINAVICA.
62(3):211-217, 1983.

Side effects of hormonal contraceptives from an internal medicine
viewpoint, by J. Dabels. ZEITSCHRIFT FUR DIE GESAMTE
INNERE MEDIZIN. 38(22):254-256, November 15, 1983.

Side effects of oral contraceptives, by A. G. Khomasuridze. AKUSHER-
STVO I GINEKOLOGIIA. (11):27-29, November 1983.

The significance of pregnancy among adolescents choosing abortion
as compared to those continuing pregnancy, by M. Morin-
Gonthier, et al. JOURNAL OF REPRODUCTIVE MEDICINE.
29(4):255-259, April 1984.

Silicone devices for tubal occlusion: radiographic description and
evaluation, by M. E. Fischer, et al. RADIOLOGY. 151(3):601-602,
June 1984.

A simple method for estimating the contraceptive prevalence required to reach a fertility target, by J. Bongaarts. STUDIES IN
FAMILY PLANNING. 15(4):184, July-August 1984.

Simple sterilization (methyl cranoacrylate injection), by K. Jenkins.
MACLEAN'S. 97:46b, September 3, 1984.

Simulation modeling perspectives of the Bangladesh family planning and female education system, by J. H. Teel, et al. BE-
HAVIORAL SCIENCE. 29(3):145-161, July 1984.

Small families: promoting population stabilization [in developing
countries; cites lessons from India and China], by J. Jacobsen.
TRANSNATIONAL PERSPECTIVES. 9(2):15-18, 1983.

Small testicles could thwart new male pill, by A. la Guardia. NEW
SCIENTIST. 101:8, February 23, 1984.

Social and clinical correlates of postpartum sterilization in the
United States, 1972 and 1980, by W. D. Mosher, et al. PUBLIC
HEALTH REPORTS. 99:128-137, March-April 1984.

Social anxiety, sexual behavior, and contraceptive use, by M. R.

Leary, et al. JOURNAL OF PERSONALITY AND SOCIAL PSYCHOL-
OGY. 45(6):1347-1354, December 1983.

The social effects of contraception, by J. N. Santamaria. LINACRE
QUARTERLY. 51:114-127, May 1984.

A social judgment of behavior modeling upon racial attitudes, by E.
D. Schmikl. DISSERTATION ABSTRACTS INTERNATIONAL: B.
45(5), November 1984.

Social justice perspective needed on abortion issue, by D. C. Maguire.
NATIONAL CATHOLIC REPORTER. 20:16, August 17, 1984.

Social marketing of contraceptives in Bangladesh, by W. P. Schellstede, et al. STUDIES IN FAMILY PLANNING. 15:30-39, January-
February 1984.

Social, spatial and political determinants of U. S. abortion rates, by
N. F. Henry, et al. SOCIAL SCIENCE AND MEDICINE. 16(9):987-
996, 1982.

The social, theological and biological context of abortion: tenth
anniversary reflections on Roe V. Wade, by G. H. Williams.
LINACRE QUARTERLY. 50:335-354, November 1983.

Societal trends, Church beliefs support NFP methods, by L. Gallahue.
HOSPITAL PROGRESS. 64(12):54-56; 60, December 1983.

Socio-economic and demographic study of factors influencing
fertility control in India, by S. K. Chaudhuri. JOURNAL OF THE
INDIAN MEDICAL ASSOCIATION. 181(5-6):99-101, September
1983.

Socio-economic status and use of contraceptives among unmarried
primigravidas in Cape Town, by D. A. Whitelaw. SOUTH
AFRICAN MEDICAL JOURNAL. 64(18):712-715, October 22,
1983.

Some are more equal, by V. G. Kulkarni. FAR EASTERN ECONOMIC
REVIEW. 124:31-32, June 21, 1984.

Some data on natural fertility, by L. Henry. SOCIAL BIOLOGY. 29:145-
156, Spring-Summer 1982.

Some epidemiological data on spontaneous abortion in Hungary,
1971-1980, by A. Czeizel, et al. JOURNAL OF EPIDEMIOLOGY

AND COMMUNITY HEALTH. 38(2):143-148, June 1984.

Some observations on family planning education in China, by M. V. Hamburg. HYGIE. 3(2):21-24, June 1984.

Some organizational alternatives to increased support for reproductive and contraceptive research, by J. I. Rosoff. FAMILY PLANNING PERSPECTIVES. 16(1):28-31, January-February 1984.

Soul searching, by I. L. Horowitz. SOCIETY. 21:4-8, March-April 1984.

Source of prescription contraceptives and subsequent pregnancy among young women, by M. Zelnik, et al. FAMILY PLANNING PERSPECTIVES. 16:6-13, January-February 1984.

South Carolina rapists given choice: castration or 30 years. CRIME VICTIMS DIGEST. 1(3):6, December 1983.

South Carolina rapists weight choice: castration or 30 years. CORRECTIONS DIGEST. 14(25):9, November 30, 1983.

Spanish abortionist gets 12 years. SPARE RIB. 37:9, December 1983.

Spatial and temporal aspects of contraceptive adoption: an analysis of contemporary fertility behavior in Costa Rica. DISSERTATION ABSTRACTS INTERNATIONAL: A. 45(5), November 1984.

Spermicides; safe?, by K. Freifeld, et al. HEALTH. 15:8, December 1983.

Sponge; the latest contraceptive device debuts with some interesting (but questionable) features, by K. Freifeld, et al. HEALTH. 15:56, July 1983.

Spontaneous abortions among dental assistants, factory workers, painters, and gardening workers: a follow up study, by L. Z. Heidam. JOURNAL OF EPIDEMIOLOGY AND COMMUNITY HEALTH. 38(2):149-155, June 1984.

Spontaneous abortions among factory workers. The importance of gravidity control, by L. Z. Heidam. SCANDINAVIAN JOURNAL OF SOCIAL MEDICINE. 11(3):81-85, 1983.

Spontaneous abortions among laboratory works; a follow up study, by L. Z. Heidam. JOURNAL OF EPIDEMIOLOGY AND COMMUNITY HEALTH. 38(1):36-41, March 1984.

Spontaneous abortions among rubber workers and congenital malformations in their offspring, by M. L. Lindbohm, et al. SCANDINAVIAN JOURNAL OF WORK, ENVIRONMENT AND HEALTH. 9(Suppl 2):85-90, 1983.

Spontaneous abortions and twinning, by M. Zahalkova, et al. ACTA GENETICAE MEDICAE ET GEMELLOLOGIAE: TWIN RESEARCH. 33(1):25-26, 1984.

Spontaneous abortions following Three Mile Island accident [letter], by C. J. Johnson. AMERICAN JOURNAL OF PUBLIC HEALTH. 74(5):520, May 1984.

Spontaneous abortion in proven intact pregnancies [letter], by G. C. Christiaens, et al. LANCET. 2(8402):571-572, September 8, 1984.

Spontaneous abortions, stillbirths, and birth defects in families of agricultural pilots, by C. C. Roan, et al. ARCHIVES OF ENVIRON-MENTAL HEALTH. 39(1):56-60, January-February 1984.

Spousal notification and the right of privacy. Scheinberg v. Smith. CHICAGO-KENT LAW REVIEW. 59:1129-1151, 1983.

Spousal notification: an unconstitutional limitation on a woman's right to privacy in the abortion decision. HOFSTRA LAW RE-VIEW. 12:531-560, Winter 1984.

State funding cutoff for abortions may be constitutionally protected. THE FAMILY LAW REPORTER: COURT OPINIONS. 10(3):1041-1042, November 15, 1983.

The state of the thrombocytic component of the hemostasis system in patients with infection and septic shock, by A. D. Makatsariia, et al. SOVETSKAIA MEDITSINA. (4):34-39, 1984.

State of the world. HUMANIST. 44:45-46, July-August 1984.

State protection of the unborn after Roe v. Wade: a legislative proposal. STETSON LAW REVIEW. 13:237-266, Winter 1984.

Statement and proposals of the regional Chinese Catholic Bishops' Conference on the issue should abortion be legalized? L'OSSER-VATORE ROMANO. (30):11-12, July 23, 1984.

Statement on pluralism and abortion. ORIGINS. 14:414, December 6, 1984.

The statistical evaluation of natural methods of family planning, by T. W. Hilgers. IRNFP. 8:226-264, Fall 1984.

Sterilization. JOURNAL OF FAMILY LAW. 20(4):781-784, August 1981-82.

Sterilization, abortion a way of life, by T. Ackerman. REGISTER. 60:10, August 12, 1984.

Sterilization and nidation [letter]. UGESKRIFT FOR LAEGER. 145(47):3676, November 21, 1983.

Sterilization-associated deaths: a global survey, by L. T. Strauss, et al. INTERNATIONAL JOURNAL OF GYNAECOLOGY AND OBSTETRICS. 22(1):67-75, February 1984.

Sterilization at the time of cesarean section: tubal ligation or hysterectomy?, by I. Bukovsky, et al. CONTRACEPTION. 28(4):349-356, October 1983.

Sterilization by colpoceliotomy, by W. Heidenreich. FORTSCHRITTE DER MEDIZIN. 101(41):1855-1859, November 3, 1983.

Sterilization: cross-country chaos, by D. Winn. SUNDAY TIMES. July 15, 1984, p. 36.

Sterilization has little effect on menstrual cycles. AMERICAN FAMILY PHYSICIAN. 29:262, March 1984.

Sterilization in Canberra, by D. Lucas. JOURNAL OF BIOSOCIAL SCIENCE. 16:335, 1984.

Sterilization in Honduras: assessing the unmet demand, by B. Janowitz, et al. STUDIES IN FAMILY PLANNING. 14(10):252, October 1983.

Sterilization of the mentally retarded. The rules change but the results remain the same, by R. M. Soskin. MEDICINE AND LAW. 2(3):267-276, 1983.

Sterilization of women at a county hospital 1969-1981, by P. E. Bordahl, et al. TIDSSKRIFT FOR DEN NORSKE LAEGEFORENING. 103(23):1618-1619, August 20, 1983.

Steroid-induced thrombogenesis in rats, by J. R. Reel, et al. INTERNATIONAL JOURNAL OF FERTILITY. 28(3):169-172, 1983.

Steroidal contraception in the '80s. The role of current and new products, by J. J. Speidel. JOURNAL OF REPRODUCTIVE MEDICINE. 28(11):759-769, November 1983.

Steroidogenesis inhibitors. 1. Adrenal inhibitory and interceptive activity of trilostane and related compounds, by R. G. Christiansen, et al. JOURNAL OF MEDICINAL CHEMISTRY. 27(7):928-931, July 1984.

Strategists work to sound the death knell for abortion: What will it take to overturn Roe v. Wade, by R. Frame. CHRISTIANITY TODAY. 28:74, May 18, 1984.

Stress and spontaneous abortion: a controlled study, by P. Santonastaso, et al. MEDICINA PSICOSOMATICA. 28(1):3-14, January-March 1983.

Student choices and effectiveness, by L. H. Schilling. JOURNAL OF AMERICAN COLLEGE HEALTH. 32(6):239-243, June 1984.

Studies find no link between pill use and development of pituitary tumors. FAMILY PLANNING PERSPECTIVES. 15:283, November-December 1983.

Studies on Aristolochia III. Isolation and biological evaluation of constitutents of Aristolochia indica roots for fertility-regulating activity, by C. T. Che, et al. JOURNAL OF NATURAL PRODUCTS. 47(2):331-341, March-April 1984.

Studies on the role of intestinal bacteria in metabolism of synthetic and natural steroid hormones, by H. Adlercreutz, et al. JOURNAL OF STEROID BIOCHEMISTRY. 20(1):217-229, January 1984.

Study of the endometrium following voluntary interruption of pregnancy in relation to the contraceptive method used following abortion, by J. B. Sindayirwanya, et al. JOURNAL DE GYNECOLOGIE, OBSTETRIQUE ET BIOLOGIE DE LA REPRODUCTION. 12(4):351-362, 1983.

Study of impotent men raises a question about vasectomy, by S. Stanik, et al. AMERICAN FAMILY PHYSICIAN. 28:180, August 1983.

Study of pregnancies of women with copper intrauterine devices, by A. Albert, et al. REPRODUCTION. 7(1-2):25-32, 1983.

A study of the serum factor 'X' in women with pathological pregnancy and during delivery, by J. B. Lukanov. FOLIA MEDICA. 25(3):19-24, 1983.

A study of women on the progestogen only pill, by M. C. Robertson. PRACTITIONER. 228(1390):435-439, April 1984.

Study on the factors associated with contraceptive discontinuations in Bangkok, by T. Chumnijarakij, et al. CONTRACEPTION. 29(3):241-249, March 1984.

Study on plasma prolactin and immunoreactive-prolactin released from decidua in normal pregnancy and abortion, by T. Kubota, et al. ASIA-OCEANIA JOURNAL OF OBSTETRICS AND GYNAE-COLOGY. 10(2):225-234, June 1984.

Study shows that IUDs pose a long-term risk. NEW SCIENTIST. 103:22, September 20, 1984.

Subchorionic bleeding in threatened abortion: sonographic findings and significance, by S. R. Goldstein, et al. AJR. 141(5):975-978, November 1983.

Subsequent reproductive outcome in couples with repeated pregnancy loss, by J. FitzSimmons, et al. AMERICAN JOURNAL OF MEDICAL GENETICS. 16(4):583-587, December 1983.

Substituted judgment: a modern application, by M. J. Gormley. NEW ENGLAND JOURNAL ON CRIMINAL AND CIVIL CONFINE-MENT. 10(2):353-382, 1984.

Suction curettage, by E. C. English. JOURNAL OF FAMILY PRAC-TICE. 17(6):1065-1070, December 1983.

Suit charges subsidy for religious views. E/SA. 12:35, April 1984.

Sulphation of contraceptive steroids, by F. S. Khan, et al. JOURNAL OF STEROID BIOCHEMISTRY. 19(5):1657-1660, November 1983.

Sulprostone for preoperative cervical dilatation in primigravidae scheduled for late first trimester termination of pregnancy, by F. Jerve, et al. ARCHIVES OF GYNECOLOGY. 233(3):199-203, 1983.

Supply-demand disequilibria and fertility changes in Africa: toward a more appropriate economic approach, by J. E. Kocher. SOCIAL BIOLOGY. 30:41-58, Spring 1983.

Supreme Court holds anti-abortion law unconstitutional: A summary of the court's decision; abortion foes falter in Senate, fight on in House, by D. E. Kulp. OFF OUR BACKS. 13:19; 20, August-September 1983.

—. An analysis of the court's decision: its strength and weaknesses, by N. Hunter. OFF OUR BACKS. 13:19-20, August-September 1983.

Supreme court review, by S. Bernstein. TRIAL. 19(12):20; 22, December 1983.

Surgery and circulating antiprothrombinase-type anti-coagulant in the Soulier-Boffa syndrome, by C. Martin, et al. ANNALES FRANCAISES D'ANESTHESIE ET DE REANIMATION. 3(4):306-308, 1984.

Surgery in utero on a two-headed monster. The value of echography, by H. Serment, et al. JOURNAL DE GYNECOLOGIE, OBSTETRIQUE ET BIOLOGIE DE LA REPRODUCTION. 13(2):197-203, 1984.

Surgical and chemical vasectomy in the cat, by M. H. Pineda, et al. AMERICAN JOURNAL OF VETERINARY RESEARCH. 4(2):291-300, February 1984.

The surgical solution: the writings of activist physicians in the early days of eugenical sterilization, by P. Reilly. PERSPECTIVES IN BIOLOGY AND MEDICINE. 26:637-656, Summer 1983.

The surgical technic and vaso-vasostomy, by M. Andersen, et al. UGESKRIFT FOR LAEGER. 145(39):3012-3013, September 26, 1983.

Surgically treated focal nodular hyperplasia, by S. Pap, et al. ORVOSI HETILAP. 125(20):1201-1203, May 13, 1984.

Surprise contraceptive: Canadian zoologist stumbles upon compound to control male fertility, by R. Spence. EQUINOX. 3:16, January-February 1984.

A survey of different approaches to management of menstrual disturbances in women using injectable contraceptives, by I. S. Fraser. CONTRACEPTION. 28(4):385-397, October 1983.

Swedish abortion practice. One should talk about abortion. The staff needs therapy, by I. Andersson. KRANKENPLFEGE JOURNAL. 21(10):6, October 1, 1983.

Swedish midwifery society's reply to SHSTF. JORDEMODERN. 97(5):151-154, May 1984.

Symptoms of emotional distress in a family planning service: stability over a four-week period, by A. Winokur, et al. BRITISH JOURNAL OF PSYCHIATRY. 144:395-399, April 1984.

Synthesis and pregnancy terminating activity of 2-arylimidazo [2,1-a] isoquinolines and isoindoles, by E. Toja, et al. ARZENEIMITTEL-FORSCHUNG. 33(9):1222-1225, 1983.

Synthesis of dl-17-phenyl-18,19,20-trinorprostaglandin F2 alpha methyl ester and its 15-epimer, by Y. L. Wu, et al. YAO HSUEH HSUEH PAO. 18(5):351-355, May 1983.

Systemic changes during the use of hormonal contraceptives, by I. A. Manuilova, et al. AKUSHERSTVO I GINEKOLOGIIA. (11):14-17, November 1983.

Systemic effects of oral contraceptives, by T. M. Kelly. WESTERN JOURNAL OF MEDICINE. 141(1):113-116, July 1984.

T-cell subset distribution in chronically aborting women [letter], by A. Bertotto, et al. LANCET. 1(8368):108, January 14, 1984.

Taking our health into our hands, by K. Hodge. GUARDIAN. 36 (24):1, Spring 1984.

Talking sense on population [Reagan administration stand on cutting aid to governments that sanction abortion]. NATIONAL REVIEW. 36:15-16, August 10, 1984.

Teaching ethics in nursing: a handbook for use of the case-study approach, by M. L. Applegate, et al. NLN PUBLICATIONS. (41-1963):1-81, 1984.

Teenage abortion in the United States, by W. Cates, Jr., et al. PUBLIC HEALTH REVIEWS. 11(4):291-310, October-December 1983.

Teenage fertility in developed nations: 1971-1980, by C. F. Westoff, et al. FAMILY PLANNING PERSPECTIVES. 15(3):105, May-June 1983.

Teenage pregnancies and abortion, by J. E. Morgenthau. MT. SINAI

JOURNAL OF MEDICINE. 51(1):18-19, January-February 1984.

Teenage pregnancy and childbearing: why the difference between countries? FAMILY PLANNING PERSPECTIVES. 15:104-105, May-June 1983.

Teenage pregnancy and public policy, by D. L. Gilchrist, et al. SOCIAL SERVICE REVIEW. 57:307-322, June 1983.

Teenage pregnancy prevention: an Atlanta program, by M. F. Hill, et al. URBAN HEALTH. 13(2):26-29, March 1984.

Teenagers and fertility control: legal and ethical issues for doctors, by V. Wootten. HEALTHRIGHT. 3:6-9, February 1984.

The ten most common questions concerning abortion, by W. Odell, et al. OUR SUNDAY VISITOR. 72:3+, January 22, 1984.

Teratology study with the synthetic prostaglandin ONO-802 given intravaginally to rabbits, by J. A. Petrere, et al. TERATO-GENESIS, CARCINOGENESIS AND MUTAGENESIS. 4(2):225-231, 1984.

Termination of early pregnancy by ONO-802 suppositiories, by C. F. Zhang. CHUNG HUA FU CHAN KO TSA CHIH. 18(3):150-153, July 1983.

The termination of early pregnancy in the mouse by beta-momor-charian, by W. Y. Chan, et al. CONTRACEPTION. 29(1):91-100, January 1984.

Termination of midtrimester pregnancies with extraovular 0.1% ethacridine lactate. Accurate method for estimation of blood loss. Role of spartein sulfate, by R. M. Laul, et al. ASIA-OCEANIA JOURNAL OF OBSTETRICS AND GYNAECOLOGY. 10(2):185-189, June 1984.

Termination of pregnancy by general practitioners, by H. J. Rieger. DEUTSCHE MEDIZINISCHE WOCHENSCRIFT. 109(33):1259-1261, August 17, 1984.

Termination of pregnancy during the third trimester [letter]. NEW ENGLAND JOURNAL OF MEDICINE. 311(4):264-265, July 26, 1984.

Termination of pregnancy in teenagers, by D. Krishnamoni, et al.

CANADIAN JOURNAL OF PSYCHIATRY. 28(6):457-461, October 1983.

Termination of second-trimester pregnancy by laminaria and intramuscular injections of 15-methyl PGF2 alpha or 16-phenoxy-omega-17,18,19,20-tetranor PGE2 methyl sulfonylamide. A randomized study, by M. Bygdeman, et al. ACTA OBSTETRICIA ET GYNECOLOGICA SCANDINAVICA. 62(5):535-537, 1983.

Termination of very early pregnancy by RU 486— an anti-progestational compound, by L. Kovacs, et al. CONTRACEPTION. 29(5): 399-410, May 1984.

Theologian resigns after signing abortion statement, by J. T. Beifuss. NATIONAL CATHOLIC REPORTER. 20:21, October 19, 1984.

Theologians brief press on Church's birth control position. REGISTER. 60:3, August 5, 1984.

A theoretical analysis of antecedents of young couple's fertility decisions, by L. J. Beckman, et al. DEMOGRAPHY. 20:519-534, November 1983.

Therapeutic abortion and nursing care, by H. Hulme. NURSING TIMES. 179(41):54; 56-58; 60, October 12-18, 1983.

Therapeutic abortions, by M. Achour, et al. MAROC MEDICAL. 5(2):184-190, June 1983.

Therapeutic interruption of pregnancy in the second trimester after preparation of the cervix with prostaglandins F2 alpha, by B. Maria, et al. JOURNAL DE GYNECOLOGIE, OBSTETRIQUE ET BIOLOGIE DE LA REPRODUCTION. 12(5):545-552, 1983.

Therapeutic uses of contraceptive steroids, by G. C. Starks. JOURNAL OF FAMILY PRACTICE. 19(3):315-321, September 1984.

Therapy of primary aldosteronism with trilostane, by B. Winterberg, et al. SCHWEIZERISCHE MEDIZINISCHE WOCHENSCHRIFT. 113(46):1735-1738, November 19, 1983.

Thirty years of family planning in India, by R. Ledbetter. ASIAN SURVEY. 24:736-758, July 1984.

30 years of patient education in the use of pessaries: personal history of Mrs. Taki Hanyu. The past and present of education in pessary

use, by T. Hanyu, et al. JOSANPU ZASSHI. 37(3):178-186, March 1983.

This amendment could kill women. HARVARD WOMEN'S LAW JOURNAL. 7:287-301, Spring 1984.

Thomasma reassessing his abortion stand?, by M. Meehan. REGISTER. 60:1+, October 7, 1984.

3D display of stillbirth in Indonesian obstetrics part 4: Contraception as preventive determinant?, by S. Sastrawinata, et al. SOZIAL- UND PRAVENTIVMEDIZIN. 29(2):98-101, 1984.

Three methods for gradual cervical dilatation prior to vacuum aspiration in late first trimester pregnancy, by S. Sema, et al. CONTRACEPTION. 28(3):223-231, September 1983.

Three years of experience after post-abortal insertion of Nova-T and Copper-T-200, by N. C. Nielsen, et al. ACTA OBSTETRICIA ET GYNECOLOGICA SCANDINAVICA. 63(3):261-264, 1984.

Three years experience with copper T-200, by S. D. Kanitkar, et al. JOURNAL OF THE INDIAN MEDICAL ASSOCIATION. 80(9-10): 148-149, May 1983.

Thrombosis, abortion, cerebral disease, and the lupus anticoagulant, by G. R. V. Hughes. BRITISH MEDICAL JOURNAL. 287:1088-1089, October 15, 1983.

Thyroid function during treatment with a new oral contraceptive combination containing desogestrel, by I. M. Penttila, et al. EUROPEAN JOURNAL OF OBSTETRICS, GYNECOLOGY AND REPRODUCTIVE BIOLOGY. 16(4):269-274, December 1983.

A ticking population bomb, by M. Whitaker. NEWSWEEK. 103:43, June 25, 1984.

Time bomb or myth: the population problem, by R. S. McNamara. FOREIGN AFFAIRS. 62:1107-1131, Summer 1984.

The timing of family formation: structural and societal factors in the Asian context, by R. R. Rindfuss, et al. JOURNAL OF MARRIAGE AND THE FAMILY. 46:205-214, February 1984.

Title X and its critics, by J. I. Rosoff, et al. FAMILY PLANNING PERSPECTIVES. 16(3):111-113; 115-116; 119, May-June 1984.

To abort is to destroy one's son or daughter, by J. T. Burtchaell. NATIONAL CATHOLIC REPORTER. 20:11, October 5, 1984.

To be born, to die: individual rights in the '80s: birth, by L. Reaves. AMERICAN BAR ASSOCIATION JOURNAL. 70:27-28, February 1984.

Today, the sponge, by E. Frank. NEW YORK. 117:68-69, February 27, 1984.

Today's contraceptives: what's what? What's best?, by W. S. Ross. READER'S DIGEST. 123(739):217-218; 220-222; 225-226, November 1983.

Too many teen pregnancies. FAMILY PLANNING PERSPECTIVES. 16(1):4, January-February 1984.

Top court upholds right to advertise condoms. EDITOR AND PUBLISHER-THE FOURTH ESTATE. 116:34, July 2, 1983.

Topics in radiology/case of the month. Acute dyspnea in a young women taking birth control pills, by T. E. Goffman, et al. JAMA. 251(11):1465-1466, March 16, 1984.

Torts— birth control. THE FAMILY LAW REPORTER. 10(29):1402, May 22, 1984.

Total ligation syndrome. Does it exist?, by R. C. Strickler. POST-GRADUATE MEDICINE. 75(1):233; 237, January 1984.

Towards a theory of history, by P. Colinvaux. COEVOLUTION QUARTERLY. 41:94, Spring 1984.

Toxic abortion agent making a comeback. LRN. 46:19, November 1983.

Toxic shock and the sponge, by B. Day. GUARDIAN. 36(15):4, January 18, 1984.

Toxic-shock syndrome and the vaginal contraceptive sponge. MMWR. 33(4):43-44; 49, February 3, 1984.

Toxic shocker, by E. J. Tracy. FORTUNE. 110:48, July 23, 1984.

A toxic way to abort . . . ingesting quinine. EMERGENCY MEDICINE. 16(1):75; 78, January 15, 1984.

The traditions of probabilism and the moral status of the early embryo, by C. A. Tauer. THEOLOGICAL STUDIES. 45(1):3-33, 1984.

Trail blazing . . . in the area of family planning research, by T. Standley, et al. WORLD HEALTH. December 1983, pp. 8-10.

Transferring health and family planning service innovations to the public sector: an experiment in organization development in Bangladesh, by J. F. Phillips, et al. STUDIES IN FAMILY PLANNING. 15(2):62, March-April 1984.

Treatment for habitual aborters. AMERICAN JOURNAL OF NURSING. 84:494, April 1984.

The trend toward judicial recognition of wrongful life: a dissenting view, by B. Kennedy. UCLA LAW REVIEW. 31:474, December 1983.

Trends and differentials in Moslem fertility, by M. H. Nagi. JOURNAL OF BIOSOCIAL SCIENCE. 16:189-204, April 1984.

Trends in mortality from carcinoma of the liver and the use of oral contraceptives, by D. Forman, et al. BRITISH JOURNAL OF CANCER. 48(3):349-354, September 1983.

Trends in postpartum contraceptive choice, by C. H. Debrovner, et al. OBSTETRICS AND GYNECOLOGY. 63(1):65-70, January 1984.

Trial by fire/feminist health clinic, by L. Averill. NORTHWEST PASSAGE. 24(11):1, June 1984.

Trichomoniasis— incidence in pill users and associated pap smear abnormalities, by B. Pillay, et al. MALAYSIAN JOURNAL OF PATHOLOGY. 2:59-62, August 1979.

The trimester approach: how long can the legal fiction last? MERCER LAW REVIEW. 35:891-913, Spring 1984.

Triploidy, partial mole and dispermy. An investigation of 12 cases, by S. E. Procter, et al. CLINICAL GENETICS. 26(1):46-51, July 1984.

Tubal lesions after sterilization [letter], by A. McCausland. FERTILITY AND STERILITY. 42(3):493-495, September 1984.

Tubal ligation and mini-laparotomy in an outpatient setting, by F.

R. Hurlbutt, et al. HAWAII MEDICAL JOURNAL. 42(7):156-157, July 1983.

Tubal ligations and menstrual cycles, by E. Michaels. CHATELAINE. 57:20, June 1984.

Tubal polyps, epithelial inclusions, and endometriosis after tubal sterilization, by J. Donnez, et al. FERTILITY AND STERILITY. 41(4):564-568, April 1984.

Tubal rupture in a sterilized woman, by S. Kruger, et al. UGESKRIFT FOR LAEGER. 145(47):3667, November 21, 1983.

Tubal sterilization, by M. Dubois. REVUE MEDICALE DE LIEGE. 39(7):265-266, April 1, 1984.

Tubal sterilization among women of reproductive age, United States, update for 1979-1980, by V. I. Moses, et al. MMWR SURVEILLANCE SUMMARY. 32(3):9SS-14SS, August 1983.

Tubal sterilization using laser coagulation, by P. Bailer. FORTSCHRITTE DER MEDIZIN. 101(43):1977, November 17, 1983.

Tubal sterilization performed in freestanding, ambulatory-care surgical facilities in the United States in 1980, by J. R. Greenspan, et al. JOURNAL OF REPRODUCTIVE MEDICINE. 29(4):237-241, April 1984.

Tunnel vision, by S. N. Chakravarty. FORBES. 133:21+, May 21, 1984.

XXII Scandinavian Congress of Obstetrics and Gynecology. Helsinki, Finland, June 7-10, 1982. Abstracts. ACTA OBSTETRICIA ET GYNECOLOGICA SCANDINAVICA [SUPPL]. 116:1-112, 1983.

Two-phase teratology study with the synthetic prostaglandin ONO-802 given intravaginally to rats, by J. A. Petrere, et al. TERATOGENESIS, CARCINOGENESIS AND MUTAGENESIS. 4(2):233-243, 1984.

Two studies find no link between use of oral contraceptives and development of pituitary tumors. FAMILY PLANNING PERSPECTIVES. 15(6):283-284, November-December 1983.

UN defends tactics for population control, by F. Pearce. NEW SCIENTIST. 103:4, August 9, 1984.

145

U. S. bishops advise Democrats to emphasize life. OUR SUNDAY VISITOR. 73:8, June 24, 1984.

U. S. bishops seek to clear electoral confusion by reiterating opposition to abortion and nuclear arms, by S. Askin. NATIONAL CATHOLIC REPORTER. 20:1+, October 19, 1984.

U. S. bucks the tide on birth control [decision to halt family planning funds for countries promoting abortions]. U. S. NEWS AND WORLD REPORT. 97:8, August 20, 1984.

U. S. inflicts "mortality" on a world fit to burst, by R. Righter. SUNDAY TIMES. August 5, 1984, p. 11.

U. S. population stance makes World bank edgy, by F. Harrison. FINANCIAL POST. 78:16, July 14, 1984.

U. S. says no to overseas abortion funding. CHRISTIANITY TODAY. 28:75-76, September 7, 1984.

U. S. switch on family planning raises fear about economic development: the new limits on use of U. S. funds by international groups that support abortions have buoyed right-to-life groups and worried population experts, by B. Stokes. NATIONAL JOURNAL. 16:1476-1479, August 4, 1984.

Ultra low dose OC. RN. 46:130, May 1983.

Ultrasonic measurement of ovarian follicles during chronic LRH agonist treatment for contraception, by C. Bergquist, et al. CONTRACEPTION. 28(2):125-133, August 1983.

An ultrasonographic study on the pathophysiology of threatened abortion, by M. Kawano. SHIKOKU ACTA MEDICA. 40(1):1-17, 1984.

Unaltered lipoprotein and carbohydrate metabolism during treatment with contraceptive subdermal implants containing ST-1435, by V. Odlind, et al. UPSALA JOURNAL OF MEDICAL SCIENCES. 89(2):151-158, 1984.

Understandable but mistaken: law, morality and the Canadian Catholic Church, by A. DeValk. STUDY SESSIONS: CANADIAN CATHOLIC HISTORICAL ASSOCIATION. 49:87-109, 1982.

Uneasy freedom: women's experiences of contraception, by M. Benn, et al. WOMEN'S STUDIES INTERNATIONAL FORUM. 7(4):219-225, 1984.

Unemancipated minors' rights of access to contraceptives without parental consent or notice— the squeal rule and beyond. OKLA-HOMA CITY UNIVERSITY LAW REVIEW. 8:219-250, Summer 1983.

A unified psychological model of contraceptive behavior, by L. T. Condelli. DISSERTATION ABSTRACTS INTERNATIONAL: B. 45(4), October 1984.

Unintended pregnancy and the risks/safety of birth control methods, by L. Klein. JOGN NURSING. 13(5):287-289, September-October 1984.

Unisex birth control. AMERICAN FAMILY PHYSICIAN. 29:385+, March 1984.

United nations conference rewards contraceptive technology, by F. Pearce. NEW SCIENTIST. 103:24, August 16, 1984.

Unsocial issues [R. Reagan speaks on abortion and school prayer]. NEW REPUBLIC. 190:9-10, February 27, 1984.

An unwanted baby boom, by M. Beck. NEWSWEEK. 103:47, April 30, 1984.

Unwanted life. BRITISH MEDICAL JOURNAL [CLIN RES]. 289 (6444):565, September 1, 1984.

Unwanted pregnancies terminated by indicated abortion: A study in unconscious motivational factors, by G. S. Canzano. DISSERTATION ABSTRACTS INTERNATIONAL: B. 45(5), November 1984.

Unwanted pregnancy. A failure of contraceptive education, by W. Fielding, et al. JOURNAL OF REPRODUCTIVE MEDICINE. 28(12): 847-850, December 1983.

Unwanted pregancy: a failure of contraceptive education [letter], by P. A. Poma. JOURNAL OF REPRODUCTIVE MEDICINE. 29(6): 61, June 1984.

Update on natural birth control, by S. Katz. CHATELAINE. 57:16, January 1984.

Urban black adolescents who obtain contraceptive services before or after their first pregnancy. Psychosocial factors and contraceptive use, by E. W. Freeman, et al. JOURNAL OF ADOLESCENT HEALTH CARE. 5(3):183-190, July 1984.

Urinary concentrations of steroid glucuronides in women taking oral contraceptives, by M. A. Shaw, et al. CONTRACEPTION. 28(1):69-75, July 1983.

Urinary porphyrin pattern in liver damage, by C. M. de Rover, et al. FOOD AND CHEMICAL TOXICOLOGY. 22(3):241-243, March 1984.

Urinary tract infections among diaphragm users, by E. M. Wall, et al. JOURNAL OF FAMILY PRACTICE. 18(5):707-711, May 1984.

The use of biodegradable norethisterone implants as a six-month contraceptive system, by R. Rivera, et al. FERTILITY AND STERILITY. 42(2):228-232, August 1984.

Use of circulating progesterone and estradiol levels to predict outcome of pregnancy in cases of threatened abortion, by B. Adelusi, et al. EAST AFRICAN MEDICAL JOURNAL. 60(5):323-327, May 1983.

Use of clomiphene in habitual abortion due to lutein insufficiency, by G. Del Papa, et al. MINERVA GINECOLOGIA. 35(10):677-679, October 1983.

Use of contraceptive drugs in cardiac patients, by F. X. Veray. BOLETIN-ASOCIACION MEDICA DE PUERTO RICO. 75(6):253-254, June 1983.

Use of contraceptives in Norway, by L. Ostby. TIDSSKRIFT FOR DEN NORSKE LAEGEFORENING. 103(26):1793-1797, September 20, 1983.

The use of 15-methylated derivative of prostaglandin F2a for the therapeutic termination of pregnancy and management of late fetal death, by A. Antsaklis, et al. INTERNATIONAL SURGERY. 69(1):63-68, January-March 1984.

Use of a new synthetic prostaglandin (sulprostone) in the interruption of pregnancy after the first 90 days, by A. Segre, et al. MINERVA GINECOLOGIA. 35(10):681-687, October 1983.

Use of oral contraceptives and the occurrence of breast cancer, by I.

Baksaas, et al. TIDSSKRIFT FOR DEN NORSKE LAEGEFORE-NING. 104(22):1390-1392, August 10, 1984.

Use of oral contraceptives in Denmark in 1983, by O. Lidegaard. UGESKRIFT FOR LAEGER. 146(15):1172-1174, April 9, 1984.

Use of Ovidon, Rigevidon and Postinor for contraception, by V. I. Kulakov, et al. AKUSHERSTVO I GINEKOLOGIIA. (11):22-24, November 1983.

The use of real-time ultrasound as an aid during difficult therapeutic abortion procedures, by R. L. Goldenberg, et al. AMERICAN JOURNAL OF OBSTETRICS AND GYNECOLOGY. 148(6):826-827, March 15, 1984.

Use of tocolysis as a routine method of preventing spontaneous abortions and premature labor, by Kh. Veselinov. AKUSHER-STVO I GINEKOLOGIIA. 22(2):93-97, 1983.

Use of a urinary balloon catheter in abortions after the 20th week of gestation and in premature labor, by K. Iordanov, et al. AKUSHERSTVO I GINEKOLOGIIA. 22(2):97-99, 1983.

An user acceptability study of vaginal spermicides in combination with barrier methods or an IUCD, by C. Black, et al. CONTRACEP-TION. 28(2):103-110, August 1983.

User's perception of the contraceptive vaginal ring: a field study in Brazil and the Dominican Republic, by E. E. Hardy, et al. STUDIES IN FAMILY PLANNING. 14(1):284-290, November 1983.

The uses of chastity and other paths to sexual pleasures, by G. Greer. MS. 12:53+, April 1984.

Uterine embolization in a patient with postabortal hemorrhage, by F. P. Haseltine, et al. OBSTETRICS AND GYNECOLOGY. 63 (Suppl 3):78S-80S, March 1984.

Uterine rupture as a complication of second-trimester abortion when using prostaglandin F2 alpha together with other oxytocic agents, by H. Malmstrom, et al. ACTA OBSTETRICIA ET GYNECOLOGICA SCANDINAVICA. 63(3):271-272, 1984.

Vaccination against spontaneous abortion in mice, by G. Chaouat, et al. JOURNAL OF REPRODUCTIVE IMMUNOLOGY. 5(6):389-392, November 1983.

Vaginal administration of 15-methyl-PGF2 alpha-methyl ester prior to vacuum aspiration. Peri- and postoperative complications, by S. Nilsson, et al. ACTA OBSTETRICIA ET GYNECOLOGICA SCANDINAVICA. 62(6):599-602, 1983.

Vaginal cleansing at vacuum aspiration abortion does not reduce the risk of postoperative infection, by C. Lundh, et al. ACTA OBSTETRICIA ET GYNECOLOGICA SCANDINAVICA. 62(3):275-277, 1983.

Vaginal contraception: an overview, by D. A. Edelman. INTERNATIONAL JOURNAL OF GYNAECOLOGY AND OBSTETRICS. 22(1): 11-17, February 1984.

Vaginal mechanical contraceptive devices, by M. Smith, et al. CANADIAN MEDICAL ASSOCIATION JOURNAL. 129(7):699-701, October 1, 1983.

Vaginal removal of the ovaries in association with vaginal hysterectomy, by C. V. Capen, et al. JOURNAL OF REPRODUCTIVE MEDICINE. 28(9):589-591, 1983.

Validation of questionnaire reported miscarriage, malformation and birth weight, by G. Axelsson, et al. INTERNATIONAL JOURNAL OF EPIDEMIOLOGY. 13(1):94-98, March 1984.

Value of cervical encirclage in the treatment of midtrimester abortion, by S. Nnatu. INTERNATIONAL JOURNAL OF GYNAECOLOGY AND OBSTETRICS. 21(6):469-472, December 1983.

Value of routine histologic studies in spontaneous abortion, by G. Stranz, et al. ZENTRALBLATT FUR GYNAEKOLOGIE. 105(23): 1542-1545, 1983.

Variations in historical natural fertility patterns and the measurement of fertility control, by P. R. Hinde, et al. JOURNAL OF BIOSOCIAL SCIENCE. 16(3):309-321, July 1984.

Vascular complications of oral contraception. In whom and how to prevent them?, by V. Beaumont, et al. PRESSE MEDICALE. 12(47):2977-2981, December 24, 1983.

Vasectomies and health. DISCOVER. 5:11, January 1984.

Vasectomy and health: results from a large cohort study, by F. J. Massey, Jr., et al. JAMA. 252:1023-1029, August 24, 1984.

Vasectomy and nonfatal myocardian infarction: continued observation indicates no elevation of risk, by A. M. Walker, et al. JOURNAL OF UROLOGY. 130(5):936-937, 1983.

Vasectomy failure using an open-ended technique, by M. Goldstein. FERTILITY AND STERILITY. 40(5):699-700, November 1983.

Vasectomy for contraception, by J. C. Rageth, et al. SCHWEIZERISCHE MEDIZINISCHE WOCHENSCHRIFT. 113(34):1191-1198, August 27, 1983.

Vasectomy/heart disease link questioned. RN. 46:19, September 1983.

Vasectomy in the framework of contraception, by H. Stamm, et al. GYNAEKOLOGISCHE RUNDSCHAU. 24(2):85-97, 1984.

Vasectomy reversal [letter]. MEDICAL JOURNAL OF AUSTRALIA. 140(11):681, May 26, 1984.

Vasectomy reversal. Review of 475 microsurgical vasovasostomies, by E. Owen, et al. MEDICAL JOURNAL OF AUSTRALIA. 140(7): 398-400, March 31, 1984.

Vasectomy safe and simple. POPULATION REPORTS. 11(5):D-61, November-December 1983.

Vasectomy study. AMERICAN FAMILY PHYSICIAN. 29:383, January 1984.

Vasectomy the unpopular choice, by J. C. Horn. PSYCHOLOGY TODAY. 18:17, June 1984.

Vasocclusion sterility induced by ethanol, prostaglandin or ascorbic acid in male rats, by M. R. Chinoy, et al. ENDOCRINOLOGIA EXPERIMENTALIS. 18(1):65-77, March 1984.

Vasovasostomy: current state of the art, by L. R. Cos, et al. UROLOGY. 22(6):567-575, December 1983.

Vasovasostomy in rabbits after vasectomy or vas occlusion by tantalum clip, by N. K. Lohiya, et al. JOURNAL OF REPRODUCTION AND FERTILITY. 71(1):243-248, May 1984.

Vasovasostomy: what to tell the patient who wants a vasectomy reversal, by D. T. Vetrosky, et al. PHYSICIAN ASSISTANT. 8(5): 130; 132; 134+, May 1984.

Vatican orders hospitals to stop tubal ligations. OUR SUNDAY VISITOR. 72:8, December 11, 1983.

Viability of alpha-momorcharin-treated mouse blastocysts in the pseudopregnant uterus, by P. P. Tam, et al. JOURNAL OF REPRODUCTION AND FERTILITY. 71(2):567-572, July 1984.

The viability of the trimester approach. UNIVERSITY OF BALTIMORE LAW REVIEW. 13:322-345, Winter 1984.

A Virginia college bans an antiabortion painting: a five-month-old fetus is part of the artwork, by R. Frame. CHRISTIANITY TODAY. 28:42+, March 2, 1984.

Visit to an abortion clinic, by D. C. Maguire. NATIONAL CATHOLIC REPORTER. 20:9+, October 5, 1984.

Visit to Nepal. 9. Family planning in Nepal, by T. Akita. KANGO-GAKU ZASSHI. 47(9):1066-1068, September 1983.

Vitamin B6 status and static muscle function. 2 case reports, by J. C. Wirth. ANNALS OF NUTRITION AND METABOLISM. 28(4): 240-244, 1984.

Voice of tradition: genetic counseling in a liberal Jewish context, by F. L. Weiss. RECONSTRUCTIONIST. 49:26-32, April-May 1984.

Voluntarily childless women: traditional or nontraditional, by S. Bram. SEX ROLES. 10:195-206, February 1984.

Voluntary childlessness and the women's liberation movement, by G. A. Shea. POPULATION AND ENVIRONMENT. 6(1):17, Spring 1983.

Voluntary female sterilization: psychosocial motivations and effects, by E. Garcia Hassey, et al. GINECOLOGIA Y OBSTETRICIA DE MEXICO. 50(307):301-305, November 1982.

Voluntary interruption of pregnancy in adolescents from 13 to 18 years of age. Clinical and sociologic analysis of 295 cases, by M. Vekemans, et al. JOURNAL DE GYNECOLOGIE, OBSTETRIQUE ET BIOLOGIE DE LA REPRODUCTION. 13(1):21-30, 1984.

Voluntary sterilization in North Tyneside, by K. Carnegie-Smith. JOURNAL OF BIOSOCIAL SCIENCE. 16(2):249-257, April 1984.

Voluntary termination of pregnancy, by T. B. Schneider. JOGN

NURSING. 13(Suppl 2):77s-84s, March-April 1984.

Walking away from Omelas, by R. Doerflinger. OUR SUNDAY VISITOR. 73:10, October 7, 1984.

The war between the women, by K. Luker. FAMILY PLANNING PERSPECTIVES. 16:105-110, May-June 1984.

A war on abortions, by S. Masterman. MACLEAN'S. 97:12, April 23, 1984.

Warner-Lambert tests condom ads on radio, by P. Sloan. ADVERTISING AGE. 55:29, July 2, 1984.

Wattleton blasts Reagan on harsh abortion stand. JET. 66:39, August 6, 1984.

What do American Catholics really thinks about abortion?, by R. Doerflinger. OUR SUNDAY VISITOR. 72:4+, January 22, 1984.

What do we know about occupational sterility, abortion, and fetal abnormalities?, by M. Kringelbach, et al. UGESKRIFT FOR LAEGER. 145(43):3348-3351, October 24, 1983.

What do we mean by prolife?, by R. R. Roach. REGISTER. 60:1+, January 29, 1984.

What future/national abortion campaign. SPARE RIB. 35:26, October 1983.

What information should women applying for abortion receive?, by G. N. Rivrud. TIDSSKRIFT FOR DEN NORSKE LAEGEFORENING. 103(31):2109, November 10, 1983.

What is a pregnancy? A question for programs of in vitro fertilization, by H. W. Jones, Jr., et al. FERTILITY AND STERILITY. 40(6):728-733, December 1983.

What is wrong with the [Manitoba] therapeutic abortion committee system? CANADIAN DIMENSION. 17:6, November 1983.

What limits for abortion?, by P. Davies. DAILY TELEGRAPH. January 21, 1984, p. 11.

What a pro-lifer can expect in medicine, interview with Kathy, Beck-Coon, by R. A. Hanley. CATHOLIC DIGEST. 48:109-112, February 1984.

What's new: can't make doctor pay for rearing unplanned child, by
    J. Ashman. AMERICAN BAR ASSOCIATION JOURNAL. 70:138-
    139, September 1984.

What's new: family planning clinics not required to squeal, by A.
    Ashman. AMERICAN BAR ASSOCIATION JOURNAL. 70:140,
    March 1984.

When dreams die, by C. G. Irvin. NURSING. 14(6):32, June 1984.

When family planning is necessary, by T. Harford. GUARDIAN.
    July 18, 1984, p. 23.

When the fever cools. FORBES. 134:10, July 16, 1984.

When is termination of pregnancy during the third trimester
    morally justifiable?, by F. A. Chervenak, et al. NEW ENGLAND
    JOURNAL OF MEDICINE. 310:501-504, February 23, 1983.

When religion mixes with politics. U. S. NEWS AND WORLD RE-
    PORT. 97:8, August 20, 1984.

Where the best contraceptive is plenty of money, by R. del Quiaro.
    GUARDIAN. August 7, 1984, p. 8.

Which parent owns the child? [father denied right to stop abortion],
    by B. Amiel. MACLEAN'S. 97:17, April 16, 1984.

Which pill?, by J. Drife. BRITISH MEDICAL JOURNAL [CLIN RES].
    287(6403):1397-1398, November 12, 1983.

Which pill? [letter]. BRITISH MEDICAL JOURNAL [CLIN RES]. 287
    (6405):1625-1626, November 26, 1983.

White House briefing eyes prolife alternatives, by J. Manney.
    REGISTER. 60:1+, May 20, 1984.

White House paper on population may be less than it seemed, by
    J. Frawley. REGISTER. 60:1+, July 8, 1984.

Who are the bigots? NATIONAL REVIEW. 36:17-18, October 19, 1984.

Who plans your family?, by N. Cavnar. NEW COVENANT. 13:13-16,
    February 1984.

Why Depo-Provera became respectable [injectable contraceptive].
    NEW SCIENTIST. 102:9, April 19, 1984.

Why do inadvertent pregnancies occur in oral contraceptive users? Effectiveness of oral contraceptive regimens and interfering factors, by I. S. Fraser, et al. CONTRACEPTION. 27(6):531-551, June 1983.

Why a lag in male-oriented birth control?, by J. E. Brody. NEW YORK TIMES. October 16, 1983, sec 4, p. 18.

Why men act like boys about birth control, by D. Weinberg. MADE-MOISELLE. 90:236+, August 1984.

Why should Catholic hospitals promote abortion, sterilization alternatives? HOSPITAL PROGRESS. 65:67-68, February 1984.

Will prenatal diagnosis with selective abortion affect society's attitude toward the handicapped?, by A. G. Motulsky, et al. PROGRESS IN CLINICAL AND BIOLOGICAL RESEARCH. 128:277-291, 1983.

With prolife activism increasing, abortion clinics feel the squeeze, by M. Meehan. REGISTER. 60:1+, April 8, 1984.

Woman's failure to use contraceptives not valid defense in paternity action. THE FAMILY LAW REPORTER. 10(41):1561-1562, August 21, 1984.

Woman's or baby's rights? Genes make the difference [letter], by P. M. Nicholls, et al. CANADIAN MEDICAL ASSOCIATION JOURNAL. 131(5):426; 428, September 1, 1984.

Women, abortion, and autonomy. CHRISTIANITY AND CRISIS. 44:51-52, March 5, 1984.

Women's reactions to late miscarriage, stillbirth and perinatal death, by A. Lovell. HEALTH VISITOR. 56(9):325-327, September 1983.

The wonderful world of contraception, by F. Pearce. NEW SCIEN-TIST. 103:8, August 30, 1984.

World Bank, U. S. at odds on population, by C. Holden. SCIENCE. 225:396, July 27, 1984.

The World Fertility Survey and Contraceptive Prevalence Surveys: a comparison of substantive results, by J. E. Anderson, et al. STUDIES IN FAMILY PLANNING. 15(1):1-13, Janaury-February 1984.

Wrongful birth and wrongful conception: the legal and moral issues, by P. Donovan. FAMILY PLANNING PERSPECTIVES. 16(2):64-69, March-April 1984.

Wrongful birth and wrongful life in Texas, by M. G. Young. TEXAS MEDICINE. 80(5):74-75, May 1984.

'Wrongful birth' lawsuits raise complex social issues, by C. Cancila. AMERICAN MEDICAL NEWS. 26(38):2; 24, October 14, 1983.

X-chromosome hyperploidy in couples with multiple spontaneous abortions, by W. Holzgreve, et al. OBSTETRICS AND GYNE-COLOGY. 63(2):237-240, February 1984.

Yet more pill problems, by A. Henry. SPARE RIB. 1(37):12, December 1983.

Young U. S. women delaying motherhood: 25 percent may remain childless. FAMILY PLANNING PERSPECTIVES. 15:224, September-October 1983.

Your birth control: is it still right for you?, by J. E. Rodgers. GLAMOUR. 82:162+, June 1984.

Youth and contraception education. A study among the pupils of post-compulsory schools in Bergen and its surroundings, by F. D. Alsaker, et al. TIDSSKRIFT FOR DEN NORSKE LAEGEFORE-NING. 104(17-18):1206-1209, June 20, 1984.

PERIODICAL LITERATURE

SUBJECT INDEX

ABORTION: GENERAL

ABO incompatibility and reproductive failure. I. Prenatal selection, by T. Schaap, et al. AMERICAN JOURNAL OF HUMAN GENETICS. 36(1):143-151, January 1984.

Abortion [letter]. MEDICAL JOURNAL OF AUSTRALIA. 140(11): 681, May 26, 1984.

Abortion [letter]. MEDICAL JOURNAL OF AUSTRALIA. 141(2): 131-132, July 21, 1984.

Abortion [leltter]. NEW ZEALAND MEDICAL JOURNAL. 96(744): 987, November 1983.

Abortion [letter], by C. A. Kaufmann. JOGN NURSING. 13(2):131-2, March-April 1984.

Abortion [letter], by K. McAll. MEDICAL JOURNAL OF AUSTRALIA. 141(1):65-66, July 7, 1984.

Abortion [letter], by J. E. McArthur. NEW ZEALAND MEDICAL JOURNAL. 97(756):341, May 23, 1984.

Abortion activists mark January anniversary, by S. Hyde. GAY COMMUNITY. 11(28):1, February 4, 1984.

Abortion advocates stress access, by J. Irvine. GAY COMMUNITY. 11(26):3, January 21, 1984.

Abortion and contraception: apples and oranges, by H. J. Byrne. AMERICA. 151:272-275, November 3, 1984.

Abortion and its cost. REGISTER. 60:2, January 29, 1984.

Abortion and the potentiality principle, by D. B. Annis. SOUTH-
ERN JOURNAL OF PHILOSOPHY. 22:155-164, Summer 1984.

Abortion and self-defense, by M. Davis. PHILOSOPHY AND
PUBLIC AFFAIRS. 13:175-207, Summer 1984.

Abortion at 10 to 12 weeks using a plastic syringe or electric
aspirator, by E. Borko, et al. JUGOSLAVENSKA GINE-
KOLOGIJA I OPSTETRICIJA. 23(1-2):17-20, January-April
1983.

Abortion by ordeal. FAMILY PLANNING PERSPECTIVES. 15:
258, November-December 1983.

Abortion cells model reaction to drugs. NEW SCIENTIST. 103:18,
August 30, 1984.

Abortion clause fight kills ERA. NATIONAL CATHOLIC RE-
PORTER. 20:4, November 25, 1983.

Abortion: a clear and constant teaching, by J. R. Quinn. ORIGINS.
14:413-414, December 6, 1984.

Abortion: the demographic argument [letter], by B. Frazer.
CANADIAN MEDICAL ASSOCIATION JOURNAL. 130(4):340,
February 15, 1984.

Abortion denied— outcome of mothers and babies, by C. Del
Campo. CANADIAN MEDICAL ASSOCIATION JOURNAL.
130(4):361-362; 366, February 15, 1984.

Abortion: it can't be left to personal choice, by J. T. Burtchaell.
ST. ANTHONY MESSENGER. 92:16-20, October 1984.

Abortion, limited medical resources, and the meaning of health
care, by K. Anderson, et al. JOURNAL OF AMERICAN
COLLEGE HEALTH. 32(5):231-232, April 1984.

Abortion 1982 [letter], by J. E. McArthur. NEW ZEALAND MEDI-
CAL JOURNAL 96(745):1032, December 14, 1983.

Abortion 1983: the controversy continues: II., by J. M. Healey. CONNECTICUT MEDICINE. 48(6):413, June 1984.

Abortion offices bombed, by U. Vaid. GAY COMMUNITY. 12(1):6, July 14, 1984.

Abortion on demand, by J. J. Rovinsky. MT. SINAI JOURNAL OF MEDICINE. 51(1):12-14, January-February 1984.

Abortion: predicting the complexity of the decision-making process, by M. L. Friedlander, et al. WOMEN AND HEALTH. 9:43-54, September 1984.

Abortion rights offensive launched, by N. Hoodbhoy. GUARDIAN. 36(15):4, January 18, 1984.

Abortion: who decides?, by F. Horan, et al. NURSING TIMES. 80(10):16-17, March 7-13, 1984.

Abortion— the woman in conflict, by L. Bier. FORTSCHRITTE DER MEDIZIN. 102(19):78-79, May 17, 1984.

About TOP risks and about mammography, by E. Trimmer. MIDWIFE, HEALTH VISITOR AND COMMUNITY NURSE. 20(9):322-330, September 1984.

Absorption, excretion and tissue residue in feedlot heifers injected with the synthetic prostaglandin, fenprostalene, by R. V. Tomlinson, et al. JOURNAL OF ANIMAL SCIENCE. 59(1): 164-169, July 1984.

The acceptable holocaust?, by V. P. Miceli. HOSPITAL PEER REVIEW. 85:56-62, November 1984.

Acute poisoning caused by inhalation of an aerosol spray used for waterproofing, by K. J. Christensen, et al. UGESKRIFT FOR LAEGER. 146(4):274-275, January 23, 1984.

Admission of abortion patients, by Enjoubault. INFIRMIERE FRANCAISE. (253):15-16, March 1984.

Advanced abdominal pregnancy with a live fetus, by C. Strehl, et al. GINEKOLKOLOGIA POLSKA. 55(2):147-150, February 1984.

Aggressive cervical cerclage [letter], by P. Bergsjo. AMERICAN JOURNAL OF OBSTETRICS AND GYNECOLOGY. 149(2):240-241, May 15, 1984.

Alive or dead? The eye of the beholder, by C. Del Campo, et al. CANADIAN JOURNAL OF SURGERY. 26(5):394-5, September 1983.

Antiemetic efficacy of droperidol and metoclopramide, by S. E. Cohen, et al. ANESTHESIOLOGY. 60(1):67-69, January 1984.

Anti-Ro antibodies and abortions in women with SLE [letter], by R. G. Hull, et al. LANCET. 2(8359):1138, November 12, 1983.

Apropos of a case for deductions and conclusions in gynecologic practice, by Kh. Durveniashki. AKUSHERSTVO I GINE-KOLOGIIA. 23(3):270-271, 1984.

An assessment of pre-operative microbial screening on the prevention of post-abortion pelvic inflammatory disease, by A. M. Mills. BRITISH JOURNAL OF OBSTETRICS AND GYNAE-COLOGY. 91(2):182-186, February 1984.

Background factors of defective contraception in abortion-seeking patients, by A. Lalos, et al. LAKARTIDNINGEN. 80(26-27):2646-2648, June 29, 1983.

Bankrolling the pro-choice machine, by M. Meehan. REGISTER. 60:1+, January 29, 1984.

Behind the lines, by D. Browning. TEXAS MEDICINE. 12:5+, September 1984.

Bernardin: abortion is a public issue. REGISTER. 60:2, October 14, 1984.

Bernardin on prolife future, by M. Meehan. REGISTER. 59:1+, December 4, 1983.

Better advice is needed both before and after abortion, by U. Claesson, et al. LARKARTIDNINGEN. 81(4):220-222, January 25, 1984.

The CMA abortion survey [letter]. CANADIAN MEDICAL ASSOCIATION JOURNAL. 129(12):1259-1260, December 15, 1983.

Case of successful treatment of a patient with an extremely severe form of gynecologic tetanus, by V. L. Rabinovich, et al. ANESTEZIOLOGIIA I REANIMATOLOGIIA. (6):58-59, November-December 1983.

Cause-effect relation between abortion and herpes infection, by N. D. Kolomiets, et al. AKUSHERSTVO I GINEKOLOGIIA. (3):62-64, March 1984.

Cervical dilatation using PGF2 alpha gel before voluntary interruption of pregnancy during the first trimester, by B. Maria, et al. JOURNAL DE GYNECOLOGIE, OBSTETRIQUE ET BIOLOGIE DE LA REPRODUCTION. 12(7):789-794, 1983.

Cervical dilatation with 16,16-dimethyl-trans-delta 2-PGE1 methyl ester (Cervagem) prior to vacuum aspiration. A double-blind, placebo-controlled randomized study, by N. J. Christensen, et al. CONTRACEPTION. 29(5):457-464, May 1984.

Chaff from the Charter's threshing floor, by M. Shumiatcher. MANITOBA LAW JOURNAL. 13:435-443, 1983.

Changes in lipid peroxidation indices and their correction in women before artifical interruption of pregnancy, by G. N. Kryzhanovskii, et al. AKUSHERSTVO I GINEKOLOGIIA. (3):34-35, March 1984.

Characteristics of the course and management of pregnancy and labor in women at risk for abortion, by L. N. Chernomaz, et al. AKUSHERSTVO I GINEKOLOGIIA. (12):34-35, December 1983.

Choice of termination of pregnancy. The significance of demographic and social factors, by N. K. Rasmussen, et al. UGESKRIFT FOR LAEGER. 145(48):3758-3764, November 28, 1983.

Chromosomal aberrations and chromosomal polymorphism in families with reproductive failure, by G. Vulkova. FOLIA MEDICA. 25(3):11-18, 1983.

Chronic toxoplasmosis in pregnant women— an epidemiological and social problem, by C. Jezyna, et al. ZENTRALBLATT FUR BAKTERIOLOGIE, MIKROBIOLOGIE UND HYGIENE. 177(1-2):96-102, January 1983.

Clinical evaluation of uterine hemorrhage in early pregnancy, by J. Krzysiek. GINEKOLOGIA POLSKA. 55(2):109-114, February 1984.

Clinical use of RU 486: control of the menstrual cycle and effect on the hypophyseal-adrena axis, by R. C. Gaillard, et al. ANNALES D'ENDOCRINOLOGIE. 44(5):345-346, 1983.

Clinico-experimental evaluation on the use of sulprostone, new PGE2 derivative. I. Interruption of pregnancy in the first trimester, by I. Stoppelli, et al. MINERVA GINECOLOGIA. 35(12):819-823, December 1983.

— . II. Interruption of pregnancy in the second trimester, by I. Stoppelli, et al. MINVERVA GINECOLOGIA. 35(12):825-828, December 1983.

— . III. Its use in some aspects of obstetric pathology, by I. Stoppelli, et al. MINERVA GINECOLOGIA. 35(12):829-831, December 1983.

Clinico-pathologic study on the action of yuanhuadine in mid-trimester abortion, by Q. W. Wang. CHUNG HUA FU CHAN KO TSA CHIH. 18(3):154-156, July 1983.

Clostridium welchii infection after amniocentesis, by R. E. Fray, et al. BRITISH MEDICAL JOURNAL [CLIN RES]. 288(6421):901-902, March 24, 1984.

Comparative study of various intracervically administered PG gel preparations for termination of first trimester pregnancies, by W. Rath, et al. CONTRACEPTION. 28(3):209-222, September 1983.

Comparison of rigid and flexible cannulae for early abortion without cervical dilatation, World Health Organization Task Force on Sequelae of Abortion. STUDIES IN FAMILY PLANNING. 15(2):79-83, March-April 1984.

Compensation for damages due to failure to interrupt pregnancy. MMW. 126(6):128-131, February 10, 1984.

Consequences of chorionic biopsy [letter]. NEW ENGLAND JOURNAL OF MEDICINE. 310(17):1121, April 26, 1984.

Considerations on the possible immune nature of abortions, by E. Laureti. MINERVA GINECOLOGIA. 36(1-2):15-16, January-February 1984.

Continued pregnancy after failed first-trimester abortion, by W. L. Fielding, et al. OBSTETRICS AND GYNECOLOGY. 63(3): 421-424, March 1984.

The contraceptive habits of women applying for termination of pregnancy, by K. Sidenius, et al. UGESKRIFT FOR LAEGER. 145(48):3721-3724, November 28, 1983.

Correlation between emotional reaction to loss of an unborn child and lymphocyte response to mitogenic stimulation in women, by S. Naor, et al. ISRAEL JOURNAL OF PSYCHIATRY AND RELATED SCIENCES. 20(3):231-239, 1983.

Correlation of human chorionic gonadotropin secretion in early pregnancy failure with size of gestational sac and placental histology, by P. Jouppila, et al. OBSTETRICS AND GYNECOLOGY. 63(4):537-542, April 1984.

Damages and the 'unwanted child'. BRITISH MEDICAL JOURNAL [CLIN RES]. 288(6412):244-245, January 21, 1984.

Day-case anaesthesia for termination of pregnancy. Evaluation of a total intravenous anaesthetic technique, by T. W. Ogg, et al. ANAESTHESIA. 38(11):1042-1046, November 1983.

Demands made on general practice by women before and after an abortion, by D. Berkeley, et al. JOURNAL OF THE ROYAL COLLEGE OF GENERAL PRACTITIONERS. 34(263):310-315, June 1984.

Detection of subclinical abortion by assay of pregnancy specific beta 1 glycoprotein, by A. G. Ahmed, et al. BRITISH MEDICAL JOURNAL [CLIN RES]. 288(6411):113, January 14, 1984.

Development in the number of legal terminations of pregnancy, by L. B. Knudsen. UGESKRIFT FOR LAEGER. 145(48):3753-3758, November 18, 1983.

The development of obstetrics and gynecology: dramatically decreased maternal mortality. Far-seeing points of view in the question of abortion, by K. Hagenfeldt. LAKARTIDNINGEN. 80(45):4299-4302, November 9, 1983.

Diagnostic value of plasma progesterone in nonendocrine incipient abortions in the first trimester, by E. Rachev. AKUSHERSTVO I GINEKOLOGIIA. 22(4):270-273, 1983.

Does the aborted baby feel pain?, by P. Kaler. LIGUORIAN. 72:18-22, November 1984.

Does a fetus feel pain?. SCIENCE. 5:8+, May 1984.

Drainage of postabortion hematometra by Foley catheter, by M. Borten, et al. AMERICAN JOURNAL OF OBSTETRICS AND GYNECOLOGY. 149(8):908-909, August 15, 1984.

The effect of partusisten on uterine motility stimulated by blood serum from pregnant women with certain pathological manifestations, by J. Lukanov, et al. FOLIA MEDICA. 25(3):25-29, 1983.

Effects of abortion on subsequent pregnancies, by B. Adelusi. AFRICAN JOURNAL OF MEDICINE AND MEDICAL SCIENCES. 12(2):65-69, June 1983.

The effects of an antiprogesterone steroid in women: interruption of the menstrual cycle and of early pregnancy, by W. Herrmann, et al. COMPTES RENDUS DES SEANCES DE L'ACADEMIE DES SCIENCE [III]. 296(13):591, 1983.

The effects of prostaglandins in colpocytology, by J. Kobilkova, et al. CESKOSLOVENSKA GYNEKOLOGIE. 49(1):14-17, February 1984.

Efficacy and safety of low-dose 15-methyl prostaglandin F2 alpha for cervical ripening in the first trimester of pregnancy, by F. Arias. AMERICAN JOURNAL OF OBSTETRICS AND GYNECOLOGY. 149(1):100-101, May 1, 1984.

Eleven years later, the struggle still goes on, by M. Meehan. REGISTER. 60:1+, January 22, 1984.

End runs around choice, by H. Lessinger. GUARDIAN. 36(22):2, March 7, 1984.

Endocrine forms of infertility as a risk factor for the failure to carry a subsequent pregnancy to term, by D. V. Vasadze, et al. AKUSHERSTVO I GINEKOLOGIIA. (2):17-21, February 1984.

Endocrinologic events in early pregnancy failure, by M. O. Aspillaga, et al. AMERICAN JOURNAL OF OBSTETRICS AND GYNECOLOGY. 147(8):903-908, December 15, 1983.

Estimation of blood loss in second-trimester dilatation and extraction, by G. Woodward. OBSTETRICS AND GYNECOLOGY. 63(2):230-232, February 1984.

Etiological factors in sterility and infertility as risk factors in future pregnancies, by D. Avramovic, et al. JUGOSLAVENSKA GINEKOLOGIJA I OPSTETRICIJA. 23(3-4):68-71, May-August 1983.

Experience with a specialized office (consultation) for abortion, by N. K. Mironycheva, et al. AKUSHERSTVO I GINEKOLOGIIA. (1):64-66, January 1984.

Factors responsible for abortion, by Y Shimono, et al. KANGO GIJUTSU. 30(3):370-373, February 1984.

Familial case of a balanced chromosomal translocation as a cause of reproductive failure, by V. Georgieva, et al. AKUSHERSTVO I GINEKOLOGIIA. 22(5):409-414, 1983.

Fate of subsequent pregnancies in relation to the outcome of previous pregnancies, by F. A. Szczotka, et al. PROBLEMY MEDYCYNY WIEKU ROZWOJOWEGO. 8:238-245, 1979.

Fertilization and early pregnancy loss in healthy women attempting conception, by Y. C. Smart, et al. CLINICAL REPRODUCTION AND FERTILITY. 1(3):177-184, September 1982.

First experience with extra-amniotic intrauterine administration of prostaglandin F2 alpha, by L. Rotta. CESKOSLOVENSKA GYNEKOLOGIE. 48(9):643-647, November 1983.

A Gemeprost vaginal suppository for cervical priming prior to termination of first trimester pregnancy, by P. Kajanoja, et al. CONTRACEPTION. 29(3):251-260, March 1984.

Genetics, amniocentesis, and abortion, by K. Hirschhorn. MT. SINAI JOURNAL OF MEDICINE. 51(1):15-17, January-February 1984.

Genetics and morality, by M. H. Shapiro. CENTER MAGAZINE. 16:9-15, July-August 1983.

Having a life versus being alive, by T. Kushner. JOURNAL OF MEDICAL ETHICS. 10(1):5-8, March 1984.

Hedonism returns, by S. Weatherbe. ALBERTA REPORT. 11:33, July 9, 1984.

Heterotopic tissue in the uterus, by W. Kanski, et al. PATOLOGIA POLSKA. 34(2):195-203, April-June 1983.

The historical dimensions of infanticide and abortion: the experience of classical Greece, by R. H. Feen. LINACRE QUARTERLY. 51:248-254, August 1984.

Human chorionic gonadotropin levels in complete and partial

hydatidiform moles and in nonmolar abortuses, by E. B. Smith, et al. AMERICAN JOURNAL OF OBSTETRICS AND GYNECOLOGY. 149(2):129-132, May 15, 1984.

Human lives, human rights, by J. J. O'Connor. ORIGINS. 14:291-301, October 25, 1984.

Ideology and opposition to abortion: trends in public opinion, 1972-1980, by C. H. Deitch. ALTERNATIVE LIFESTYLES. 6(1):6-26, Fall 1983.

If men got pregnant, abortion-sacrament, by E. Lubetsky. BROOMSTICK. 6(4):29, July 1984.

Immediate postabortion insertion of an IUD, by H. Lehfeldt. EUROPEAN JOURNAL OF OBSTETRICS, GYNECOLOGY AND REPRODUCTIVE BIOLOGY. 17(2-3):141-147, May 1984.

Incomplete pregnancy, by N. M. Pobedinskii, et al. AKUSHER-STVO I GINEKOLOGIIA. (12):22-25, December 1983.

Increased risk of abortion after genetic amniocentesis in twin pregnancies, by C. Palle, et al. PRENATAL DIAGNOSIS. 3(2):83-89, April-June 1983.

Inevitable abortion, by D. Rutledge. NURSING MIRROR. 158(6): Midwifery Forum: v, viii, February 8, 1984.

Inhibition of 3-beta-hydroxy steroid dehydrogenase activity in first trimester human pregnancy with trilostane and WIN 32729, by Z. M. van der Spuy, et al. CLINICAL ENDOCRINOLOGY. 19(4):521-531, October 1983.

Insertion of the Multiload Cu 250 IUD immediately after abortion or labor, by L. Morup, et al. UGESKRIFT FOR LAEGER. 146(14):1046-1048, April 2, 1984.

Interruption of early pregnancy in the monkey with mestranol and 5-oxa-17-phenyl-18,19,20-trinor prostaglandin F1 alpha methyl ester, by J. W. Wilks. BIOLOGY OF REPRODUCTION. 30(4):886-893, May 1984.

InterVarsity withdraws a book opposed by prolifers, by R. Frame.

CHRISTIANITY TODAY. 28:63+, September 21, 1984.

Intramuscular administration of 15(S) methyl prostaglandins F2 alpha for midtrimester abortion, by G. Sakunthala, et al. ASIA-OCEANIA JOURNAL OF OBSTETRICS AND GYNAECOLOGY. 10(2):191-195, June 1984.

Intrauterine incarcerated bowel following uterine perforation during an abortion: a case report, by P. S. Dunner, et al. AMERICAN JOURNAL OF OBSTETRICS AND GYNECOLOGY. 147(8):969-970, December 15, 1983.

Intubation, aspiration prophylaxis in midtrimester abortions? [letter], by D. J. Dehring, et al. ANESTHESIOLOGY. 61(2):223-225, August 1984.

Is wide availability of abortion essential to national population growth control programs? Experiences of 116 countries, by S. D. Mumford, et al. AMERICAN JOURNAL OF OBSTETRICS AND GYNECOLOGY. 149(6):639-645, July 15, 1984.

It takes death, by M. O'Brien. SPARE RIB. (141):9, April 1984.

It's time to move on abortion. REGISTER. 60:2, November 11, 1984.

Jail term over, no regrets, by D. Goldkamp. REGISTER. 60:7, February 5, 1984.

The kindest month, by M. Richards. CLERGY REVIEW. 68:382, November 1983.

Krol defends single issue of abortion as a top priority, by M. Meehan. REGISTER. 60:1+, November 25, 1984.

Late abortions [letter], by C. Woodroffe, et al. LANCET. 1(8374): 454, February 25, 1984.

Late abortions: there is madness in our methods. PRACTITIONER. 228(1389):247; 249, March 1984.

Light microscopy and electron microscopy observation on the

placenta and viscera of fetus in mid-stage abortion induced by Radix euphorbiae Kansui, by T. W. Yu. CHUNG HSI I CHIEH HO TSA CHIH. 4(4):201-202, April 1984.

Listeriosis in mother and fetus during the first trimester of pregnancy. Case report, by R. Pezeshkian, et al. BRITISH JOURNAL OF OBSTETRICS AND GYNAECOLOGY. 91(1):85-86, January 1984.

Locus of control and decision to abort, by P. N. Dixon, et al. PSYCHOLOGICAL REPORTS. 54(2):547-553, April 1984.

The lupus-anticoagulant: clinical and obstetric implications, by W. F. Lubbe, et al. NEW ZEALAND MEDICAL JOURNAL. 97(758):398-402, June 27, 1984.

Lupus nephropathy and pregnancy. A study of 26 pregnancies in patients with systemic lupus erythematosus and nephritis, by E. Imbasciati, et al. NEPHRON. 36(1):46-51, 1984.

Maguire urges pluralism, jailed prolifer heartsick, by M. Meehan. REGISTER. 60:1+, September 30, 1984.

The Maguires bring abortion issue to a turbulent boil, by M. Meehan. REGISTER. 60:1+, May 27, 1984.

Matters of conscience: all in the line of duty?, by M. Kenny. NURSING MIRROR. 158(20):22-23, May 16, 1984.

Medical experts affirm that life begins at conception. OUR SUNDAY VISITOR. 73:8, November 4, 1984.

Menstrual disorder after medical termination of pregnancy, by J. Mitra, et al. JOURNAL OF THE INDIAN MEDICAL ASSOCIATION. 82(1):4-6, January 1984.

Metabolic pathways of the contragestational agent, 3-(2-ethylphenyl)-5-(3-methoxyphenyl)-1H-1,2,4-triazol (DL 111-IT), in the rat, by A. Assandri, et al. XENOBIOTICA. 14(6):429-443, June 1984.

Methods for the study of the experimental interruption of pregnancy by ornithine decarboxylase inhibitors: effects of DL-alpha-difluoromethylornithine, by J. R. Fozard, et al. METHODS IN ENZYMOLOGY. 94:213-216, 1983.

Methods of terminating pregnancy and acute complications, by L. Heisterberg. UGESKRIFT FOR LAEGER. 145(48):3711-3715, November 28, 1983.

Methods to determine success of attempts to terminate early gestation pregnancies with prostaglandin vaginal suppositories, by P. F. Brenner, et al. CONTRACEPTION. 28(2):111-124, August 1983.

Midtrimester abortion: techniques and complications, by J. J. LaFerla. CLINICAL PERINATOLOGY. 10(2):305-320, June 1983.

Mini-abortion, the determination of its effectiveness and the present method of performing it at the Institute for Maternal and Child Care, by F. Havranek, et al. CESKOSLOVENSKA GYNEKOLOGIE. 49(1):23-26, February 1984.

Mini-abortion— 3 years' experience in the district of Mlada Boleslav, by V. Divecky, et al. CESKOSLOVENSKA GYNEKOLOGIE. 48(5):362-363, June 1983.

Mixed feelings on abortion, by S. Egan. SPARE RIB. 1(40):21, March 1984.

More cautionary labeling appears on isotretinoin, by C. Marwick. JAMA. 251(24):3208-3209, June 22-29, 1984.

More conflict over abortion, by J. G. Deedy. TABLET. 238:810-811, August 25, 1984.

Negative psychological sequelae and psychiatric sequelae of abortion obtained in a hospital: possible application of an evaluation scale, by G. R. Brera, et al. MINERVA PSICHIATRICA. 24(1):19-24, January-March 1983.

New importance in the social aspects of the care of the pregnant woman, by Z. Stembera. CESKOSLOVENSKA GYNECOLOGIE. 48(9):633-637, November 1983.

New sure-death abortion method. REGISTER. 60:2, September 9, 1984.

Nitrous oxide and termination of pregnancy [letter], by M. Mikhael, et al. ANAESTHESIA. 38(11):1103-1104, November 1983.

No time limit on maintaining "dead" mother to save fetus?. MEDICAL WORLD NEWS. 24:20-21, May 9, 1983.

Observation: contraceptive method use following an abortion, by S. K. Henshaw. FAMILY PLANNING PERSPECTIVES. 16(2):75-77, March-April 1984.

Obstetric ultrasonography: recent observations in first trimester of pregnancy, by J. F. Pedersen, et al. EUROPEAN JOURNAL OF RADIOLOGY. 4(2):167-168, May 1984.

On this picket line, trouble, by V. Warner. REGISTER. 60:1+, May 13, 1984.

The other side of the question. . . the adverse affects of abortion, by J. Robinson. NURSING MIRROR. 158(20):20-21, May 16, 1984.

Outcome of delivery subsequent to vacuum-aspiration abortion in nulliparous women, by O. Meirik, et al. ACTA OBSTETRICIA ET GYNECOLOGICA SCANDINAVICA. 62(5):499-509, 1983.

A painful experience, by L. Hardie. NURSING TIMES. 80(18):64, May 2-8, 1984.

Parental occupation and cytogenetic studies in abortuses, by M. Hatch. PROGRESS IN CLINICAL AND BIOLOGICAL RESEARCH. 160:475-483, 1984.

Parental origin of autosomal trisomies, by T. Hassold, et al. ANNALS OF HUMAN GENETICS. 48(Pt 2):129-144, May 1984.

Pondering direct action: acting out of anger or love?, by P. Sheehan. OUR SUNDAY VISITOR. 73:3, May 13, 1984.

Possible herpesvirus role in abortion studied, by M. F. Goldsmith. JAMA. 251(23):3067-3068, June 15, 1984.

Post-abortion depression: study of cases and controls, by S. Arturo Roizblatt, et al. ACTAS LUSO-ESPANOLAS DE NEUROLOGIA Y PSIQUIATRIA. 11(5):391-394, September-October 1983.

Post-abortion reconcilation growing, by B. J. Hubbard. NATIONAL CATHOLIC REPORTER. 20:1+, October 19, 1984.

Preabortion cervical dilatation with a low-dose prostaglandin suppository. A comparison of two analogs, by N. H. Lauersen, et al. JOURNAL OF REPRODUCTIVE MEDICINE. 29(2):133-135, February 1984.

Pregnancy interruption in the GDR. KRANKENPFLEG JOURNAL. 21(10):10-11, October 1, 1983.

Pregnancy outcome in diabetics with other endocrine disorders [letter], by K. J. Cruickshanks, et al. LANCET. 1(8377):629-630, March 17, 1984.

Pregnancy-resolution decisions. What if abortions were banned?, by J. G. Murphy, et al. JOURNAL OF REPRODUCTIVE MEDICINE. 28(11):789-797, November 1983.

Pregnancy suppression by antibodies to gestation-specific riboflavin carrier protein. NUTRITION REVIEWS. 41:130-132, April 1983.

Preoperative cervical dilatation in abortion during the first trimester with sulprostone, by B. O. Schulz, et al. GEBURTSHILFE UND FRAUENHEILKUNDE. 44(3):185-187, March 1984.

Preoperative cervical dilatation with a single long-acting prostaglandin analog suppository. An alternative to traumatic mechanical dilatation before surgical evacuation, by D. R. Kent, et al. JOURNAL OF REPRODUCTIVE MEDICINE. 28(11):778-780, November 1983.

Prevention of uterine perforation during curettage abortion, by

D. A. Grimes, et al. JAMA. 251(16):2108-2111, April 27, 1984.

Prince Edward Island: the abortion battle goes on— and on, by K. Jones. ATLANTIC INSIGHT. 6:13, June 1984.

Prolife update in a year of small successes, by M. Meehan. REGISTER. 59:1+, December 11, 1983.

Prolifers hit Polish paper, by J. Higgins. REGISTER. 60:1+, February 26, 1984.

Prostaglandins in gynecology and obstetrics, by E. Bakali, et al. MAROC MEDICAL. 5(4):285-292, December 1983.

Psychiatric and ethical aspects of the termination of pregnancy, by B. Bron. FORTSCHRITTE DER NEUROLOGIE-PSYCHIATRIE. 51(10):342-354, October 1983.

Quinine toxicity in pregnancy, by M. E. Rivera-Alsina, et al. BOLETIN-ASOCIACION MEDICA DE PUERTO RICO. 76(3): 114-115, March 1984.

Rabbinic comment: abortion, by D. M. Feldman. MT. SINAI JOURNAL OF MEDICINE. 51(1):20-24, January-February 1984.

Randomized comparison of prostaglandin treatment in hospital or at home with vacuum aspiration for termination of early pregnancy, by A. S. Rosen, et al. CONTRACEPTION. 29(5): 423-435, May 1984.

Ray Flynn and lesbian/gay liberation. GAY COMMUNITY. 12(11):4, September 29, 1984.

The reality of abortion, by R. Diamond. NEW DIRECTIONS FOR WOMEN. 13:5, November-December 1984.

Recent Cases: Children, by A. Bainham. THE JOURNAL OF SOCIAL WELFARE LAW. September 1984, pp. 290-292.

Reducing misclassification errors through questionnaire design, by C. J. Hogue. PROGRESS IN CLINICAL AND BIOLOGICAL

RESEARCH. 160:81-97, 1984.

Repetitive requests for voluntary abortions, by B. Mattauer, et al. ANNALES MEDICO-PSYCHOLOGIQUES. 142(1):151-164, January 1984.

Reproductive endocrinology: new problems call for new solutions, by J. E. Tyson. DIAGNOSTIC MEDICINE. 7(4):24-31, April 1984.

Reproductive health update. HORIZONS. 2(3):18, June 1984.

Reproductive performance among DES exposed daughters compared with that of their mothers, by T. G. Kirkhope. OHIO STATE MEDICAL JOURNAL. 79(11):867-869, November 1983.

Reproductive risks for translocation carriers: cytogenetic study and analysis of pregnancy outcome in 58 familes, by G. Neri, et al. AMERICAN JOURNAL OF MEDICAL GENETICS. 16(4):535-561, December 1983.

Request for abortion after the 12th week, by C. W. Schmidt. ZEITSCHRIFT FUR AERZTLICHE FORTBILDUNG. 77(23): 975-977, 1983.

Response to termination of pregnancy for genetic reasons, by J. Lloyd, et al. ZEITSCHRIFT FUR KINDERCHIRURGIE. 38(Suppl 2):98-99, December 1983.

Retained fetal bones in chronic tubal pregnancy, by D. M. Avery, et al. AMERICAN JOURNAL OF OBSTETRICS AND GYNECOLOGY. 149(7):794-795, August 1, 1984.

A review of psychiatric aspects for termination of pregnancy, by H. V. Perea. CEYLON MEDICAL JOURNAL. 28(1):42-47, March 1983.

Right-to-life meeting: destroying stereotypes, by G. Palumbo. NATIONAL CATHOLIC REPORTER. 20:5, September 7, 1984.

Role of maternal prolactin in early pregnancy failure, by P. Jouppila, et al. OBSTETRICS AND GYNECOLOGY. 64(3):373-375, September 1984.

Ruptured appendix after elective abortion. A case report, by S. Pine, et al. JOURNAL OF REPRODUCTIVE MEDICINE. 28(10):691-693, October 1983.

The safety of fetoscopy: (II). Effect on maternal plasma levels of 13,14-dihydro-15-oxo-prostaglandin F2 alpha, by K. H. Nicolaides, et al. PRENATAL DIAGNOSIS. 3(2):97-100, April-June 1983.

The sanctity of life. RECONSTRUCTIONIST. 49:5, February 1984.

Seamless garment issue tied up with controversy. OUR SUNDAY VISITOR. 72:3, April 15, 1984; 3, April 22, 1984.

Second-trimester abortion by extra-amniotic instillation of Rivanol combined with intravenous administration of oxytocin or prostaglandin F2 alpha, by I. Klinte, et al. ACTA OBSTETRICIA ET GYNECOLOGICA SCANDINAVICA. 62(4):303-306, 1983.

Second-trimester amniocentesis and termination of pregnancy, by A. C. Turnbull, et al. BRITISH MEDICAL BULLETIN. 39(4):315-321, October 1983.

Seeking the middle ground, prolife quarterly struggles hard to survive, by G. Erlandson. REGISTER. 59:1+, December 18, 1983.

Selective reduction in cases of multiple pregnancy, by R. Jeny, et al. ANNALES DE RADIOLOGIE. 26(5):446, June-July 1983.

Self-induced: a Red Deer woman stabs her own foetus, by R. Lenz, et al. ALBERTA REPORT. 11:22, August 6, 1984.

Septicemias of obstetrico-gynecological origin: clinical and therapeutical aspects, by H. de la Cuadra, et al. REVISTA MEDICA DE CHILE. 112(1):36-42, January 1984.

Serial multiple laminaria and adjunctive urea in late outpatient

dilatation and evacuation abortion, by W. M. Hern. OBSTET-
RICS AND GYNECOLOGY. 63(4):543-549, April 1984.

Serologic research of toxoplasmosis, cytomegalovirus infection
and listeriosis in women with and without previous abortion,
by V. Amato Neto, et al. REVISTA DO INSTITUTO DE
MEDICINA TROPICAL DE SAO PAULO. 25(2):62-66, March-
April 1983.

Serum complement levels and perinatal outcome in pregnancies
complicated by systemic lupus erythematosus, by L. D. Devoe,
et al. OBSTETRICS AND GYNECOLOGY. 63(6):796-800, June
1984.

Serum prolactin levels following abortion in normal and molar
pregnancy, by O. Shinkawa, et al. NIPPON SANKA FUJINKA
GAKKAI ZASSHI. 36(6):911-916, June 1984.

Shake hands with a prolife peacemaker; interview, by J. Loesch.
U. S. CATHOLIC. 49:22-28, May 1984.

Showdown on abortion: polarized views, by J. Bell. NEW
DIRECTIONS FOR WOMEN. 13(5):15, September 1984.

The significance of pregnancy among adolescents choosing abor-
tion as compared to those continuing pregnancy, by M.
Morin-Gonthier, et al. JOURNAL OF REPRODUCTIVE
MEDICINE. 29(4):255-259, April 1984.

Statement on pluralism and abortion. ORIGINS. 14:414, December 6, 1984.

Sterilization, abortion a way of life, by T. Ackerman. REGISTER.
60:10, August 12, 1984.

Steroidogenesis inhibitors. 1. Adrenal inhibitory and interceptive activity of trilostane and related compounds, by R. G.
Christiansen, et al. JOURNAL OF MEDICINAL CHEMISTRY.
27(7):928-931, July 1984.

Study of the endometrium following voluntary interruption of
pregnancy in relation to the contraceptive method used

following abortion, by J. B. Sindayirwanya, et al. JOURNAL DE GYNECOLOGIE, OBSTETRIQUE ET BIOLOGIE DE LA REPRODUCTION. 12(4):351-362, 1983.

A study of the serum factor X in women with pathological pregnancy and during delivery, by J. B. Lukanov. FOLIA MEDICA. 25(3):19-24, 1983.

Study of plasma prolactin and immunoreactive-prolactin released from decidua in normal pregnancy and abortion, by T. Kubota, et al. ASIA-OCEANIA JOURNAL OF OBSTETRICS AND GYNAECOLOGY. 10(2):225-234, June 1984.

Suction curettage, by E. C. English. JOURNAL OF FAMILY PRACTICE. 17(6):1065-1070, December 1983.

Sulprostone for preoperative cervical dilatation in primigravidae scheduled for late first trimester termination of pregnancy, by F. Jerve, et al. ARCHIVES OF GYNECOLOGY. 233(3):199-203, 1983.

Surgery and circulating antiprothrombinase-type anticoagulant in the Soulier-Boffa syndrome, by C. Martin, et al. ANNALES FRANCAISES D ANESTHESIE ET DE REANIMATION. 3(4):306-308, 1984.

Surgery in utero on a two-headed monster. The value of echography, by H. Serment, et al. JOURNAL DE GYNECOLOGIE, OBSTETRIQUE ET BIOLOGIE DE LA REPRODUCTION. 13(2): 197-203, 1984.

Synthesis and pregnancy terminating activity of 2-arylimidazo [2,1-a]isoquinolines and isoindoles, by E. Toja, et al. ARZNEIMITTEL-FORSCHUNG. 33(9):1222-1225, 1983.

Synthesis of dl-17-phenyl-18,19,20-trinorprostaglandin F2 alpha methyl ester and its 15-epimer, by Y. L. Wu, et al. YAO HSUEH HSUEH PAO. 18(5):351-355, May 1983.

T-cell subset distribution in chronically aborting women [letter], by A. Bertotto, et al. LANCET. 1(8368):108, January 14, 1984.

Taking our health into our hands, by K. Hodge. GUARDIAN. 36(24):1, Spring 1984.

The ten most common questions concerning abortion, by W. Odell, et al. OUR SUNDAY VISITOR. 72:3+, January 22, 1984.

Termination of early pregnancy by ONO-802 suppositories, by C. F. Zhang. CHUNG HUA FU CHAN KO TSA CHIH. 18(3):150-153, July 1983.

Termination of midtrimester pregnancies with extraovular 0.1% ethacridine lactate. Accurate method for estimation of blood loss. Role of spartein sulfate, by R. M. Laul, et al. ASIA-OCEANIA JOURNAL OF OBSTETRICS AND GYNAECOLOGY. 10(2):185-189, June 1984.

Termination of pregnancy by general practitioners, by H. J. Rieger. DEUTSCHE MEDIZINISCHE WOCHENSCHRIFT. 109(33):1259-1261, August 17, 1984.

Termination of pregnancy during the third trimester [letter]. NEW ENGLAND JOURNAL OF MEDICINE. 311(4):264-265, July 26, 1984.

Termination of very early pregnancy by RU 486 an antiprogestational compound, by L. Kovacs, et al. CONTRACEPTION. 29(5):399-410, May 1984.

Thomasma reassessing his abortion stand?, by M. Meehan. REGISTER. 60:1+, October 7, 1984.

Three years of experience after post-abortal insertion of Nova-T and Copper-T-200, by N. C. Nielsen, et al. ACTA OBSTETRICIA ET GYNECOLOGICA SCANDINAVICA. 63(3):261-264, 1984.

Time bomb or myth: the population problem, by R. S. McNamara. FOREIGN AFFAIRS. 62:1107-1131, Summer 1984.

Toxic abortion agent making a comeback. RN. 46:19, November 1983.

Triploidy, partial mole and dispermy. An investigation of 12 cases, by S. E. Procter, et al. CLINICAL GENETICS. 26(1):46-51, July 1984.

Use of a urinary balloon catheter in abortions after the 20th week of gestation and in premature labor, by K. Iordanov, et al. AKUSHERSTVO I GINEKOLOGIIA. 22(2):97-99, 1983.

Uterine embolization in a patient with postabortal hemmorr-hage, by F. P. Haseltine, et al. OBSTETRICS AND GYNE-COLOGY. 63(3 Suppl):78S-80S, March 1984.

Value of cervical encirclage in the treatment of midtrimester abortion, by S. Nnatu. INTERNATIONAL JOURNAL OF GYNAECOLOGY AND OBSTETRICS. 21(6):469-472, December 1983.

The viability of the trimester approach. UNIVERSITY OF BALTI-MORE LAW REVIEW. 13:322-345, Winter 1984.

What do we know about occupational sterility, abortion, and fetal abnormalities:, by M. Kringelbach, et al. UGESKRIFT FOR LAEGER. 145(43):3348-3351, October 24, 1983.

What do we mean by prolife?, by R. R. Roach. REGISTER. 60:1+, January 29, 1984.

What information should women applying for abortion receive?, by G. N. Rivrud. TIDSSKRIFT FOR DEN NORSKE LAEGEFORENING. 103(31):2109, November 10, 1983.

What is pregnancy? A question for programs of in vitro fertiliza-tion, by H. W. Jones, Jr., et al. FERTILITY AND STERILITY. 40(6):728-733, December 1983.

What a pro-lifer can expect in medicine, interview with Kathy Beck-Coon, by R. A. Hanley. CATHOLIC DIGEST. 48:109-112, June-July 1983.

With prolife activism increasing, abortion clinics feel the squeeze, by M. Meehan. REGISTER. 60:1+, April 8, 1984.

Woman's or baby's rights? Genes make the difference [letter],

by P. M. Nicholls, et al. CANADIAN MEDICAL ASSOCIA-
TION JOURNAL. 131(5):426; 428, September 1, 1984.

When dreams die, by C. G. Irvin. NURSING. 14(6):96, June
1984.

Voluntary termination of pregnancy, by T. B. Schneider.
JOGN NURSING. 13(2 Suppl):77S-84S, March-April 1984.

AFRICA
Attitudes toward abortion and contraception among Nigerian
secondary school girls, by A. U. Oronsaye, et al. INTER-
NATIONAL JOURNAL OF GYNAECOLOGY AND OBSTET-
RICS. 21(5):423-426, October 1983.

AUSTRALIA
Attitude to abortion, attitude to life and conservation in
Australia, by J. J. Ray. SOCIOLOGY AND SOCIAL RE-
SEARCH. 68:236-246, January 1984.

The public funding of abortion services: comparative developments in the United States and Australia, by K. A. Petersen. INTERNATIONAL AND COMPARATIVE LAW
QUARTERLY. 33:158-180, January 1984.

BANGLADESH
Risks and costs of illegally induced abortion in Bangladesh,
by A. R. Khan, et al. JOURNAL OF BIOSOCIAL SCIENCE.
16:89-98, January 1984.

CANADA
Battling 'foeticide' [Alberta] therapeutic committees are
under pressure, by S. McCarthy. ALBERTA REPORT.
11:45, May 28, 1984.

Campaign against reproductive choice in Manitoba, by P.
Mitchell. CANADIAN DIMENSION. 17:4, November 1983.

Choice: a divisive issue [Manitoba], by P. Mitchell. CANA-
DIAN DIMENSION. 17:5-6, November 1983.

Dismembering the United way: Edmonton's BCs battle as an

CANADA

abortion referral agency joins, by T. Philip, et al. AL-
BERTA REPORT. 11:32; 35-36, July 9, 1984.

Dis-united: Catholics divorce the [Edmonton] charity federation, by G. Herchak. ALBERTA REPORT. 11:40, July
16, 1984.

Doctors in Canada hauled/antiabortion, by P. Habermann.
MILITANT. 48(2):20, January 27, 1984.

"The politics of abortion: trends in Canadian fertility policy",
by M. F. Bishop. ATLANTIS. 9:105-117, Fall 1983.

The politics of abortion: trends in Canadian fertility policy,
by L. D. Collins, et al. ATLANTIS. 7(2):2-20, 1982.

Reproductive choice [Manitoba]. CANADIAN DIMENSION.
17:3, November 1983.

A setback for Morgentaler, by R. Block. MACLEANS. 97:46,
July 30, 1984.

What is wrong with the [Manitoba] therapeutic abortion
committee system?. CANADIAN DIMENSION. 17:6,
November 1983.

Which parent owns the child? [father denied right to stop
abortion], by B. Amiel. MACLEANS. 97:17, April 16,
1984.

CHINA

Eugenic theory in contemporary mainland China: popularizing the knowledge of eugenics and advocating optimal
births vigorously, by S. Dongsheng. MANKIND QUARTER-
LY. 24:167-184, Winter 1983.

Statement and proposals of the regional Chinese Catholic
Bishops' Conference on the issue should abortion be
legalized?. OR. (30):11-12, July 23, 1984.

Sterilization, abortion a way of life, by T. Ackerman. REGIS-
TER. 60:10, August 12, 1984.

DENMARK
Postpartum and postabortion mental health in Denmark
[letter], by H. P. David, et al. FAMILY PLANNING
PERSPECTIVES. 15(4):156, July-August 1983.

DEVELOPING COUNTRIES
U. S. inflicts "morality" on a world fit to burst, by R. Righter.
SUNDAY TIMES. August 5, 1984, p. 11.

FINLAND
Parental occupational exposure and spontaneous abortions
in Finland, by M. L. Lindbohm, et al. AMERICAN JOUR-
NAL OF EPIDEMIOLOGY. 120(3):370-378, September
1984.

GREAT BRITAIN
Abortion in England, 1919-1939: Legal theory and Social
practice, by B. L. Brookes. DISSERTATION ABSTRACTS
INTERNATIONAL: A. 45(1), July 1984.

Abortion: quicker, therefore earlier [Britain]. ECONOMIST.
290:53-54, January 21, 1984.

The horrors of late abortion. TABLET. 238:99-100, February
4, 1984.

What limits for abortion?, by P. Davies. TELEGRAPH.
January 21, 1984, p. 11.

HUNGARY
Some epidemiological data on spontaneous abortion in
Hungary, 1971-80, by A. Czeizel, et al. JOURNAL OF
EPIDEMIOLOGY AND COMMUNITY HEALTH. 38(2):143-
148, June 1984.

INDIA
Abortion surveillance, 1979-1980, by P. R. Lang, et al. MMWR.
32(2):1SS-7SS, May 1983.

INDIA
Characteristics of first trimester abortion patients at an urban Indian clinic, by S. Bahl Dhall, et al. STUDIES IN FAMILY PLANNING. 15(2):93-97, March-April 1984.

IRELAND
Abortion referendum in Ireland, by J. Marcus. WORLD TODAY. 39:413-416, November 1983.

Ireland: bishops' pawns [constitutional amendment that would bar legalization of abortion]. ECONOMIST. 287: 44+, April 9, 1983.

Ireland outlaws abortion, by R. Boyd. SPARE RIB. 1(35):15, October 1983.

Ireland: rights for the unborn. ECONOMIST. 288:39-40, September 3, 1983.

Irish bamboozlement, by P. Kirby. COMMONWEAL. 111:26+, January 13, 1984.

The pro-life amendment to the constitution: one year later, by K. McNamara. OR. (43):11, October 22, 1984.

Seamus Bond to the rescue. ECONOMIST. 288:60-61, September 17-23, 1983.

MEXICO
Effects of synthetic steroid contraceptives on biliary lipid composition of normal Mexican women, by G. Etchegoyen, et al. CONTRACEPTION. 27(6):591-603, June 1983.

POLAND
Abortion and contraception in Poland, by M. Okólski. STUDIES IN FAMIY PLANNING. 14(11):263-274, November 1983.

PORTUGAL
Off the backstreets. ECONOMIST. 290:51, February 4, 1984.

ROMANIA
Dateline: Romania: a war on abortions, by S. Masterman.
MACLEANS. 97:12, April 23, 1984.

SINGAPORE
Psychosocial aspects of repeat abortions in Singapore— a
preliminary report, by W. F. Tsoi, et al. SINGAPORE
MEDICAL JOURNAL. 25(2):116-121, April 1984.

SOUTH AMERICA
Cytogenetic findings in 318 couples with repeated spontaneous abortion: a review of experience in British Columbia,
by J. T. Pantzar, et al. AMERICAN JOURNAL OF MEDI-
CAL GENETICS. 17(3):615-620, March 1984.

SOUTH KOREA
Abortion in South Korea, by P. Marx. HOSPITAL PEER
REVIEW. 85:46-51, October 1984.

SPAIN
Opinion poll: evaluation and analysis. What the Spanish
nursing profession thinks about abortion. REVISTA
DE ENFERMAGEN. 6(60):12-17; 19-21, July 1983.

Spanish abortionist gets 12 years. SPARE RIB. 1(37):9,
December 1983.

SWEDEN
Pregnancy outcome among women in a Swedish rubber plant,
by O. Axelson, et al. SCANDINAVIAN JOURNAL OF
WORK, ENVIRONMENT AND HEALTH. 9(Suppl 2):79-83,
1983.

Swedish abortion practice. One should talk about abortion.
The staff needs therapy, by I. Andersson. KRANKEN-
PFLEG JOURNAL. 21(10):6, October 1, 1983.

Swedish Midwifery Society's reply to SHSTF (Swedish
Association for Health Care and Nursing Employees).
JORDEMODERN. 97(5):151-154, May 1984.

UNITED STATES
Abortion and dialogue, by D. R. Carlin, Jr. AMERICA. 151:64, August 18-25, 1984.

The abortion decision for Minnesota minors: who decides?. WILLIAM MITCHELL LAW REVIEW. 9:194-215, 1983.

Abortion money pours into North Carolina to defeat Jesse Helms, by M. Meehan. REGISTER. 60:1+, August 19, 1984.

Abortion: the role of public officials; New York bishops' statement. ORIGINS. 13:759-760, April 26, 1984.

Abortion services in the United States, 1981 and 1982, by S. K. Henshaw, et al. FAMILY PLANNING PERSPECTIVES. 16(3):119-127, May-June 1984.

Abortion surveillance: preliminary analysis— United States, 1981. MMWR. 33(26):373-375, July 6, 1984.

The Americas: patterns are changing, by J. C. Abcede. WORLD HEALTH. June 1984, pp. 21-23.

Changes in rates of spontaneous fetal deaths reported in Upstate New York vital records by gestational age, 1968-78, by P. K. Cross. PUBLIC HEALTH REPORTS. 99:212-215, March-April 1984.

Colorado bishops endorse Amendment No. 3. ORIGINS. 14:223-224, September 20, 1984.

Constitutional law— fourteenth amendment— right to abortion— regulatory framework— standard of review— the United States Supreme Court has held that the state may not, in its regulation of abortion, deviate from accepted medical practice, and that all pre-viability abortion regulation shall be subject to strict scrutiny under the compelling state interest standard of substantive due process analysis— City of Akron v. Akron Center for Reproductive Health, Inc. DUQUESNE LAW REVIEW. 22:767-785, Spring 1984.

UNITED STATES
Constitutional law— New Jersey statute prohibiting Medicaid funding for abortions except where medically necessary to preserve the life of the mother violates the equal protection clause of the New Jersey Constitution— Right to Choose v. Byrne. TEMPLE LAW QUARTERLY. 56:983-1011, 1983.

Creating and controlling a medical market: abortion in Los Angeles after liberalization, by M. S. Goldstein. SOCIAL PROBLEMS. 31:514-529, June 1984.

A debate over sovereign rights [U. S. cuts off funds to family planning agencies that promote abortion, by L. Lopez. TIME. 124:34, August 20, 1984.

ERA and abortion; Pennsylvania court ruling. ORIGINS. 13:699-704, March 29, 1984.

Epizootics of ovine abortion due to Toxoplasma gondii in north central United States, by J. P. Dubey, et al. JOURNAL OF THE AMERICAN VETERINARY MEDICAL ASSOCIATION. 184(6):657-660, March 15, 1984.

How freedom of thought is smothered in America: a pluralistic society demands that Christian values be heard, by C. Horn. CHRISTIANITY TODAY. 28:12-17, April 6, 1984.

The impact of U. S. family planning programs on births, abortions and miscarriages, 1970-1979, by J. D. Forrest. SOCIAL SCIENCE AND MEDICINE. 18(6):461-465, 1984.

LAPAC announces deadly dozen, by M. Meehan. REGISTER. 60:1+, May 6, 1984.

New Jersey Court recognizes limited "wrongful life" action. THE FAMILY LAW REPORTER. 10(44):1603-1604, September 11, 1984.

Ovine abortion and neonatal death due to toxoplasmosis in Montana, by J. C. Rhyan, et al. JOURNAL OF THE AMERI-

UNITED STATES
ICAN VETERINARY MEDICAL ASSOCIATION. 184(6):
661-664, March 15, 1984.

Pennsylvania court uses ERA to strike down abortion limits,
by C. McDonnell. REGISTER. 60:1+, March 25, 1984.

Polybrominated biphenyls and fetal mortality in Michigan,
by C. G. Humble, et al. AMERICAN JOURNAL OF PUBLIC
HEALTH. 74(10):1130-1132, October 1984.

Population and U. S. policy. NATIONAL REVIEW. 36:13-14,
September 7, 1984.

Population: trading places [U. S. restrictions on family planning aid to discourage abortions], by R. Watson. NEWS-
WEEK. 104:50, August 20, 1984.

The public funding of abortion services: comparative developments in the United States and Australia, by K. A. Petersen. INTERNATIONAL AND COMPARATIVE LAW
QUARTERLY. 33:158-180, January 1984.

Report shows abortion rate declining slightly in U. S. OUR
SUNDAY VISITOR. 73:8, July 22, 1984.

Social justice perspective needed on abortion issue, by D. C.
Maguire. NATIONAL CATHOLIC REPORTER. 20:16,
August 17, 1984.

Social, spatial and political determinants of U. S. abortion
rates, by N. F. Henry, et al. SOCIAL SCIENCE AND
MEDICINE. 16(9):987-996, 1982.

Spontaneous abortions following Three Mile Island accident
[letter], by C. J. Johnson. AMERICAN JOURNAL OF
PUBLIC HEALTH. 74(5):520, May 1984.

Teenage abortion in the United States, by W. Cates, Jr., et al.
PUBLIC HEALTH REVIEWS. 11(4):291-310, October-
December 1983.

UNITED STATES
U. S. inflicts "morality" on a world fit to burst, by R. Righter. SUNDAY TIMES. August 5, 1984, p. 11.

World Bank, U. S. at odds on population, by C. Holden. SCIENCE. 225:396, July 27, 1984.

Wrongful birth and wrongful life in Texas, by M. G. Young. TEXAS MEDICINE. 80(5):74-75, May 1984.

ABORTION: ATTITUDES
Abortion: a pro-life view, by R. J. Adamek. USA TODAY. 112:98, May 1984.

Abortion: predicting the complexity of the decision-making process, by M. L. Friedlander, et al. WOMEN AND HEALTH. 9:43-54, September 1984.

Attitude to abortion, attitude to life and conservatism in Australia, by J. J. Ray. SOCIOLOGY AND SOCIAL RESEARCH. 68:236-246, January 1984.

Attitudes and behavioral intentions about abortion, by B. K. Singh, et al. POPULATION AND ENVIRONMENT: BEHAVIORAL SOCIAL ISSUES. 6(2):84-95, Summer 1983.

Attitudes to abortion, by J. Kemp. NURSING MIRROR. 158(17): 34-35, April 25, 1984.

Attitudes toward abortion among Catholic Mexican-American women: the effects of religiosity and education, by S. Rosenhouse-Persson, et al. DEMOGRAPHY. 20:87-98, February 1983.

Attitudes toward abortion as a means of sex selection, by R. N. Feil, et al. JOURNAL OF PSYCHOLOGY. 116:269-272, March 1984.

Attitudes toward abortion and contraception among Nigerian secondary school girls, by A. U. Oronsaye, et al. INTERNATIONAL JOURNAL OF GYNAECOLOGY AND OBSTETRICS. 21(5):423-426, October 1983.

Bernardin still tailoring his seamless garment ethic of life issues, by J. Bernardin. NATIONAL CATHOLIC REPORTER. 20:1, April 6, 1984.

Choice advocates, by C. Cracolice. NEW DIRECTIONS FOR WOMEN. 13:8, March-April 1984.

The classical roots of the personhood debate, by R. H. Feen. FAITH AND REASON. 9:120-127, Summer 1983.

A course on mothering and the right to abortion. WOMEN'S STUDIES QUARTERLY. 11:32-34, Winter 1983.

Determinants of attitudes toward abortion in the American electorate, by J. S. Legge, Jr. WESTERN POLITICAL QUARTERLY. 36:479-490, September 1983.

The ethics of choice— after my amniocentesis, Mike and I faced the toughest decision of our lives, by R. Rapp. MS. 12:97-100, April 1984.

Family and community factors associated with infant deaths that might be preventable, by E. M. Taylor, et al. BRITISH MEDICAL JOURNAL. 287:871-874, September 24, 1983.

Gender roles and premarital contraception, by P. L. MacCorquodal. JOURNAL OF MARRIAGE AND THE FAMILY. 46(1):57-63, February 1984.

Having a life versus being alive, by T. Kushner. JOURNAL OF MEDICAL ETHICS. 10(1):5-8, March 1984.

How can they sleep, by J. J. Timmerman. REFORMED JOURNAL. 34(2):2, February 1984.

Interview with Ellen Kruger, by E. Kruger. CANADIAN DIMENSION. 17:8-9, November 1983.

Interview with Muriel Smith, by M. Smith. CANADIAN DIMENSION. 17:7-8, November 1983.

Mercy or murder? Ethical dilemmas in newborn care, by M.

Klitsch. FAMILY PLANNING PERSPECTIVES. 15:143-145, May-June 1983.

Moral controversies and the policymaking process: Lowi's framework applied to the abortion issue, by R. Tatalovich, et al. POLICY STUDIES REVIEW. 3(2):207-222, February 1984.

The moral status of the bodies of persons, by S. A. Ketchum. SOCIAL THEORY AND PRACTICE. 10(1):25-38, 1984.

The moral status of the human embryo: a tradition recalled. JOURNAL OF MEDICAL ETHICS. 10:38-44, March 1984.

On an inconsistency in Thomson's abortion argument, by R. Gibson. PHILOSOPHICAL STUDIES. 46:131-139, July 1984.

Pastoral teaching links abortion, nuclear threat in call for ethic of life, by J. McManus. NATIONAL CATHOLIC REPORTER. 20:8, May 11, 1984.

Plea to love aborters, by S. Weatherbe. ALBERTA REPORT. 11:31, January 9, 1984.

A prescription for the prevention of birth defects, by H. C. Slavkin. USA TODAY. 112:87-89, March 1984.

Pro-lifers regroup for new battles. AMERICAN JOURNAL OF NURSING. 83:1270, September 1983.

A social judgment of behavior modeling upon racial attitudes, by E. D. Schmikl. DISSERTATION ABSTRACTS INTERNATIONAL: B. 45(5), November 1984.

Substituted judgment: a modern application, by M. J. Gormley. NEW ENGLAND JOURNAL ON CRIMINAL AND CIVIL CONFINEMENT. 10(2):353-382, 1984.

The traditions of probabilism and the moral status of the early embryo, by C. A. Tauer. THEOLOGICAL STUDIES. 45(1):3-33, 1984.

The trend toward judicial recognition of wrongful life: a dissenting view, by B. Kennedy. UCLA LAW REVIEW. 31:473, December 1983.

Unwanted pregnancies terminated by indicated abortion: a study in unconscious motivational factors, by G. S. Canzano. DISSERTATION ABSTRACTS INTERNATIONAL: B. 45(5), November 1984.

When is termination of pregnancy during the third trimester morally justifiable?, by F. A. Chervenak, et al. NEW ENGLAND JOURNAL OF MEDICINE. 310:501-504, February 23, 1983.

Women, abortion, and autonomy. CHRISTIANITY AND CRISIS. 44:51-52, March 5, 1984.

ABORTION: COMPLICATIONS
Absence of coagulation changes in voluntary abortions by aspiration [letter], by M. T. Cousin, et al. ANNALES FRANCAISES D'ANESTHESIE ET DE REANIMATION. 1(4):453, 1982.

Adjunctive use of Laminaria tents for termination of early midtrimester pregnancy with intramuscular 15(S)-15-methyl PGF2 alpha, by N. N. Chowdhury, et al. ASIA-OCEANIA JOURNAL OF OBSTETRICS AND GYNAECOLOGY. 9(2):173-179, June 1983.

Effect of abortion on premature labor, by N. Bogdnov, et al. AKUSHERSTVO I GINEKOLOGIIA. 22(2):100-104, 1983.

Evaluation of tubal patency in post-abortal infertile women, by S. Roopnarinesingh, et al. WEST INDIAN MEDICAL JOURNAL. 32(3):168-171, September 1983.

Human chorionic gonadotropin and pregnancy-specific beta-1-glycoprotein in predicting pregnancy outcome and in association with early pregnancy vomiting, by A. Kauppila, et al. GYNECOLOGIC AND OBSTETRIC INVESTIGATION. 18(1): 49-53, 1984.

Interrupted pregnancy as an indicator of poor prognosis in T1, 2, NO, MO primary breast cancer, by H. E. Ownby, et al.

BREAST CANCER RESEARCH AND TREATMENT. 3(4):339-344, 1983.

Intrauterine small bowel entrapment and obstruction complicating suction abortion, by C. R. McArdle, et al. GASTROINTESTINAL RADIOLOGY. 9(3):239-240, 1984.

The new neonatal dilemma: live births from late abortions, by N. K. Rhoden. GEORGETOWN LAW JOURNAL. 72:1451-1509, June 1984.

Previous abortions exert favourable effects on the prognosis of breast cancer patients, by M. Yoshimoto, et al. GAN NO RINSHO. 30(7):777-784, June 1984.

Quantitative measurement of blood loss in medical termination of pregnancy, by L. Gupta, et al. INDIAN JOURNAL OF MEDICAL RESEARCH. 78:49-52, July 1983.

Thrombosis, abortion, cerebral disease, and the lupus anticoagulant, by G. R. V. Hughes. BRITISH MEDICAL JOURNAL. 287:1088-1089, October 15, 1983.

Vaginal administration of 15-methyl-PGF2 alpha-methyl ester prior to vacuum aspiration. Peri- and postoperative complications, by S. Nilsson, et al. ACTA OBSTETRICA ET GYNECOLOGICA SCANDINAVICA. 62(6):599-602, 1983.

Vaginal cleansing at vacuum aspiration abortion does not reduce the risk of postoperative infection, by C. Lundh, et al. ACTA OBSTETRICA ET GYNECOLOGICA SCANDINAVICA. 62(3):275-277, 1983.

ABORTION: EDUCATION
Attitudes toward abortion among Catholic Mexican-American women: the effects of religiosity and education, by S. Rosenhouse-Persson, et al. DEMOGRAPHY. 20:87-98, February 1983.

ABORTION: HABITUAL
Balanced translocation as one of the genetic causes of habitual abortion, by J. Szabo, et al. ORVOSI HETILAP. 125(2):67-70, January 8, 1984.

Congenital uterine malformations as indication for cervical suture (cerclage) in habitual abortion and premature delivery, by H. Abramovici, et al. INTERNATIONAL JOURNAL OF FERTILITY. 28(3):161-164, 1983.

Etiologic factors and subsequent reproductive performance in 195 couples with a prior history of habitual abortion, by B. Stray-Pedersen, et al. AMERICAN JOURNAL OF OBSTETRICS AND GYNECOLOGY. 148(2):140-146, January 15, 1984.

Evaluation and management of habitual abortion, by A. De-Cherney, et al. BRITISH JOURNAL OF HOSPITAL MEDICINE. 31(4):261-262; 266-268, April 1984.

Factors related to subsequent reproductive outcome in couples with repeated pregnancy loss, by J. FitzSimmons, et al. AMERICAN JOURNAL OF MEDICAL GENETICS. 18(3):407-411, July 1984.

Habitual abortion and uterine malformations, by A. J. Audebert, et al. ACTA EUROPAEA FERTILITATIS. 14(4):273-278, July-August 1983.

Habitual abortion: parental sharing of HLA antigens, absence of maternal blocking antibody, and suppression of maternal lymphocytes, by A. M. Unander, et al. AMERICAN JOURNAL OF REPRODUCTIVE IMMUNOLOGY. 4(4):171-178, December 1983.

Maternal-paternal histocompatibility: lack of association with habitual abortions, by J. R. Oksenberg, et al. FERTILITY AND STERILITY. 42(3):389-395, September 1984.

Prevalence of antinuclear antibodies in patients with habitual abortion and in normal and toxemic pregnancies, by I. Garcia-De La Torre, et al. RHEUMATOLOGY INTERNATIONAL. 4(2):87-89, 1984.

Prevention of habitual abortion and prematurity by early total occlusion of the external os uteri, by E. Saling. EUROPEAN JOURNAL OF OBSTETRICS, GYNECOLOGY AND REPRODUCTIVE BIOLOGY. 17(2-3):165-170, May 1984.

ABORTION: HABITUAL

Treatment for habitual aborters. AMERICAN JOURNAL OF NURSING. 84:494, April 1984.

Use of clomiphene in habitual abortion due to lutein insufficiency, by G. Del Papa, et al. MINERVA GINECOLOGIA. 35(10):677-679, October 1983.

ABORTION: HISTORY
Induced abortion and fertility: a quarter century of experience in Eastern Europe, by T. Frejka. POPULATION AND DEVELOPMENT REVIEW. 9:494-520, September 1983.

Laminaria— a modern cervix dilatation method with more than a 100-year history, by A. Jonasson. JORDEMODERN. 97(6): 187-195, June 1984.

ABORTION: ILLEGAL
Risks and costs of illegally induced abortion in Bangladesh, by A. R. Khan, et al. JOURNAL OF BIOSOCIAL SCIENCE. 16(1): 89-98, January 1984.

ABORTION: INCOMPLETE
Incomplete abortion and hydrometrosis in a squirrel monkey (Saimiri sciureus), by M. M. Swindle, et al. LABORATORY ANIMAL SCIENCE. 34(3):290-292, June 1984.

ABORTION: INDUCED
Clinico-ultrasonic aspects of the diagnosis of complications after induced abortion in the first trimester, by L. P. Bakuleva, et al. AKUSHERSTVO I GINEKOLOGIIA. (12):53-55, December 1983.

Coagulopathy and induced abortion methods: rates and relative risks, by M. E. Kafrissen, et al. AMERICAN JOURNAL OF OBSTETRICS AND GYNECOLOGY. 147(3):344-345, October 1, 1983.

Duration of induced abortion in the second trimester in relation to placental insertion, by E. Rachev, et al. AKUSHERSTVO I GINEKOLOGIIA. 22(5):349-354, 1983.

Early and late complications of induced abortion, by A. A.

Radionchenko, et al. SOVETSKAIA MEDITSINA. (7):113-115, 1983.

Effect of repeated induced abortions on female reproductive function, by I. B. Frolov. AKUSHERSTVO I GINEKOLOGIIA. (2): 44-47, February 1984.

Fertility after induced abortion: a prospective follow-up study, by P. G. Stubblefield, et al. OBSTETRICS AND GYNECOLOGY. 63(2):186-193, February 1984.

Foetal cell leak (FCL) studies in spontaneous and induced abortion, by R. R. Kulkarni, et al. INDIAN JOURNAL OF MEDICAL RESEARCH. 78:824-827, December 1983.

The incidence of repeat induced abortion in a randomly selected group of women. A retrospective study, by J. F. Heinrich, et al. JOURNAL OF REPRODUCTIVE MEDICINE. 29(4):260-264, April 1984.

Induced abortion in the early stages of pregnancy. CESKOSLO-VENSKA GYNEKOLOGIE. 48(6):456-457, July 1983.

Kinetic studies on prostaglandin concentrations in the amniotic fluid during rivanol-induced abortion, by Z. R. Zhou, et al. YAO HSUEH HSUEH PAO. 18(8):569-571, August 1983.

Medical indication of induced abortion and its criticism [letter]. ORVOSI HETILAP. 124(45):2773-2774, November 6, 1983.

Nursing of unmarried teenagers undergoing induced abortion— a description of their care in case studies, by K. Hirano, et al. KANGOGAKU ZASSHI. 47(6):648-652, June 1983.

Outcome of first delivery after second trimester two-stage induced abortion. A controlled historical cohort study, by O. Meirik, et al. ACTA OBSTETRICIA ET GYNECOLOGICA SCANDI-NAVICA. 63(1):45-50, 1984.

Plasma hormone concentrations in induced abortion with local prostaglandin administration in the first trimester, by W. Rath, et al. ZENTRALBLATT GYNAKOLOGIE. 105(15):961-971, 1983.

Prostaglandin F2 alpha, oxytocin, and uterine activation in hypertonic saline-induced abortions, by A. R. Fuchs, et al. AMERICAN JOURNAL OF OBSTETRICS AND GYNECOLOGY. 150(1):27-32, September 1, 1984.

Psychiatric sequelae of induced abortion, by M. Gibbons. JOURNAL OF THE ROYAL COLLEGE OF GENERAL PRACTITIONERS. 34(260):146-50, March 1984.

Radiographic findings in cervix uteri after prostaglandin abortion induction, by P. Kajanoja, et al. ACTA OBSTETRICIA ET GYNECOLOGICA SCANDINAVICA. 62(3):253-256, 1983.

Reactions to induced abortion [letter]. UGESKRIFT FOR LAEGER. 145(48):3781-3782, November 28, 1983.

Termination of second-trimester pregnancy by laminaria and intramuscular injections of 15-methyl PGF2 alpha or 16-phenoyx-omega-17,18,19 20-tetranor PGE2 methyl sulfonylamide. A randomized study, by M. Bygdeman, et al. ACTA OBSTETRICIA ET GYNECOLOGICA SCANDINAVICA. 62(5):535-537, 1983.

ABORTION: INDUCED: COMPLICATIONS

Complications in pregnancy following abortion induced with PGF2 alpha, by G. Koinzer, et al. ZENTRALBLATT FUR GYNAEKOLOGIE. 106(2):120-125, 1984.

Complications of induced abortion— personal observations, by J. Krasnodebski, et al. POLSKI TYGODNIK LEKARSKI. 38(41):1271-1273, October 10, 1983.

Levels of serum lipids during abortion induced by a hypertonic saline solution, by A. S. Sane, et al. JOURNAL DE GYNECOLOGIE, OBSTETRIQUE ET BIOLOGIE DE LA REPRODUCTION. 12(5):477-480, 1983.

Observation: contraceptive method use following an abortion, by S. K. Henshaw. FAMILY PLANNING PERSPECTIVES. 16(2):75-77, March-April 1984.

Omentum presenting at the vulva after a normal labor and

delivery. An unusual late complication of induced abortion, by D. E. Marsden. ACTA OBSTETRICIA ET GYNECOLOGICA SCANDINAVICA. 63(3):277-278, 1984.

ABORTION: LAWS AND LEGISLATION
Abortion and the body politic: an anthropological analysis of legislative activity in Massachusetts, by K. R. Scharf. DISSERTATION ABSTRACTS INTERNATIONAL: A. 45(3), September 1984.

Abortion and the law, by M. M. Cuomo. ORIGINS. 14:301-303, October 25, 1984.

Abortion: court unmoved. ECONOMIST. 287:32-33, June 25, 1983.

Abortion: from Roe [Roe v. Wade] to Arkon [City of Akron v. Akron Center for Reproductive Health Inc.], changing standards of analysis. CATHOLIC UNIVERSITY LAW REVIEW. 33:393-428, Winter 1984.

Abortion group says Church violates tax laws. OUR SUNDAY VISITOR. 73:8, October 14, 1984.

Abortion in England, 1919-1939: Legal theory and Social practice, by B. L. Brookes. DISSERTATION ABSTRACTS INTERNATIONAL: A. 45(1), July 1984.

Abortion law on trial/Morgentaler, by G. Rodgerson. BODY POLITIC. 1(12):11, April 1984.

Abortion money pours into North Carolina to defeat Jesse Helms, by M. Meehan. REGISTER. 60:1+, August 19, 1984.

Abortion— Provisions of city abortion ordinance requiring hospitalization for all abortions performed after the first trimester of pregnancy, notification and consent of parents before performance of abortions on unmarried minors, conveyance by attending physician of specific statements to insure informed consent, delay of twenty-four hours between the time a woman signs a consent form and the time an abortion is performed, and disposal of the fetus in a humane and sanitary manner are violations of the constitutional right of privacy. City of Akron v. Akron Center for Reproductive Health, Inc. JOURNAL OF FAMILY LAW. 22:159-167, 1983-1984.

Abortion, religion and the law, by D. R. Carlin, Jr. AMERICA. 151:356-358, December 1, 1984.

Abortion/rights of juvenile mother— Nebraska. JUVENILE AND FAMILY LAW DIGEST. 16(2):107-108, February 1984.

Abortion rights: where do we go from here?, by R. Copelon. MS. 12:146, October 1983.

Abortion's penalty: go to jail, by E. Bader. GUARDIAN. 36(43):2, September 5, 1984.

Anniversary of legalized abortion, by F. Simon. NORTHWEST PASSAGE. 24(7):6, February 1984.

The anti abortion amendments, by S. Poggi. GAY COMMUNITY. 11(45):3, June 2, 1984.

Anti sex lobby on the move. SPARE RIB. 1(40):17, March 1984.

Archbishop says politicans must fight abortion laws. OUR SUNDAY VISITOR. 73:8, October 28, 1984.

Arizona unborn dumped as waste, by V. Warner. REGISTER. 60:1+, April 1, 1984.

Beyond baby Doe, by M. Lipsyte. NEW DIRECTIONS FOR WOMEN. 13:8, January-February 1984.

CA2 enjoins implementation of government's "squeal rule". THE FAMILY LAW REPORTER: COURT OPINIONS. 10(2):1024-1025, November 8, 1983.

Can abortion be legally jusified?, by W. Esser. MEDICINE AND LAW. 3(3):205-216, 1984.

Clinical estimation of the duration of pregnancy in legal

abortion— are doctors biased by their knowledge of the duration of amenorrhoea?, by T. Gjorup, et al. METHODS OF INFORMATION IN MEDICINE. 23(2):96-98, April 1984.

Colorado bishops endorse Amendment No. 3. ORIGINS. 14:223-224, September 20, 1984.

Confidentiality and the abortion act [letter], by J. Chambers. LANCET. 1(8369):165, January 21, 1984.

Congenital abnormalities in legal abortions at 20 weeks' gestation or later, by E. Alberman, et al. LANCET. 1(8388):1226-1228, June 2, 1984.

Constitutional law— the "aborted" evolution of fetal rights after Roe v. Wade. WESTERN NEW ENGLAND LAW REVIEW. 6:535-553, 1983.

Constitutional law— fourteenth amendment— right to abortion— regulatory framework— standard of review— the United States Supreme Court has held that the state may not, in its regulation of abortion, deviate from accepted medical practice, and that all pre-viability abortion regulation shall be subject to strict scrutiny under the compelling state interest standard of substantive due process analysis— City of Akron v. Akron Center for Reproductive Health, Inc. DUQUESNE LAW REVIEW. 22:767-785, Spring 1984.

Constitutional law— right to privacy— municipal roadblock to abortion denounced— City of Arkon v. Akron Center for Reproductive Health, Inc. SETON HALL LAW REVIEW. 14:658-682, 1984.

Constitutional law— state constitutional law— equal protection— state statute restricting the provision of medicaid funds to abortions medically necessary to preserve the mother's life violates state equal protection standards and therefore must be construed to require funding of all abortions necessary to preserve the mother's life or health. Right to Choose v. Byrne. RUTGERS LAW JOURNAL. 14:217-231, Fall 1982.

Criminal law— murder— intentional killing of viable fetus not murder— Hollis v. Commonwealth. NORTHERN KENTUCKY LAW REVIEW. 11:213-227, 1984.

Counseling and the abortion issue, by P. J. Riga. JOURNAL OF PASTORAL COUNSELING. 17:44-55, Fall-Winter 1982.

Current technology affecting Supreme Court abortion jurisprudence, by M. Buckley. NEW YORK LAW SCHOOL LAW REVIEW. 27(4):1221-1260, 1982.

Dateline: Romania: a war on abortions, by S. Masterman. MACLEANS. 97:12, April 23, 1984.

A decade of cementing the mosaic of Roe v. Wade: is the composite a message to leave abortion alone?. UNIVERSITY OF TOLEDO LAW REVIEW. 15:681-753, Winter 1984.

Defending the right to abortion, by Reiman, et al. AGAINST THE CURRENT. 2(4):31, Winter 1984.

Dorothy, my sister-in-love [in-law with Down's syndrome], by W. Wangerin. CHRISTIANITY TODAY. 28:66, August 10, 1984.

Equal protection of the laws and the 14th amendment: value or humanity?, by P. J. Riga. LINCARE QUARTERLY. 51:176-180, May 1984.

Exactly whose right to life is it, by J. Pasternak. GUARDIAN. 36(17):3, February 1, 1984.

Experts hammer away at Roe vs. Wade logic, by A. J. Zwerneman. REGISTER. 60:1+, April 15, 1984.

The fallacy of time limits . . . therapeutic abortions, by J. Finch. NURSING MIRROR. 158(20):24-25, May 16, 1984.

The fetus and the law— whose life is it anyway?, by J. Gallagher. MS. 12:62+, September 1984.

The fetus, under criminal law is considered a complete human being from the onset of labor pains. FORTSCHRITTE DER MEDIZIN. 102(10):92, March 15, 1984.

The fetus under Section 1983: still struggling for recognition, by P. T. Czepiga. SYRACUSE LAW REVIEW. 34:1029-1066, August 1983.

Forum assesses abortion rights crisis, by J. Irvine. GAY COMMUNITY. 11(45):3, June 2, 1984.

Freedom and/or separation: the constitutional dilemma of the First Amendment, by L. Pfeffer. UNION SEMINARY QUARTERLY REVIEW. 38(3):337-359, 1984.

Gender, the judiciary, and U. S. public opinion, by G. S. Swan. JOURNAL OF SOCIAL, POLITICAL AND ECONOMIC STUDIES. 8(3):323-341, 1983.

Genetic screening, eugenic abortion, and Roe v. Wade: how viable is Roe's viability standard?. BROOKLYN LAW REVIEW. 50:113-142, Fall 1983.

H. L. v. Matheson— a minor decision about parental notice. UTAH LAW REVIEW. 1982:949-961, 1982.

Health personnel in the matter of legal abortion: physicians and other personnel should have the right to refuse to perform abortions, by L. Jacobsson, et al. LAKARTIDNINGEN. 80(39): 3541-3545, September 28, 1983.

The Human Life Bill: some issues and answers, by H. J. Hyde. NEW YORK LAW SCHOOL LAW REVIEW. 27:1077-1100, 1982.

Human life— its value and sanctity, by W. E. Power. CHAC REVIEW. 11(2):19-20, June 1983.

Hysterectomy as treatment for complications of legal abortion, by D. A. Grimes, et al. OBSTETRICS AND GYNECOLOGY. 63(4):457-462, April 1984.

Ireland: bishops' pawns [constitutional amendment that would bar legalization of abortion]. ECONOMIST. 287:44+, April 9, 1983.

Judicial decision [Medhurst v. Medhurst] that takes us back to pre-barbarian, by T. Byfield. ALBERTA REPORT. 11:52, April 16, 1984.

Late sequela of legal abortion, by E. B. Obel. UGESFRIFT FOR LAEGER. 145(48):3716-3721, November 28, 1983.

Law: the fallacy of time limits, by J. Finch. NURSING MIRROR. 158(20):24-25, May 16, 1984.

Legal abortion and placenta previa, by D. A. Grimes, et al. AMERICAN JOURNAL OF OBSTETRICS AND GYNECOLOGY. 149(5):501-504, July 1, 1984.

Legal abortion in Georgia, 1980, by A. M. Spitz. JOURNAL OF THE MEDICAL ASSOCIATION OF GEORGIA. 73(2):87-91, February 1984.

The legality of abortion by prostaglandin, by G. Wright. THE CRIMINAL LAW REVIEW. June 1984, pp. 347-349.

Limiting state regulation of reproductive decisions, by L. H. Glantz. AMERICAN JOURNAL OF PUBLIC HEALTH. 74:168-169, February 1984.

New Jersey court recognizes limited "wrongful life" action. THE FAMILY LAW REPORTER. 10(44):1603-1604, September 11, 1984.

New life for the doctrine of unconstitutional conditions?— Committee to Defend Reproductive Rights v. Myers. WASHINGTON LAW REVIEW. 779:679-707, July 1983.

The 1983 Supreme Court abortion decisions: impact on hospitals, a conflict with Baby Doe?, by R. A. Carlson. HEALTH LAW VIGIL. 6(21):2-7, October 14, 1983.

NOW vs. Judge: abortion used as morality test, by V. Quade. AMERICAN BAR ASSOCIATION JOURNAL. 70:40, May 1984.

O'Connor says politicos must fight abortion with laws. REGISTER. 60:2, October 28, 1984.

Parents, judges, and a minor's abortion decision: third party participation and the evolution of a judicial alternative, by W. Green. AKRON LAW REVIEW. 17:87-110, Summer 1983.

Passage of child abuse bill applauded by U. S. Senator. CRIME VICTIMS DIGEST. 1(12):5-6, September 1984.

Paternal child-support tort parallels for the abortion on maternal demand era: the work of Regan, Levy and Duncan, by G. S. Swan. GLENDALE LAW REVIEW. 5:151-187, 1981-1982.

A political party is born: single-issue advocacy and the New York State election law, by R. J. Spitzer. NATIONAL CIVIC REVIEW. 73:321-328, July-August 1984.

Prenatal diagnosis of fetal disorders: issues and implications part 2, by D. Beeson, et al. BIRTH. 10(4):233-241, Winter 1983.

Prolife social worker facing new jail term, by D. Goldkamp. REGISTER. 60:1+, October 21, 1984.

The public health effects of legal abortion in the United States, by C. Tietze. FAMILY PLANNING PERSPECTIVES. 16(1):26-28, January-February 1984.

Public remains closely divided on Supreme Court's 1973 abortion ruling: 5-point decline since '81 in percent feeling abortions should be outlawed. GALLUP REPORT. August 1983, p. 16-18.

Public support for legal abortion continues, although polls show conflicting trends in 1983. FAMILY PLANNING PERSPECTIVES. 15(6):279-281, November-December 1983.

Reagan's war on abortion, by M. Kramer. NEW YORK. 17:27+, September 24, 1984.

Rejection of husband's claim to stop wife's abortion, by J. K. Bentil. SOLICITOR'S JOURNAL. 128:288-290, April 27, 1984.

The right to privacy: Roe v. Wade revisited, by P. A. Smith. JURIST. 43(2):289-317, 1983.

Saving the unborn earns a jail cell, by D. Goldkamp. REGISTER. 59:1+, December 11, 1983.

Setback for Morgentaler, by R. Block. MACLEANS. 97:46, July 30, 1984.

The social, theological and biological context of abortion: 10th anniversary reflections on Roe v. Wade, by G. H. Williams. LINACRE QUARTERLY. 50:335-354, November 1983.

Spousal notification and the right of privacy. Scheinberg v. Smith. CHICAGO-KENT LAW REVIEW. 59:1129-1151, 1983.

State funding cutoff for abortions may be constitutionally protected. THE FAMILY LAW REPORTER: COURT OPINIONS. 10(3):1041-1042, November 15, 1983.

State protection of the unborn after Roe v. Wade: a legislative proposal, by M. C. Walker, et al. STETSON LAW REVIEW. 13:237-266, Winter 1984.

Strategists work to sound the death knell for abortion: What will it take to overturn Roe v. Wade, by R. Frame. CHRISTIANITY TODAY. 28:74, May 18, 1984.

Suit charges subsidy for religious views [Adolescent Family Life Act denies funds to "pro-choice" organizations]. E/SA. 12:35, April 1984.

Supreme court holds anti-abortion law unconstitutional: A summary of the court's decision; abortion foes falter in Senate, fight on in House, by D. E. Kulp. OFF OUR BACKS. 13:19; 20, August-September 1983.

—. An analysis of the court's decision: its strength and weaknesses, by N. Hunter. OFF OUR BACKS. 13:19; 20, August-September 1983.

Supreme court review, by S. Bernstein. TRIAL. 19(12):20; 22, December 1983.

This amendment could kill women. HARVARD WOMEN'S LAW JOURNAL. 7:287-301, Spring 1984.

To be born, to die: individual rights in the '80s: birth, by L. Reaves.

AMERICAN BAR ASSOCIATION JOURNAL. 70:27-28, February 1984.

The trimester approach: how long can the legal friction last?. MERCER LAW REVIEW. 35:891-913, Spring 1984.

Which parent owns the child?, by B. Amiel. MACLEANS. 97:17, April 16, 1984.

What future/national abortion campaign. SPARE RIB. 1(35):26, October 1983.

Wrongful birth and wrongful conception: the legal and moral issues, by P. Donovan. FAMILY PLANNING PERSPECTIVES. 16(2):64-69, March-April 1984.

ABORTION: MISSED
Extraamniotic infusion of prostaglandin F2 alpha in normal saline for termination of midtrimester missed abortion, by O. E. Jaschevatzky, et al. EUROPEAN JOURNAL OF OBSTET- RICS GYNECOLOGY AND REPRODUCTIVE BIOLOGY. 15(3): 185-187, July 1983.

Fetus papyraceus— 11 cases, by E. Daw. POSTGRADUATE MEDICAL JOURNAL. 59(695):598-600, September 1983.

Intracervical instillation of PGE2-gel in patients with missed abortion or intrauterine fetal death, by G. Ekman, et al. ARCHIVES OF GYNECOLOGY. 233(4):241-245, 1983.

Missed abortion presenting as a vascular tumour on hystero- salpingography, by A. Ho. BRITISH JOURNAL OF RADIOL- OGY. 57(673):102-103, January 1984.

ABORTION: MORTALITY AND MORTALITY STATISTICS
The development of obstetrics and gynecology: dramatically decreased maternal mortality. Far-seeing points of view in the question of abortion, by K. Hagenfeldt. LAKARTIDNIN- GEN. 80(45):4299-4302, November 9, 1983.

Polybrominated biphenyls and fetal mortality in Michigan, by C. G. Humble, et al. AMERICAN JOURNAL OF PUBLIC

HEALTH. 74(10):1130-1132, October 1984.

ABORTION: PSYCHOLOGY AND PSYCHIATRY
Abortion: identity and loss, by W. Quinn. PHILOSOPHY AND
PUBLIC AFFAIRS. 13:3-24, Winter 1984.

A common tragedy . . . miscarriage, by J. Moore. COMMUNITY
OUTLOOK. June, 1984, p. 210.

A comparison of crisis variables among groups of women experiencing induced abortion, by G. C. Polk. DISSERTATION
ABSTRACTS INTERNATIONAL: B. 45(3), September 1984.

Comparison of first-time and repeat abortions, by E. Michaels.
CHATELAINE. 57:16, October 1984.

Lithium and pregnancy. A cohort study on manic-depressive
women, by B. Kallen, et al. ACTA PSYCHIATRICA SCANDI-
NAVICA. 68(2):134-139, August 1983.

Matters of conscience: the other side of the question, by J. Robinson. NURSING MIRROR. 158(20):20-21, May 16, 1984.

Psychiatric sequelae of induced abortion, by M. Gibbons. JOUR-
NAL OF THE ROYAL COLLEGE OF GENERAL PRACTI-
TIONERS. 34(260):146-150, March 1984.

Say, brother, by L. Holder. ESSENCE. 14:22, March 1984.

When dreams die, by C. G. Irvin. NURSING. 14(6):32, June 1984.

ABORTION: REPEATED
C heterochromatin variation in couples with recurrent early
abortions, by A. Maes, et al. JOURNAL OF MEDICAL GENE-
TICS. 20(5):350-356, October 1983.

Campylobacter enteritis associated with recurrent abortions in
agammaglobulinemia, by A. Pines, et al. ACTA OBSTET-
RICIA ET GYNECOLOGICA SCANDINAVICA. 62(3):279-280,
1983.

Couples with repeat spontaneous abortions: chromosome ab-

normalities, by F. Hecht, et al. ARIZONA MEDICINE. 41(8):
530-532, August 1984.

Cytogenetic findings in 318 couples with repeated spontaneous
abortion: a review of experience in British Columbia, by J.
T. Pantzar, et al. AMERICAN JOURNAL OF MEDICAL GENE-
TICS. 17(4):615-620, March 1984.

Cytogenetic study in 50 couples with recurrent abortions, by M.
Maraeli, et al. GYNECOLOGIC AND OBSTETRIC INVESTIGA-
TION. 17(2):84-88, 1984.

Cytogenetic survey in couples with recurrent fetal wastage, by
J. P. Fryns, et al. HUMAN GENETICS. 65(4):336-354, 1984.

Determinants of immuological responsiveness in recurrent
spontaneous abortion, by P. M. Johnson, et al. TRANSPLAN-
TATION. 38(3):280-284, September 1984.

Effect of repeated induced abortions on female reproductive
function, by I. B. Frolov. AKUSHERSTVO I GINEKOLOGIIA.
(2):44-47, February 1984.

Endometrial ossification associated with repeated abortions, by
S. Degani, et al. ACTA OBSTETRICIA ET GYNECOLOGICA
SCANDINAVICA. 62(3):281-282, 1983.

Etiology of recurrent pregnancy losses and outcome of subsequent
pregnancies, by J. H. Harger, et al. OBSTETRICS AND GYNE-
COLOGY. 62(5):574-581, November 1983.

Histocompatibility and recurrent abortion [letter], by J. A.
McIntyre, et al. FERTILITY AND STERILITY. 41(4):653-
654, April 1984.

Immune factors and recurrent abortion: a review, by C. W. Redman. AMERICAN JOURNAL OF REPRODUCTIVE IMMUNOL-
OGY. 4(4):179-181, December 1983.

Immunological analysis of women with repeated spontaneous
abortions, by J. Bousquet, et al. GYNECOLOGIC AND OBSTET-
RIC INVESTIGATION. 17(3):113-119, 1984.

Immunological factors and recurrent fetal loss [letter], by J. S. Scott. LANCET. 1(8386):1122, May 19, 1984.

Immunopathologic factors contributing to recurrent spontaneous abortion in humans, by A. E. Beer. AMERICAN JOURNAL OF REPRODUCTIVE IMMUNOLOGY. 4(4):182-184, December 1983.

The incidence of repeat induced abortion in a randomly selected group of women. A retrospective study, by J. F. Heinrich. JOURNAL OF REPRODUCTIVE MEDICINE. 29(4):260-264, April 1984.

Lupus anticoagulant, recurrent abortion, and prostacyclin production by cultured smooth muscle cells [letter], by C. de Castellarnau, et al. LANCET. 2(8359):1137-1138, November 12, 1983.

Luteal phase inadequacy and a chromosomal anomaly in recurrent abortion, by A. C. Wentz, et al. FERTILITY AND STERILITY. 41(1):142-143, January 1984.

Maternal blocking antibodies, the fetal allograft, and recurrent abortion. LANCET. 2(8360):1175-1176, November 19, 1983.

Minimizing risk of repeated pregnancy loss, by A. C. Cruz, et al. JOURNAL OF THE FLORIDA MEDICAL ASSOCIATION. 70(9):728-731, September 1983.

Preliminary experience with the use of human chorionic gonadotrophin therapy in women with repeated abortion, by J. Svigos. CLINICAL REPRODUCTION AND FERTILITY. 1(2): 131-135, June 1982.

Prognosis for couples who have experienced repeated pregnancy loss, by D. N. Abuelo, et al. FERTILITY AND STERILITY. 40(6):844-845, December 1983.

Psychosocial aspects of repeat abortions in Singapore— a preliminary report, by W. F. Tsoi, et al. SINGAPORE MEDICAL JOURNAL. 25(2):116-121, April 1984.

Recurrent abortion— a review, by G. M. Stirrat. BRITISH JOUR-
NAL OF OBSTETRICS AND GYNAECOLOGY. 90(10):881-883,
October 1983.

Repeat abortion. AMERICAN FAMILY PHYSICIAN. 30:262,
August 1984.

Repeat abortion: is it a problem?, by C. Berger, et al. FAMILY
PLANNING PERSPECTIVES. 16(2):70-75, March-April 1984.

Repeated pregnancy loss, by J. FitzSimmons, et al. AMERICAN
JOURNAL OF MEDICAL GENETICS. 16(1):7-13, September
1983.

Subsequent reproductive outcome in couples with repeated pregnancy loss, by J. FitzSimmons, et al. AMERICAN JOURNAL
OF MEDICAL GENETICS. 16(4):583-587, December 1983.

ABORTION: RESEARCH
Antifertility and uterine activity of Plumbago rosea in rats, by R.
Lal, et al. INDIAN JOURNAL OF MEDICAL RESEARCH.
78:287-290, August 1983.

Brucella ovis-induced abortion in ewes, by M. C. Libal, et al.
JOURNAL OF THE AMERICAN VETERINARY MEDICAL
ASSOCIATION. 183(5):553-554, September 1983.

Clinical and analytic hormone studies of the suitability of
estrumate for induction of mummified fetus expulsion in
cattle, by D. Ruetschi, et al. SCHWEIZER ARCHIV FUER
TIERHEILKUNDE. 126(6):323-329, June 1984.

Effects of alpha-trichosanthin and alpha-momorcharin on the
development of peri-implantation mouse embryos, by L. K.
Law, et al. JOURNAL OF REPRODUCTION AND FERTILITY.
69(2):597-604, November 1983.

Mechanisms of fetal demise in pregnant mice immunized to
murine alpha-fetoprotein, by G. J. Mizejewski, et al. AMERI-
CAN JOURNAL OF REPRODUCTIVE IMMUNOLOGY. 5(1):32-
38, January-February 1984.

Pathogenesis of in utero infections with abortogenic and non-abortogenic alpha viruses in mice, by A. R. Milner, et al. JOURNAL OF VIROLOGY. 50(1):66-72, April 1984.

Reproductive hazards in the workplace. Development of epidemilogic research, by P. J. Landrigan, et al. SCANDINAVIAN JOURNAL OF WORK, ENVIRONMENT AND HEALTH. 9(2 Spec No): 83-88, April 1983.

Septic abortion caused by Salmonella heidelberg in a white-handed gibbon, by J. D. Thurman, et al. JOURNAL OF THE AMERICAN VETERINARY MEDICAL ASSOCIATION. 183:1325-1326, December 1, 1983.

'Sex and society': Gotland project. A research project in primary health services, by B. Stokstad, et al. SYKEPLEIEN. 70(17): 16-17, October 5, 1983.

Teratology study with the synthetic prostaglandin ONO-802 given intravaginally to rabbits, by J. A. Petrere, et al. TERATO-GENESIS, CARCINOGENESIS AND MUTAGENESIS. 4(2): 225-231, 1984.

The termination of early pregnancy in the mouse by beta-momorcharin, by W. Y. Chan, et al. CONTRACEPTION. 29(1):91-100, January 1984.

Vaccination against spontaneous abortion in mice, by G. Chaouat, et al. JOURNAL OF REPRODUCTIVE IMMUNOL-OGY. 5(6):389-392, November 1983.

Viability of alpha-momorcharin-treated mouse blastocysts in the pseudopregnant uterus, by P. P. Tam, et al. JOURNAL OF REPRODUCTION AND FERTILITY. 71(2):567-72, July 1984.

ABORTION: SEPTIC
Anti-lipopolysaccharide immunotherapy in management of septic shock of obstetric and gynaecological origin, by E. Lachman, et al. LANCET. 1(8384):981-983, May 5, 1984.

Campylobacter coli septicaemia associated with septic abortion, by M. Kist, et al. INFECTION. 12(2):88-90, March-April 1984.

Campylobacter septic abortion, by P. M. Jost, et al. SOUTHERN MEDICAL JOURNAL. 77(7):924, July 1984.

Erythema nodosum and Campylobacter fetus infection, by F. Garcier, et al. ANNALES DE DERMATOLOGIE ET DE VENEREOLOGIE. 110(5):449-453, 1983.

Dilated cardiomyopathy and thyrotoxicosis complicated by septic abortion, by G. D. Hankins, et al. AMERICAN JOURNAL OF OBSTETRICS AND GYNECOLOGY. 149(1):85-86, May 1, 1984.

Septic abortion: clinical aspects, diagnosis, treatment, by V. A. Kulavskii. AKUSHERSTVO I GINEKOLOGIIA. (2):73-78, February 1984.

Septic abortion in Wellington 1960-1979, by J. M. Shepherd, et al. NEW ZEALAND MEDICAL JOURNAL. 97(756):322-324, May 23, 1984.

The state of the thrombocytic component of the hemostasis system in patients with infection and septic shock, by A. D. Makatsariia, et al. SOVETSKAIA MEDITSINA. (4):34-39, 1984.

ABORTION: SEPTIC: COMPLICATIONS
Experience with combined treatment using hemosorptica in the generalized suppurative-septic infection of puerperae and women with septic abortion, by G. I. Gerasimovich, et al. AKUSHERSTVO I GINEKOLOGIIA. (2):60-61, February 1984.

ABORTION: SPONTANEOUS
Additional data on spontaneous abortion and facial cleft malformations, by J. C. Bear. CLINICAL GENETICS. 24(6): 407-412, December 1983.

The age of incidence of spontaneous abortion, by Y. Shiina, et al. HOKKAIDO IGAKU ZASSHI. 59(1):17-20, January 1984.

Aneuploidy in recurrent spontaneous aborters: the tendency to parental nondisjunction, by F. Hecht, et al. CLINICAL GENETICS. 26(1):43-45, July 1984.

Causes of spontaneous abortion, by H. J. Huisjes. NEDERLANDS TIJDSCHRIFT VOOR GENEESKUNDE. 127(49):2241-2246, December 3, 1983.

Changes in rates of spontaneous fetal deaths reported in Upstate New York vital records by gestational age, 1968-78, by P. K. Cross. PUBLIC HEALTH REPORTS. 99:212-215, March-April 1984.

Correlation between morphological and cytogenetical findings in spontaneous abortions, by H. Muntefering, et al. VER-HANDLUNGEN DER DEUTSCHEN GESELLSCHAFT FUR PATHOLOGIE. 66:372-377, 1982.

Couples with repeat spontaneous abortions: chromosome abnormalities, by F. Hecht, et al. ARIZONA MEDICINE. 41(8): 530-532, August 1984.

Cytogenetic findings in 318 couples with repeated spontaneous abortion: a review of experience in British Columbia, by J. T. Pantzar, et al. AMERICAN JOURNAL OF MEDICAL GENE-TICS. 17(3):615-620, March 1984.

Cytogenetic observations on 24 couples with spontaneous abortions, by J. F. Xu. CHUNG HUA I HSUEH TSA CHIH. 63(6): 365-367, June 1983.

Cytogenetic studies in couples with multiple spontaneous abortions, by W. Schempp, et al. ACTA ANTHROPOGENETICA. 7(2):113-118, 1983.

Cytogenetic studies in spontaneous abortuses, by T. Andrews, et al. HUMAN GENETICS. 66(1):77-84, 1984.

Cytogenetic study of married couples with recurrent spontaneous abortions, by V. G. Kroshikina, et al. TSITOLOGIYA I GENETIKA. 18(3):229-230, May-June 1984.

Determinants of immunological responsiveness in recurrent spontaneous abortion, by P. M. Johnson, et al. TRANSPLAN-TATION. 38(3):280-284, September 1984.

ELISA antibodies to cytomegalovirus in pregnant patients: prevalence in and correlation with spontaneous abortion, by M. Luerti, et al. BIOLOGICAL RESEARCH IN PREGNANCY AND PERINATOLOGY. 4(4):181-183, 1983.

Effect of plasma substitute solutions on the immunologic indices of pregnant women with spontaneous abortions, by V. V. Shcherbakova, et al. AKUSHERSTVO I GINEKOLOGIIA. (3):68-71, March 1984.

Effect of spontaneous abortion in the first pregnancy on the course of subsequent pregnancy, labor, puerperium and the state of the newborn infant, by S. Lembrych, et al. WIADOMOSCI LEKARSKIE. 37(2):122-127, January 1984.

Endometriosis and spontaneous abortion, by M. Groll. FERTILITY AND STERILITY. 41(6):933-935, June 1984.

Etiology of infertility in monkeys with endometriosis: luteinized unruptured follicles, luteal phase defects, pelvic adhesions, and spontaneous abortions, by R. S. Schenken, et al. FERTILITY AND STERILITY. 41(1):122-130, January 1984.

Foetal cell leak (FCL) studies in spontaneous and induced abortion, by R. R. Kulkarni, et al. INDIAN JOURNAL OF MEDICAL RESEARCH. 78:824-827, December 1983.

Grieving characteristics after spontaneous abortion: a management approach, by P. C. Leppert, et al. OBSTETRICS AND GYNECOLOGY. 64(1):119-122, July 1984.

High resolution chromosome studies in couples with multiple spontaneous abortions, by T. L. Yang-Feng. DISSERTATION ABSTRACTS INTERNATIONAL: B. 45(9), March 1985.

Hormonal treatment of spontaneous abortion, by A. Katsulov. AKUSHERSTVO I GINEKOLOGIIA. 23(1):82-88, 1984.

Human chorionic gonadotropin in maternal plasma after induced abortion, spontaneous abortion, and removed ectopic pregnancy, by J. A. Steier, et al. OBSTETRICS AND GYNECOLOGY. 64(3):391-394, September 1984.

Immunological analysis of women with repeated spontaneous
abortions, by J. Bousquet, et al. GYNECOLOGIC AND OB-
STETRIC INVESTIGATION. 17(3):113-119, 1984.

Immunological aspects of spontaneous and habitual abortion,
by W. R. Jones. CLINICAL REPRODUCTION AND FERTILITY.
1(3):244-246, September 1982.

Immunopathologic factors contributing to recurrent spontaneous
abortion in humans, by A. E. Beer. AMERICAN JOURNAL
OF REPRODUCTIVE IMMUNOLOGY. 4(4):182-184, December
1983.

Lymphocyte-reactive antibodies and spontaneous abortion
[letter], by P. M. Johnson, et al. LANCET. 2(8362):1304-
1305, December 3, 1983.

Oxytocic drugs and anaesthesia. A controlled clinical trial of
ergometrine, syntocinon and normal saline during evacuation of the uterus after spontaneous abortion, by D. Beeby,
et al. ANAESTHESIA. 39(8):764-767, August 1984.

Recurrent spontaneous abortion, by B. J. Poland. EUROPEAN
JOURNAL OF OBSTETRICS, GYNECOLOGY AND REPRODUC-
TIVE BIOLOGY. 16(6):369-375, March 1984.

Recurrent spontaneous abortion in human pregnancy: results
of immunogenetical, cellular, and humoral studies, by J. A.
McIntyre, et al. AMERICAN JOURNAL OF REPRODUCTIVE
IMMUNOLOGY. 4(4):165-170, December 1983.

Reliability of reporting of spontaneous abortion [letter], by W. H.
James. AMERICAN JOURNAL OF OBSTETRICS AND GYNE-
COLOGY. 147(4):473, October 15, 1983.

Ring chromosome 21 in a healthy woman with three spontaneous
abortions, by K. Rhomberg. HUMAN GENETICS. 67(1):120,
1984.

Selection bias in studies of spontaneous abortion among occupational groups, by G. Axelsson. JOURNAL OF OCCUPATIONAL
MEDICINE. 26(7):525-528, July 1984.

Some epidemiological data on spontaneous abortion in Hungary, 1971-80, by A. Czeizel, et al. JOURNAL OF EPIDEMIOLOGY AND COMMUNITY HEALTH. 38(2):143-148, June 1984.

Spontaneous abortions among dental assistants, factory workers, painters, and gardening workers: a follow up study, by L. Z. Heidam. JOURNAL OF EPIDEMIOLOGY AND COMMUNITY HEALTH. 38(2):149-155, June 1984.

Spontaneous abortions among factor workers. The importance of gravity control, by L. Z. Heidam. SCANDINAVIAN JOURNAL OF SOCIAL MEDICINE. 11(3):81-85, 1983.

Spontaneous abortions among laboratory workers: a follow up study, by L. Z. Heidam. JOURNAL OF EPIDEMIOLOGY AND COMMUNITY HEALTH. 38(1):36-41, March 1984.

Spontaneous abortions among rubber workers and congenital malformations in their offspring, by M. L. Lindbohm, et al. SCANDINAVIAN JOURNAL OF WORK, ENVIRONMENT AND HEALTH. 9(Suppl 2):85-90, 1983.

Spontaneous abortions and twinning, by M. Zahalkova, et al. ACTA GENETICAE MEDICAE ET GEMELLOLOGIAE: TWIN RESEARCH. 33(1):25-26, 1984.

Spontaneous abortions following Three Mile Island accident [letter], by C. J. Johnson. AMERICAN JOURNAL OF PUBLIC HEALTH. 74(5):520, May 1984.

Spontaneous abortion in proven intact pregnancies [letter], by G. C. Christiaens, et al. LANCET. 2(8402):571-572, September 8, 1984.

Spontaneous abortions, stillbirths, and birth defects in families of agricultural pilots, by C. C. Roan, et al. ARCHIVES OF ENVIRONMENTAL HEALTH. 39(1):56-60, January-February 1984.

Stress and spontaneous abortion: A controlled study, by P. Santonastaso, et al. MEDICINA PSICOSOMATICA. 28(1):3-14, January-March 1983.

Use of tocolysis as a routine method of preventing spontaneous abortions and premature labor, by Kh. Veselinov. AKUSHER-STVO I GINEKOLOGIIA. 22(2):93-97, 1983.

Value of routine histologic studies in spontaneous abortion, by G. Stranz, et al. ZENTRALBLATT FUR GYNAEKOLOGIE. 105(23):1542-1545, 1983.

X-chromosome hyperploidy in couples with multiple spontaneous abortions, by W. Holzgreve, et al. OBSTETRICS AND GYNECOLOGY. 63(2):237-240, February 1984.

ABORTION: SPONTANEOUS: COMPLICATIONS
Immune complex and complement levels in spontaneous abortions and normal pregnancy, by S. Saitoh, et al. NIPPON SANKA FUJINKA GAKKAI ZASSHI. 35(11):1981-1990, November 1983.

The in vitro effect of grandiflorenic acid and zoapatle aqueous crude extract upon spontaneous contractility of the rat uterus during oestrus cycle, by E. Bejar, et al. JOURNAL OF ETHNOPHARMACOLOGY. 11(1):87-97, June 1984.

On the treatment of early and late toxicoses in pregnancy and spontaneous abortion, by Y. Lukanov, et al. FOLIA MEDICA. 25(4):50-53, 1983.

Protective antibodies and spontaneous abortion [letter], by R. W. Beard, et al. LANCET. 2(8358):1090, November 5, 1983.

The psychodynamics of spontaneous abortion, by J. M. Stack. AMERICAN JOURNAL OF ORTHOPSYCHIATRY. 54(1):162-167, January 1984.

ABORTION: STATISTICS
ARIMA models of seasonal variation in U. S. birth and death rates, by K. C. Land, et al. DEMOGRAPHY. 20:541-568, November 1983.

Induced abortion and fertility: a quarter century of experience in Eastern Europe, by T. Frejka. POPULATION AND DEVELOPMENT REVIEW. 9:494-520, September 1983.

A mysterious drop in the abortion rate. NEWSWEEK. 104:26, July 16, 1984.

A "profile" population delegation?, by C. Holden. SCIENCE. 224: 1321-1322, June 22, 1984.

ABORTION: TECHNIQUES
Effects of prostaglandin E2 analogue suppository on blood loss in suction abortion, by M. S. Sidhu, et al. OBSTETRICS AND GYNECOLOGY. 64(1):128-130, July 1984.

Experimental study on reanastomosis of the ductus deferens, by N. N. Rodrigues, Jr., et al. ACTAS UROLOGICAS ESPANOLAS. 7(2):155-160, March-April 1983.

Midtrimester pregnancy termination: a study of the cost effectiveness of dilation and evacuation in a free-standing facility, by T. Crist, et al. NORTH CAROLINA MEDICAL JOURNAL. 44(9):549-551, September 1983.

Observation: contraceptive method use following an abortion, by S. K. Henshaw. FAMILY PLANNING PERSPECTIVES. 16:75-76, March-April 1984.

Postabortal contraception with norethisterone enanthate injections, by P. Lahteenmaki, et al. CONTRACEPTION. 27(6): 553-562, June 1983.

Prenatal exposure to diethylstilbestrol (DES) and the development of sexually dimorphic cognitive abilities and cerebral lateralization, by M. Hines, et al. DEVELOPMENTAL PSYCHOLOGY. 20:81-94, January 1984.

Reflections on midtrimester pregnancy termination by dilation and evacuation in a free-standing facility, by R. T. Parker. NORTH CAROLINA MEDICAL JOURNAL. 44(9):537, September 1983.

Serum folate concentrations during pregnancy in women with epilepsy: relation to antiepileptic drug concentrations, number of seizures, and fetal outcome, by V. K. Hiilesmaa, et al. BRITISH MEDICAL JOURNAL. 287:577-579, August 27, 1983.

Three methods for gradual cervical dilatation prior to vacuum aspiration in late first trimester pregnacy, by S. Sema, et al. CONTRACEPTION. 28(3):223-231, September 1983.

ABORTION: THERAPEUTIC

Battling 'foeticide' [Alberta] therapeutic committees are under pressure, by S. McCarthy. ALBERTA REPORT. 11:45, May 28, 1984.

Ethical contradiction of the therapeutic use of aborted fetuses and modern medical interventions [letter]. ORVOSI HETILAP. 125(15):919-920, April 8, 1984.

The fallacy of time limits . . . therapeutic abortions, by J. Finch. NURSING MIRROR. 158(20):24-25, May 16, 1984.

Postcoital contraception: awareness of the existence of postcoital contraception among students who have had a therapeutic abortion, by L. H. Schilling. JOURNAL OF AMERICAN COLLEGE HEALTH. 32(6):244-246, June 1984.

Sequelae of therapeutic abortion [letter], by J. F. Cattanach. MEDICAL JOURNAL OF AUSTRALIA. 141(5):316-317, September 1, 1984.

Sequelae of therapeutic abortion, by I. S. Fraser. MEDICAL JOURNAL OF AUSTRALIA. 140(11):639-640, May 26, 1984.

Therapeutic abortion and nursing care, by H. Hulme. NURSING TIMES. 79(41):54-60, October 12-18, 1983.

Therapeutic abortions, by M. Achour, et al. MAROC MEDICAL. 5(2):184-190, June 1983.

Therapeutic interruption of pregnancy in the second trimester after preparation of the cervix with prostaglandins F2 alpha, by B. Maria, et al. JOURNAL DE GYNECOLOGIE, OBSTETRIQUE ET BIOLOGIE DE LA REPRODUCTION. 12(5):545-552, 1983.

Therapy of primary aldosteronism with trilostane, by B. Winterberg, et al. SCHWEIZERISCHE MEDIZINISCHE WOCHEN-

SCHRIFT. 113(46):1735-1738, November 19, 1983.

The use of 15-methylated derivative of prostaglandin F2a for the therapeutic termination of pregnancy and management of late fetal death, by A. Antsaklis, et al. INTERNATIONAL SURGERY. 69(1):63-68, January-March 1984.

The use of real-time ultrasound as an aid during difficult therapeutic abortion procedures, by R. L. Goldenberg, et al. AMERICAN JOURNAL OF OBSTETRICS AND GYNECOLOGY. 148(6): 826-827, March 15, 1984.

What is wrong with the [Manitoba] therapeutic abortion committee system?. CANADIAN DIMENSION. 17:6, November 1983.

ABORTION: THREATENED

Activity of the adrenergic nervous system in the pathophysiology of pregnancy and labor. I. Dopamine beta-hydroxylase (DBH) activity in the plasma of women with physiological pregnancy, threatened and completed abortion and threatened and completed premature labor, by H. Zrubek, et al. GINEKOLOGIA POLSKA. 55(3):161-170, March 1984.

Cholesterol, triglyceride and apolipoprotein concentrations in the serum and lipoprotein fractions in the first trimester of normal pregnancy and threatened abortion, by L. Marianowski, et al. GINEKOLOGIA POLSKA. 55(3):177-184, March 1984.

Clinico-immunologic studies in threatened abortion, by L. S. Dzoz, et al. AKUSHERSTVO I GINEKOLOGIIA. (12):28-29, December 1983.

Complete surgical obliteration of the cervix uteri (Szendi's technic) in the treatment of threatened premature labor, by L. Cesak. CESKOSLOVENSKA GYNEKOLOGIE. 48(3):195-197, April 1983.

Diagnostic procedures in threatened abortion, by J. B. Hertz. OBSTETRICS AND GYNECOLOGY. 64(2):223-229, August 1984.

Effect of serum on lymphocyte chromatin properties in threatened abortion, by V. S. Tolmachev. AKUSHERSTVO I GINEKOLOGIIA. (10):51-54, October 1983.

Effects of laser-puncture therapy in threatened abortion on the hormone content of the blood, by G. G. Dzhvehenava, et al. AKUSHERSTVO I GINEKOLOGIIA. (12):32-33, December 1983.

Immunologic indicators in theatened abortion, by V. V. Shcher-bakova, et al. AKUSHERSTVO I GINEKOLOGIIA. (12):29-31, December 1983.

Plasma renin substrate in the prediction of pregnancy outcome in threatened abortion, by A. S. Siimes, et al. BRITISH JOURNAL OF OBSTETRICS AND GYNAECOLOGY. 90(12):1186-1192, December 1983.

Prognosis of threatened abortion and serum levels of TBG, by S. Wanibe, et al. KAKU IGAKU. 21(2):155-163, February 1984.

Prognostic predictions of threatened abortion. A comparison between real-time ultrasound, clinical assessment and urinary human chorionic gonadotropin (HCG), by S. K. Ping. AUSTRALIA AND NEW ZEALAND JOURNAL OF OBSTETRICS AND GYNAECOLOGY. 23(2):99-102, May 1983.

Prognostic value of biochemical tests in the assessment of fetal outcome in threatened abortion, by H. T. Salem, et al. BRI-TISH JOURNAL OF OBSTETRICS AND GYNAECOLOGY. 91(4):382-385, April 1984.

Prognostic value of changes in serum histaminase (DAO) activity in cases of threatened abortion, by K. Kaminski, et al. PRZEGLAND LEKARSKII. 41(2):205-207, 1984.

Prognostic value of immunoglobulin determination in women with threatened abortion, by H. Donat, et al. ZENTRALBLATT FUR GYNAEKOLOGIE. 106(12):814-826, 1984.

Properties of chromatin of peripheral blood lymphocytes in women with threatened abortion, by V. S. Tolmachev, et al. BIULLETIN EKSPERIMENTALNOI BIOLOGII I MEDITSINY.

97(2):181-183, February 1984.

Serum AFP concentration in threatened abortion, by J. Woyton, et al. WIADOMOSCI LEKARSKIE. 36(17):1411-1414, September 1, 1983.

Serum ferritin levels in normal pregnancy and in women in threatened abortion and premature labor, by M. Sirakov, et al. AKUSHERSTVO I GINEKOLOGIIA. 23(1):10-13, 1984.

Subchorionic bleeding in threatened abortion: sonographic findings and significance, by S. R. Goldstein, et al. AJR. 141(5):975-978, November 1983.

An ultrasonographic study on the pathophysiology of threatened abortion, by M. Kawano. SHIKOKU ACTA MEDICA. 40(1): 1-17, 1984.

Use of circulating progesterone and estradiol levels to predict outcome of pregnancy in cases of threatened abortion, by B. Adelusi, et al. EAST AFRICAN MEDICAL JOURNAL. 60(5):323-327, May 1983.

ABORTION: VOLUNTARY
Absence of coagulation changes in voluntary abortions by aspiration [letter], by M. T. Cousin, et al. ANNALES FRANCAISES D'ANESTHESIE ET DE REANIMATION. 1(4):453, 1982.

Study of the endometrium following voluntary interruption of pregnancy in relation to the contraceptive method used following abortion, by J. B. Sindayirwanya, et al. JOURNAL DE GYNECOLOGIE, OBSTETRIQUE ET BIOLOGIE DE LA REPRODUCTION. 12(4):351-362, 1983.

Voluntary termination of pregnancy, by T. B. Schneider. JOGN NURSING. 13(2 Suppl):77S-84S, March-April 1984.

ABORTION AND COLLEGE STUDENTS
Awareness of the existence of postcoital contraception among students who have had a therapeutic abortion, by L. H. Schilling. JOURNAL OF AMERICAN COLLEGE HEALTH.

32(6):244-246, June 1984.

Exposure to solvents and outcome of pregnancy in university laboratory employees, by G. Axelsson, et al. BRITISH JOURNAL OF INDUSTRIAL MEDICINE. 41(3):305-312, August 1984.

Postcoital contraception: awareness of the existence of postcoital contraception among students who have had a therapeutic abortion, by L. H. Schilling. JOURNAL OF AMERICAN COLLEGE HEALTH. 32:244-246, June 1984.

A Virginia college bans an antiabortion painting [M. C. Carroll vs. Mary Washington College], by R. Frame. CHRISTIANITY TODAY. 28:42+, March 2, 1984.

ABORTION AND CRIMINALS
A toxic way to abort . . . ingesting quinine. EMERGENCY MEDICINE. 16(1):75; 78, January 15, 1984.

ABORTION AND ERA
Abortion clause fight kills ERA. NATIONAL CATHOLIC REPORTER. 20:4, November 25, 1983.

Abortion, related issues are snags in ERA battle, by D. Johnson. REGISTER. 59:1+, December 4, 1983.

Bishops' ERA position avoids equality issue for abortion statement, by Sister M. Fiedler. NATIONAL CATHOLIC REPORTER. 20:30, June 8, 1984.

Court flips ruling that ERA permits abortion, by J. McManus, et al. NATIONAL CATHOLIC REPORTER. 20:6, October 5, 1984.

ERA, abortion linked, by J. Feuerherd. NATIONAL CATHOLIC REPORTER. 20:8, September 14, 1984.

ERA, abortion linked in future of pro-life struggle, by W. A. Ryan. OUR SUNDAY VISITOR. 72:3, January 29, 1984.

ERA and abortion/a legal link, by J. Pasternak. GUARDIAN. 36(26):2, April 4, 1984.

ERA and abortion; Pennsylvania court ruling. ORIGINS. 13: 699-704, March 29, 1984.

E. R. A. and abortion: really separate issues?, by D. Johnson, et al. AMERICA. 150:432-437, June 9, 1984.

Gender, the judiciary, and U. S. public opinion, by G. S. Swan. JOURNAL OF SOCIAL, POLITICAL AND ECONOMIC STUDIES. 8(3):323-341, 1983.

NCCB undertakes study of ERA implications. ORIGINS. 13:778, May 3, 1984.

Pennsylvania court uses ERA to strike down abortion limits, by C. McDonnell. REGISTER. 60:1+, March 25, 1984.

ABORTION AND ECONOMICS
Abortion and its cost. REGISTER. 60:2, January 29, 1984.

The Medicaid cutoff and abortion services for the poor, by S. K. Henshaw, et al. FAMILY PLANNING PERSPECTIVES. 16(4):170-172; 177-180, July-August 1984.

Midtrimester pregnancy termination: a study of the cost effectiveness of dilation and evacuation in a free-standing facility, by T. Crist, et al. NORTH CAROLINA MEDICAL JOURNAL. 44(9):549-551, September 1983.

ABORTION AND THE HANDICAPPED
Will prenatal diagnosis with selective abortion affect society's attitude toward the handicapped?, by A. G. Motulsky, et al. PROGRESS IN CLINICAL AND BIOLOGICAL RESEARCH. 128:277-291, 1983.

ABORTION AND HORMONES
Changes in blood chorionic gonadotropin, progesterone levels and estradiol in midterm labor induced by rivanol, by F. Y. Liu. CHUNG HUA FU CHAN KO TSA CHIH. 19(2):114-115, April 1984.

Comparison of two prostaglandins used to terminate midtrimester pregnancy, by K. S. Gookin, et al. SOUTHERN MEDICAL

JOURNAL. 77(6):717-718; 721, June 1984.

Dinoprostone or sulprostone. Comparison of 2 analogs of prostaglandin for the interruption of pregnancy in the second trimester, by B. Bourrit, et al. JOURNAL DE GYNECOLOGIE, OBSTETRIQUE ET BIOLOGIE DE LA REPRODUCTION. 13(1):87-90, 1984.

Effects of laser-puncture therapy in threatened abortion on the hormone content of the blood, by G. G. Dzhvebenave, et al. AKUSHERSTVO I GINEKOLOGIIA. (12):32-33, December 1983.

Hormonal treatment of spontaneous abortion, by A. Kasulov. AKUSHERSTVO I GINEKOLOGIIA. 23(1):82-88, 1984.

Increased decidual prostaglandin E concentration in human abortion, by O. E. Jaschevatzky, et al. BRITISH JOURNAL OF OBSTETRICS AND GYNAECOLOGY. 90(10):958-960, October 1983.

Induced abortion with two prostaglandin F2 alpha analogues in mares: plasma progesterone changes, by W. van Leeuwen, et al. VETERINARY QUARTERLY. 5(3):97-100, July 1983.

Kinetic studies on prostaglandin concentrations in the amniotic fluid during rivanol-induced abortion, by Z. R. Zhou, et al. YAO HSUEH HSUEH PAO. 18(8):569-571, August 1983.

Late abortion and prostaglandin, by L. W. Sorbye. SYKEPLEIEN. 71(6):13, March 20, 1984.

The legality of abortion by prostaglandin, by G. Wright. THE CRIMINAL LAW REVIEW. June 1984, pp. 347-349.

Maternal plasma estradiol and progesterone levels during therapeutic abortion induced by 16,16 dimethyl PGE2 p-benzaldehyde semicarbazone ester, by K. C. Tan, et al. PROSTAGLANDINS LEUKOTRIENES AND MEDICINE. 14(2):215-224, May 1984.

Midtrimester abortion. Intra-amniotic instillation of hyperosmolar urea and prostaglandin F2 alpha v dilatation and evacuation, by M. E. Kafrissen, et al. JAMA. 251(7):916-919, February 17, 1984.

Postcoital contraceptive efficacy and hormonal profile of Lepidium capitatum, by M. M. Singh, et al. PLANTA MEDICA. 50(2):154-157, April 1984.

Predictive value of hormone determinations in the first half of pregnancy, by I. Gerhard, et al. EUROPEAN JOURNAL OF OBSTETRICS, GYNECOLOGY AND REPRODUCTIVE BIOLOGY. 17(1):1-17, April 1984.

Randomized comparison of prostaglandin treatment in hospital or at home with vacuum aspiration for termination of early pregnancy, by A. S. Rosen, et al. CONTRACEPTION. 29(5): 423-435, May 1984.

Randomized trial of intracervical prostaglandin E2 gel and intraamniotic prostaglandin F2 alpha for induction of second trimester abortion, by S. Stampe Sorenson, et al. CONTRACEPTION. 29(2):171-179, February 1984.

Sex-hormone-binding globulin (SHBG) in serum in threatened abortion, by J. B. Hertz, et al. ACTA ENDOCRINOLOGICA. 104(3):381-384, November 1983.

Use of a new synthetic prostaglandin (sulprostone) in the interruption of pregnancy after the first 90 days, by A. Segre, et al. MINERVA GINECOLOLOGIA. 35(10):681-687, October 1983.

Uterine rupture as a complication of second-trimester abortion when using prostaglandin F2 alpha together with other oxytocic agents, by H. Malmstrom, et al. ACTA OBSTETRICIA ET GYNECOLOGICA SCANDINAVICA. 63(3):271-272, 1984.

ABORTION AND HOSPITALS

Beds for abortion: McMurray's new hospital sparks a pro-mill move, by T. Philip. ALBERTA REPORT. 10:37, October 24, 1983.

The 1983 Supreme Court abortion decisions: impact on hospitals, a conflict with Baby Doe?, by R. A. Carlson. HEALTH LAW VIGIL. 6(21):2-7, October 14, 1983.

Nurse protests spur hospitals to limit second-trimester abortions. RN. 46:13, June 1983.

Randomized comparison of prostaglandin treatment in hospital or at home with vacuum aspiration for termination of early pregnancy, by A. S. Rosen, et al. CONTRACEPTION. 29(5): 423-435, May 1984.

Why should Catholic hospitals promote abortion sterilization alternatives?. HOSPITAL PROGRESS. 65:67-68, February 1984.

ABORTION AND INSURANCE
Foes of abortion start a prolife insurance company [American Pro Life Assurance Society, Illinois]. CHRISTIANITY TO-DAY. 28:43, February 3, 1984.

ABORTION AND LITERATURE
Bibliographie sur l'avortement, by F. Fourgeroux. REVUE FRANCAISE SOCIOLOGIE. 23:527-535, July-September 1982.

Pro-choice perspectives, by D. Andrusko, et al. COMMONWEAL. 111:183+, March 23, 1984.

Quick-bibs: abortion, by B. Ott. AMERICAN LIBRARIES. 15:691, November 1984.

ABORTION AND MALES
Husband has no standing to enjoin wife from having an abortion. THE FAMILY LAW REPORTER: COURT OPINIONS. 10(21): 1284, March 27, 1984.

Out-of-wedlock abortion and delivery: the importance of the male partner, by J. M. Robbins. SOCIAL PROBLEMS. 31(3): 334-350, February 1984.

Rejection of husband's claim to stop wife's abortion, by J. K. Bentil. SOLICITORS' JOURNAL. 128:288-290, April 27, 1984.

Selected psychosocial characteristics of males: their relationship to contraceptive use and abortion, by D. Andres, et al. PERSONAL AND SOCIAL PSYCHOLOGY BULLETIN. 9:387-396, September 1983.

Spousal notification: an unconstitutional limitation on a woman's right to privacy in the abortion decision. HOFSTRA LAW REVIEW. 12:531-560, Winter 1984.

ABORTION AND THE MENTALLY RETARDED
Abortion and euthanasia of Down's syndrome children—the parents' view, by B. Shepperdson. JOURNAL OF MEDICAL ETHICS. 9(3):152-157, September 1983.

Making up her mind: consent, pregnancy and mental handicap, by R. Higgs. JOURNAL OF MEDICAL ETHICS. 9(4):219-226, December 1983.

ABORTION AND NURSES
All in the line of duty? . . . Many nurses feel ambivalent towards abortion, by M. Kenny. NURSING MIRROR. 158(20):22-23, May 16, 1984.

Case studies for students: a companion to teaching ethics in nursing, by M. L. Applegate, et al. NLN PUBLICATIONS. (41-1963A):1-36, 1984.

The nature of nursing care of women seeking an abortion, by F. Hebert, et al. INFIRMIERE CANADIENNE. 26(5):25-28, May 1984.

Nurse protests spur hospitals to limit second-trimester abortions. RN. 46:13, June 1983.

Nurses in conflict. A survey, by B. Jamtback. KRANKENPFLEG JOURNAL. 21(10):7, October 1, 1983.

Nursing Mirror midwifery forum. Problems in pregnancy: inevitable abortion, by D. Rutledge. NURSING MIRROR. 158(6): v; viii, February 8, 1984.

Opinion poll: evaluation and analysis. What the Spanish nursing profession thinks about abortion. REVISTA DE ENFERMA-GEN. 6(60):12-17; 19-21, July 1983.

Teaching ethics in nursing: a handbook for use of the case-study approach, by M. L. Applegate, et al. NLN PUBLICATIONS. (41-1963):1-81, 1984.

Therapeutic abortion and nursing care, by H. Hulme. NURSING TIMES. 79(41):54; 56-58; 60, October 12-18, 1983.

ABORTION AND PARENTAL CONSENT

Abortion— Provisions of city abortion ordinance requiring hospitalization for all abortions performed after the first trimester of pregnancy, notification and consent of parents before performance of abortions on unmarried minors, conveyance by attending physician of specific statements to insure informed consent, delay of twenty-four hours between the time a woman signs a consent form and the time an abortion is performed, and disposal of the fetus in a humane and sanitary manner are violations of the constitutional right of privacy. City of Akron v. Akron Center for Reproductive Health, Inc. JOURNAL OF FAMILY LAW. 22:159-167, 1983-1983.

CA2 enjoins implementation of government's "squeal rule." THE FAMILY LAW REPORTER: COURT OPINIONS. 10(2): 1024-1025, November 8, 1983.

Spousal notification and the right of privacy. Scheinberg v. Smith. CHICAGO-KENT LAW REVIEW. 59:1129-1151, 1983.

Which parent owns the child? [father denied right to stop abortion], by B. Amiel. MACLEANS. 97:17, April 16, 1984.

ABORTION AND PHYSICIANS

Abortion as a medical career choice: entrepreneurs, community physicians, and others, by M. S. Goldstein. JOURNAL OF HEALTH AND SOCIAL BEHAVIOR. 25(2):211-229, June 1984.

Canadian MDs challenge antiabortion, by M. Jones. MILITANT. 48(15):15, April 27, 1984.

The doctor couldn't bear to watch, by J. Sobran. CONSERVATIVE

DIGEST. 10:38, August 1984.

The ethical challenge. Is the physician allowed to do what he must do?. MMW. 126(6):132-136, February 10, 1984.

Health personnel in the matter of legal abortion: physicians and other personnel should have the right to refuse to perform abortions, by L. Jacobsson, et al. LAKARTIDNINGEN. 80(39): 3541-3545, September 28, 1983.

ABORTION AND PLANNED PARENTHOOD
Anti-choice terrorists strike again [at Annapolis, Maryland, Planned Parenthood clinic and the National Abortion Federation's Washington, D. C., headquarters], by F. Elliott. OFF OUR BACKS. 14:5, August-September 1984.

ABORTION AND POLICE
Facing trial, former police chief has no regrets for his prolife activism, by P. Sheehan. REGISTER. 60:1+, July 15, 1984.

ABORTION AND POLITICS
Abortion activists mark January anniversary, by S. Hyde. GAY COMMUNITY. 11(28):1, February 4, 1984.

The abortion issue in the 1980 elections, by D. Granberg, et al. FAMILY PLANNING PERSPECTIVES. 15:231-238, September-October 1983.

Abortion, politics and the bishops. COMMONWEAL. 111:163-165, March 23, 1984.

Another weary round/abortion debate, by A. Hayford. BRIAR-PATH. 13(2):14, March 1984.

Archbishop John O'Connor's strong stand on abortion makes him a holy terror to Democrats. PEOPLE WEEKLY. 22:47-48, October 1, 1984.

Archbishop says politicians must fight abortion laws. OUR SUNDAY VISITOR. 73:8, October 28, 1984.

The bishops and the politics of abortion, by M. Meehan.

COMMONWEAL. 111:169-173, March 23, 1984.

Bishops' letter on politics: healthy declaration or exhortation to consider abortion above all?, by R. B. Shaw, et al. NATIONAL CATHOLIC REPORTER. 20:8-9, August 31, 1984.

Casting a vote for life, by G. C. Zahn. AMERICA. 151:337-339, November 24, 1984.

A Catholic woman in the White House?. COMMONWEAL. 111: 419-421, August 10, 1984.

Church and Cuomo. COMMONWEAL. 111:517-518, October 5, 1984.

The church-state debate [M. Cuomo vs. Catholic bishops on abortion], by C. Krauthammer. NEW REPUBLIC. 191:15-18, September 17-24, 1984.

Club of life, tied to LaRouche, is courting U. S. prolife mainstream, by T. Ackerman. REGISTER. 60:1+, April 1, 1984.

Confused Cuomo, angry Safire attack bishop, by W. F. Gavin. HUMAN EVENTS. 44:12+, September 22, 1984.

Conscience and politics, by B. G. Mitchell. TABLET. 238:966-968, October 6, 1984.

Court flips ruling that ERA permits abortion, by J. McManus, et al. NATIONAL CATHOLIC REPORTER. 20:6, October 5, 1984.

Cuomo wants political realism in abortion debate, by M. Scheiber. OUR SUNDAY VISITOR. 73:8, September 30, 1984.

Determinants of attitudes toward abortion in the American electorate, by J. S. Legge, Jr. WESTERN POLITICAL QUARTERLY. 36:479-490, September 1983.

ERA and abortion: Pennsylvania court ruling. ORIGINS. 13:699-704, March 29, 1984.

Facing trial, former police chief has no regrets for his prolife activism, by P. Sheehan. REGISTER. 60:1+, July 15, 1984.

Federal abortion alternatives cut by Reagan administration, by N. Cohodas. CONGRESSIONAL QUARTERLY WEEKLY REPORT. 42:2949-2955, November 17, 1984.

Ferraro's fuzzy thinking on abortion, by T. A. Mitchell. HUMAN EVENTS. 44:11, August 18, 1984.

Ferraro's pro-abortion record, by M. Stanton Evans. HUMAN EVENTS. 44:9+, October 6, 1984.

Few in Congress vote the seamless garment, by M. Meehan. REGISTER. 60:1+, December 9, 1984.

The governor and the bishops [M. Cuomo at Notre Dame]. NEW REPUBLIC. 191:7-9, October 8, 1984.

Group working to make Democratic Party pro-life, by P. Sheehan. OUR SUNDAY VISITOR. 73:4, October 21, 1984.

Hard-line stand [Reagan administration considers cutting aid to governments that sanction abortion]. TIME. 124:21, July 2, 1984.

The Human Life Bill: some issues and answers, by H. J. Hyde. NEW YORK LAW SCHOOL LAW REVIEW. 27:1077-1100, 1982.

Hyde and go seek: a response to Representative Hyde, by H. F. Pilpel. NEW YORK LAW SCHOOL LAW REVIEW. 27(4):1101-1123, 1982.

Hyde: standing up for what's right, by D. De Celles. REGISTER. 60:2, October 7, 1984.

Jesse Jackson changes position on abortion, by M. Meehan. REGISTER. 59:1+, November 20, 1983.

Latest polls show that public support for legal abortion continues. FAMILY PLANNING PERSPECTIVES. 15:279-280, November-December 1983.

March for Life. CHRISTIANITY TODAY. 28:53, March 2, 1984.

Mayor, neighbors unite against abortion facility. REGISTER. 60:2, January 1, 1984.

More debate on abortion, by M. Beck. NEWSWEEK. 104:27, September 24, 1984.

Naral's new way, by V. Rosenquist. SOUTHERN EXPOSURE. 12:26-31, January-February 1984.

O'Connor defends obsession of abortion, by D. Ryan. NATIONAL CATHOLIC REPORTER. 21:23, October 26, 1984.

Of many things [speech by H. J. Hyde on Catholic Church and abortion], by G. W. Hunt. AMERICA. 151:inside cover, October 6, 1984.

Patchy garment [G. Ferraro's stand on abortion], by D. R. Carlin, Jr. COMMONWEAL. 111:422-423, August 10, 1984.

Personal abortion opinions shake political platforms. OUR SUNDAY VISITOR. 73:3, August 19, 1984.

Politics and abortion, by K. L. Woodward. NEWSWEEK. 104:66-67, August 20, 1984.

The politics of abortion, by J. G. Deedy. TABLET. 238:262-263, August 11, 1984.

The politics of abortion: trends in Canadian fertility policy, by L. D. Collins, et al. ATLANTIS. 7(2):2-20, 1982.

Prelate uncomfortable with Reagan's approach to issues. REGISTER. 60:2, October 21, 1984.

Prolife activists reject both nukes and abortion, hold national gathering, by M. Meehan. REGISTER. 60:1+, June 17, 1984.

A "prolife" population delegation?, by C. Holden. SCIENCE. 224: 1321-1322, June 22, 1984.

Prolifers claim they'll make headway in the new Congress, by M. Meehan. REGISTER. 60:1+, November 18, 1984.

Prolifers criticize Ferraro record, by M. Meehan. REGISTER. 60:1+, July 29, 1984.

Prolifers gear up for election-year battles. CHRISTIANITY TODAY. 28:65-66, September 7, 1984.

Public support for legal abortion continues, although polls show conflicting trends in 1983. FAMILY PLANNING PERSPECTIVE. 15(6):279-281, November-December 1983.

Pulpit politics [Bishop J. W. Malone criticizes pro-choice politicians]. TIME. 124:26, August 20, 1984.

Reagan courts Catholics on abortion, relief aid, by S. Askin, et al. NATIONAL CATHOLIC REPORTER. 20:7, May 18, 1984.

Reagan: no funds to groups that promote abortion, by J. Friedland. NATIONAL CATHOLIC REPORTER. 20:4, August 3, 1984.

Reagan's war on abortion, by M. Kramer. NEW YORK. 17:27+, September 24, 1984.

Religion and politics: clearing the air. COMMONWEAL. 111:451-452, September 7, 1984.

Religion comes first [M. Cuomo's attack on Catholic position], by J. Sobran. NATIONAL REVIEW. 36:16, September 7, 1984.

Religious belief and public morality [M. Cuomo's Notre Dame speech], by C. M. Whelan. AMERICA. 151:156; 159-163, September 29, 1984.

Religious influence and congressional voting on abortion, by B. W. Daynes, et al. JOURNAL FOR THE SCIENTIFIC STUDY OF RELIGION. 23(2):197-200, 1984.

A response to Governor Cuomo, by H. J. Hubbard. ORIGINS. 14:304, October 25, 1984.

Right to Life president continues the abortion battle, interview with Jean Eleanor Doyle, by B. Kennedy. OUR SUNDAY VISITOR. 72:4, January 22, 1984.

Ronald Reagan on abortion. NEWSWEEK. 103:23, April 30, 1984.

Scrutiny of Ferraro remarks on abortion only deepens worry, by M. Meehan. REGISTER. 60:1+, September 2, 1984.

Senate panel agrees to relax federal abortion restrictions. CONGRESSIONAL QUARTERLY WEEKLY REPORT. 42:1592, June 29, 1984.

Social, spatial and political determinants of U. S. abortion rates, by N. F. Henry, et al. SOCIAL SCIENCE AND MEDICINE. 16(9):987-996, 1982.

Strategists work to sound the death knell for abortion [Roe v. Wade], by R. Frame. CHRISTIANITY TODAY. 28:74, May 18, 1984.

Talking sense on population [Reagan administration stand on cutting aid to governments that sanction abortion]. NATIONAL REVIEW. 36:15-16, August 10, 1984.

Unsocial issues [R. Reagan speaks on abortion and school prayer]. NEW REPUBLIC. 190:9-10, February 27, 1984.

The war between the women, by K. Luker. FAMILY PLANNING PERSPECTIVES. 16:105-110, May-June 1984.

Wattleton blasts Reagan on harsh abortion stand. JET. 66:39, August 6, 1984.

When religion mixes with politics [abortion issue and the Catholic church]. U. S. NEWS AND WORLD REPORT. 97:8, August 20, 1984.

White House briefing eyes prolife alternatives, by J. Manney. REGISTER. 60:1+, May 20, 1984.

Who are the bigots?. NATIONAL REVIEW. 36:17-18, October 19, 1984.

Abortion and the archbishop [J. J. O'Connor], by J. Klein. NEW YORK. 17:36-43, October 1, 1984.

Abortion and the Christian story, by M. K. Duffey. LINACRE QUARTERLY. 51:60-69, February 1984.

Abortion and dialogue, by D. R. Carlin, Jr. AMERICA. 151:64, August 18-25, 1984.

Abortion group says Church violates tax laws. OUR SUNDAY VISITOR. 73:8, October 14, 1984.

Abortion is not a 'religious issue', by J. Hart. HEALTH EDUCATION. 44:9, October 13, 1984.

Abortion, politics, and the bishops. COMMONWEAL. 111:163-165, March 23, 1984.

Abortion: a pro-life view, by R. J. Adamek. USA TODAY. 112:98, May 1984.

Abortion, religion and the law, by D. R. Carlin, Jr. AMERICA. 151:356-358, December 1, 1984.

Abortion: a religious issue?, by Sister M. M. Mooney. LINACRE QUARTERLY. 51:53-59, February 1984.

Abortion: the role of public officials; New York bishops' statement. ORIGINS. 13:759-760, April 26, 1984.

Archbishop: Ferraro misstated abortion teaching. OUR SUNDAY VISITOR. 73:5, September 23, 1984.

Archbishop John O'Connor's strong stand on abortion makes him a holy terror to Democrats. PEOPLE WEEKLY. 22:47-48, October 1, 1984.

Archbishop John J. O'Connor, interview by J. C. O'Neill. OUR SUNDAY VISITOR. 73:3+, October 14, 1984.

Archbishop, governor, and veep [J. J. O'Connor's statement on Catholic principles and abortion], by M. Novak. NATIONAL

REVIEW. 36:45, September 21, 1984.

Archbishop Law calls abortion primordial darkness, by B. F. Law. OUR SUNDAY VISITOR. 72:8, April 8, 1984.

Archbishop says politicans must fight abortion laws. OUR SUNDAY VISITOR. 73:8, October 28, 1984.

Attitudes toward abortion among Catholic Mexican-American women: the effects of religiosity and education, by S. Rosenhouse-Persson, et al. DEMOGRAPHY. 20:87-98, February 1983.

Baptists and freedom: some reminders and remembrances of our past for the sake of our present, by H. Moody. AMERICAN BAPTIST QUARTERLY. 3(1):4-15, March 1984.

The bishops and the politics of abortion, by M. Meehan. COMMONWEAL. 111:169-173, March 23, 1984.

Bishops' ERA position avoids equality issue for abortion statement, by Sister M. Fiedler. NATIONAL CATHOLIC REPORTER. 20:30, June 8, 1984.

Bishops' letter on politics: healthy declaration or exhortation to consider abortion above all?, by R. B. Shaw, et al. NATIONAL CATHOLIC REPORTER. 20:8-9, August 31, 1984.

Breaking through the stereotypes, by S. Callahan, et al. COMMONWEAL. 111:520-523, October 5, 1984.

Carr resigns from women's pastoral, by C. Hays. REGISTER. 60:1+, October 21, 1984.

Catholic teaching on abortion in a secular society, by D. E. Pilarczyk. OUR SUNDAY VISITOR. 73:6, October 7, 1984.

Catholic theologians clash on abortion, by M. Meehan. REGISTER. 60:1+, July 1, 1984.

A Catholic woman in the White House?. COMMONWEAL. 111:419-421, August 10, 1984.

Catholics and abortion; interview with Frances Kissling, by M. Meehan. REGISTER. 60:1+, May 20, 1984.

Choicers courting Catholic academics, by J. F. Hitchcock. REGISTER. 60:1+, June 3, 1984.

Chromosome anomalies in 136 couples with a history of recurrent abortions, by U. Diedrich, et al. HUMAN GENETICS. 65(1):48-52, 1983.

The church and abortion, perception and reality, by P. Zagano. COMMONWEAL. 111:173-175, March 23, 1984.

Church and Cuomo. COMMONWEAL. 111:517-518, October 5, 1984.

The church-state debate [M. Cuomo vs. Catholic bishops on abortion], by C. Krauthammer. NEW REPUBLIC. 191:15-18, September 17-24, 1984.

Coitus-related cervical cancer risk factors: trends and differentials in racial and religious groups, by G. E. Hendershot. AMERICAN JOURNAL OF PUBLIC HEALTH. 73:299-301, March 1983.

Colorado bishops endorse Amendment No. 3. ORIGINS. 14:223-224, September 20, 1984.

Commentary on abortion article, by T. J. O'Donnell. LINACRE QUARTERLY. 51:11-13, February 1984.

Confused Cuomo, angry Safire attack bishop, by W. F. Gavin. HUMAN EVENTS. 44:12+, September 22, 1984.

Consistent ethic of life: morally correct, tactically necessary, by J. L. Bernardin. ORIGINS. 14:120-122, July 12, 1984.

Continental war [Roman Catholic church], by L. Cohen, et al. ALBERTA REPORT. 11:34, July 9, 1984.

A critique of two theological papers, by G. G. Grisez. HOMILETIC AND PASTORAL REVIEW. 84:10-15, July 1984.

Dan Maguire on Catholic theology and abortion; interview with Daniel Charles Maguire, by M. Meehan. REGISTER. 60:1+, October 21, 1984.

Dis-united: Catholics divorce the [Edmonton] charity federation, by G. Herchak. ALBERTA REPORT. 11:40, July 16, 1984.

The efficacy of religious participation in the national debates over abolitionism and abortion, by M. C. Sernett. JOURNAL OF RELIGION. 64:205-220, April 1984.

The governor and the bishops [M. Cuomo at Notre Dame]. NEW REPUBLIC. 191:7-9, October 8, 1984.

Grim reapers for hire, by R. E. Burns. U. S. CATHOLIC. 49:2, June 1984.

Healing the women who sorrow, by K. Arriaga. REGISTER. 60:1+, September 30, 1984.

How Catholic can an abortion be?, by M. Meehan. REGISTER. 60:1+, May 20, 1984.

How freedom of thought is smothered in America: a pluralistic society demands that Christian values be heard, by C. Horn. CHRISTIANITY TODAY. 28:12-17, April 6, 1984.

In God's image: a statement on the sanctity of human life. ORIGINS. 14:151-153, August 9, 1984.

Ireland: bishops' pawns [constitutional amendment that would bar legalization of abortion]. ECONOMIST. 287:44+, April 9, 1983.

Jewish-Christian feminist dialogue: a wholistic vision, by D. McCauley, et al. UNION SEMINARY QUARTERLY REVIEW. 38(2):147-190, 1983.

Liberals shun abortion as single issue, by S. Askin. NATIONAL CATHOLIC REPORTER. 20:10, September 28, 1984.

Moral leadership and partisanship [obligations of Catholic

public officials], by J. A. Califano. AMERICA. 151:164-165, September 29, 1984.

Not a single-issue Church, bishops say. ORIGINS. 14:217-218, September 20, 1984.

OSV/Gallup report: abortion limits favored, by J. Castelli. OUR SUNDAY VISITOR. 73:8, December 9, 1984.

Original sin and the unborn, by A. L. Garcia. CONCORDIA THEOLOGICAL QUARTERLY. 47:147-152, April 1983.

The pols and the bishops. NATIONAL REVIEW. 36:18-19, October 5, 1984.

Pope reaffirms Humanae Vitae, by T. C. Fox. NATIONAL CATHOLIC REPORTER. 20:1+, July 20, 1984.

Pressing the abortion issue; the Catholic view, by E. Magnuson. TIME. 124:18-20, September 24, 1984.

Probabilism and abortion, by D. C. Maguire. CHRISTIAN CENTURY. 101:174, February 15, 1984.

Rating the press on pro-life questions, by J. J. Higgins. LIGUORIAN. 72:26-31, October 1984.

Reagan courts Catholics on abortion, relief aid, by S. Askin, et al. NATIONAL CATHOLIC REPORTER. 20:7, May 18, 1984.

Religion and politics: clearing the air. COMMONWEAL. 111:451-452, September 7, 1984.

Religion and politics: interview with David Patrick O'Keefe, interviewed by M. Arnold. REGISTER. 60:1+, April 22, 1984.

Religion comes first [M. Cuomo's attack on Catholic position], by J. Sobran. NATIONAL REVIEW. 36:16, September 7, 1984.

Religious belief and public morality, by C. M. Whelan. AMERICA. 151:159-163, September 229, 1984.

Religous influence and congressional voting on abortion, by B.

W. Daynes, et al. JOURNAL FOR THE SCIENTIFIC STUDY OF RELIGION. 23(2):197-200, June 1984.

Religious leaders join to back abortion funding [Michigan]. JET. 66:29, April 30, 1984.

Respect for life, sexual morality, and opposition to abortion, by T. G. Jelen. REVIEW OF RELIGIOUS RESEARCH. 25:220-231, March 1984.

The Roman Catholic Church and abortion: an historical perspective, by D. T. De Marco. HOMILETIC AND PASTORAL REVIEW. 84:59-66, July 1984; 84:68+, August-September 1984.

Rules for liberals [Catholics opposed to abortion], by D. R. Carlin, Jr. COMMONWEAL. 111:486-487, September 21, 1984.

The social, theological and biological context of abortion: tenth anniversary reflections on Roe v. Wade, by G. H. Williams. LINACRE QUARTERLY. 50:335-354, November 1983.

Statement and proposals of the regional Chinese Catholic Bishops' Conference on the issue should abortion be legalized? L'OSSERVATORE ROMANO. (30):11-12, July 23, 1984.

Suit charges subsidy for religious views. E/SA. 12:35, April 1984.

Theologian resigns after signing abortion statement, by J. T. Beifuss. NATIONAL CATHOLIC REPORTER. 20:21, October 19, 1984.

To abort is to destroy one's son or daughter, by J. T. Burtchaell. NATIONAL CATHOLIC REPORTER. 20:11, October 5, 1984.

The tradition of probabilism and the moral status of the early embryo, by C. A. Tauer. THEOLOGICAL STUDIES. 45:3-33, March 1984.

U. S. bishops advise Democrats to emphasize life. OUR SUNDAY VISITOR. 73:8, June 24, 1984.

U. S. bishops seek to clear electoral confusion by reiterating opposition to abortion and nuclear arms, by S. Askin. NATIONAL CATHOLIC REPORTER. 20:1+, October 19, 1984.

A Virginia college bans an antiabortion painting: a five-month-old fetus is part of the artwork, by R. Frame. CHRISTIANITY TODAY. 28:42+, March 2, 1984.

Voice of tradition: genetic counseling in a liberal Jewish context, by F. L. Weiss. RECONSTRUCTIONIST. 49:26-32, April-May 1984.

Walking away from Omelas, by R. Doerflinger. OUR SUNDAY VISITOR. 73:10, October 7, 1984.

What do American Catholics really think about abortion?, by R. Doerflinger. OUR SUNDAY VISITOR. 72:4+, January 22, 1984.

When religion mixes with politics [abortion issue and the Catholic Church]. U. S. NEWS AND WORLD REPORT. 97:8, August 20, 1984.

Why should Catholic hospitals promote abortion sterilization alternatives?. HOSPITAL PROGRESS. 65:67-68, February 1984.

ABORTION AND TELEVISION
Pro-lifers protest abortion as subject on TV sitcom. OUR SUNDAY VISITOR. 72:8, February 19, 1984.

ABORTION AND YOUTH
The abortion decision for Minnesota minors who decides?. WILLIAM MITCHELL LAW REVIEW. 9:194-215, 1983.

Abortion— Provisions of city abortion ordinance requiring hospitalization for all abortions performed after the first trimester of pregnancy, notification and consent of parents before performance of abortions on unmarried minors, conveyance by attending physician of specific statements to insure informed consent, delay of twenty-four hours between the time a woman signs a consent form and the time an abortion is performed, and disposal of the fetus in a humane and sanitary manner are violations of the constitutional right of privacy. City of Akron v. Akron Center for Reproductive Health, Inc. JOURNAL OF FAMILY LAW. 22:159-167, 1983-1984.

Attitudes toward abortion and contraception among Nigerian secondary school girls, by A. U. Oronsaye, et al. INTERNATIONAL JOURNAL OF GYNAECOLOGY AND OBSTETRICS. 21(5):423-426, October 1983.

CA 2 enjoins implementation of government's "squeal rule." THE FAMILY LAW REPORTER: COURT OPINIONS. 10(2): 1024-1025, November 8, 1983.

A cultural and historical perspective on pregnancy-related activity among U. S. teenagers, by A. C. Washington. JOURNAL OF BLACK PSYCHOLOGY. 9(1):1-28, August 1982.

Factors discriminating pregnancy resolution decisions of unmarried adolescents, by M. Eisen, et al. GENETIC PSYCHOLOGY MONOGRAPHS. 108(1st half):69-95, August 1983.

How does abortion affect a family's other children, by S. Katz. CHATELAINE. 57:16, March 1984.

Judging teenagers: how minors fare when they seek court-authorized abortions, by P. Donovan. FAMILY PLANNING PERSPECTIVES. 15(6):259-262; 264-267, November-December 1983.

Medical risks of teenage pregnancy, by J. A. Straton, et al. AUSTRALIAN FAMILY PHYSICIAN. 12(6):474; 477-478; 480, June 1983.

The risks associated with teenage abortion, by W. Cates, Jr., et al. NEW ENGLAND JOURNAL OF MEDICINE. 309:621-624, September 15, 1983.

Significance of pregnancy among adolescents choosing abortion as compared to those continuing pregnancy, by M. Morin-Gonthier, et al. JOURNAL OF REPRODUCTIVE MEDICINE. 29(4):255-259, 1984.

Spousal notification and the right of privacy. Scheinberg v. Smith. CHICAGO-KENT LAW REVIEW. 59:1129-1151, 1983.

Teenage abortion in the United States, by W. Cates, Jr., et al. PUBLIC HEALTH REVIEWS. 11(4):291-310, October-December 1983.

Teenage pregnancies and abortion, by J. E. Morgenthau. MT. SINAI JOURNAL OF MEDICINE. 51(1):18-19, January-February 1984.

Termination of pregnancy in teenagers, by D. Krishnamoni, et al. CANADIAN JOURNAL OF PSYCHIATRY. 28(6):457-461, October 1983.

Voluntary interruption of pregnancy in adolescents from 13 to 18 years of age. Clinical and sociologic analysis of 295 cases, by M. Vekemans, et al. JOURNAL DE GYNECOLOGIE, OBSTETRIQUE ET BIOLOGIE DE LA REPRODUCTION. 13(1):21-30, 1984.

Which parent owns the child? [father denied right to stop abortion], by B. Amiel. MACLEANS. 97:17, April 16, 1984.

ABORTION CLINICS
Abortion clinics firebombed, by C. Oliver. NEW WOMEN'S TIMES. 10(1):1, January 1984.

Abortion clinics and rights attacked, by E. Bader. GUARDIAN. 36(40):6, July 25, 1984.

Abortion clinics under fire, by M. Snell. MOTHER JONES. 9:8, November 1984.

Abortion risks for teens as low or lower than risks for older women. FAMILY PLANNING PERSPECTIVES. 15(6):282-283, November-December 1983.

Acts of terror [eleventh act of terrorism against abortion clinics, when Planned Parenthood of Maryland's Annapolis center was bombed]. NEW DIRECTIONS FOR WOMEN. 13:1+, September-October 1984.

Adolescent pregnancy program stresses family counseling, educational services, by B. A. McNeil, et al. HOSPITAL PROGRESS. 65(5):12-14; 31, May 1984.

Characteristics of first trimester abortion patients at an urban Indian clinic, by S. Bahl Dhall, et al. STUDIES IN FAMILY PLANNING. 15(2):93-97, March-April 1984.

Clinic arson suspect goes to trial, by D. Mathiason. GUARDIAN. 36(44):4, September 12, 1984.

Everett womens clinic firebombed, by A. Fine. NORTHWEST PASSAGE. 24(6):4, January 1984.

The reality of abortion, by R. Diamond. NEW DIRECTIONS FOR WOMEN. 13:5, November-December 1984.

Rightist charged in Washington. Antiabortion bombing, by L. Hickler. MILITANT. 48(29):24, August 3, 1984.

Trial by fire/feminist health clinic, by L. Averill. NORTHWEST PASSAGE. 24(11):1, June 1984.

Visit to an abortion clinic, by D. C. Maguire. NATIONAL CATHOLIC REPORTER. 20:9, October 5, 1984.

ABORTION COUNSELING
Abortion counseling, by A. Broome. NURSING MIRROR. 158(20):19-20, May 16, 1984.

Counseling and the abortion issue, by P. J. Riga. JOURNAL OF PASTORAL COUNSELING. 17:44-55, Fall-Winter 1982.

SHSTF's answer to the abortion committee: support patient and personnel and expand contraceptive counseling, by A. Widen. VARDFACKET. 8(3):42-45, February 9, 1984.

Voice of tradition: genetic counseling in a liberal Jewish context, by F. L. Weiss. RECONSTRUCTIONIST. 49:26-32, April-May 1984.

ABORTION FUNDING
Abortion and its cost. REGISTER. 60:2, January 29, 1984.

Abortion ban eased in Labor-HHS money bill, by J. Hook. CONGRESSIONAL QUARTERLY WEEKLY REPORT. 42:2359-2360, September 29, 1984.

Abortion books— a bumper crops, by D. Andrusko. NATIONAL CATHOLIC REPORTER. 20:9, February 24, 1984.

Constitutional law— fourteenth amendment— right to abortion— regulatory framework— standard of review— the United States Supreme Court has held that the state may not, in its regulation of abortion, deviate from accepted medical practice, and that all pre-viability abortion regulation shall be *subject to strict scrutiny under the compelling state interest standard of substantive due process analysis— City of Akron v. Akron Center for Reproductive Health, Inc. DUQUESNE LAW REVIEW. 22:767-785, Spring 1984.

A debate over sovereign rights [U. S. cuts off funds to family planning agencies that promote abortion], by L. Lopez. TIME. 124:34, August 20, 1984.

Elections may decide future of abort funds, by M. Meehan. REGISTER. 60:1+, November 4, 1984.

Funding the abortion pros, by M. Meehan. REGISTER. 60:1+, January 15, 1984.

The public funding of abortion services: comparative developments in the United States and Australia, by K. A. Petersen. INTERNATIONAL AND COMPARATIVE LAW QUARTERLY. 33:158-180, January 1984.

Public funding of contraceptive, sterilization and abortion services, 1982, by B. Nestor, et al. FAMILY PLANNING PERSPECTIVES. 16(3):128-133, May-June 1984.

Public support for legal abortion continues, although polls show conflicting trends in 1983. FAMILY PLANNING PERSPEC-TIVES. 15(6):279-282, November-December 1983.

Reagan: no funds to groups that promote abortion, by J. Friedland. NATIONAL CATHOLIC REPORTER. 20:4, August 3, 1984.

State funding cutoff for abortions may be constitutionally protected. THE FAMILY LAW REPORTER: COURT OPINIONS. 10(3):1041-1042, November 15, 1983.

Suit charges subsidy for religious views. E/SA. 12:35, April 1984.

Talking sense on population [Reagan administration stand on cutting aid to governments that sanction abortion]. NATION-AL REVIEW. 36:15-16, August 10, 1984.

U. S. bucks the tide on birth control [decision to halt family planning funds for countries promoting abortions]. U. S. NEWS AND WORLD REPORT. 97:8, August 20, 1984.

U. S. says no to overseas abortion funding. CHRISTIANITY TODAY. 28:75-76, September 7, 1984.

BIRTH CONTROL: GENERAL
Birth control centers. Are they a necessary supplement to primary health care?, by T. Bull-Njaa, et al. TIDSSKRIFT FOR DEN NORSKE LAEGEFORENING. 103(26):1798-1802, September 20, 1983.

Birth control coercion on the horizon?, by J. Cavanaugh-O'Keefe. REGISTER. 60:1+, August 26, 1984.

Birth control/custommade child, by A. Barclay. WOMEN AND HEALTH. 9(1):83, Spring 1984.

Birth control— damages— torts. THE FAMILY LAW REPORTER: COURT OPINIONS. 10(16):1219, February 21, 1984.

Birth control discontinuance as a diffusion process, by E. G. Porter. STUDIES IN FAMILY PLANNING. 15(1):20-29, January-February 1984.

Birth control: lucky dip [diagnostic kit by Boots-Celltech Diagnostics]. ECONOMIST. 290:84-85, February 18, 1984.

Birth control manual, by L. Kapplow. EAST WEST. 14(2):86, February 1984.

Birth control: new data on women's choices. RN. 47:14, January 1984.

Birth control [ovulation method], by R. A. Jonas. MS. 13:54+, August 1984.

Birth-control reliability, by J. Whitlow. ESSENCE. 14:36+, February 1984.

Birth control socialization: how to avoid discussing the subject, by J. Aldous. POPULATION AND ENVIRONMENT. 6(1):27, Spring 1983.

Civil liberties, by N. Hentoff. INQUIRY. 7(2):25, January 1984.

Early birth controllers of B. C., by M. F. Bishop. BC STUDIES. (61):64-84, Spring 1984.

Family and marriage textbook banned from 28 Philadelphia schools, by M. R. Day. NATIONAL CATHOLIC REPORTER. 20:7, September 28, 1984.

Historical ways of controlling population: a commentary, by W. J. Kramer. IRNFP. 8:20-33, Spring 1984.

Humanae Vitae revisited: the argument goes on, by J. M. Dominian. TABLET. 238:1052-1053, October 27, 1984.

The life they saved was yours, by B. Weinhouse. LADIES HOME JOURNAL. 101:30+, January 1984.

Lucky dip [urine analysis]. ECONOMIST. 290:84-85, February 18, 1984.

PW interviews [G. Greer], by W. Smith. PUBLISHERS WEEKLY. 225:61-62, May 25, 1984.

Proxies for birth control, by D. G. Sloan. SOCIOLOGICAL FOCUS. 17:77-81, January 1984.

Recent cases: children, by A. Bainham. THE JOURNAL OF SOCIAL WELFARE LAW. September 1984, pp. 287-290.

Some data on natural fertility, by L. Henry. SOCIAL BIOLOGY. 29:145-156, Spring-Summer 1982.

State of the world. HUMANIST. 44:45-46, July-August 1984.

Torts—birth control. THE FAMILY LAW REPORTER. 10(29): 1402, May 22, 1984.

U. S. population stance makes World bank edgy, by F. Harrison. FINANCIAL POST. 78:16. July 14, 1984.

Your birth control: is it still right for you?, by J. E. Rodgers. GLAMOUR. 82:162+, June 1984.

AFRICA
Africa faces up to overpopulation, by A. Marshall. NEW SCIENTIST. 101:10-11, February 2, 1984.

CANADA
Condom conundrum: a birth control gimmick raises hackles in Calgary. ALBERTA REPORT. 11:13, March 5, 1984.

Teen sex clinic may expand: furore in Calgary pushes the service to capacity, by B. Wilford, et al. ALBERTA RE-PORT. 10:36, October 24, 1983.

Understandable but mistaken: law, morality and the Canadian Catholic Church 1966-1969, by A. De Valk. STUDY SESSIONS: CANADIAN CATHOLIC HISTORICAL ASSO-CIATION. 49:87-109, 1982.

CHINA
Consequences of China's new population policy, by S. L. Wong. CHINA QUARTERLY. June 1984, pp. 220-240.

The growth of China's population, 1949-1982, by A. J.

CHINA
Jowett. GEOGRAPHICAL JOURNAL. 150:155-170, July 1984.

Induced fertility transition: impact of population planning and socio-economic change in the People's Republic of China, by H. Y. Tien. POPULATION STUDIES. 38:385-400, November 1984.

New look at happiness. BEIJING REVIEW. 26:27-28, February 14, 1983.

Population China, by N. Keyfitz. SCIENTIFIC AMERICAN. 250:38-47, February 1984.

The rural Chinese fertility transition: a report from Shifang Xian, Sichuan, by W. R. Lavely. POPULATION STUDIES. 38:365-384, November 1984.

Soul searching, by I. L. Horowitz. SOCIETY. 21:4-8, March-April 1984.

An unwanted baby boom, by M. Beck. NEWSWEEK. 103:47, April 30, 1984.

INDIA
Barren policy, by B. Hartmann, et al. GUARDIAN. April 27, 1984, p. 9.

Husband-wife inconsistencies in contraceptive use responses, by M. A. Koenig, et al. POPULATION STUDIES. 38:281-298, July 1984.

IRELAND
Bitter pills for Garret the Good, by R. Ford. TIMES. November 15, 1984, p. 16.

Inducing the birth of change in Ireland, by R. F. TIMES. May 21, 1984, p. 10

SOUTH AMERICA
Brazil tries birth control. WORLD PRESS REVIEW. 31:54, February 1984.

UNITED STATES
Birth control knowledge, attitudes and practice: a comparison of working and middle class Puerto Rican and white American women, by V. A. Borras. DISSERTATION ABSTRACTS INTERNATIONAL: B. 45(10), April 1985.

The people problem [U. S. position on birth control aid]. AMERICA. 151:62, August 18-25, 1984.

Salt Lake City: Baby City, U. S. A., by E. Stansfield. HUMANIST. 44:19+, May-June, 1984.

U. S. bucks the tide on birth control [decision to halt family planning funds for countries promoting abortions]. U. S. NEWS AND WORLD REPORT. 97:8, August 20, 1984.

BIRTH CONTROL: ATTITUDES
Birth control knowledge, attitudes and practice: a comparison of working and middle class Puerto Rican and white American women, by V. A. Borras. DISSERTATION ABSTRACTS INTERNATIONAL: B. 45(10), April 1985.

BIRTH CONTROL: DEVELOPING COUNTRIES
Child-spacing effects on infant and early child mortality, by J. Hobcraft, et al. POPULATION INDEX. 49:585-618, Winter 1983.

How nations govern growth. SCHOLASTIC UPDATE. 116:18-19, March 2, 1984.

Small families: promoting population stabilization [in developing countries], by J. Jacobsen. TRANSNATIONAL PERSPECTIVES. 9(2):15-18, 183.

A ticking population bomb, by M. Whitaker. NEWSWEEK. 103:43, June 25, 1984.

U. S. inflicts "morality" on a world fit to burst, by R. Righter. SUNDAY TIMES. August 5, 1985, p. 11.

BIRTH CONTROL: HISTORY
Black women in double jeopardy: a perspective on birth control,

by K. H. Gould. HEALTH AND SOCIAL WORK. 9(2):96-105, Spring 1984.

BIRTH CONTROL: LAWS AND LEGISLATION
Can effective birth control be legislated? An analysis of factors that predict birth control utilization, by J. G. Murphy, et al. JOURNAL OF PUBLIC HEALTH POLICY. 5(2):198-212, June 1984.

Understandable but mistaken: law, morality and the Canadian Catholic Church 1966-1969, by A. De Valk. STUDY SESSIONS: CANADIAN CATHOLIC HISTORICAL ASSOCIATION. 49:87-109, 1982.

BIRTH CONTROL: MALES
Birth of a new role for men, by T. Prentice. TIMES. September 24, 1984, p. 9.

Contraception? No, but we're careful, by J. Richters. HEALTH-RIGHT. 3:30-35, November 1984.

Why a lag in male-oriented birth control?, by J. E. Brody. NEW YORK TIMES. October 16, 1983, sec 4, p. 18.

Why men act like boys about birth control, by D. Weinberg. MADEMOISELLE. 90:236+, August 1984.

BIRTH CONTROL: METHODS
And now, propranolol for birth control? RN. 47:107, February 1984.

Computerized birth control, by S. Katz. CHATELAINE. 56:18, November 1983.

BIRTH CONTROL: NATURAL
Rhythm: 1. Periodic abstinence, by H. Ratner. IRNFP. 8:162-169, Summer 1984.

Update on natural birth control, by S. Katz. CHATELAINE. 57:16, January 1984.

Unintended pregnancy and the risks/safety of birth control
methods, by L. Klein. JOGN NURSING. 13(5):287-289,
September-October 1984.

BIRTH CONTROL: RESEARCH
Pill research professor in bid to halt inquiry, by G. Maslen.
TIMES HIGHER EDUCATION SUPPLEMENT. 621:9,
September 28, 1984.

BIRTH CONTROL AND HORMONES
Placental hormone for birth control. SCIENCE NEWS. 124:74,
July 30, 1983.

BIRTH CONTROL AND POLITICS
White House paper on population may be less than it seemed, by
J. Frawley. REGISTER. 60:1+, July 8, 1984.

BIRTH CONTROL AND RELIGION
The Catholic Church's view on population, by A. W. Smith.
SCHOLASTIC UPDATE. 116:3, March 2, 1984.

Feeling like a stranger in my own Church, by K. Matthews.
IRNFP. 8:121-130, Summer 1984.

John Paul argues forcefully against population planning.
REGISTER. 60:3, June 24, 1984.

John Paul II and Humanae Vitae, by S. C. Wroblewski. HOMILE-
TIC AND PASTORAL REVIEW. 85:52-55, October 1984.

Nun urges NFP as humane alternative. REGISTER. 60:3, July 8,
1984.

Pope hits birth control. NATIONAL CATHOLIC REPORTER.
20:4+, August 31, 1984.

Theologians brief press on Church's birth control position.
REGISTER. 60:3, August 5, 1984.

Understandable but mistaken: law, morality and the Canadian
Catholic Church 1966-1969, by A. De Valk. STUDY SES-

SIONS: CANADIAN CATHOLIC HISTORICAL ASSOCIATION. 49:87-109, 1982.

Voice of tradition: genetic counseling in a liberal Jewish context, by F. L. Weiss. RECONSTRUCTIONIST. 49:26-32, April-May 1984.

BIRTH CONTROL AND YOUTH
Adolescents' communication styles for learning about birth control from mass media, by R. De Pietro, et al. HEALTH EDUCATION QUARTERLY. 10(2):106-119, Summer 1983.

Teen sex clinic may expand: furore in Calgary pushes the service to capacity, by B. Wilford, et al. ALBERTA REPORT. 10:36, October 24, 1983.

BIRTH CONTROL FUNDING
The people problem [U. S. position on birth control aid]. AMERICA. 151:62, August 18-25, 1984.

CASTRATION
Castration for rapists criticized. THE NATIONAL SHERIFF. 36(1):32, Feburary-March 1984.

CONTRACEPTIVES: GENERAL
Abortion and contraception: apples and oranges, by H. J. Byrne. AMERICA. 151:272-275, November 3, 1984.

About postcoital contraception, by E. Trimmer. MIDWIFE, HEALTH VISITOR AND COMMUNITY NURSE.

Actinomyces in the female genital tract. A preliminary report, by G. C. Grice, et al. BRITISH JOURNAL OF VENEREAL DISEASES. 59(5):317-319, October 1983.

Angiographic indications of vasculitis in four cases of acute cerebrovascular accidents while taking contraceptives, by C. Mestre, et al. REVISTA CLINICA ESPANOLA. 171(1):27-30, October 1983.

Azoospermia induced by 19-nortestosterone [letter], by R. F. Parrott. LANCET. 1(8379):731, March 31, 1984.

Background factors of defective contraception in abortion-seeking patients, by A. Lalos, et al. LAKARTIDNINGEN. 80(26-27):2646-2648, June 29, 1983.

Benzalkonium chloride tampons. Local tolerance and effects on cervix mucus, by R. Erny, et al. JOURNAL DE GYNECOLOGIE OBSTETRIQUE ET BIOLOGIE DE LA REPRODUCTION. 12(7):767-774, 1983.

Breast feeding . . . its contraceptive effects is increasingly forgotten in the worldwide trend toward bottle feeding, by R. V. Short. SCIENTIFIC AMERICAN. 250(4):35-41, April 1984.

Budd-Chiari syndrome following pregnancy, by F. V. Covillo, et al. MISSOURI MEDICINE. 81(7):356-358, July 1984.

Cardiomyopathy with hepatic necrosis after several years of using Norbiogest Spofa, by M. Brozman, et al. BRATISLAVSKE LEKARSKE LISTY. 80(5):603-609, November 1983.

Clinical study of the secondary effects associated with taking a triphasic anti-ovulatory contraceptive, by M. Vekemans. REVUE MEDICALE DE BRUZELLES. 5(1):13-19, January 1984.

Compliance with therapeutic regimens, by S. Jay, et al. JOURNAL OF ADOLESCENT HEALTH CARE. 5(2):124-136, April 1984.

Contraception and unwanted pregnancy, by N. E. Adler. CONTRACEPTION. 5(4):28-34, Winter 1984.

Contraception: antibodies an answer?, by J. Silberner. SCIENCE NEWS. 126:46, July 21, 1984.

The contraception controversy. TABLET. 237:1199-1200, December 10, 1983.

Contraception: fad and fashion, by A. Kessler, et al. WORLD HEALTH. June 1984, p. 24.

Contraception for adolescents, by M. Broome. PRACTITIONER.

228(1391):493-498, May 1984.

Contraception: helping patients choose, by L. G. Cupit. JOGN NURSING (SUPPL). 13(2):23S-9S, March-April 1984.

Contraception: the hope that failed, by A. Lake. LADIES HOME JOURNAL. 101(8):83-85; 137-138; 142+, August 1984.

Contraception in the perimenopausal years, by J. A. Need. CLINICAL REPRODUCTION AND FERTILITY. 1(4):332-335, December 1982.

Contraception? No, but we're careful, by J. Richters. HEALTH-RIGHT. 3:30-35, November 1984.

Contraception tomorrow, by C. C. Standley, et al. INTERNA-TIONAL NURSING REVIEW. 31(3):73-75, May-June 1984.

Contraception with an LHRH agonist: effect on gonadotrophin and steroid secretion patterns, by H. Kuhl, et al. CLINICAL ENDOCRINOLOGY. 21(2):179-188, August 1984.

Contraceptive knowledge, contraceptive use, and pregnancy risk experience among young Manawatu women, by A. D. Trlin, et al. NEW ZEALAND MEDICAL JOURNAL. 96(746):1055-1058, December 28, 1983.

Contraceptive methods and epilepsy. Consideration on its physiopathogenesis, by J. G. Speciali, et al. ARQUIVOS DE NEUROPSIQUIATRIA. 41(4):332-336, December 1983.

Contraceptive preparations of plant origin, by V. V. Korkhov, et al. AKUSHERSTVO I GINEKOLOGIIA. (11):8-10, November 1983.

Contraceptive self-efficacy: a primary prevention strategy, by R. A. Levinson. JOURNAL OF SOCIAL WORK AND HUMAN SEXUALITY. 3(1):1-15, 1984.

Contraceptives and acute salpingitis, by L. Svensson, et al. JAMA. 251(19):2553-2555, May 18, 1984.

Cottonseed contraceptive update, by J. Silberner. SCIENCE

NEWS. 126:60, July 28, 1984.

Determination of progestational potency: a review, by G. I. Swyer. JOURNAL OF THE ROYAL SOCIETY OF MEDICINE. 77(5):406-409, May 1984.

Dominance and control, by G. Corea. AGENDA. 4(3):20, May 1984.

The effect of different contraceptive treatments on the serum concentration of dehydroepiandrosterone sulfate, by K. L. Klove, et al. CONTRACEPTION. 29(4):319-324, April 1984.

Effects of contraceptive vaginal ring treatment on vaginal bacteriology and cytology, by A. Schwan, et al. CONTRA-CEPTION. 28(4):341-347, October 1983.

Eggs to order, by J. S. Biggs. MEDICAL JOURNAL OF AUSTRALIA. 140(10):572-573, May 12, 1984.

Etiological studies of secondary hypertension. e. Drug-induced hypertension, by E. Kato. NIPPON RINSHO. 42(2):390-398, February 1984.

Evaluation of the in vivo efficacy of a new vaginal contraceptive agent in stumptailed macaques, by L. J. Zaneveld, et al. FERTILITY AND STERILITY. 41(3):455-459, March 1984.

Extent of vaginal absorption of sulphated polysaccharide from A-gen 53 in the rabbit, by S. G. Wood, et al. CONTRACEPTION. 29(4):375-383, April 1984.

Further investigations on the cytological effects of some contra-ceptives, by A. Kabarity, et al. MUTATION RESEARCH. 135(3):181-188, March 1984.

Gynecological services utilization by contraceptive clients: a cost analysis, by J. G. Zapka, et al. JOURNAL OF AMERI-CAN COLLEGE HEALTH. 32(2):66-72, October 1983.

Immunization with spermatozoal peptide antigens resulting in immuno-suppression of fertility rates in female rats, by L. Mettler, et al. ANDROLOGIA. 15(6):670-675, November-December 1983.

Incremental program of contraceptive care of women, by H. G. Neumann, et al. ZEITSCHRIFT FUR AERZTLICHE FORT-BILDUNG. 77(20):841-843, 1983.

Inhibin contraception. AMERICAN FAMILY PHYSICIAN. 29:396, May 1984.

Interception (postcoital contraception), by J. G. Schenker, et al. HAREFUAH. 105(7):176-177, October 2, 1983.

Intracervical release of ST-1435 for contraception, by H. Kurunmäki, et al. CONTRACEPTION. 29(5):411-421, May 1984.

An intravaginal contraceptive device for the delivery of an acrosin and hyaluronidase inhibitor, by P. J. Burck, et al. FERTILITY AND STERILITY. 41(2):314-318, February 1984.

Lack of association between contraceptive usage and congenital malformations in offspring, by S. Linn, et al. AMERICAN JOURNAL OF OBSTETRICS AND GYNECOLOGY. 147(8): 923-928, December 1, 1983.

Latest developments in contraception [letter], by E. L. Billings. MEDICAL JOURNAL OF AUSTRALIA. 140(6):381-382, March 17, 1984.

Long-acting contraceptive agents: aliphatic and alicyclic carboxylic esters of levonorgestrel, by A. Shafiee, et al. STEROIDS. 41(3):349-359, March 1983.

Long-acting contraceptive agents: analysis and purification of steroid esters, by S. A. Matlin, et al. STEROIDS. 41(3):361-367, March 1983.

Long-acting contraceptive agents: design of the WHO Chemical Synthesis Programme, by P. Crabbe, et al. STEROIDS. 41(3): 243-253, March 1983.

Long-acting contraceptive agents: levonorgestrel esters of unsaturated acids, by A. S. Wan, et al. STEROIDS. 41(3):339-348, March 1983.

Medical intervention, by D. Gould. NEW SCIENTIST. 98:485-486, May 19, 1983.

Medroxyprogesterone acetate. Biochemical and clinical aspects, by A. R. Ayala, et al. GINECOLOGICA Y OBSTETRICIA DE MEXICO. 50(305):253-259, September 1982.

Monoclonal antibody to a human germ cell membrane glyco-protein that inhibits fertilization, by R. K. Naz, et al. SCIENCE. 225:342-344, July 20, 1984.

Monoclonal sperm antibodies: their potential for investigations of sperms as target of immunological contraception, by L. Mettler, et al. AMERICAN JOURNAL OF REPRODUCTIVE IMMUNOLOGY. 5(3):125-128, April-May 1984.

Motives for pregnancy, birth and parenthood. Results of an empirical study of females using contraceptives, by O. Mittag, et al. PSYCHOTHERAPIE, PSYCHOSOMATIK, MEDIZINISCHE PSYCHOLOGIE. 34(1):20-24, January 1984.

Mrs. Gillick's campaign. LANCET. 2(8363):1346, December 10, 1983.

Myth of the month. HEALTH. 16:64, March 1984.

A new look at antifertility vaccines, by D. J. Anderson, et al. FERTILITY AND STERILITY. 40(5):557-571, November 1983.

New roads to contraception, by J. E. Jirasek. CESKOSLOVENSKA GYNEKOLOGIE. 48(10):764-768, December 1983.

A new strategy for preventing unintended teenage childbearing... social and welfare needs of disadvantaged adolescents must be addressed, by J. G. Dryfoos. FAMILY PLANNING PERSPECTIVES. 16(4):193-195, July-August 1984.

A new superagonist of GnRH for inhibition of ovulation in

women, by S. J. Nillius, et al. UPSALA JOURNAL OF MEDICAL SCIENCES. 89(2):147-150, 1984.

New techniques in contraception: gossypol, vaccines and GnRH analogues, by R. J. Aitken. PROCEEDINGS OF THE ANNUAL SYMPOSIUM OF THE EUGENICS SOCIETY. 19:1-18, 1983.

Nutritional and medicinal factors in biliary cholesterol lithiasis, by E. Loizeau. REVUE MEDICALE DE LA SUISSE ROMANDE. 104(3):179-184, March 1984.

Ovarian function, bleeding control and serum lipoproteins in women using contraceptive vaginal rings releasing five different progestins, by T. Ahren, et al. CONTRACEPTION. 28(4):315-317, October 1983.

Perceived availability of contraceptives and family limitation, by J. D. Teachman, et al. HUMAN ORGANIZATION.

Pharmacokinetic and 'potency' of contraceptive steroids [letter], by D. J. Back, et al. LANCET. 1(8369):171, January 21, 1984.

Pharmocokinetic interaction of contraceptive steroids with prednisone and prednisolone, by B. M. Frey, et al. EUROPEAN JOURNAL OF CLINICAL PHARMACOLOGY. 26(4):505-511, 1984.

Postcoital contraception, by M. Farkas. AKUSHERSTVO I GINEKOLOGIIA. (11):31-33, November 1983.

Postcoital contraception, by R. Wyss, et al. SCHWEIZERISCHE RUNDSCHAU FUR MEDIZIN PRAXIS. 73(9):283-286, February 28, 1984.

Postcoital pregnancy interception, by D. Llewellyn-Jones. MEDICAL JOURNAL OF AUSTRALIA. 141(7):407-408, September 29, 1984.

Postpartum and post-abortum contraception, by A. A. Yuzpe. UNION MEDICALE DU CANADA. 113(3):191-194, March 1984.

Postpartum contraception, by J. H. Meuwissen. NEDERLANDS

TIJDSCHRIFT VOOR GENEESKUNDE. 128(12):565-567, March 24, 1984.

A preliminary study of the antifertility effect of Vicoa indica in albino rats, by M. Gandhi, et al. INDIAN JOURNAL OF MEDICAL RESEARCH. 78:724-725, November 1983.

Prevention of conception— fate of prevention. The achievements of Ernst Gräfenberg and the reaction of gynecology in his time, by H. Ludwig. ZENTRALBLATT FÜR GYNAEKOLOGIE. 105(18):1197-1205, 1983.

The prevention of procreation: contraception, by D. C. Overduin, et al. IRNFP. 8:131-144, Summer 1984.

A quest for better contraception: the Ford Foundation's contribution to reproductive science and contraceptive development 1959-1983, by R. Hertz. CONTRACEPTION. 29(2):107-142, February 1984.

Reasons for not using contraceptives: an international comparison, by N. K. Nair, et al. STUDIES IN FAMILY PLANNING. 15:84-92, March-April 1984.

Reversible azoospermia induced by the anabolic steroid 19-nortestosterone, by T. Schurmeyer, et al. LANCET. 1(8374): 417-410, February 1984.

Rigevidon (clinical trial of the preparation), by V. Kliment, et al. THERAPIA HUNGARY. 29(2):94-95, 1981.

Role of alkaline phosphatase in contraception— a review, by P. C. Das. ACTA PHYSIOLOGICA ET PHARMACOLOGICA BULGARICA. 9(2):74-78, 1983.

Role of gestagens in contraception and the treatment of menstruation disorders in women, by L. Grzeniewski. WIADOMOSCI LEKARSKIE. 36(21):1779-1787, November 1, 1983.

Scanning electron microscopy and x-ray microanalysis of foreign bodies associated with Silastic implants in humans, by A. H. Tatum, et al. CONTRACEPTION. 28(6):543-552, December 1983.

The secretion of human chorionic gonadotropin-like substance in women employing contraceptive measures, by S. C. Huang, et al. JOURNAL OF CLINICAL ENDOCRINOLOGY AND METABOLISM. 58(4):646-653, April 1984.

Self images and contraceptive behavior, by K. McKinney, et al. BASIC AND APPLIED SOCIAL PSYCHOLOGY. 5(1):37-57, March 1984.

Sex-related differences in clinical drug response: implications for women's health, by J. Hamilton, et al. JOURNAL OF THE AMERICAN MEDICAL WOMEN'S ASSOCIATION. 38(5):126-132, September-October 1983.

Silicone devices for tubal occlusion: radiographic description and evaluation, by M. E. Fischer, et al. RADIOLOGY. 151(3): 601-602, June 1984.

A simple method for estimating the contraceptive prevalence required to reach a fertility target, by J. Bongaarts. STUDIES IN FAMILY PLANNING. 15(4):184, July-August 1984.

Social anxiety, sexual behavior, and contraceptive use, by M. R. Leary, et al. JOURNAL OF PERSONALITY AND SOCIAL PSYCHOLOGY. 45(6):1347-1354, December 1983.

The social effects of contraception, by J. N. Santamaria. LINACRE QUARTERLY. 51:114-127, May 1984.

Social marketing of contraceptives in Bangladesh, by W. P. Schellstede, et al. STUDIES IN FAMILY PLANNING. 15:30-39, January-February 1984.

Socio-economic status and use of contraceptives among unmarried primigravidas in Cape Town, by D. A. Whitelaw. SOUTH AFRICAN MEDICAL JOURNAL. 64(18):712-715, October 22, 1983.

Steroidal contraception in the '80s. The role of current and new products, by J. J. Speidel. JOURNAL OF REPRODUCTIVE MEDICINE. 28(11):759-769, November 1983.

Study of the endometrium following voluntary interruption of pregnancy in relation to the contraceptive method used following abortion, by J. B. Sindayirwanya, et al. JOURNAL DE GYNECOLOGIE, OBSTETRIQUE ET BIOLOGIE DE LA REPRODUCTION. 12(4):351-362, 1983.

Sulphation of contraceptive steroids, by F. S. Khan, et al. JOURNAL OF STEROID BIOCHEMISTRY. 19(5):1657-1660, November 1983.

Surgically treated focal nodular hyperplasia, by S. Pap, et al. ORVOSI HETILAP. 125(20):1201-1203, May 13, 1984.

Today's contraceptives: what's new? What's best?, by W. S. Ross. READER'S DIGEST. 123(739):217-218; 220-222; 225-226, November 1983.

Trends in postpartum contraceptive choice, by C. H. Debrovner, et al. OBSTETRICS AND GYNECOLOGY. 63(1):65-70, January 1984.

XXII Scandiniavian Congress of Obstetrics and Gynecology, Helsinki, Finland, June 7-10, 1982. Abstracts. ACTA OBSTETRICA ET GYNECOLOGICA SCANDINAVICA [SUPPL]. 116:1-112, 1983.

Ultrasonic measurement of ovarian follicles during chornic LRH agonist treatment for contraception, by C. Bergquist, et al. CONTRACEPTION. 28(2):125-133, August 1983.

Uneasy freedom: women's experiences of contraception, by M. Benn, et al. WOMEN'S STUDIES INTERNATIONAL FORUM. 7(4):219-225, 1984.

United Nations conference rewards contraceptive technology, by F. Pearce. NEW SCIENTIST. 103:24, August 16, 1984.

Urinary porphyrin pattern in liver damage, by C. M. de Rover, et al. FOOD AND CHEMICAL TOXICOLOGY. 22(3):241-243, March 1984.

Use of contraceptive drugs in cardiac patients, by F. X. Veray. BOLETIN-ASOCIACION MEDICA DE PUERTO RICO.

75(6):253-254, June 1983.

Vaginal contraception: an overview, by D. A. Edelman. INTER-NATIONAL JOURNAL OF GYNAECOLOGY AND OBSTETRICS. 22(1):11-17, February 1984.

Vaginal mechanical contraceptive devices, by M. Smith, et al. CANADIAN MEDICAL ASSOCIATION JOURNAL. 129(7): 699-701; 710, October 1, 1983.

Vasectomy in the framework of contraception, by H. Stamm, et al. GYNAEKOLOGISCHE RUNDSCHAU. 24(2):85-97, 1984.

Vitamin B6 status and static muscle function. Two case reports, by J. C. Wirth, et al. ANNALS OF NUTRITION AND ME-TABOLISM. 28(4):240-244, 1984.

The wonderful world of contraception, by F. Pearce. NEW SCIENTIST. 103:8 August 30, 1984.

The World Fertility Survey and Contraceptive Prevalence Surveys: a comparison of substantive results, by J. E. Anderson, et al. STUDIES IN FAMILY PLANNING. 15(1):1-13, January-February 1984.

AFRICA
Attitudes toward abortion and contraception among Nigerian secondary school girls, by A. U. Oronsaye, et al. INTER-NATIONAL JOURNAL OF GYNAECOLOGY AND OBSTET-RICS. 21(5):423-426, October 1983.

Charactistics of contraceptive acceptors in an urban Nigerian setting, by O. Ayangade. INTERNATIONAL JOURNAL OF GYNAECOLOGY AND OBSTETRICS. 22(1):59-66, February 1984.

Decision-making in regard to the use of contraceptives after confinement: a study among urban black women (in Afrikaans), by G. Erasmus. SOUTH AFRICAN JOURNAL OF SOCIOLOGY. 15(2):94-97, 1984.

Motives of deficienty, want and illness in the conception of the godhead within the chasidic mysticism, by J. Mendel-

AFRICA
sohn. ANALYTISCHE PSYCHOLOGIE. 14(3):165-185, August 1983.

AUSTRALIA
Guidelines on vasectomy and oral contraceptives. Medical Task Force of the Australian Federation of Family Planning Associations. MEDICAL JOURNAL OF AUSTRALIA. 140(11):669-670, May 26, 1984.

BANGLADESH
Reasons for discontinuing contraception among women in Bangkok, by S. Sunyavivat, et al. WHO BULLETIN. 61(5):861-865, 1983.

Study on the factors associated with contraceptive discontinuations in Bangkok, by T. Chumnijarakij, et al. CONTRACEPTION. 29(3):241-249, March 1984.

BELGIUM
Contraceptive pill use, urinary sodium and blood pressure. A population study in two Belgian towns, by J. Staessen et al. ACTA CARDIOLOGICA. 39(1):55-64, 1984.

BRAZIL
User's perception of the contraceptive vaginal ring: a field study in Brazil and the Dominican Republic, by E. E. Hardy, et al. STUDIES IN FAMILY PLANNING. 14(11): 284-290, November 1983.

Where the best contraceptive is plenty of money, by R. del Quiaro. GUARDIAN. August 7, ;1984, p. 8.

CANADA
A plea for corporate conscience [product liability suit against A. H. Robins in Dalkon Shield case], by M. W. Lord. HARPERS. 268:13-14, June 1984.

Surprise contraceptive: Canadian zoologist stumbles upon compound to control male fertility, by R. Spence. EQUINOX. 3:16, January-February 1984.

CONTRACEPTIVES

CARIBBEAN
Oral contraception and cerebral thrombosis in a Jamaican,
by A. Campbell, et al. WEST INDIAN MEDICAL JOURNAL.
32(3):191-193, September 1983.

CHINA
Mosher case enters final phase, by M. Sun. SCIENCE. 224:
701, May 18, 1984.

Oral contraceptives and mortality from circulatory system
diseases: an epidemiologic study in Taiwan, by L. P.
Chow, et al. INTERNATIONAL JOURNAL OF GYNAE-
COLOGY AND OBSTETRICS. 21(4):297-304, August 1983.

The population of China, by N. Keyfitz. SCIENTIFIC AMERI-
CAN. 250(2):38-47, February 1984.

COSTA RICA
Spatial and temporal aspects of contraceptive abortion: an
analysis of contemporary fertility behavior in Costa
Rica. DISSERTATION ABSTRACTS INTERNATIONAL:
A. 45(5), November 1984.

DOMINICAN REPUBLIC
Users' perception of the contraceptive vaginal ring: a field
study in Brazil and the Dominican Republic, by E. E.
Hardy, et al. STUDIES IN FAMILY PLANNING. 14:284,
November 1983.

DENMARK
Use of oral contraceptives in Denmark in 1983, by O.
Lidegaard. UGESKRIFT FOR LAEGER. 146(15):1172-
1174, April 9, 1984.

EGYPT
Blood hormone levels in Egyptian women on norethisterone
oenanthate, by F. M. Saleh, et al. CONTRACEPTION.
28(1):41-51, July 1983.

A prospective study of Norplant Implants and the TCu 380Ag
IUD in Assiut, Egypt, by M. M. Shaaban, et al. STUDIES IN
FAMILY PLANNING. 14(6-7):163, June-July 1983.

GREAT BRITAIN
British pill victims win right to sue in U. S. NEW SCIENTIST.
102:8, May 31, 1984.

Sexual behavior and contraceptive practice at Oxford and
Aberdeen Universities, by P. Anderson, et al. JOURNAL
OF BIOSOCIAL SCIENCE. 16(2):287-290, April 1984.

HUNGARY
Development of hormonal contraception in the Hungarian
People's Republic, by G. Seregélyi. AKUSHERSTVO I
GINEKOLOGIIA. (4):70-72, April 1984.

INDONESIA
3D display of stillbirth in Indonesian obstetrics Part 4:
Contraception as preventive determinant?, by S.
Sastrawinata, et al. SOZIAL-UND PRAVENTIV-
MEDIZIN. 29(2):98-101, 1984.

KOREA
Perceived availability of contraceptives and family limitation, by J. D. Teachman, et al. HUMAN ORGANIZATION.
42:123-131, Summer 1983.

MEXICO
A clinical study of norethisterone enanthate in rural
Mexico, by C. Walther Meade, et al. STUDIES IN FAMILY
PLANNING. 15(3):143, May-June 1984.

Contraceptive effectiveness in Mexico, by H. Garrison.
DISSERTATION ABSTRACTS INTERNATIONAL: A.
45(3), September 1984.

Perceived availability of contraceptives and family limita-
tions, by J. D. Teachman, et al. HUMAN ORGANIZATION.
42:123-131, Summer 1983.

NORWAY
Use of contraceptives in Norway, by L. Ostby. TIDSSKRIFT
FOR DEN NORSKE LAEGEFORENING. 103(26):1793-1797,
September 20, 1983.

CONTRACEPTIVES

POLAND
Abortion and contraception in Poland, by M. Okolski.
STUDIES IN FAMILY PLANNING. 14(11):263-274,
November 1983.

SINGAPORE
Comparative studies of intrauterine devices in Singapore,
by T. McCarthy, et al. CONTRACEPTIVE DELIVERY
SYSTEMS. 4(3):219-226, 1983.

SOUTH AMERICA
Impact of accessiblity of contraceptives on contraceptive
prevalence in Guatemala, by C. H. Chen, et al. STUDIES
IN FAMILY PLANNING. 14(11):275-283, November 1983.

Menstrual regulation and contraception in Bangladesh:
competing or complmentary?, by H. H. Akhter, et al.
INTERNATIONAL JOURNAL OF GYNAECOLOGY AND
OBSTETRICS. 22(2):137-143, April 1984.

Menstrual regulation versus contraception in Bangladesh:
characteristics of the acceptors, by H. H. Akhter, et al.
STUDIES IN FAMILY PLANNING. 14(12 Pt 1):318-323,
December 1983.

Norplant Implants and the Tcu 200 IUD: a comparative
study in Equador, by P. Marangoni, et al. STUDIES IN
FAMILY PLANNING. 14(6-7):177, June-July 1983.

SOUTHEAST ASIA
Contraceptive use and program development: new information from Indonesia, by J. A. Ross, et al. INTERNATIONAL
FAMILY PLANNING PERSPECTIVES. 9:68-77, October
1983.

Perceptions and acceptability of Norplant implants in
Thailand, by S. Satayapan. STUDIES IN FAMILY
PLANNING. 14(6-7):170, June-July 1983.

SWEDEN
Sexual and contraceptive experience among teenagers in
Uppsala, Sweden, by E. Weiner, et al. UPSALA JOURNAL
OF MEDICAL SCIENCES. 89(2):171-178, 1984.

SWITZERLAND
Contraception: answers of wives and husbands compared in a survey of Swiss couples, by F. Hopflinger, et al. JOURNAL OF BIOSOCIAL SCIENCE. 16:259-268, April 1984.

UNITED STATES
An analysis of access to contraceptive care in western Pennsylvania, by S. E. Milligan. DISSERTATION ABSTRACTS INTERNATIONAL: A. 45(5), November 1984.

The association between smoking and sexual behavior among teens in U. S. contraceptive clinics, by L. S. Zabin. AMERICAN JOURNAL OF PUBLIC HEALTH. 74(3):261-263, March 1984.

British pill victims win right to sue in U. S. NEW SCIENTIST. 102:8, May 31, 1984.

Contraceptive patterns of religious and racial groups in the United States, 1955-1976: convergence and distinctiveness, by W. D. Mosher, et al. STUDIES IN FAMILY PLANNING. 15:101-111, May-June 1984.

World Bank, U. S. at odds on population, by C. Holden. SCIENCE. 225:396, July 27, 1984.

YUGOSLAVIA
Mortality in women of reproductive age due to diseases of the circulatory system caused by the use of oral contraceptives in Yugoslava, by J. Ananijevic-Pandey, et al. ACTA MEDICA JUGOSLAVIA. 37(3):185-195, 1983.

CONTRACEPTIVES: ADVERTISING
Advertising contraceptives on TV; the push is on, by J. Butler. OUR SUNDAY VISITOR. 73:5, November 25, 1984.

Down under: contraceptive ad sector is fertile ground for debate, by C. Pritchard. MARKETING. 89:15, September 3, 1984.

Encare contraceptive breaking ad barriers, by N. Giges. ADVERTISING AGE. 55:3+, March 19, 1984.

Judge tells Dalkon Shield producer to confess, by S. Tarnoff. BUSINESS INSURANCE. 18:66-67, March 12, 1984.

Marketing enables population control group to boost results, by K. Higgins. MARKETING NEWS. 17:12-13, October 14, 1983.

Robins to appeal Dalkon award, by B. Densmore. BUSINESS INSURANCE. 17:2+, December 26, 1983.

Top court upholds right to advertise condoms. EDITOR AND PUBLISHER-THE FOURTH ESTATE. 116:34, July 2, 1983.

Warner-Lambert tests condom ads on radio, by P. Sloan. ADVERTISING AGE. 55:29, July 2, 1984.

CONTRACEPTIVES: ATTITUDES
Attitudes toward abortion and contraception among Nigerian secondary school girls, by A. J. Oronsaye, et al. INTER-NATIONAL JOURNAL OF GYNAECOLOGY AND OBSTETRICS. 21(5):423-426, October 1983.

Attitudinal and motivational factors in contraception among women, by P. Kumar, et al. PERSPECTIVES IN PSYCHO-LOGICAL RESEARCHES. 6(1):27-31, April 1983.

Effect of religiosity on sex attitudes, experience and contraception among university students, by N. Notzer, et al. JOURNAL OF SEX AND MARITAL THERAPY. 10(1):57-62, Spring 1984.

Gender roles and premarital contraception, by P. L. Mac-Corquodale. JOURNAL OF MARRIAGE AND THE FAMILY. 46(1):57-63, February 1984.

Males and contraception: the relationship between contraceptive knowledge, attitudes and behavior, by D. A. Foss-Goodman. DISSERTATION ABSTRACTS INTERNATIONAL: B. 45(10), April 1985.

Motives of deficiency, want and illness in the conception of the godhead within the chasidic mysticism, by J. Mendelsohn. ANALYTISCHE PSYCHOLOGIE. 14(3):165-185, August 1983.

Predicting contraceptive behavior from attitudes: a comparison of within- versus across-subjects procedures, by A. Davidson, et al. JOURNAL OF PERSONALITY AND SOCIAL PSYCHOLOGY. 45(5):997-1009, November 1983.

Sex, contraception and parenthood: experience and attitudes among urban black young men, by S. D. Clark, Jr., et al. FAMILY PLANNING PERSPECTIVES. 16(2):77, March-April 1984.

CONTRACEPTIVES: COMPLICATIONS
Contraceptive could kill. NEW SCIENTIST. 98:437, May 19, 1983.

CONTRACEPTIVES: DEVELOPING COUNTRIES
Contraceptive availability and use in five developing countries [Costa Rica, Thailand, Colombia, Honduras, and Nepal], by R. M. Cornelius, et al. STUDIES IN FAMILY PLANNING. 14:302-317, December 1983.

IUD-associated hospitalzation in less developed countries, by I. C. Chi, et al. AMERICAN JOURNAL OF PUBLIC HEALTH. 74(4):353-357, April 1984.

Implications of future fertility trends for contraceptive practice, by J. Bongaarts. POPULATION AND DEVELOPMENT REVIEW. 10:341-352, June 1984.

CONTRACEPTIVES: FEMALE
Characteristics of women who stop using contraceptives, by C. R. Hammerslough. FAMILY PLANNING PERSPECTIVES. 16(1):14-18, January-February 1984.

Contraception for the older woman, by P. Bowen-Simpkins. BRITISH JOURNAL OF OBSTETRICS AND GYNAECOLOGY. 91(6):513-515, June 1984.

Contraceptive practices of female runners [letter], by J. M. Lutter. FERTILITY AND STERILITY. 40(4):551, October 1983.

Measurement issues involved in examining contraceptive use among young single women, by E. S. Herold. POPULATION AND ENVIRONMENT. 4(2):128-144, Summer 1981.

Predicting male and female contraceptive behavior: a discriminant analysis of groups high, moderate, and low in contraceptive effectiveness, by B. D. Geis, et al. JOURNAL OF PERSONALITY AND SOCIAL PSYCHOLOGY. 46(3):669-680, March 1984.

Recognizing DMPA as a contraceptive [letter], by T. F. Britton. AMERICAN JOURNAL OF NURSING. 84(3):306, March 1984.

Sources of prescription contraceptives and subsequent pregnancy among young women, by M. Zelnik, et al. FAMILY PLANNING PERSPECTIVES. 16(1):6, January-February 1984.

Today, the sponge, by E. Frank. NEW YORK. 17:68-69, February 27, 1984.

Unisex birth control. AMERICAN FAMILY PHYSICIAN. 29:385+, March 1984.

CONTRACEPTIVES: FEMALE: BARRIER
The cap that fits, by R. Porter. TIMES LITERARY SUPPLEMENT. March 16, 1984, p. 265.

The cervical cap: a retrospective study of an alternative contraceptive technique, by J. M. Johnson. AMERICAN JOURNAL OF OBSTETRIC AND GYNECOLOGY. 148(5):604-608, March 1, 1984.

Contraceptive sponge. AMERICAN FAMILY PHYSICIAN. 28: 256, July 1983.

The contraceptive sponge: easy— but is it safe?, by A. B. Eagan. MS. 12:94-95, January 1984.

Contraceptive sponge selling despite opposition. AMERICAN JOURNAL OF NURSING. 83:1372, October 1983.

Contraceptives: back to the barriers, by R. Serlin. NEW SCIENTIST. 91:281-284, July 30, 1984.

Custom cervical cap reentering clinical trials, by K. Prupes. JAMA. 250(15):1946-1947, October 21, 1983.

The Dalkon shield case: a plea for corporate conscience, by M. W. Lord. IRNFP. 8:181-188, Fall 1984.

Dalkon shield removal. AMERICAN FAMILY PHYSICIAN. 28: 241, August 1983.

The diaphragm: an accomplice in recurrent urinary tract infections, by L. Gillespie. UROLOGY. 24(1):25-30, July 1984.

Encare contraceptive breaking ad barriers, by N. Giges. ADVERTISING AGE. 55:3+, March 19, 1984.

Nursing protocol for diaphragm contraception, by C. J. Pyle. NURSE PRACTITIONER. 9(3):35; 38; 40, March 1984.

Preliminary findings on used cervical caps, by M. Smith, et al. CONTRACEPTION. 29(6):527-533, June 1984.

Sponge; the latest contraceptive device debuts with some interesting (but questionable) features, by K. Freifeld, et al. HEALTH. 15:56, July 1983.

An user acceptability study of vaginal spermicides in combination with barrier methods or an IUCD, by C. Black, et al. CONTRACEPTION. 28(2):103-110, August 1983.

When the fever cools [contraceptive spong marketing by VLI Corp.]. FORBES. 134:10, July 16, 1984.

CONTRACEPTIVES: FEMALE: BARRIER: COMPLICATIONS
A. H. Robins hauls a judge into court [M. W. Lord accused of taking sides in Dalkon Shield liability case]. BUSINESS WEEK. July 16, 1984, p. 27-28.

All contraceptives have problems: toxic-shock syndrome and the vaginal contraceptive sponge. NORTH CAROLINA MEDICAL JOURNAL. 45(3):197-198, March 1984.

Contraceptive sponge linked to toxic shock. AMERICAN FAMILY PHYSICIAN. 29:16, February 1984.

Depth charge in the womb [Dalkon Shield controversy]. PROGRESSIVE. 48:10, May 1984.

Leads from the MMWR. Toxic-shock syndrome and the vaginal contraceptive sponge. JAMA. 251(8):1015-1016, February 24, 1984.

A panel tries to judge a judge [M. W. Lord's remarks challenged by A. H. Robins Co. in Dalkon Shield case], by M. S. Serrill. TIME. 124:88, July 23, 1984.

A plea for corporate conscience [produce liability suit against A. H. Robins in Dalkon Shield case], by M. W. Lord. HARPERS. 268:13-14, June 1984.

Toxic shock and the sponge, by B. Day. GUARDIAN. 36(15):4, January 18, 1984.

Toxic-shock syndrome and the vaginal contraceptive sponge. MMWR. 33(4):43-44; 49, February 3, 1984.

Toxic shocker [fear has cooled VLI's contraceptive sponge], by E. J. Tracy. FORTUNE. 110:48, July 23, 1984.

Urinary tract infections among diaphragm users, by E. M. Wall, et al. JOURNAL OF FAMILY PRACTICE. 18(5):707-711, May 1984.

CONTRACEPTIVES: FEMALE: IUD
The acceptability of the copper 7, multiload 250 and copper T 220c intrauterine devices, by H. Hutapea, et al. CONTRA-CEPTIVE DELIVERY SYSTEMS. 5(1):11-16, 1984.

A comparative evaluation of three intrauterine devices, by P. M. Ditchik, et al. CONTRACEPTIVE DELIVERY SYSTEMS. 5(2):117-122, 1984.

A comparative study of Lippes loop and Delta loop intrauterine devices in early postpartum, by S. Chompootaweep, et al. CONTRACEPTION. 28(5):399-404, 1983.

Copper loss from the copper-T model Tcu220C, by M. Thiery, et al. CONTRACEPTION. 26(3):295-302, 1982.

Discontinued use of intrauterine contraceptive device and pregnancy loss, by A. A. Levin, et al. AMERICAN JOURNAL OF OBSTETRICS AND GYNECOLOGY. 149(7):768-771, August 1, 1984.

Effect of polyphloretin phosphate on the contraceptive action of a polyethylene intrauterine device in rats, by M. R. Chaudhury. CONTRACEPTION. 28(2):171-180, 1983.

Failure of post-coital contraception after insertion of an intrauterine device. Case report, by A. A. Kubba, et al. BRITISH JOURNAL OF OBSTETRICS AND GYNAECOLOGY. 91(6): 596-597, June 1984.

Failure to insert an intrauterine device, by I. C. Chi, et al. CONTRACEPTIVE DELIVERY SYSTEMS. 4(3):207-212, 1983.

Immediate postabortion insertion of an IUD, by H. Lehfeldt. EUROPEAN JOURNAL OF OBSTETRICS, GYNECOLOGY AND REPRODUCTIVE BIOLOGY. 17(2-3):141-147, May 1984.

Inhibition of rat embryonic development by the intrauterine administration of alpha-difluoromethylornithine, by J. D. Mendez, et al. CONTRACEPTION. 28(1):93-98, July 1983.

Insertion of the Multiload Cu 250 IUD immediately after abortion or labor, by L. Morup, et al. UGESKRIFT FOR LAEGER. 146(14):1046-1048, April 2, 1984.

Intrauterine contraceptive device insertion with suture fixation at cesarean section, by B. H. Liu, et al. CHINESE MEDICAL JOURNAL. 96(2):141-144, 1983.

Intrauterine devices. Their role in family planning care. WHO OFFSET PUBLICATION. (750:1-53, 1983.

Norplant implants and the Tcu 200 IUD: a comparative study in Equador, by P. Marangoni, et al. STUDIES IN FAMILY PLANNING. 14(6-7):177, June-July 1983.

Performance of multiload intrauterine device models with different copper loads, by M. Thiery, et al. CONTRACEPTIVE DELIVERY SYSTEMS. 4(3):227-230, 1983.

Postcoital IUD insertion, a review, by M. R. van Santen, et al. GEBURTHSILFE UND FRAUENHEILKUNDE. 44(4):266-272, April 1984.

Prediction of inflammatory complications in female reproductive organs when using the intrauterine contraceptive device, umbrella, by immunochemical determination of the serum content of individual inflammation protein in female blood, by Z. A. Chiladze, et al. AKADEMIYA NAUK GRUZINSKOI S. S. R. SOOBSHCHENIYA. 107(2):421-424, 1982.

A prospective study of Norplant Implants and the Tcu 380Ag IUD in Assiut, Egypt, by M. M. Shaaban, et al. STUDIES IN FAMILY PLANNING. 14(6-7):163, June-July 1983.

Report on the experience with 2829 prescriptions for IUD at Modena family counseling centers, by G. Masellis, et al. MINERVA GINECOLOGIA. 36(3):127-132, March 1984.

Risk of PID five times greater from Dalkon Shield than from other IUDs. FAMiLY PLANNING PERSPECTIVES. 15:225-226, September-October 1983.

Study of pregnancies of women with copper intrauterine devices, by A. Albert, et al. REPRODUCCION. 7(1-2):25-32, 1983.

Three years of experience after post-abortal insertion of Nova-T and Copper-T-200, by N. C. Nielsen, et al. ACTA OBSTETRICA ET GYNECOLOGICA SCANDINAVICA. 63(3):261-264, 1984.

Three years experience with copper T-200, by S. D. Kanitkar, et al. JOURNAL OF THE INDIAN MEDICAL ASSOCIATION. 80(9-10):148-149, May 1983.

Tunnel vision [A. H. Robins' Dalkon Shield intrauterine device], by S. N. Chakravarty. FORBES. 133:21+, May 21, 1984.

An user acceptability study of vaginal spermicides in combination with barrier methods or an IUCD, by C. Black, et al. CONTRACEPTION. 28(2):103-110, August 1983.

At risk for PID . . . the IUD. EMERGENCY MEDICINE. 16(1):107; 110, January 15, 1984.

Corrosion and weight loss from copper wire in the lincoid intrauterine device in utero, by S. Kaivola, et al. CONTRACEPTIVE DELIVERY SYSTEMS. 5(2):105-108, 1984.

IUD-associated hospitalization in less developed countries, by I. C. Chi, et al. AMERICAN JOURNAL OF PUBLIC HEALTH. 74(4):353-357, April 1984.

IUD risk in lactation. AMERICAN FAMILY PHYSICIAN. 28:359, October 1983.

Marketing enables population control group to boost results, by K. Higgins. MARKETING NEWS. 17:12-13, October 14, 1983.

Pelvic infections and the IUD. AMERICAN JOURNAL OF NURSING. 83:1374, October 1983.

Prognosis of pathological menstrual bleeding caused by the use of the intrauterine contraceptive Umbrella by immunochemical determination of some components of the fibrimolytic system, by Z. Z. Chiladze, et al. AKADEMIYA NAUK GRUZINSKOI S. S. R. SOOBSHCHENIYA. 107(3):613-616, 1982.

Study shows that IUDs pose a long-term risk. NEW SCIENTIST. 103:22, September 20, 1984.

CONTRACEPTIVES: FEMALE: IMPLANTED
Flowers of Hibiscus rosa-sinensis, a potential source of contragestative agent: I. effect of benzene extract on implantation of mouse, by S. N. Kabir, et al. CONTRACEPTION. 29(4): 385-397, April 1984.

A four-year clinical study of Norplant Implants, by I. Sivin, et al. STUDIES IN FAMILY PLANNING. 14(6-7):184, June-July 1983.

Implants: better than the pill? [levonorgestrel]. USA TODAY. 112:13, February 1984.

Norplant Implants and the Tcu 200 IUD: a comparative study in Equador, by P. Marangoni, et al. STUDIES IN FAMILY PLANNING. 14(6-7):177, June-July 1983.

Perceptions and acceptability of Norplant Implants in Thailand, by S. Satayapan. STUDIES IN FAMILY PLANNING. 14(6-7): 170, June-July 1983.

A Prospective study of Norplant Implants and the Tcu 380Ag IUD in Assiut, Egypt, by M. M. Shaaban, et al. STUDIES IN FAMILY PLANNING. 14(6-7):163, June-July 1983.

Unaltered lipoprotein and carbohydrate metabolism during treatment with contraceptive subdermal implants containing ST-1435, by V. Odlind, et al. UPSALA JOURNAL OF MEDICAL SCIENCES. 89(2):151-158, 1984.

The use of biodegradable norethisterone implants as a six-month contraceptive system, by R. Rivera, et al. FERTILITY AND STERILITY. 42(2):228-232, August 1984.

CONTRACEPTIVES: FEMALE: INJECTED
Acceptability of depo-provera [letter], by S. Basnayake, et al. LANCET. 1(8373):390, February 18, 1984.

Clinical evaluation of an improved injectable microcapsule contraceptive system, by L. R. Beck, et al. AMERICAN JOURNAL OF OBSTETRICS AND GYNECOLOGY. 147(7):815-821, December 1, 1983.

Depo approved, by A. Henry. SPARE RIB. 143:12, June 1984.

Depo Provera being used in Seattle. NORTHWEST PASSAGE. 24(9):5, April 1984.

Depo-Provera— ethical issues in its testing and distribution, by M. Potts, et al. JOURNAL OF MEDICAL ETHICS. 10(1):9-20, March 1984.

The Depo-Provera public hearing, by F. C. Dening. MIDWIVES CHRONICLE. 96(1146):246, July 1983.

Depo Provera/shot that sterilizes, by J. Slaughter. CHANGES. 6(7):4, July 1984.

Experiences with Depo-Provera as a contraceptive agent, by E. Kollstedt, et al. JORDEMODERN. 97(1-2):18-20, January-February 1984.

FDA considers Depo-Provera as contraceptive, by M. F. Docksai. TRIAL. 19:16, March 1983.

Health: mass use of injectable contraception, by V. Balasubrahmanyan. ECONOMIC AND POLITICAL WEEKLY. 19:371, March 3, 1984.

Long acting injectable hormonal contraceptives, by I. S. Fraser. CLINICAL REPRODUCTION AND FERTILITY. 1(1):67-88, March 1982.

Method failure pregnancy rates with depo provera and a local substitute [letter], by E. B. McDaniel, et al. LANCET. 1(8389):1293, June 9, 1984.

Multinational comparative clinical trial of long-acting injectable contraceptives: norethisterone enanthate given in two dosage regimens and depot-medroxyprogesterone acetate. Final report. CONTRACEPTION. 28(1):1-20, July 1983.

No increased risk of cancer with Depo-Provera contraception. NURSES DRUG ALERT. 7(11):87, November 1983.

Norethisterone levels in maternal serum and milk after intramuscular injection of norethisterone oenanthate as a contraceptive, by K. Fotherby, et al. CONTRACEPTION. 28(5):405-411, November 1983.

Postabortal contraception with norethisterone enanthate injections, by P. Lahteenmaki, et al. CONTRACEPTION. 27(6):553-562, June 1983.

Return of fertility after use of the injectable contraceptive Depo Provera: up-dated data analysis, by T. Pardthaisong. JOURNAL OF BIOSOCIAL SCIENCE. 16:23-24, January 1984.

Why Depo-Provera became respectable [injectable contraceptive]. NEW SCIENTIST. 102:9, April 19, 1984.

CONTRACEPTIVES: FEMALE: ORAL
Adolescent use of oral contraceptives, by M. A. Babington. PEDIATRIC NURSING. 10(2):111-114, March-April 1984.

The (anti-cancer?) pill, by A. Rowand. SCIENCE NEWS. 125: 404, June 30, 1984.

Biphasic oral contraceptives, by S. C. Sasso. MCN. 9(2):101, March-April 1984.

Contraceptive pills and cancer. MIDWIFE, HEALTH VISITOR AND COMMUNITY NURSE. 19(11):419; 443, November 1983.

The effect of combined oral contraceptive steroids on the gonadotropin responses to LH-RH in lactating women with regular menstrual cycles resumed, by K. Ryu, et al. CONTRACEPTION. 27(6):605-617, June 1983.

The effect of cotrimoxazole on oral contraceptive steroid: in women, by S. F. Grimmer, et al. CONTRACEPTION. 28(1): 53-59, July 1983.

Effect of exercise and oral contraceptive agents on fibrinolytic potential in trained females, by I. A. Huisveld, et al. JOURNAL OF APPLIED PHYSIOLOGY. 56(4):906-913, April 1984.

Effect of peer counselors on adolescent compliance in use of oral contraceptives, by M. S. Jay, et al. PEDIATRICS. 73(2):126-131, February 1984.

Guidelines on vasectomy and oral contraceptives. Medical Task Force on the Australian Federation of Family Planning Associations. MEDICAL JOURNAL OF AUSTRALIA. 140(11): 669-670, May 26, 1984.

Hepatic tumors and oral contraceptives, by J. L. Vaur. IN-FIRMIERE FRANCAISE. (253):17-18, March 1984.

An ill for every pill?, by A. Cotter. NURSING TIMES. 79(46):12-14, November 16-21, 1983.

Influence of augmented Hageman factor (Factor XII) titers on the cryoactivation of plasma prorenin in women using oral contraceptive agents, by E. M. Gordon, et al. JOURNAL OF CLINICAL INVESTIGATION. 72(5):1833-1838, November 1983.

Interaction between oral contraceptives and griseofluvin, by C. P. van Dijke, et al. BRITISH MEDICAL JOURNAL [CLIN RES]. 288(6424):1125-1126, April 14, 1984.

Interaction of drugs with steroidal oral contraceptives, by K. Dvorak. CESKOSLOVENSKA GYNEKOLOGIE. 48(3):222-228, April 1983.

Morning-after pill. AMERICAN FAMILY PHYSICIAN. 27:250, May 1983.

Nutritional consequences of oral contraceptives, by M. G. Emery, et al. FAMILY AND COMMUNITY HEALTH. 6(3):23-30, November 1983.

Oral contraceptive use and fibrocystic breast disease of different histologic classifications, by C. C. Hsieh, et al. JNCI. 72(2): 285-290, February 1984.

Ovarian function is effectively inhibited by a low-dose triphasic oral contraceptive containing ethinylestradiol and levonor-gestrel, by U. J. Gaspard, et al. CONTRACEPTION. 29(4):305-318, April 1984.

Pill the morning after. SCIENCE NEWS. 125:59, January 28, 1984.

The pill/taking stock of consequences, by A. Hayford. BRIAR-PATH. 13(6):28, July 1984.

Prudence and the pills, by A. Veitch. GUARDIAN. January 18, 1984, p. 11.

A recent review on the use of copper IUDs. IPPF RESEARCH IN REPRODUCTION. 15(3):1, July 1983.

Reduced plasminogen activator content of the endometrium

in oral contraceptive users, by B. Casslen, et al. CONTRACEP-
TION. 28(2):181-188, August 1983.

Severe and prolonged oral contraceptive jaundice, by D. A. Lieberman, et al. JOURNAL OF CLINICAL GASTROENTEROLOGY.
6(2):145-148, April 1984.

Topics in radiology/case of the month. Acute dyspnea in a young
woman taking birth control pills, by T. E. Goffman, et al.
JAMA. 251(11):1465-1466, March 16, 1984.

Ultra low dose OC. RN. 46:130, May 1983.

Use of oral contraceptives in Denmark in 1983, by O. Lidegaard.
UGESKRIFT FOR LAEGER. 146(15):1172-1174, April 9, 1984.

Which pill?, by J. Drife. BRITISH MEDICAL JOURNAL [CLIN
RES]. 287(6403):1397-1399, November 12, 1983.

Which pill? [letter]. BRITISH MEDICAL JOURNAL [CLIN RES].
287(6405):1625-1626.

CONTRACEPTIVES: FEMALE: ORAL: COMPLICATIONS
Balancing the risks of the pill [to an increased risk of developing
certain cancers]. ECONOMIST. 289:91, October 29, 1983.

Benign liver tumors following long-term use of oral contraceptives. I. Results of image-producing diagnostic procedures
of incidental intraoperatively discovered tumors, by F.
Reichenbach, et al. ZENTRALBLATT FUR CHIRURGIE.
108(15):947-954, 1983.

—. II. Clinical diagnosis and therapy, by F. Reichenbach, et al.
ZENTRALBLATT FUR CHIRURGIE. 108(15):955-966, 1983.

Breast cancer and oestrogen content of oral contraceptives
[letter], by P. Bye. LANCET. 1(8370):223, January 28, 1984.

Breast cancer and oral contraceptive use, by L. Rosenberg, et al.
AMERICAN JOURNAL OF EPIDEMIOLOGY. 119(2):167-176,
February 1984.

Breast cancer and oral contraceptive use: a case-control study, by D. T. Janerich, et al. JOURNAL OF CHRONIC DISEASES. 36(9):639-646, 1983.

Breast cancer and oral contraceptives [letter]. LANCET. 2(8359): 1145-1146, November 12, 1983.

Breast cancer and oral contraceptives: reply to critics [letter], by M. C. Pike, et al. LANCET. 2(8364):1414, December 17, 1983.

Breast cancer in young women and use of oral contraceptives: possible modifying effect of formulation and age at use, by M. C. Pike, et al. LANCET. 2(8356):926-930, October 22, 1983.

British pill victims win right to sue in U. S. NEW SCIENTIST. 102:8, May 31, 1984.

Cancer and the pill [letter]. LANCET. 2(8395):166, July 21, 1984.

Cancer and the pill, by E. Grant. ECOLOGIST. 14(2):68-76, 1983.

Cancer and the pill; the mountain which brough forth a mouse, by L. Offerhaus, et al. NEDERLANDS TIJDSCHRIFT VOOR GENEESKUNDE. 128(2):78-79, January 14, 1984.

A case of multiple thromboses: review of the cardiovascular complications of oral contraceptives, by C. Hanssen, et al. REVUE MEDICALE DE LIEGE. 39(11):495-499, June 1, 1984.

Cerebral arterial occlusion and intracraial venous thrombosis in a woman taking oral contraceptives, by F. Monton, et al. POSTGRADUATE MEDICAL JOURNAL. 60(704):426-428, June 1984.

Cervical cytological screening for users of oral contraceptives [letter], by R. W. Burslem. LANCET. 2(8356):968, October 22, 1983.

Cigarettes, contraceptive drugs and lipidogenesis in the female, by J. Lederer. SEMAINES DES HOPITAUX DE PARIS. 59(49):3413-3416, December 29, 1983.

Clinical data on the use of current oral contraceptives, by M. L. Krymskaia, et al. AKUSHERSTVO I GINEKOLOGIIA. (11): 19-22, November 1983.

The contraceptive pill and vascular accidents, by M. Lancet. HAREFUAH. 104(3):107-108, February 1, 1983.

Contraceptive pills and cancer [letter], by O. E. Iversen. TIDSSKRIFT FOR DEN NORSKE LAEGEFORENING. 104(3):186-187, January 30, 1984.

Digestive complications of oral contraceptives: a case of extensive digestive necrosis in a young woman, by E. Carpentier, et al. ANNALES DE CHIRURGIE. 38(4):305-308, May 1984.

Doctors dismiss link between the pill and cancer. NEW SCIENTIST. 100:559, November 24, 1983.

Drug interactions with oral contraceptives: a review, by F. X. Veray. BOLETIN-ASOCIACION MEDICA DE PUERTO RICO. 75(8):361-362, August 1983.

Effect of long-term use of composite steroid contraceptives on serum lipids in women, by Z. X. Li. CHUNG HUA FU CHAN KO TSA CHIH. 18(2):98-100, April 1983.

The effect of oral contraceptive therapy and of pregnancy on serum folate levels of rural Sri Lankan women, by N. S. Hettiarachchy, et al. BRITISH JOURNAL OF NUTRITION. 50(3):495-501, November 1983.

Effect of oral contraceptives on the formation of cholesterol crystals in gallbladder bile, by R. Pinero, et al. GEN. 36(4): 244-250, October-December 1982.

The effect of a progestin-only oral contraceptive on lactation, by M. F. McCann. DISSERTATION ABSTRACTS INTERNATIONAL: B. 45(8), February 1984.

Effects of tobacco smoking and oral contraceptive use on theophylline disposition, by M. J. Gardner, et al. BRITISH JOURNAL OF CLINICAL PHARMACOLOGY. 16(3):271-280, September 1983.

Ethanol metabolism in women taking oral contraceptives, by M. K. Jones, et al. ALCOHOLISM. 8(1):24-28, January-February 1984.

Exercise may offset lipid alterations in pill users. PHYSICIAN AND SPORTSMEDICINE. 12:42, June 1984.

Factor VII in plasma of women taking oral contraceptives. Lack of cold activation under blood bank conditions, by U. Seligsohn, et al. TRANSFUSION. 24(2):171-172, March-April 1984.

Female urethral pressure profile; reproducibility, axial variation and effects of low dose oral contraceptives, by J. M. Van Geelen, et al. JOURNAL OF UROLOGY. 131(2):394-398, February 1984.

Fertility disorders after taking contraceptive tablets, by G. Godo, et al. ORVOSI HETILAP. 125(6):313-316, February 5, 1984.

A flurry about the pill. NEW ZEALAND MEDICAL JOURNAL. 96(745):1009, December 14, 1983.

Focal nodular hyperplasia of great extent in the liver after taking oral contraceptives, by A. Szecseny, et al. ORVOSI HETILAP. 125(12):687-691, March 18, 1984.

Hemolytic-uremic syndrome caused by estrogen-progestagen combined oral contraceptives [letter], by A. Otero Gonzalez, et al. MEDICINA CLINICA. 82(18):824, May 12, 1984.

Hepatic adenomas and oral contraceptives, by M. C. Jimenez Garrido, et al. REVISTA ESPANOLA DE LAS ENFERMEDADES DEL APARATO DIGESTIVO. 65(1):71-75, January 1984.

Hepatic cell adenoma and peliosis hepatis in women using oral contraceptives, by F. C. Schmitt, et al. ARQUIVOS DE GASTROENTEROLOGIA. 20(4):153-155, October-December 1984.

Hepatocellular carcinoma and oral contraceptives, by B. E. Henderson, et al. BRITISH JOURNAL OF CANCER. 48(3):437-440, September 1983.

How dangerous is the pill?, by G. Cannon. NEW SCIENTIST. 100:601-602, November 24, 1983.

IUDs and pelvic inflammatory disease. SCIENCE NEWS. 124: 127, August 20, 1983.

IUD's and the risks of disease, by S. Katz. CHATELAINE. 57:16, January 1984.

IUDs stimulate interferon release. NEW SCIENTIST. 99:848, September 22, 1983.

Ill effects from pill paper, by B. Dixon. NEW SCIENTIST. 101:50, March 15, 1984.

Increased risk for cancer of the breast due to previous medication, by R. W. de Levin, et al. ARCHIV FUR GESCHWULST-FORSCHUNG. 54(2):153-158, 1984.

Increased urinary androgen levels in patients with carcinoma in situ of the breast with onset while taking oral contraceptives, by G. Secreto, et al. CANCER DETECTION AND PREVENTION. 6(4-5):439-442, 1983.

Lack of correlation between contraceptive pills and Down's syndrome, by A. Ericson, et al. ACTA OBSTETRICIA ET GYNECOLOGICA SCANDINAVICA. 62(50:511-514, 1983.

Lack of an elevated risk of malignant melanoma in relation to oral contraceptive use, by S. P Helmrich, et al. JNCI. 72(3):617-620, March 1984.

Leads from the MMWR. Oral contraceptive use and the risk of breast cancer in young women. JAMA. 252(3):326-327, July 20, 1984.

Long-term follow-up of children whose mothers used oral contraceptives prior to conception, by S. Magidor, et al. CONTRACEPTION. 29(3):203-214, March 1984.

Long-term survival after resection of a hepatocellular carcinoma with lymph node metastasis and discontinuation of oral contraceptives, by O. T. Terpstra, et al. AMERICAN JOURNAL OF GASTROENTEROLOGY. 79(6):474-478, June 1984.

Massive hemoperitoneum from rupture of richly vascularized benign liver tumours in women on oral contraceptives, by B. B. Kroon, et al. NETHERLANDS JOURNAL OF SURGERY. 36(3):85, June 1984.

Melanoma, pregnancy and oral contraception, by G. Veen, et al. NEDERLANDS TIJDSCHRIFT VOOR GENEESKUNDE. 127(41): 1865-1868, October 8, 1983.

Melanoma, pregnancy and oral contraception [letter], by T. A. van der Ploeg-Phaff. NEDERLANDS TIJDSCHRIFT VOOR GENEESKUNDE. 127(48):2210, November 26, 1983.

Mitotic and apoptotic response of breast tissue to oral contraceptives [letter], by T. J. Anderson. LANCET. 1(8368):99-100, January 14, 1984.

More worries about the pill. NATURE. 305(5937):749-750, October 27-November 2, 1983.

Neoplasia of the cervix uteri and contraception: a possible adverse effect of the pill, by M. P. Vessey, et al. LANCET. 2(8356): 930-934, October 22, 1983.

New products [Ouvtest 77 Baby Computer (for natural family planning) PMT-eze (for premenstrual tension and as a nutritional supplement for women using oral contraceptives); Synphasic (oral contraceptive), by L. Wray. HEALTHRIGHT. 3:35-38, May 1984.

No pill-cancer link. FDA CONSUMER. 18:4, May 1984.

Oral contraceptive use and fibrocystic breast disease among pre- and postmenopausal women, by G. S. Berkowitz, et al. AMERICAN JOURNAL OF EPIDEMIOLOGY. 120(1):87-96, July 1984.

Oral contraceptive use and the risk of breast cancer in young women. MMWR. 33(25):353-354, June 29, 1984.

Oral contraceptives and acute viral hepatitis [letter], by C. Dolz Abadia, et al. MEDICINA CLINICA. 82(17):782, May 5, 1984.

Oral contraceptives and benign breast disease: a case-control study, by S. Franceschi, et al. AMERICAN JOURNAL OF OBSTETRICS AND GYNECOLOGY. 149(6):602-606, July 15, 1984.

Oral contraceptives and benign tumors of the liver, by J. G. Fitz. WESTERN JOURNAL OF MEDICINE. 140(2):260-267, February 1984.

Oral contraceptives and breast cancer. LANCET. 2(8395):145, July 21, 1984.

Oral contraceptives and breast cancer, by A. Kalache, et al. BRITISH JOURNAL OF HOSPITAL MEDICINE. 30(4):278-283, October 1983.

Oral contraceptives and breast cancer [letter]. LANCET. 2(8360): 1201-1202, November 19, 1983.

Oral contraceptives and breast cancer [letter], by K. McPherson, et al. LANCET. 2(8364):1414-1415, December 17, 1983.

Oral contraceptives and breast cancer rates [letter], by M. C. Pike, et al. LANCET. 1(8373):389, February 18, 1984.

Oral contraceptives and breast-cancer rates [letter], by R. A. Wiseman. LANCET. 1(8380):791, April 7, 1984.

Oral contraceptives and breast cancer rates [letter], by R. A. Wiseman. LANCET. 2(8364):1415-1416, December 17, 1983.

Oral contraceptives and cancer [letter]. LANCET. 2(8357):1018-1020, October 29, 1983.

Oral contraceptives and cancer [letter]. LANCET. 2(8358):1081, November 5, 1983.

Oral contraceptives and cancer [letter], by A. Pedersen. LANCET.

2(8361):1259, November 26, 1983.

Oral contraceptives and cancer. FDA DRUG BULLETIN. 14(1):2-3, April 1984.

Oral contraceptives and cardiovascular complications, by V. Murad. ARQUIVOS BRASILEIROS DE CARDIOLOGIA. 40(3):215-221, March 1983.

Oral contraceptives and cardiovascular disease— aspects of lipid metabolism, by N. Crona, et al. LAKARTIDNINGEN. 81(6): 425-427, February 8, 1984.

Oral contraceptives and cardiovascular mortality, by I. Stucker, et al. REVUE D'EPIDEMIOLOGIE ET DE SANTE PUBLIQUE. 32(1):16-24, 1984.

Oral contraceptives and cervical cancer [letter]. LANCET. 2(8359):1146-1147, November 12, 1983.

Oral contraceptives and cervical cancer [letter], by L. Andolsek, et al. LANCET. 2(8362):1310, December 3, 1983.

Oral contraceptives and cervical cancer [letter], by M. P. Vessey, et al. LANCET. 2(8363):1358-1359, December 10, 1983.

Oral contraceptives and deep venous thrombosis with pulmonary embolism, by R. T. Bouche, et al. JOURNAL OF FOOT SURGERY. 21(4):297-301, Winter 1982.

Oral contraceptives and endometrial cancer [letter], by E. S. Maxey. JAMA. 250(16):2111, October 28, 1983.

Oral contraceptives and mortality from circulatory system diseases: an epidemiologic study in Taiwan, by L. P. Chow, et al. INTERNATIONAL JOURNAL OF GYNAECOLOGY AND OBSTETRICS. 21(4):297-304, August 1983.

Oral contraceptives and neoplasia. LANCET. 2(8356):947-948, October 22, 1983.

Oral contraceptives and prolactinomas: which caused what?

NURSES DRUG ALERT. 7(9):71-72, September 1983.

Oral contraceptives and the risk of cancer, by K. E. Sapire. SOUTH AFRICAN MEDICAL JOURNAL. 64(25):964-965, December 10, 1983.

Oral contraceptives and stroke, by W. T. Longstreth, Jr., et al. STROKE. 15(4):747-750, July-August 1984.

Oral contraceptives and stroke: findings in a large prospective study, by M. P. Vessey, et al. BRITISH MEDICAL JOURNAL [CLIN RES]. 289(6444):530-531, September 1, 1984.

Oral contraceptives, carbohydrate metabolism and diabetes mellitus, by J. M. Ekoe, et al. SEMAINES DES HOPITAUX DE PARIS. 59(45):3162-3166, December 8, 1983.

Oral contraceptives may promote cancer. SCIENCE NEWS. 124:127, August 20, 1983.

Oral contraceptives, pregnancy, and endogenous oestrogen in gall stone disease— a case-control study, by R. K. Scragg, et al. BRITISH MEDICAL JOURNAL [CLIN RES]. 288(6433): 1795-1799, June 16, 1984.

Oral contraceptives, pregnancy, and focal nodular hyperplasia of the liver, by L. D. Scott, et al. JAMA. 251(11):1461-1463, March 16, 1984.

Oral contraceptives: the risks in perspective, by R. G. Kanell. NURSE PRACTITIONER. 9(9):25-26; 28-29; 62, September 1984.

PID and IUD use. AMERICAN FAMILY PHYSICIAN. 30:272, July 1984.

Paying a high price for the bill, by R. Block. MACLEANS. 97:52, April 30, 1984.

Pill affected older women more. NEW SCIENTIST. 101:21, January 12, 1984.

Pill and cancer. AMERICAN FAMILY PHYSICIAN. 29:383+, January 1984.

The pill and cancer of the breast and cervix uteri, by A. Pedersen. UGESKRIFT FOR LAEGER. 146(14):1063-1066, April 2, 1984.

Pill and tumors. AMERICAN FAMILY PHYSICIAN. 28:372+, November 1983.

The pill, breast and cervical cancer, and the role of progestogens in arterial disease, by R. Lincoln. FAMILY PLANNING PERSPECTIVES. 16(2):55-63, March-April 1984.

Pill— cancer link re-examined, by F. Lesser. NEW SCIENTIST. 100:264, October 27, 1983.

The pill the morning after. SCIENCE NEWS. 125:59, January 28, 1984.

Pill questions that remain unanswered. NEW SCIENTIST. 100: 247, October 27, 1983.

Pill revisited; new cancer link?, by J. Silberner. SCIENCE NEWS. 124:279, October 29, 1983.

Plasma renin substrate, renin activity, and aldosterone levels in a sample of oral contraceptive users from a community survey, by S. Z. Goldhaber, et al. AMERICAN HEART JOURNAL. 107(1):119-122, January 1984.

Presence of the Beaumont protein in serum of oral contraceptive users, by D. C. Collins, et al. FERTILITY AND STERILITY. 40(4):490-496, October 1983.

Progestagen 'potency' and breast cancer [letter], by G. I. Swyer. LANCET. 2(8364):1416, December 17, 1983.

A prospective cohort study of oral contraceptives and cancer of the endometrium, by E. J. Trapido. INTERNATIONAL JOURNAL OF EPIDEMIOLOGY. 12(3):297-300, September 1983.

Rheumatoid arthritis and oral contraceptives. AMERICAN

FAMILY PHYSICIAN. 28:309-310, November 1983.

Side effects of oral contraceptives, by A. G. Khomasuridze.
AKUSHERSTVO I GINEKOLOGIIA. (11):27-29, November 1983.

Studies find no link between pill use and development of
pituitary tumors. FAMILY PLANNING PERSPECTIVES.
15:283, November-December 1983.

Systemic effects of oral contraceptives, by T. M. Kelly. WESTERN
JOURNAL OF MEDICINE. 141(1):113-116, July 1984.

Use of oral contraceptives and the occurrence of breast cancer,
by I. Baksaas, et al. TIDSSKRIFT FOR DEN NORSKE
LAEGEFORENING. 104(22):1390-1392, August 10, 1984.

Yet more pill problems, by A. Henry. SPARE RIB. 37:12, December 1983.

CONTRACEPTIVES: FEMALE: POSTCOITAL
About postcoital contraception, by E. Trimmer. MIDWIFE,
HEALTH VISITOR AND COMMUNITY NURSE. 19(11):434,
November 1983.

Our experience with the clinical trial of postinor— an oral
hormonal preparation for postcoital contraception, by D.
Vasilev, et al. AKUSHERSTVO I GINEKOLOGIIA. 22(3):239-
242, 1983.

Post-coital contraception, by J. R. Ashton, et al. JOURNAL OF
THE ROYAL COLLEGE OF GENERAL PRACTITIONERS.
34(260):175-176, March 1984.

CONTRACEPTIVES: HISTORY
Ernst Gräfenberg: the life and work of the specialist of Kiel
on the hundreth anniversary of his birth on 26 September
1881, by K. Semm, et al. INTERNATIONAL JOURNAL OF
FERTILITY. 28(3):141-148, 1983.

History of contraception and a look to the future, by O. Käser.
GEBURTSHILFE UND FRAUENHEILKUNDE. 43(Suppl 1):
2-7, June 1983.

Towards a theory of history, by P. Colinvaux. COEVOLUTION. 41:94, Spring 1984.

CONTRACEPTIVES: IRREVERSIBLE

Medical counseling and activities of the Specialty Committee— final conclusions drawn from current trends in irreversible contraception, by J. Rothe, et al. ZEITSCHRIFT FUR AERZTLICHE FORTBILDUNG. 78(2):57-60, 1984.

CONTRACEPTIVES: LAWS AND LEGISLATION

A. H. Robins hauls a judge into court [M. W. Lord accused of taking sides in Dalkon Shield liability case]. BUSINESS WEEK. July 16, 1984, pp. 27-28.

Blowing the whistle on the squeal rule [defunct regulation requiring clinics to inform parents if daughters are given contraceptives is still on the books], by D. Gates. NEWSWEEK. 104:18, September 24, 1984.

The Depo-Provera public hearing, by F. C. Dening. MIDWIVES CHRONICLE. 96(1146):246, July 1983.

FDA considers Depo-Provera as contraceptive, by M. F. Docksai. TRIAL. 19:16, March 1983.

Minors' rights of privacy: access to contraceptives without parental notification. JOURNAL OF JUVENILE LAW. 7:99-115, 1983.

Playing safe, keeping quiet, by W. Cooper. GUARDIAN. June 29, 1984, p. 11.

The role of epidemiology in the regulation of oral contraceptives, by S. Sobel. PUBLIC HEALTH REPORTS. 99(4):350-354, July-August 1984.

Top court upholds right to advertise condoms. EDITOR AND PUBLISHER-THE FOURTH ESTATE. 116:34, July 2, 1983.

Unemancipated minors' rights of access to contraceptives without parental consent or notice— the squeal rule and beyond. OKLAHOMA CITY UNIVERSITY LAW REVIEW. 8:219-250, Summer 1983.

Woman's failure to use contraceptives not valid defense in paternity action. THE FAMILY LAW REPORTER. 10(41): 1561-1562, August 21, 1984.

CONTRACEPTIVES: MALE

An ancient method and a modern scourge: the condom as a barrier against herpes [letter], by L. S. Kish, et al. JOURNAL OF THE AMERICAN ACADEMY OF DERMATOLOGY. 9(5): 769-770, November 1983.

Androgenisation of female partners of men on medroxyprogesterone acetate/percutaneous testosterone contraception [letter], by D. Delanoe, et al. LANCET. 1(8371):276, February 4, 1984.

Antifertility actions of alpha-chlorohydrin in the male, by A. R. Jones. AUSTRALIAN JOURNAL OF BIOLOGICAL SCIENCES. 36(4):333-350, 1983.

Are men ready to share the burden?, by F. Lesser. NEW SCIENTIST. 101:37-38, January 5, 1984.

A barrier to HSV . . . the condom. EMERGENCY MEDICINE. 16(11):135; 136, June 15, 1984.

Condom conundrum: a birth control gimmick raises hackles in Calgary. ALBERTA REPORT. 11:13, March 5, 1984.

Contraception: answers of wives and husbands compared in a survey of Swiss couples, by F. Hopflinger, et al. JOURNAL OF BIOSOCIAL SCIENCE. 16:259-268, April 1984.

The control of male fertility by 1,2,3-trihydroxypropane (THP; glycerol): rapid arrest of spermatogenesis without altering libido, accessory organs, gonadal steroidogenesis, and serum testosterone, LH and FSH, by J. P. Wiebe, et al. CONTRACEPTION. 29(3):291-302, March 1984.

Copper intravas device (IVD) and male contraception, by M. M. Kapur, et al. CONTRACEPTION. 29(1):45-54, January 1984.

Effect of (+)-gossypol on fertility in male hamsters, by D. P.

Wallter, et al. JOURNAL OF ANDROLOGY. 4(4):276-279, July-August 1983.

Efficacy of the condom as a barrier to the transmission of cytomegalovirus, by S. Katznelson, et al. JOURNAL OF INFECTIOUS DISEASES. 150(1):155-157, July 1984.

Evaluation of steroids as contraceptives in men, by M. Foegh. ACTA ENDOCRINOLOGICA [SUPPL]. 260::3-48, 1983.

Gossypol prospects. LANCET. 1(8386):1108-1109, May 19, 1984.

Herpes simplex virus transmission: condom studies, by M. A. Conant, et al. SEXUALLY TRANSMITTED DISEASES. 11(2):94-95, April-June 1984.

Ionized copper as contraceptive in male rhesus monkey, by S. S. Riar, et al. ANDROLOGIA. 16(2):116-117, March-April 1984.

Judge tells Dalkon Shield producer to confess, by S. Tarnoff. BUSINESS INSURANCE. 18:66-67, March 12, 1984.

Male adolescent sexual behavior, the forgotten partner: a review, by M. L. Finkel, et al. JOURNAL OF SCHOOL HEALTH. 53(9):544-547, November 1983.

Male contraception, by A. Demoulin. REVUE MEDICALE DER LIEGE. 39(7):266-272, April 1, 1984.

Male contraceptive. ENVIRONMENT. 25:23-24, October 1983.

Male contraceptive. SCIENCE DIMENSION. 16(1):7, 1984.

Males and contraception: the relationship between contraceptive knowledge, attitudes and behavior, by D. A. Foss-Goodman. DISSERTATION ABSTRACTS INTERNATIONAL: B. 45(10), April 1985.

Men's new role in pregnancy prevention. SCIENCE DIGEST. 92:88, January 1984.

New contraceptives for men. What are the prospects?, by M. R.

Prasad, et al. INTERNATIONAL JOURNAL OF ANDROLOGY. 6(4):305-309, August 1983.

The possible use of phenoxybenzamine as a male contraceptive drug: studies on male rats, by G. F. Paz, et al. CONTRACEP-TION. 29(2):189-195, February 1984.

Predicting male and female contraceptive behavior: a discriminant analysis of groups high, moderate, and low in contraceptive effectiveness, by B. D. Geis, et al. JOURNAL OF PERSONALITY AND SOCIAL PSYCHOLOGY. 46(3):669-680, March 1984.

Prospect of gossypol as a contraceptive agent for men, by H. P. Lei. YAO HSUEH HSUEH PAO. 18(5):321-324, May 1983.

A review of the current status in male contraceptive studies, by S. Gombe. EAST AFRICAN MEDICAL JOURNAL. 60(4):203-211, April 1983.

Search for male contraceptive complicated by adverse effects, by T. Ziporyn. JAMA. 252(9):1101-1103, September 7, 1984.

Selected psychosocial characteristics of males: their relationship to contraceptive use and abortion, by D. Andres, et al. PERSONALITY AND SOCIAL PSYCHOLOGY BULLETIN. 9(3):387-396, September 1983.

Sex, contraception and parenthood: experience and attitudes among urban black young men, by S. D. Clark, Jr., et al. FAMILY PLANNING PERSPECTIVES. 16:77-82, March-April 1984.

Small testicles could thwart new male pill, by A. la Guardia. NEW SCIENTIST. 101:8, February 23, 1984.

Title X and its critics, by J. L. Rosoff, et al. FAMILY PLANNING PERSPECTIVES. 16(3):111-113; 115-116; 119, May-June 1984.

Unisex birth control. AMERICAN FAMILY PHYSICIAN. 29:385+, March 1984.

Warner-Lambert tests condom ads on radio, by P. Sloan. ADVERTISING AGE. 55:29, July 2, 1984.

CONTRACEPTIVES: MALE: ORAL
The pill for men: available soon?, by W. Frese. MAX PLANCK SOCIETY SCIENCE NEWSLETTER. June 1984, p. 8.

Phenoxybenzamine— an effective male contraceptive pill, by Z. T. Homonnai, et al. CONTRACEPTION. 29(5):479-491, May 1984.

CONTRACEPTIVES: METHODS
Antifertility vaccines [letter], by R. Bronson, et al. FERTILITY AND STERILITY. 41(5):786-787, May 1984.

Breast feeding is contraceptive. NEW SCIENTIST. 102:23, May 3, 1984.

Clinical use of Rigevidon, Ovidon and Postinor, by V. N. Serov, et al. AKUSHERSTVO I GINEKOLOGIIA. (11):17-19, November 1983.

The contraceptive sponge: easy— but is it safe?, by A. B. Eagan. MS. 12:94-95, January 1984.

Failure of post-coital contraception after insertion of an intrauterine device. Case report, by A. A. Kubba, et al. BRITISH JOURNAL OF OBSTETRICS AND GYNAECOLOGY. 91(6):596-597, June 1984.

Morphologic evidence for vaginal toxicity of Delfen contraceptive cream in the rat, by L. Tryphonas, et al. TOXICOLOGY LETTERS. 20(3):289-295, March 1984.

Observation: contraceptive method use following an abortion, by S. K. Henshaw. FAMILY PLANNING PERSPECTIVES. 16(2):75-77, March-April 1984.

Perceptions of contraceptive methods: a multidimensional scaling analysis, by V. J. Callan, et al. JOURNAL OF BIO-SOCIAL SCIENCE. 16:277-286, April 1984.

Practical viewpoints of various preventive methods with emphasis on alternative minipills, by A. K. Mansson. JORDE-MODERN. 96(6):159-164, June 1983.

Putting the sex back into contraception, by R. Shapiro. COMMUNITY OUTLOOK. April 1984, pp. 123-126; 128-129; 131.

Rigevidon and Ovidon in the therapy of menstrual cycle disorders, by V. N. Prilepskaia, et al. AKUSHERSTVO I GINEKOLOGIIA. (11):24-27, November 1983.

Spermicides: safe?, by K. Freifeld, et al. HEALTH. 15:8, December 1983.

A survey of different approaches to management of menstrual disturbances in women using injectable contraceptives, by I. S. Fraser. CONTRACEPTION. 28(4):385-397, October 1983.

Use of Ovidon, Rigevidon and Postinor for contraception, by V. I. Kulakov, et al. AKUSHERSTVO I GINEKOLOGIIA. (11):22-24, November 1983.

When the fever cools [VLI's new contraceptive device]. FORBES. 134:10, July 16, 1984.

CONTRACEPTIVES: MORTALITY AND MORTALITY STATISTICS
Mortality among young black women using contraceptives, by H. W. Ory, et al. JAMA. 251(8):1044-1048, February 24, 1984.

Mortality in women of reproductive age due to diseases of the circulatory system caused by the use of oral contraceptives in Yugoslavia, by J. Ananijevic-Pandey, et al. ACTA MEDICA JUGOSLAVIA. 37(3):185-195, 1983.

CONTRACEPTIVES: ORAL
Absence of antibodies to ethinyl estradiol in users of oral contraceptive steroids, by N. H. Huang, et al. FERTILITY AND STERILITY. 41(4):587-592, April 1984.

Alpha-fetoprotein assay in patients treated with low-dose oral contraceptives, by S. Dessole, et al. CLINICAL AND EXPERI-MENTAL OBSTETRICS AND GYNECOLOGY. 11(3):76-78, 1984.

Alterations in prednisolone disposition as a result of oral contraceptive use and dose, by P. J. Meffin, et al. BRITISH JOURNAL OF CLINICAL PHARMACOLOGY. 17(6):655-664, June 1984.

Antithrombin III in oral contraceptive users and during normo-tensive pregnancy, by G. H. Weenink, et al. ACTA OBSTET-RICIA ET GYNECOLOGICA SCANDINAVICA. 63(1):57-61, 1984.

Benign hepatic adenoma associated with oral contraceptive use mimicking pelvic inflammatory disease. A case report, by J. E. Jenks, et al. JOURNAL OF REPRODUCTIVE MEDICINE. 29(3):200-203, March 1984.

Beta-adrenoceptor blocker pharmacokinetics and the oral contraceptive pill, by M. J. Kendall, et al. BRITISH JOURNAL OF CLINICAL PHARMACOLOGY. 17(Suppl 1):87S-89S, 1984.

Blood prolactin levels: influence of age, menstrual cycle and oral contraceptives, by F. Pansini, et al. CONTRACEPTION. 28(3):201-207, September 1983.

Breast feeding and contraception. The effect of low-dose oral contraceptives on the growth of the infant during breast feeding, by J. Gellen, et al. ORVOSI HETILAP. 125(4):193-196, January 22, 1984.

Breastfeeding and oral contraceptives: Tasmanian survey, by J. F. Coy, et al. AUSTRALIAN PAEDIATRIC JOURNAL. 19(3):168-171, September 1983.

Changes in serum lipoproteins in women treated with combined oral contraceptives, by P. Bellod, et al. REVISTA CLINICA ESPANOLA. 170(6):275-278, September 30, 1983.

The choice of oral contraception in 1984: general indications and specific cases, by U. Gaspard. REVUE MEDICALE DE LIEGE. 39(7):261-265, April 1984.

Choosing an oral contraceptive, by E. Weisberg. HEALTHRIGHT. 3:12-16, February 1984.

Clinical experience with a triphasic oral contraceptive, by M. Ulstein, et al. ACTA OBSTETRICA ET GYNECOLOGICA SCANDINAVICA. 63(3):233-236, 1984.

Colonic Crohn's disease and use of oral contraception, by J. M. Rhodes, et al. BRITISH MEDICAL JOURNAL [CLIN RES]. 288(6471):595-596, February 25, 1984.

A comparative study of two estrogen dosages in combined oral contraceptives among Sudanese women, by A. S. Gerais, et al. INTERNATIONAL JOURNAL OF GYNAECOLOGY AND OB-STETRICS. 21(6):459-468, December 1983.

Contra-indications of oral contraceptives, by G. E. Lopez de la Osa. MEDICINA CLINICA. 81(9):404-406, October 1, 1983.

Differential effects of isoniazid and oral contraceptive steroids on antipyrine oxidation and acetaminophen conjugation, by H. R. Ochs, et al. PHARMACOLOGY. 28(4):188-195, 1984.

Do oral contraceptives reduce the incidence of rheumatoid arthritis? A pilot study using the Stockholm County medical information system, by P. Allebeck, et al. SCANDINAVIAN JOURNAL OF RHEUMATOLOGY. 13(2):140-146, 1984.

The effect of low dose oral contraceptives on the initial immune response to infection, by D. A. Baker, et al. CONTRACEPTION. 29(6):519-525, June 1984.

Effect of oral contraception on serum bile acid, by M. M. Shaaban, et al. INTERNATIONAL JOURNAL OF GYNAECOLOGY AND OBSTETRICS. 22(2):111-115, April 1984.

Effect of oral contraceptives on intestinal folate conjugase activity and folate absorption in rats, by J. Leichter, et al. DRUG-NUTRIENT INTERACTIONS. 2(1):1-6, 1983.

The effect of oral contraceptives on rat platelet membrane glyco-proteins, by B. Toor, et al. BIOCHIMICA ET BIOPHYSICA ACTA. 770(2):178-182, March 14, 1984.

Effect of various oral contraceptive combinations on dysmenorrhea, by I. Milsom, et al. GYNECOLOGIC AND OB-
STETRIC INVESTIGATION. 17(6):284-292, 1984.

Effects of oral contraceptives and of the ovarian cycle on
auditory performance at 4 and 6 kHz. Demonstration by
functional audiometry, by J. C. Petiot, et al. COMPTES
RENDUES DES SEANCES DE LA SOCIETIE DE BIOLOGIE ET
DE SES FILIALES. 178(1):105-117, 1984.

Effects of oral contraceptives on diazepam-induced psychomotor
impairment, by E. H. Ellinwood, Jr., et al. CLINICAL
PHARMACOLOGY AND THERAPUTICS. 35(3):360-366,
March 1984.

Effects of oral contraceptives on lipoprotein lipids: a prospective
study, by M. G. Powell, et al. OBSTETRICS AND GYNE-
COLOGY. 63(6):764-770, June 1984.

Effects of oral contraceptives, or lanosterol, on ADP-induced
aggregation and binding of 1251-fibrinogen to rat platelets,
by L. McGregor, et al. THROMBOSIS RESEARCH. 33(5):517-
522, March 1, 1984.

Epilepsy and oral contraceptives. A therapeutic dilemma, by
M. E. Fiol, et al. MINNESOTA MEDICINE. 66(9):551-552,
September 1983.

Ethynyl estradiol content of cervical mucus after administration
of oral contraceptive, by J. Morvay, et al. HORMONE RE-
SEARCH. 18(4):221-224, 1983.

Evaluation of risk factors associated with vascular thrombosis
in women on oral contraceptives. Possible role of anti-sex
steroid hormone antibodies, by V. Beaumont, et al. ARTERY.
11(5):331-344, 1983.

Fertility after discontinuation of oral contraceptives, by E.
Weisberg. CLINICAL REPRODUCTION AND FERTILITY.
1(4):261-272, December 1982.

Gender and oral contraceptive effects on temporary auditory
effects of noise, by J. E. Dengerink, et al. AUDIOLOGY. 23(4):
411-425, 1984.

Hepatic infarction related to oral contraceptive use, by M. B. Jacobs. ARCHIVES OF INTERNAL MEDICINE. 144(3):642-643, March 1984.

Imipramine disposition in users of oral contraceptive steroids, by D. R. Abernethy, et al. CLINICAL PHARMACOLOGY AND THERAPEUTICS. 35(6):792-797, June 1984.

Individual levels of plasma alpha 2-antiplasmin and alpha 2-macroglobulin during the normal menstrual cycle and in women on oral contraceptives low in oestrogen, by J. Jespersen, et al. THROMBOSIS AND HAEMOSTASIS. 50(2):581-585, August 30, 1983.

The influence of oral contraceptives on the frequency of acute appendicitis in different phases of the menstrual cycle, by E. Arnbjornsson. SURGERY, GYNECOLOGY AND OBSTETRICS. 158(5):464-466, May 1984.

Influence of oral contraceptives on the incidence of premalignant and malignant lesions of the cervix, by L. Andolsek, et al. CONTRACEPTION. 28(6)505-519, December 1983.

Influence of psychosocial factors on adolescent compliance with oral contraceptives, by R. H. Durant, et al. JOURNAL OF ADOLESCENT HEALTH CARE. 5(1):1-6, January 1984.

Influence of sex and oral contraceptive steroids on paracetamol metabolism, by J. O. Miners, et al. BRITISH JOURNAL OF CLINICAL PHARMACOLOGY. 16(5):503-509, November 1983.

More on reproductive mortality [letter], by R. A. Edgren. FAMILY PLANNING PERSPECTIVES. 15(4):155, July-August 1983.

'Morning-after pill' and antithrombin III, by G. H. Weenink, et al. ACTA OBSTETRICIA ET GYNECOLOGICA SCANDINAVICA. 62(4):359-363, 1983.

Oral contraception, the press and the CSM, by V. R. Bloom. JOURNAL OF THE ROYAL SOCIETY OF MEDICINE. 77(5):359, May 1984.

Oral contraceptive agents do not affect serum prolactin in normal women, by J. R. Davis, et al. CLINICAL ENDOCRINOLOGY. 20(4):427-434, April 1984.

Oral contraceptive use and the risk of epithelial ovarian cancer, by C. La Vecchia, et al. BRITISH JOURNAL OF CANCER. 50(1): 31-34, July 1984.

Oral contraceptives and benign breast disease, by T. G. Hislop, et al. AMERICAN JOURNAL OF EPIDEMIOLOGY. 120(2):273-280, August 1984.

The phasic approach to oral contraception: the triphasic concept and its clinical application, by G. V. Upton. INTERNATIONAL JOURNAL OF FERTILITY. 28(3):121-140, 1983.

The pill for men: available soon?, by W. Frese. MAX PLANCK SOCIETY SCIENCE NEWSLETTER. June 1984, p. 8.

Plasma carnitine in women. Effects of the menstrual cycle and of oral contraceptives, by A. C. Bach, et al. ARCHIVES INTER-NATIONALES DE PHYSIOLOGIE ET DE BIOCHIMIE. 91(4): 333-338, November 1983.

Plasma hormone levels in women receiving new oral contra-ceptives containing ethinyl estradiol plus levonorgestrel or desogestrel, by U. J. Gaspard, et al. CONTRACEPTION. 27(6): 577-590, June 1983.

Positive effects of oral contraceptives, by G. Colla, et al. MI-NERVA GINECOLOGIA. 35(7-8):505-510, July-August 1983.

Prevention of pregnancy with a low dosage 3-stage oral prepara-tion, by R. Gimes, et al. ZENTRALBLATT FUR GYNAE-KOLOGIE. 105(22):1436-1440, 1983.

Prevention of the prothrombotic effects of oral contraceptives with vitamin B6, by J. Koutsky, et al. CESKOSLOVENSKA GYNEKOLOGIE. 49(2):98-103, March 1984.

Prolactin plasma levels and oral contraceptives at low dosage, by S. Milia, et al. CLINICAL AND EXPERIMENTAL OBSTET-RICS AND GYNECOLOGY. 10(4):188-190, 1983.

Prolonged elevation of hypothalamic opioid peptide activity in women taking oral contraceptives, by R. F. Casper, et al. JOURNAL OF CLINICAL ENDROCRINOLOGY AND METABOLISM. 58(3):582-584, March 1984.

Rapid onset of an increase in caffeine residence time in young women due to oral contraceptive steroids, by E. C. Rietveld, et al. EUROPEAN JOURNAL OF CLINICAL PHARMACOLOGY. 26(3):371-373, 1984.

Response from women to adverse publicity about oral contraceptives, by A. Portnoy. JOURNAL OF THE ROYAL COLLEGE OF GENERAL PRACTITIONERS. 34(263):334-335, June 1984.

Results of establishing medical guidelines for selecting oral contraceptive types in family planning agencies, by P. G. Stumpf. CONTRACEPTION. 29(6):511-517, June 1984.

Riboflavin, self-report, and serum norethindrone. Comparison of their use as indicators of adolescent compliance with oral contraceptives, by S. Jay, et al. AMERICAN JOURNAL OF DISEASES OF CHILDREN. 138(1):70-73, January 1984.

The role of epidemiology in the regulation of oral contraceptives, by S. Sobel. PUBLIC HEALTH REPORTS. 99(4):350-354, July-August 1984.

Serum lipids and proteins during treatment with a new oral contraceptive combination containing desogestrel, by I. M. Penttila, et al. EUROPEAN JOURNAL OF OBSTETRICS, GYNECOLOGY AND REPRODUCTIVE BIOLOGY. 16(4):275-281, December 1983.

Serum prostaglandin F levels during menstrual cycle in women using oral contraceptives, by S. K. Garg. INTERNATIONAL JOURNAL OF CLINICAL PHARMACOLOGY, THERAPY AND TOXICOLOGY. 21(8):431-432, August 1983.

Severe intrahepatic cholestasis due to the combined intake of oral contraceptives and triacetyloleandomycin, by J. Fevery, et al. ACTA CLINICA BELGICA. 38(4):242-245, 1983.

Sex hormone profiles in oligomenorrheic adolescent girls and the effect of oral contraceptives, by R. Siegberg, et al. FERTIL-ITY AND STERILITY. 41(6):888-893, June 1984.

The short-term effects of a low-dose oral contraceptive on glucose metabolism, plasma lipids and blood clotting factors, by S. O. Skouby, et al. CONTRACEPTION. 28(5):489-499, November 1983.

Therapeutic uses of contraceptive steroids, by G. C. Starks. JOURNAL OF FAMILY PRACTICE. 19(3):315-312, September 1984.

Thyroid function during treatment with a new oral contraceptive combination containing desogestrel, by I. M. Penttila, et al. EUROPEAN JOURNAL OF OBSTETRICS, GYNECOLOGY AND REPRODUCTIVE BIOLOGY. 16(4):269-274, December 1983.

Trichomoniasis— incidence in pill users and associated pap smear abnormalities, by B. Pillay, et al. MALAYSIAN JOURNAL OF PATHOLOGY. 2:59-62, August 1979.

Urinary concentrations of steroid glucuronides in women taking oral contraceptives, by M. A. Shaw, et al. CONTRACEPTION. 28(1):69-75, July 1983.

Vascular complications of oral contraception. In whom and how to prevent them?, by V. Beaumont, et al. PRESSE MEDICALE. 12(47):2977-2981, December 24, 1983.

Why do inadvertent pregnancies occur in oral contraceptive users? Effectiveness of oral contraceptive regimens and interfering factors, by I. S. Fraser, et al. CONTRACEPTION. 27(6):531-551, June 1983.

CONTRACEPTIVES: ORAL: COMPLICATIONS
Two studies find no link between use of oral contraceptives and development of pituitary tumors. FAMILY PLANNING PERSPECTIVES. 15(6):283-284, November-December 1983.

CONTRACEPTIVES: PSYCHOLOGY AND PSYCHIATRY
Indicators of psychological well-being in a sample of employed women: an exploratory study, by M. W. O'Rourke. HEALTH

CARE FOR WOMEN, INTERNATIONAL. 5(1-3):163-177, 1984.

Matters of conscience: all in the line of duty?, by M. Kenny. NURSING MIRROR. 158(20):22-23, May 16, 1984.

Psychosexual issues in adolescent contraception, by J. G. Greer. PUBLIC HEALTH REVIEWS. 10(1):27-47, January-March 1982.

A unified psychological model of contraceptive behavior, by L. T. Condelli. DISSERTATION ABSTRACTS INTERNATIONAL: B. 45(4), October 1984.

CONTRACEPTIVES: RESEARCH
Changes in estrogen metabolism after chronic oral contraceptive administration in the rhesus monkey, by W. Slikker, Jr., et al. DRUG METABOLISM AND DISPOSITION. 12(2):148-153, March-April 1984.

Characterizations of anti-oLH beta antibodies acting as contraceptives in rhesus monkeys. II. In vivo neutralizing ability for gonadotropic hormones, by Y. Yamamoto, et al. JOURNAL OF REPRODUCTIVE IMMUNOLOGY. 5(4):195-202, July 1983.

Contraception in the dog and cat, by E. K. Jackson. BRITISH VETERINARY JOURNAL. 140(2):132-137, March-April 1984.

Contragestational effects of DL-alpha-difluoro-methylornithine, an irreversible inhibitor of ornithine decarboxylase, in the hamster, by G. Galliani, et al. CONTRACEPTION. 28(2):159-170, August 1983.

Development of six new contraceptives among 1989 goals of WHO programme. FAMILY PLANNING PERSPECTIVES. 15:226-227, September-October 1983.

The effect of alpha-chlorohydrin on the oxidation of fructose by rabbit spermatozoa in vitro, by S. A. Ford, et al. CONTRACEPTION. 28(6):565-573, December 1983.

The effect of oral contraceptives on rat platelet membrane glycoproteins, by B. Toor, et al. BIOCHIMICA ET BIOPHYSICA ACTA. 770(2):178-182, March 14, 1984.

Effect of polyphloretin phosphate on the contraceptive action of a polyethylene intrauterine device in rats, by M. R. Chaudhury. CONTRACEPTION. 28(2):171-180, 1983.

Effect of a single maximal and low multiple doses of testosterone propionate (TP) on male reproductive organs in Long Evans rats, by M. A. Bari, et al. BANGLADESH MEDICAL RESEARCH BULLETIN. 10(1):17-23, June 1984.

Effects of cyproterone acetate with combination of testosterone enanthate on seminal characteristics, androgenicity and clinical chemistry in langur monkey, by N. K. Lohiya, et al. CONTRACEPTION. 28(6):575-586, December 1983.

Given a free rein, prolific mustangs gallop into trouble [use of antifertility drug to control herds], by J. W. Turner, Jr. SMITHSONIAN. 14:88+, February 1984.

Influence of a levonorgestrel-containing contraceptive vaginal ring on plasma lipids and lipoproteins in cynomolgus monkeys, by M. R. Adams, et al. CONTRACEPTION. 28(3):253-266, September 1983.

Local anti-fertility effect of inhibin-enriched preparation (IEP) in female hamsters, by B. V. Bapat, et al. CONTRACEPTION. 29(4):367-373, April 1984.

New developments in vaginal contraception. POPULATION REPORTS [H]. (7):H157-190, January-February 1984.

Research on the effects of hormonal contraceptives on lactation: current findings, methodological considerations and future priorities, by V. J. Hull. WORLD HEALTH STATISTICS QUARTERLY. 36(2):168-200, 1983.

Research on methods of fertility regulation, by E. B. Connell. JOGN NURSING. 13(2 Suppl):50S-56S, March-April 1984.

Reversible contraception like activity of embelin in male dogs (Canis indicus Linn), by V. P. Dixit, et al. ANDROLOGIA. 15(5): 486-494, September-October 1983.

Reversible inhibition of spermatogenesis by danazol with combination of tesosterone enanthate in rabbit, by N. K. Lohiya, et al. ANDROLOGIA. 16(1):72-75, January-February 1984.

Some organizational alternatives to increase support for reproductive and contraceptive research, by J. I. Rosoff. FAMILY PLANNING PERSPECTIVES. 16(1):28-31, January-February 1984.

Steroid-induced thrombogenesis in rats, by J. R. Reel, et al. INTERNATIONAL JOURNAL OF FERTILITY. 28(3):169-172, 1983.

Studies on Aristolochia III. Isolation and biological evaluation of constitutents of Aristolochia indica roots for fertility-regulating activity, by C. T. Che, et al. JOURNAL OF NATURAL PRODUCTS. 47(2):331-341, March-April 1984.

Two-phase teratology study with the synthetic prostaglandin ONO-802 given intravaginally to rats, by J. A. Petrere, et al. TERATOGENESIS, CARCINOGENESIS AND MUTAGENESIS. 4(2):233-243, 1984.

CONTRACEPTIVES: STATISTICS
A 1984 perspective of contraceptive technology, by I. S. Fraser. HEALTHRIGHT. 3:7-11, August 1984.

CONTRACEPTIVES: TECHNIQUES
Propranolol as a novel, effective spermicide, by J. Zipper, et al. BRITISH MEDICAL JOURNAL. 287:1245-1246, October 29, 1983.

Propranolol concentrations in plasma after insertion into the vagina, by L. G. Patel, et al. BRITISH MEDICAL JOURNAL. 287:1247-1248, October 29, 1983.

User's perception of the contraceptive vaginal ring: a field study in Brazil and the Dominican Republic, by E. E. Hardy, et al. STUDIES IN FAMILY PLANNING. 14(11):284-290, November 1983.

CONTRACEPTIVES: URBAN
Characteristics of contraceptive acceptors in an urban Nigerian setting, by O. Ayangade. INTERNATIONAL JOURNAL OF

GYNACOLOGY AND OBSTETRICS. 22(1):59-66, February 1984.

CONTRACEPTIVES AND COLLEGE STUDENTS
Awareness of the existence of postcoital contraception among students who have had a therapeutic abortion, by L. H. Schilling. JOURNAL OF AMERICAN COLLEGE HEALTH. 32(6):244-246, June 1984.

Effect of religiosity on sex attitudes, experience and contraception among university students, by N. Notzer, et al. JOURNAL OF SEX AND MARITAL THERAPY. 10(1):57-62, Spring 1984.

Knowledge of contraception and use of contraceptive methods among college students in a major southeastern public university, by N. S. Palmer. DISSERTATION ABSTRACTS INTERNATIONAL: A. 45(3), September 1984.

A school-, hospital- and university-based adolescent pregnancy prevention program. A cooperative design for service and research, by L. S. Zabin, et al. JOURNAL OF REPRODUCTIVE MEDICINE. 29(6):421-426, June 1984.

Student choices and effectiveness, by L. H. Schilling. JOURNAL OF AMERICAN COLLEGE HEALTH. 32(6):239-243, June 1984.

CONTRACEPTIVES AND ECONOMICS
Postcoital contraception: student choices and effectiveness, by L. H. Schilling. JOURNAL OF AMERICAN COLLEGE HEALTH. 32(6):239-243, June 1984.

Sexual behaviour and contraceptive practice at Oxford and Aberdeen universities, by P. Anderson, et al. JOURNAL OF BIOSOCIAL SCIENCE. 16:287-290, April 1984.

CONTRACEPTIVES AND EDUCATION
Educating peers about human sexuality and birth control in natural settings: a social comparison perspective, by R. De Pietro. PATIENT EDUCATION AND COUNSELING. 6(1):39-46, 1984.

Knowledge of contraception and use of contraceptive methods

among college students in a major southeastern public university, by N. S. Palmer. DISSERTATION ABSTRACTS INTERNATIONAL: A. 45(3), September 1984.

Nursing protocol for diaphragm contraception, by C. J. Pyle. NURSE PRACTITIONER. 9(3):35; 38; 40, March 1984.

A school-, hospital and university-based adolescent pregnancy prevention program. A cooperative design for service and research, by L. S. Zabin, et al. JOURNAL OF REPRODUCTIVE MEDICINE. 29(6):421-426, June 1984.

Unwanted pregnancy. A failure of contraceptive education, by W. Fielding, et al. JOURNAL OF REPRODUCTIVE MEDICINE. 28(12):847-850, December 1983.

Unwanted pregnancy: a failure of contraceptive education [letter], by P. A. Poma. JOURNAL OF REPRODUCTIVE MEDICINE. 29(6):61, June 1984.

Youth and contraception education. A study among the pupils of post-compulsory schools in Bergen and its surroundings, by F. D. Alsaker, et al. TIDSSKRIFT FOR DEN NORSKE LAEGEFORENING. 104(17-18):1206-1209, June 20, 1984.

CONTRACEPTIVES AND FDA
Clearing carcinogenic contraceptives through the FDA [injectable contraceptive, Depo-Provera], by E. Gollub. BUSINESS AND SOCIETY REVIEW. (46):67-70, Summer 1983.

FDA considers Depo-Provera as contraceptive, by M. F. Docksai. TRIAL. 19:16, March 1983.

CONTRACEPTIVES AND HORMONES
Arterial complications of estrogen-progestogen contraception, by J. Jaillard. ANNALES DE MEDECINE INTERNE. 134(5): 416-420, 1983.

Biological properties of 1,2-trans-1(p(beta-pyrrolidinoethoxy) phenyl)-2-phenyl-oxyindane (compound E-1487): a new non-steroidal post-coital antifertility agent, by M. M. Singh, et al. INDIAN JOURNAL OF EXPERIMENTAL BIOLOGY. 21(8):432-434, August 1983.

Calcium oxalate crystal growth in normal urine: role of contraceptive hormones, by R. Tawashi, et al. UROLOGY RESEARCH. 12(1):7-9, 1984.

Cancer of the breast. Influence of hormonal contraception, by A. Gorins. PRESSE MEDICALE. 13(19):1207-1210, May 5, 1984.

Case of ectopic pregnancy after postcoital contraception with ethinyloestradiol-levonorgestrel, by A. A. Kubba, et al. BRITISH MEDICAL JOURNAL [CLIN RES]. 287(6402):1343-1344, November 5, 1983.

Changes in serum apo-lipoprotein AI and sex-hormone-binding globulin levels after treatment with two different progestins administered alone and in combination with ethinyl estradiol, by N. Crona, et al. CONTRACEPTION. 29(3):261-270, March 1984.

Characterizations of anti-oLH beta antibodies acting as contraceptives in rhesus monkeys. II. In vivo neutralizing ability for gonadotropic hormones, by Y. Yamamoto, et al. JOURNAL OF REPRODUCTIVE IMMUNOLOGY. 5(4):195-202, July 1983.

A clinical study of norethisterone enanthate in rural Mexico, by C. W. Meade, et al. STUDIES IN FAMILY PLANNING. 15(3): 143, May-June 1984.

Conception control by vaginal administration or pills containing ethinyl estradiol and dl-norgestrel, by E. M. Coutinho, et al. FERTILITY AND STERILITY. 42(3):478-481, September 1984.

Contraceptive effect of low-dosage ovulation inhibitors containing various progestagen agents, by M. Mall-Haefeli, et al. GEBURTSHILFE UND FRAUENHEILKUNDE. 44(3):177-179, March 1984.

Current trends in the development of hormonal contraception, by E. M. Vikhliaeva. AKUSHERSTVO I GINEKOLOGIIA. (11): 3-5, November 1983.

Decreased plasma phosphate under hormonal contraceptives, by W. Tschope, et al. MINERAL AND ELECTROLYTE METABOLISM. 10(2):88-91, 1984.

Development of hormonal contraception in the Hungarian People's Republic, by G. Seregelyi. AKUSHERSTVO I GINEKOLOGIIA. (4):70-72, April 1984.

Do hormones cause breast cancer?, by D. B. Thomas. CANCER. 53(3 Suppl):595-604, February 1, 1984.

Effect of hormonal contraceptives on cardiovascular function, by I. A. Manuilova, et al. AKUSHERSTVO I GINEKOLOGIIA. (11):5-8, November 1983.

The effect of sex steroids and hormonal contraceptives upon thymus and spleen on intact female rats, by H. Kuhl, et al. CONTRACEPTION. 28(6):587-560, December 1983.

Effects and side effects of hormonal contraceptives in the region of the nose, throat, and ear, by J. Bausch. HNO. 31(12):409-414, December 1983.

Effects of two estradiol/norgestrel combinations on the ovulatory pattern and on sex hormone binding globulin capacity in women around forty years of age, by A. Hagstad, et al. ACTA OBSTETRICA ET GYNECOLOGICA SCANDINAVICA. 63(4): 321-324, 1984.

Hepatic clearance of aminopyrine in the evaluation of liver function in hormonal contraception, by H. Sensing, et al. ZEIT-SCHRIFT FUR DIE GESAMTE INNERE MEDIZIN. 38(23): 622-626, December 1, 1983.

Hereditary uroporphyrinogen decarboxylase deficiency in porphyria cutanea tarda caused by hormonal contraceptives [letter], by M. Doss. DEUTSCHE MEDIZINISCHE WOCHEN-SCHRIFT. 108(48):1857-1858, December 2, 1983.

Hormonal consequences of missing the pill during the first two days of three consecutive artificial cycles, by B. M. Landgren, et al. CONTRACEPTION. 29(5):437-446, May 1984.

Hormonal contraception, by G. R. de Lima, et al. AMB. 29(7-8): 138-142, July-August 1983.

Hormonal contraception— possibilities and problems, by G.

Göretzlehner. ZEITSCHRIFT FUR GESAMTE INNERE MEDIZIN. 38(22):251-253, November 15, 1983.

Hormonal contraceptives. Past, present, and future, by J. W. Goldzieher. POSTGRADUATE MEDICINE. 75(5):75-77; 80; 83-86, April 1984.

Hormonal implants: the next wave of contraceptives, by M. Klitsch. FAMILY PLANNING PERSPECTIVES. 15:239-250, September-October 1983.

A hormone for all reasons [luteinizing hormone releasing hormone], by J. Silberner. SCIENCE NEWS. 126:60, July 28, 1984.

Immunoglobulins and hormonal contraception, by P. Fassati, et al. CESKOSLOVENSKA GYNEKOLOGIE. 48(7):475-479, August 1983.

Incidence of arterial hypertension in women taking oral hormonal contraceptive agents (femigen), by W. Mikrut. WIADOMOSCI LEKARSKIE. 36(19):1587-1592, October 1, 1983.

Individual levels of plasma alpha 2-antiplasmin and alpha 2-macroglobulin during the normal menstrual cycle and in women on oral contraceptives low in oestrogen, by J. Jespersen, et al. THROMBOSIS AND HAEMOSTASIS. 50(2):581-585, August 30, 1983.

Influence of nutritional status on pharmacokinetics of contraceptive progestogens. NUTRITION REVIEWS. 42:182-183, May 1984.

Influence of STS 557 on the mitotic activity in the endometrium of ovariectomized mice and comparison with the effects of progesterone and levonorgestrel, by M. Koch. EXPERIMENTAL AND CLINICAL ENDOCRINOLOGY. 83(3):310-314, May 1984.

Lipid and lipoprotein triglyceride and cholesterol interrelationships: effects of sex, hormone use, and hyperlipidemia, by P. W. Wahl, et al. METABOLISM. 33(6):502-508, June 1984.

Long-acting contraceptive agents: structure activity relationships in a series of norethisterone and levonorgestrel esters, by G. Bialy, et al. STEROIDS. 41(3):419-439, March 1983.

Long acting injectable hormonal contraceptives, by I. S. Fraser. CLINICAL REPRODUCTION AND FERTILITY. 1(1):67-88, March 1982.

Long-term reversible contraception with levonorgestrel-releasing Silastic rods, by S. Roy, et al. AMERICAN JOURNAL OF OBSTETRICS AND GYNECOLOGY. 148(7):1006-1013, April 1, 1984.

Luteinizing hormone-releasing hormone (LHRH) and its analogs for contraception in women: a review, by R. B. Thau. CONTRACEPTION. 29(2):143-162, February 1984.

Metabolic effects of two triphasic formulations containing ethinyl estradiol and dl-norgestrel, by R. P. Smith, et al. CONTRACEPTION. 28(2):189-199, August 1983.

Migraine and hormonal contraceptives, by W. Grassler, et al. ZEITSCHRIFT FUR AERZTLICHE FORTBILDUNG. 78(6): 229-232, 1984.

Mode of action of dl-norgestrel and ethinylestradiol combination in postcoital contraception. III. Effect of preovulatory administration following the luteinizing hormone surge on ovarian steroidogenesis, by W. Y. Line, et al. FERTILITY AND STERILITY. 40(5):631-636, November 1983.

Modification of cycle-dependent changes in the uterus by the intake of hormonal contraceptives, by W. Bartl, et al. ULTRASCHALL IN DER MEDIZIN. 5(2):74-76, April 1984.

Pharmacodynamics of a contraceptive vaginal ring releasing norethindrone and estradiol: ovarian function, bleeding control and lipoprotein patterns, by A. Victor, et al. UPSALA JOURNAL OF MEDICAL SCIENCES. 89(2):179-188, 1984.

Postmolar trophoblastic disease in women using hormonal contraception with and without estrogen, by G. L. Eddy, et al.

OBSTETRICS AND GYNECOLOGY. 62(6):736-740, December 1983.

Potency of estrogen, progestin can affect levels of cholesterol. FAMILY PLANNING PERSPECTIVES. 15:228-229, September-October 1983.

Research on the effects of hormonal contraceptives on lactation: current findings, methodological considerations and future priorities, by V. J. Hull. WORLD HEALTH STATISTICS QUARTERLY. 36(2):168-200, 1983.

Serum steroid binding protein concentrations, distribution of progestogens, and bioavailability of testosterone during treatment with contraceptives containing desogestrel or levonorgestrel, by G. L. Hammond, et al. FERTILITY AND STERILITY. 42(1):44-51, July 1984.

Sickle cell diseases and hormonal contraception, by H. M. Freie. ACTA OBSTETRICIA ET GYNECOLOGICA SCANDINAVICA. 62(3):211-217, 1983.

Side effects of hormonal contraceptives from an internal medicine viewpoint, by J. Dabels. ZEITSCHRIFT FUR DIE GESAMTE INNERE MEDIZIN. 38(22):254-256, November 15, 1983.

Studies on the role of intestinal bacteria in metabolism of synthetic and natural steroid hormones, by H. Adlercreutz, et al. JOURNAL OF STEROID BIOCHEMISTRY. 20(1):217-229, January 1984.

A study of women on the progestogen only pill, by M. C. Robertson. PRACTITIONER. 228(1390):435-439, April 1984.

Systemic changes during the use of hormonal contraceptives, by I. A. Manuilova, et al. AKUSHERSTVO I GINEKOLOGIIA. (11):14-17, November 1983.

Trends in mortality from carcinoma of the liver and the use of oral contraceptives, by D. Forman, et al. BRITISH JOURNAL OF CANCER. 48(3):349-354, September 1983.

CONTRACEPTIVES AND HORMONES

User's perception of the contraceptive vaginal ring: a field study in Brazil and the Dominican Republic, by E. E. Hardy, et al. STUDIES IN FAMILY PLANNING. 14(11):284, November 1983.

CONTRACEPTIVES AND LITERATURE
The influence of psychological and situational factors on the contraceptive behavior of single men: a review of the literature, by D. Gold, et al. POPULATION AND ENVIRONMENT: BEHAVIORAL AND SOCIAL ISSUES. 6(2):113-129, Summer 1983.

CONTRACEPTIVES AND THE MENTALLY RETARDED
Issues in fertility control for mentally retarded female adolescents: I. Sexual activity, sexual abuse, and contraception, A. Chamberlain, et al. PEDIATRICS. 73(4):445-450, April 1984.

Providing contraceptive choices for the intellectually handicapped client, by A. Rauch. HEALTHRIGHT. 2:41-43, February 1983.

CONTRACEPTIVES AND NURSES
The contraceptive context: a model for increasing nursing's involvement in family health, by J. M. Swanson, et al. MATERNAL-CHILD NURSING JOURNAL. 12(3):169-183, Fall 1983.

Nursing protocol for diaphragm contraception, by C. J. Pyle. NURSE PRACTITIONER. 9(3):35; 38; 40, March 1984.

Peers, not RNs, should teach teens oral contraception. RN. 47:14, May 1984.

The role of the midwife in family planning, by N. M. Bentley. MIDWIVES CHRONICLE. 96(1146):254, July 1983.

CONTRACEPTIVES AND PARENTAL CONSENT
Minors' right of privacy: access to contraceptives without parental notification. JOURNAL OF JUVENILE LAW. 7:99-115, 1983.

CONTRACEPTIVES AND PARENTAL CONSENT

Unemancipated minors' rights of access to contraceptives with-
out parental consent or notice— the squeal rule and beyond.
OKLAHOMA CITY UNIVERSITY LAW REVIEW. 8:219-250,
Summer 1983.

CONTRACEPTIVES AND PHYSICIANS
Attitude and behavior of physicians and medical students toward
contraception: results of a study carried out in Modena, by
G. C. Di Renzo, et al. ANNALI DI OSTETRICIA GINE-
COLOGIA, MEDICINA PERINATALE. 105(1):37-63, January-
February 1984.

Private physicians and the provision of contraceptives to
adolescents, by M. T. Orr. FAMILY PLANNING PERSPEC-
TIVES. 16:83-88, March-April 1984.

CONTRACEPTIVES AND POLITICS
The politics of contraception, by S. Bell. WOMEN AND HEALTH.
8(4):57, Winter 1983.

CONTRACEPTIVES AND RELIGION
Contraception and the rejection of God, by L. Ciccone. L'OSSER-
VATORE ROMANO. (50):9-10, December 12, 1983.

Contraceptive patterns of religious and racial groups in the
United States, 1955-1976: convergence and distinctiveness,
by W. D. Mosher, et al. STUDIES IN FAMILY PLANNING.
15:101-111, May-June 1984.

Effect of religiosity on sex attitudes, experience and contraception
among university students, by N. Notzer, et al. JOURNAL OF
SEX AND MARITAL THERAPY. 10(1):57-62, Spring 1984.

The moral act, by N. J. Rigali. HORIZONS. 10:252-266, Fall 1983.

Motives of deficiency, want and illness in the conception of the
godhead within the chasidic mysticism, by J. Mendelsohn.
ANALYTISCHE PSYCHOLOGIE. 14(3):165-185, August 1983.

CONTRACEPTIVES AND SEXUAL BEHAVIOR.
Contraception and sexually transmissible diseases, by J. Porter.
HEALTHRIGHT. 3:12-15, August 1984.

Putting the sex back into contraception, by R. Shapiro. COM-MUNITY OUTLOOK. April 11, 1984, pp. 123-131.

CONTRACEPTIVES AND SPORTS
Contraception— sports, by Dutry, et al. ARCHIVES BELGES. 41(11-12):504-510, 1983.

CONTRACEPTIVES AND YOUTH
Adolescent use of oral contraceptives, by M. A. Baginton. PEDIA-TRIC NURSING. 10(2):111-114, March-April 1984.

Adolescents' preference of source to obtain contraceptive information, by B. J. van den Berg, et al. AMERICAN JOURNAL OF OBSTETRICS AND GYNECOLOGY. 147(6):719-721, November 15, 1983.

Blowing the whistle on the squeal rule [defunct regulation requiring clinics to inform parents if daughters are given contraceptives is still on the books], by D. Gates. NEWS-WEEK. 104:18, September 24, 1984.

Consequences of teenage pregnancy and motherhood, by L. Simkins. ADOLESCENCE. 19:39-54, Spring 1984.

Contraception in adolescence: a review. 1. Psychosocial aspects, by A. D. Hofmann. WHO BULLETIN. 62(1):151-162, 1984.

—. 2. Biomedical aspects, by A. D. Hofmann. WHO BULLETIN. 62(2):331-344, 1984.

Contraception in young people, by R. Fabian. CESKOSLOVENSKA GYNEKOLOGIE. 49(3):197-198, April 1984.

Contraceptive behavior among unmarried young women: a theoretical framework for research, by C A. Nathanson, et al. POPULATION AND ENVIRONMENT. 6(1):39, Spring 1983.

Contraceptive continuation among adolescents attending family planning clinics, by F. F. Furstenberg, Jr., et al. FAMILY PLANNING PERSPECTIVES. 15(5):211-214; 216-217, September-October 1983.

Contraceptive use by adolescent females in relation to knowledge, and to time and method of contraceptive counseling, by S. A. Marcy, et al. RESEARCH IN NURSING AND HEALTH. 6(4): 175-182, December 1983.

Cognitive and behavioral methods with adolescents, by L. D. Gilchrist, et al. COGNITIVE THERAPY AND RESEARCH. 7(5): 379-388, October 1983.

Decision-making in regard to the use of contraceptives after confinement: a study among urban black woman (in Afrikaans), by G. Erasmus. SOUTH AFRICAN JOURNAL OF SOCIOLOGY. 15(2):94-97, 1984.

Digestive complications of oral contraceptives: a case of extensive digestive necrosis in a young woman, by E. Carpentier, et al. ANNALES DE CHIRURGIE. 38(4):305-308, May 1984.

Ecological factors predicting adolescent contraceptive use: implications for intervention, by L. S. Kastner. JOURNAL OF ADOLESCENT HEALTH CARE. 5(2):79-86, April 1984.

Educating peers about human sexuality and birth control in natural settings: a social comparison perspective, by R. De Pietro. PATIENT EDUCATION AND COUNSELING. 6(1): 39-46, 1984.

Effect of peer counselors on adolescent compliance in use of oral contraceptives, by M. S. Jay, et al. PEDIATRICS. 73(2):126-131, February 1984.

Effect of religiosity on sex attitudes, experience and contraception among university students, by N. Notzer, et al. JOURNAL OF SEX AND MARITAL THERAPY. 10(1):57-62, Spring 1984.

Factors associated with complicance to oral contraceptive use in an adolescent population, by P. W. Scher, et al. JOURNAL OF ADOLESCENT HEALTH CARE. 3(2):120-123, September 1982.

Family communication and teenagers contraceptive use, by F. F. Furstenberg, et al. FAMILY PLANNING PERSPECTIVES. 16(4):163-170, July-August 1984.

Gender roles and premarital contraception, by P. L. Mac-
Corquodale. JOURNAL OF MARRIAGE AND THE FAMILY.
46(1):57-63, February 1984.

High-risk young mothers: infant mortality and morbidity in
four areas in the United States, 1973-1978, by M. C. Mc-
Cormick, et al. AMERICAN JOURNAL OF PUBLIC HEALTH.
74:18-25, January 1984.

I did know how babies come into the world, by C. Esposito, et al.
ETA EVOLUTIVA. (14):5-12, February 1983.

Influence of psychosocial factors on adolescent compliance with
oral contraceptives, by R. H. Durant, et al. JOURNAL OF
ADOLESCENT HEALTH CARE. 5(1):1-6, January 1984.

Initiating contraceptive use: how do young women decide?, by J.
E. White. PEDIATRIC NURSING. 10(5):346-352, September-
October 1984.

Legislation and teenage sex. BRITISH MEDICAL JOURNAL [CLIN
RES]. 287(6408):1826, December 17, 1983.

Legislation and teenage sex [letter]. BRITISH MEDICAL JOURNAL
[CLIN RES]. 288(6412):234-235, January 21, 1984.

Male adolescent sexual behavior, the forgotten partner: a review,
by M. L. Finkel, et al. JOURNAL OF SCHOOL HEALTH. 53(9):
544-547, November 1983.

Measurement issues involved in examining contraceptive use
among young single women, by E. S. Herold. POPULATION
AND ENVIRONMENT. 4(2):128-144, Summer 1981.

Minors' right of privacy: access to contraceptives without
parental notification. JOURNAL OF JUVENILE LAW. 7:99-
115, 1983.

Mortality among young black women using contraceptives, by H.
W. Ory, et al. JAMA. 251(8):1044-1048, February 24, 1984.

Predicting adolescent sexual and contraceptive behavior: an application and test of the Fishbein model, by S. R. Jorgense, et al. JOURNAL OF MARRIAGE AND THE FAMILY. 46(1):43-55, February 1984.

Preventing adolescent pregnancy: an interpersonal problem-solving approach, by E. W. Flaherty, et al. PREVENTION IN HUMAN SERVICES. 2(3):49-64, Spring 1983.

Private physicians and the provision of contraceptives to adolescents, by M. T. Orr, et al. FAMILY PLANNING PERSPECTIVES. 16(2):83, March-April 1984.

Problems of contraception in teenage girls, by H. Barth, et al. ZENTRALBLATT FUR GYNAEKOLOGIE. 106(6):389-392, 1984.

Ribloflavin, self-report, and serum norethindrone. Comparison of their use as indicators of adolescent compliance with oral contraceptives, by S. Jay, et al. AMERICAN JOURNAL OF DISEASES OF CHILDREN. 138(1):70-73, January 1984.

A school-, hospital- and university-based adolescent pregnancy prevention program. A cooperative design for service and research, by L. S. Zabin, et al. JOURNAL OF REPRODUCTIVE MEDICINE. 29(6):421-426, June 1984.

The sentiments of love and aspirations for marriage and their association with teenage sexual activity and pregnancy, by J. W. Scott. ADOLESCENCE. 18:889-898, Winter 1983.

Sex, contraception and parenthood: experience and attitudes among urban black young men, by S. D. Clark, Jr., et al. FAMILY PLANNING PERSPECTIVES. 16(2):77-82, March-April 1984.

Sexual and contraceptive experience among teenagers in Uppsala, by E. Weiner, et al. UPSALA JOURNAL OF MEDICAL SCIENCES. 89(2):171-177, 1984.

Sexual information and contraception in adolescence, by M. P. Breton, et al. ANNALES DE PEDIATRIE. 31(3):245-249, March 1984.

Sexuality, contraception and pregnancy in the adolescent girl, by I. R. M. I. Rey-Stocker. GYNAEKOLOGISCHE RUNDSCHAU. 23(2):108-120, 1983.

Source of prescription contraceptives and subsequent pregnancy among young women, by M. Zelnik, et al. FAMILY PLANNING PERSPECTIVES. 16:6-13, January-February 1984.

Teenage pregnancy and childbearing: why the difference between countries? FAMILY PLANNING PERSPECTIVES. 15:104-105, May-June 1983.

Teenage pregnancy and public policy, by L. D. Gilchrist, et al. SOCIAL SERVICE REVIEW. 57:307-322, June 1983.

Teenage pregnancy prevention: an Atlanta program, by M. F. Hill, et al. URBAN HEALTH. 13(2):26-29, March 1984.

Too many teen pregnancies. FAMILY PLANNING PERSPEC-TIVES. 16(1):4, January-February 1984.

Unemancipated minors' rights of access to contraceptives with-out parental consent or notice— the squeal rule and beyond. OKLAHOMA CITY UNIVERSITY LAW REVIEW. 8:219-250, Summer 1983.

Urban black adolescents who obtain contraceptive services before or after their first pregnancy. Psychosocial factors and contraceptive use, by E. W. Freeman, et al. JOURNAL OF ADOLESCENT HEALTH CARE. 5(3):183-190, July 1984.

Woman's failure to use contraceptives not valid defense in paternity action. THE FAMILY LAW REPORTER. 10(41): 1561-1562, August 21, 1984.

Youth and contraception education. A study among the pupils of post-compulsory schools in Bergen and its surroundings, by F. D. Alsaker, et al. TIDSSKRIFT FOR DEN NORSKE LAEGEFORENING. 104(17-18):1206-1209, June 20, 1984.

CONTRACEPTIVE CLINICS
The association between smoking and sexual behavior among

teens in U. S. contraceptive clinics, by L. S. Zabin. AMERI-
CAN JOURNAL OF PUBLIC HEALTH. 74(3):261-263, March
1984.

Gynecological services utilization by contraceptive clients: a
cost analysis, by J. G. Zapka, et al. JOURNAL OF AMERICAN
COLLEGE HEALTH. 32(2):66-72, October 1983.

CONTRACEPTIVE COUNSELING
The art of contraceptive counseling, by J. Edwards. HEALTH-
RIGHT. 3:22-24, August 1984.

Cancer chemotherapy and contraceptive counseling, by R. H.
Parrish, 2d. DRUG INTELLIGENCE AND CLINICAL
PHARMACY. 18(1):71-72, January 1984.

Contraceptive counseling following pregnancy, by A. G. Rebholz.
FORTSCHRITTE DER MEDIZIN. 102(17): 482-484, May 3,
1984.

Contraceptive use by adolescent females in relation to knowledge, and to time and method of contraceptive counseling, by
S. A. March, et al. RESEARCH IN NURSING AND HEALTH.
6(4):175-182, December 1983.

Effect of peer counselors on adolescent compliance in use of oral
contraceptives, by M. S. Jay, et al. PEDIATRICS. 73(2):126-
131, February 1984.

Peer counselors. AMERICAN JOURNAL OF NURSING. 84:590,
May 1984.

Transferring health and family planning service innovations
to the public sector: an experiment in organization development in Bangladesh, by J. F. Phillips, et al. STUDIES IN
FAMILY PLANNING. 15(2):62-73, March-April 1984.

CONTRACEPTIVE FUNDING
Public funding of contraceptive, sterilization and abortion ser-
vices, 1982, by B. Nestor, et al. FAMILY PLANNING PERSPEC-
TIVES. 16(3):128-133, May-June 1984.

Safety last at the FDA, by D. St. Clair. GUARDIAN. 36(9):2,
July 11, 1984.

FAMILY PLANNING: GENERAL
Breast-feeding and child spacing, by P. Senanayake. HYGIE.
3(2):29-32, June 1984.

Breast-feeding and family planning policy, by V. Balasubrahmanyan. ECONOMIC AND POLITICAL WEEKLY. 18:2099,
December 10, 1983.

Building a family: unplanned events, by J. Bongaarts. STUDIES
IN FAMILY PLANNING. 15(1):14-19, January-February 1984.

Chance, choice, and the future of reproduction, by W. B. Miller.
AMERICAN PSYCHOLOGIST. 38(11):1198-1205, November
1983.

Children by choice or by chance: the perceived effects of parity,
by J. Ross, et al. SEX ROLES. 9:69-77, January 1983.

Contraceptive use by adolescent females in relation to knowledge, and to time and method of contraceptive counseling,
by S. A. March, et al. RESEARCH IN NURSING AND
HEALTH. 6(4):175-182, December 1983.

A crucial new direction for international family planning, by
F. P. Hosken. HUMANIST. 44(1):5-8; 45, January-February
1984.

Diocesan-wide NFP program reaches broad population groups.
HOSPITAL PROGRESS. 65(4):26; 28; 30, April 1984.

Dual career, delayed childbearing families: some observations,
by B. Schlesinger, et al. CANADA'S MENTAL HEALTH.
32(1):4-6, March 1984.

Evaluative methodology of a family planning service, by G.
Benussi, et al. NUOVI ANNALI D'IGIENE E MICROBIOLOGIA.
33(2-3):233-258, March-June 1982.

Family planners' accord: urgency, by T. C. Fox. NATIONAL
CATHOLIC REPORTER. 20:1+, August 17, 1984.

Family planning. PUBLIC HEALTH REPORTS. September-
October, 1983, pp. 16-24.

Family planning in a healthy, married population operationalizing the human rights approach in an Israeli health service
setting, by D. E. Block, et al. AMERICAN JOURNAL OF
PUBLIC HEALTH. 74(8):830-833, August 1984.

Family planning. A most effective preventive health measure,
by J. Rowley. HYGIE. 3(2):3-4, June 1984.

Family planning: a preventive health measure, by A. Petros-
Barvazian. WORLD HEALTH. June 1984, pp. 4-7.

A family planning risk scoring system for health care providers,
by W. N. Spellacy, et al. OBSTETRICS AND GYNECOLOGY.
63(6):846-849, June 1984.

Goals in reproductive decision making, by B. A. Nardi. AMERI-
CAN ETHNOLOGIST. 10(4):697-714, November 1983.

Good times, bad times: a study of the future path of U. S. fertility,
by D. A. Ahlburg. SOCIAL BIOLOGY. 30:17-23, Spring 1983.

Healthier mothers and children through family planning.
POPULATION REPORTS [J]. (27):J657-696, May-June 1984.

The impact of family planning on neonatal mortality, by J. C.
Caceres-Baltazar. DISSERTATIO ABSTRACTS INTER-
NATIONAL: B. 45(6), December 1984.

The influence of child spacing on child survival, by C. Desweemer.
POPULATION STUDIES. 38:47-72, March 1984.

Integrated approach to MCH and family planning [letter], by A. K.
Sood, et al. INDIAN PEDIATRICS. 20(11):876-877, November
1983.

Integrated child development services: impact on fertility regula-

tion, by M. K. Vasundhra, et al. JOURNAL OF FAMILY WEL-
FARE. 30:3-7, September 1983.

Intrauterine devices. Their role in family planning care. WHO
OFFSET PUBLICATION. (75):1-53, 1983.

Making choices. AMERICAN DEMOGRAPHICS. 6:13-14,
February 1984.

Marketing enables population control group to boost results, by
K. Higgins. MARKETING NEWS. 17:12-13, October 14, 1983.

Maternal age and overdue conceptions, by G. E. Hendershot.
AMERICAN JOURNAL OF PUBLIC HEALTH. 74(1):35-38,
January 1984.

Mixed verdict for family at U. N. population meet, by J. C.
O'Neill. OUR SUNDAY VISITOR. 73:3, September 16, 1984.

Mortality levels and family fertility goals, by J. Y. Parlange,
et al. DEMOGRAPHY. 20(4):535, November 1983.

Natural childbirth brings back good memories. NEW SCIENTIST.
96:356, November 11, 1982.

New importance in the social aspects of the care of the pregnant
woman, by Z. Stembera. CESKOSLOVENSKA GYNEKOLOGIE.
48(9):633-637, November 1983.

Obstetric and gynecological care for third world women, by J. A.
Pinotti, et al. INTERNATIONAL JOURNAL OF GYNAECOLOGY
AND OBSTETRICS. 2195):361-369, October 1983.

Perceptions about having children: are daughters different from
their mothers?, by V. J. Callan, et al. JOURNAL OF MAR-
RIAGE AND THE FAMILY. 45(3):607-612, August 1983.

Personal experience with committee family planning at the
Institute for Continuing Education of Health Personnel,
by V. Kliment, et al. CESKOSLOVENSKA GYNEKOLOGIE.
48(5):388-389, June 1983.

Popline: an overview for searchers, by D. R. Farre, et al. MEDI-

ICAL REFERENCE SERVICES QUARTERLY. 2(4):1-20, Winter 1983.

Population and health. WORLD HEALTH. June 1984, pp. 2-29.

Population explosion predicted. ENVIRONMENT. 26:22-23, July-August 1984.

The population question. SCHOLASTIC UPDATE. 116:2+, March 2, 1984.

Preventive health services: family planning. PUBLIC HEALTH REPORTS. September-October 1983, pp. 16-24.

Reproductive health services for men: is there a need?, by P. H. Gordon, et al. FAMILY PLANNING PERSPECTIVES. 16(1): 44-46, January-February 1984.

Results of establishing medical guidelines for selecting oral contraceptive types in family planning agencies, by P. G. Stumpf. CONTRACEPTION. 29(6):511-517, June 1984.

Sexually transmitted diseases and family planning. Strange or natural bedfellows?, by W. Cates, Jr. JOURNAL OF REPRODUCTIVE MEDICINE. 29(5):317-322, May 1984.

Symptoms of emotional distress in a family planning service: stability over a four-week period, by A. Winokur, et al. BRITISH JOURNAL OF PSYCHIATRY. 144:395-399, April 1984.

Voluntarily childless women: traditional or nontraditional, by S. Bram. SEX ROLES. 10:195-206, February 1984.

Voluntary childlessness and the women's liberation movement, by G. A. Shea. POPULATION AND ENVIRONMENT. 6(1):17, Spring 1983.

Who plans your family?, by N. Cavnar. NEW COVENANT. 13:13-16, February 1984.

AFRICA
Age pattern of fertility in the Sudan, by M. A. Khalifa. JOURNAL OF BIOSOCIAL SCIENCE. 15:317-324, July 1983.

Determinants of cumulative fertility in Ghana, by E. O. Tawiah. DEMOGRAPHY. 84(21):1-8, February 1984.

Marital sexual relationships and birth spacing among two Yoruba sub-groups, by L. A. Adeokun. AFRICA. 52(4): 1-14, 1982.

Supply-demand disequilibria and fertility changes in Africa: toward a more appropriate economic approach, by J. E. Kocher. SOCIAL BIOLOGY. 30:41-58, Spring 1983.

ASIA
Asian media's impact on family planning, by K. Bhupal. POPULI. 10(4):30-35, 1983.

Can Asia's population bomb be diffused?, by G. Pranay. ASIA. 6(3):16, September-October 1983.

Attitudes toward the rhythm method in the Philippines, by C. C. Verzosa, et al. STUDIES IN FAMILY PLANNING. 15:74-78, March-April 1984.

Fertility differentials in Nepal, by B. Gubhaju. JOURNAL OF BIOSOCIAL SCIENCE. 15:325-332, July 1983.

Natural family planning in the Philippines, by J. E. Laing. STUDIES IN FAMILY PLANNING. 15:49-61, March-April 1984.

The timing of family formation: structural and societal factors in the Asian context, by R. R. Rindfus, et al. JOURNAL OF MARRIAGE AND THE FAMILY. 46:205-214, February 1984.

AUSTRALIA
Family planning associations in Australia: key events from 1926 to 1983, by D. Wyndham, et al. HEALTH RIGHT. 3:7-18, November 1983.

CHINA

China's one-child families: girls need not apply [problems of female infanticide and the abuse of woman as reported in the Chinese press], by L. Landman. RF. December 1983, pp. 8-10.

China's population policy: theory and methods, by X. Qian. STUDIES IN FAMILY PLANNING. 14:295-301, December 1983.

Chinese family problems: research and trends, by Z. Wei. JOURNAL OF MARRIAGE AND THE FAMILY. 45(4):943-948, November 1983.

Family planning. BEIJING REVIEW. 26:4, August 29, 1983.

In praise of the one-child family, by J. Marshall. TIMES EDUCATIONAL SUPPLEMENT. 3513:11, October 28, 1983.

Income and other factors influencing fertility in China, by N. Birdsall, et al. POPULATION AND DEVELOPMENT REVIEW. 9:651-675, December 1983.

Increasing natality in China, by M. Cartier. POPULATION. 38:590-591, May-June 1983.

New data on nuptiality and fertility in China, by J. C. Caldwell, et al. POPULATION AND DEVELOPMENT REVIEW. 10(1):71, March 1984.

Population lid: China cajoles families and offers incentives to reduce birth rate; but one-child policy stirs resistance, hasn't ended the preference for sons, by A. Bennett. WALL STREET JOURNAL. 202:1+, July 6, 1983.

The precious child: family planning in the People's Republic of China, by D. Bulger. PERINATAL PRESS. 8(2):23-27, 1984.

Small families: promoting population stabilization [in developing countries], by J. Jacobsen. TRANSNATIONAL

CHINA
>PERSPECTIVES. 9(2):15-18, 1983.

Some observations on family planning education in China,
by M. V. Hamburg. HYGIE. 3(2):21-24, June 1984.

EGYPT
Attitudes of a group of Egyptian medical students towards
family planning, by T. el-Mehairy. SOCIAL SCIENCE
AND MEDICINE. 19(2):131-134, 1984.

EUROPE
Pronatalist population policies in some western European
countries, by H. J. Heeren. POPULATION RESEARCH
AND POLICY REVIEW. 1(2):137-152, May 1982.

GREAT BRITAIN
The family planning nurse: the present and future role of
the nurse in family planning, part 2, by A. Cowper.
NURSING TIMES. 80(13):31-33, March 28-April 3, 1984.

The family planning nurse: a centre of excellence, part 3,
by P. Holmes. NURSING TIMES. 80(13):34, March 28-
April 3, 1984.

GUAM
The rapid fertility decline in Guam natives, by S. L. Tung.
JOURNAL OF BIOSOCIAL SCIENCE. 16:231-240, April
1984.

INDIA
Action now in family planning: the role of nurse, by A. K.
Malhotra, et al. NURSING JOURNAL OF INDIA. 75(2):
27-28, February 1984.

Characteristics of family planning clients in Bangladesh, by
I. Swenson, et al. INTERNATIONAL JOURNAL OF
FERTILITY. 28(3):149-155, 1983.

Factors affecting fertility control in India: a cross-sectional
study, by K. Srinivasan, et al. POPULATION AND
DEVELOPMENT REVIEW. 10:273-296, June 1984.

INDIA

Family planning and health work at the grassroots: some issues and new concerns in the Indian context, by D. N. Saksena. HYGIE. 2(2):9-14, July 1983.

Family planning: a nurse's concern, by S. A. Samuel. NURSING JOURNAL OF INDIA. 75(5):105-106, May 1984.

Family planning top priority for Bengalees [Bangladesh], by E. C. Clift. NEW DIRECTIONS FOR WOMEN. 13:5, July-August 1983.

Fertility trends among overseas Indian populations, by A. Muthiah, et al. POPULATION STUDIES. 37(2):273, July 1983.

Ignorance of family planning methods in India: an important constraint on use, by A. M. Basu. STUDIES IN FAMILY PLANNING. 15(3):136-142, May-June 1984.

Impact of child mortality and sociodemographic attributes on family size desire: some data from urban India, by D. N. Saksena, et al. JOURNAL OF BIOSOCIAL SCIENCE. 16:119-126, January 1984.

India's family planning programme— its impact and implications, by K. Srinivasan. JOURNAL OF FAMILY WELFARE. 30:7-25, December 1983.

Integrating health services into an MCH-FP program: lessons from Matlab, Bangladesh, by J. F. Phillips, et al. STUDIES IN FAMILY PLANNING. 15(4):153-161, July-August 1984.

Marie Stopes Society's good work. NURSING JOURNAL OF INDIA. 75(6):138, June 1984.

Mortality impact of an MCH-FP program in Matlab, Bangladesh, by L. C. Chen, et al. STUDIES IN FAMILY PLANNING. 14(8-9):199-209, August-September 1983.

Simulation modeling perspectives of the Bangladesh family planning and female education system, by J. H. Teel, et al.

INDIA
BEHAVIORAL SCIENCE. 29(3):145-161, July 1984.

Small families: promoting population stabilization [in developing countries], by J. Jacobsen. TRANSNATIONAL PERSPECTIVES. 9(2):15-18, 1983.

Socio-economic and demographic study of factors influencing fertility control in India, by S. K. Chaudhuri. JOURNAL OF THE INDIAN MEDICAL ASSOCIATION. 81(5-6): 99-101, September 1983.

Thirty years of family planning in India, by R. Ledbetter. ASIAN SURVEY. 24:736-758, July 1984.

Transferring health and family planning service innovations to the public sector: an experiment in organization development in Bangladesh, by J. F. Phillips, et al. STUDIES IN FAMILY PLANNING. 15(2):62, March-April 1984.

ISRAEL
Family planning in a healthy, married population: operationalizing the human rights approach in an Israeli health service setting, by D. E. Block, et al. AMERICAN JOURNAL OF PUBLIC HEALTH. 74(8):830-833, August 1984.

JAPAN
Modern fertility patterns: contrasts between the United States and Japan, by S. P. Morgan, et al. POPULATION AND DEVELOPMENT REVIEW. 10(1):19, March 1984.

Thirty years of patient education in the use of pessaries: personal history of Mrs. Taki Hanyu. The past and present of education in pessary use, by T. Hanyu, et al. JOSANPU ZASSHI. 37(3):178-186, March 1983.

MEXICO
Family planning and maternal-child health in Mexico 1970-1980, by B. R. Ordonez. JOURNAL OF TROPICAL PEDIATRICS. 29(5):271-277, October 1983.

MEXICO
Male migration, machismo, and conjugal roles: implications
for fertility control in a Mexican municipio, by R. E.
Wiest. JOURNAL OF COMPARATIVE FAMILY STUDIES.
14(2):167-181, Summer 1983.

NEPAL
Visit to Nepal. 9. Family planning in Nepal, by T. Akita.
KANGOGAKU ZASSHI. 47(9):1066-1068, September 1983.

SINGAPORE
Some are more equal, by V. G. Kulkarni. FAR EASTERN
ECONOMIC REVIEW. 124:31-32, June 21, 1984.

SOUTH AMERICA
Community characteristics, women's education, and fertility
in Peru, by M. Tienda. STUDIES IN FAMILY PLANNING.
15(4):162, July-August 1984.

Fertility and pacification among the Mekranoti of central
Brazil, by D. Werner. HUMAN ECOLOGY. 11(2):227,
June 1983.

Quarterly versus monthly supervision of CBD family plan-
ning programs: an experimental study in northeast
Brazil, by J. R. Foreit, et al. STUDIES IN FAMILY
PLANNING. 15(3):112-120, May-June 1984.

SOUTHEAST ASIA
Advertising family planning in the press: direct response
results from Bangladesh, by P. D. Harvey. STUDIES IN
FAMILY PLANNING. 15:40-43, January-February 1984.

Family planning in Lae urban area of Papua New Guinea,
1981, by W. K. Agyei. JOURNAL OF BIOSOCIAL SCIENCE.
16(2):269-275, April 1984.

Female employment and reproductive behavior in Taiwan,
1980, by C. S. Stokes, et al. DEMOGRAPHY. 20(3):313,
August 1983.

Fertility and family planning in Papua New Guinea, by W. K.

SOUTHEAST ASIA
Agyei. JOURNAL OF BIOSOCIAL SCIENCE. 16(3):323-334, July 1984.

Practices in pregnancy and family planning of women in slum and the government housing project of the Din—Daeng community, Bangkok, 1981, by A. Leimsombat, et al. JOURNAL OF THE MEDICAL ASSOCIATION OF THAILAND. 66(Suppl 1):13-19, June 1983.

NEW ZEALAND
Childhood disadvantage and the planning of pregnancy, by D. M. Fergusson, et al. SOCIAL SCIENCE AND MEDICINE. 17(17):1223-1227, 1983.

UNITED STATES
American family building strategies in 1900: stopping or spacing, by S. E. Tolnay, et al. DEMOGRAPHY. 21(1):9, February 1984.

The changing American family, by A. Thornton, et al. POPULATION BULLETIN. 38(4):2, October 1983.

Complementarity of work and fertility among young American mothers, by F. L. Mott, et al. POPULATION STUDIES. 37(2):239, Jully 1983.

Conference on population [U. S. position on family planning], by J. L. Buckley. VITAL SPEECHES OF THE DAY. 50: 677-679, September 1, 1984.

Differential fertility in rural Erie County, New York, 1855, by M. J. Stern. JOURNAL OF SOCIAL THEORY. 16:49-64, Summer 1983.

Ethnic fertility differences in Canada, 1926-71: an examination of assimilation hypothesis, by K. G. Basavarajappa, et al. JOURNAL OF BIOSOCIAL SCIENCE. 16:45-54, January 1984.

Family planning among the urban poor: sexual politics and social policy, by M. Cummings, et al. FAMILY RELATIONS. 32:47-58, January 1983.

UNITED STATES
Family planning services from multiple provider types: an
assessment for the United States, by G. E. Hendershot.
STUDIES IN FAMILY PLANNING. 14:218-227, August-
September 1983.

Grandstand play [U. S. position on family planning aid].
NEW REPUBLIC. 191:9-10, August 27, 1984.

'Illusory' savings as a result of California's FP copayment
system. FAMILY PLANNING PERSPECTIVES. 15(6):
281-282, November-December 1983.

Mixed-up message [U. S. changes family planning position].
NATION. 239:4, July 7-14, 1984.

Modern fertility patterns: contrasts between the United
States and Japan, by S. P. Morgan, et al. POPULATION
AND DEVELOPMENT REVIEW. 10(1):19, March 1984.

On this picket line, trouble, by V. Warner. REGISTER. 60:1,
May 13, 1984.

Reproductive impairments among married couples: United
States, by W. D. Mosher, et al. HHS REPORT [PHS] 1983-
1987. 23(11), December 1982.

Sex of previous children and intentions for further births in
the United States, 1965-1976, by D. M. Sloane, et al.
DEMOGRAPHY. 20(3):353, August 1983.

A debate over sovereign rights [U. S. cuts off funds to family
planning agencies that promote abortion], by L. Lopez.
TIME. 124:34, August 20, 1984.

Population: trading places [U. S. restrictions on family
planning aid to discourage abortions], by R. Watson.
NEWSWEEK. 104:50, August 20 1984.

FAMILY PLANNING: ADVERTISING
Advertising family planning in the press: direct response results
from Bangladesh, by P. D. Harvey. STUDIES IN FAMILY
PLANNING. 15:40-43, January-February 1984.

Attitudes of a group of Egyptian medical students towards family planning, by T. el-Mehairy. SOCIAL SCIENCE AND MEDICINE. 19(2):131-134, 1984.

Knowledge, attitude and practice of family planning in Hausa women, by N. Rehan. SOCIAL SCIENCE AND MEDICINE. 18(10):839-844, 1984.

FAMILY PLANNING: DEVELOPING COUNTRIES
Conference on population [U. S. position on family planning], by J. L. Buckley. VITAL SPEECHES OF THE DAY. 50:677-679, September 1, 1984.

Declining birth rates and growing populations, by K. Davis. POPULATION RESEARCH AND POLICY REVIEW. 3(1):61-75, January 1984.

Determinants of breastfeeding in developing countries: overview and policy implications, by S. L. Huffman. STUDIES IN FAMILY PLANNING. 15(4):170, July-August 1984.

Estimating voluntary and involuntary childlessness in the developing countries, by D. L. Poston, et al. JOURNAL OF BIOSOCIAL SCIENCE. 15(4):441-452, October 1983.

Family planning in developing nations: a global concern, our concern, by L. Harriman. JOURNAL OF HOME ECONOMICS. 76(1):8-12, Spring 1984.

FAMILY PLANNING: ECONOMICS
Another look at the costs and benefits of government expenditures for family planning programs, by J. B. Healy, et al. FAMILY PLANNING PERSPECTIVES. 15(6):299-301, November-December 1983.

The effects of federal funding cuts on family planning services, 1980-1983, by A. Torres. FAMILY PLANNING PERSPECTIVES. 16(3):134-138, May-June 1984.

'Illusory' savings as a result of California's FP copayment system. FAMILY PLANNING PERSPECTIVES. 15(6;):281-282, November-December 1983.

Female employment and reproductive behavior in Taiwan, 1980, by C. S. Stokes, et al. DEMOGRAPHY. 20(3):313, August 1983.

FAMILY PLANNING: HISTORY
The career of Margaret Sanger and its impact on the family planning movement, by L. Lampe. ORVOSI HETILAP. 125(4): 221-222, January 22, 1984.

FAMILY PLANNING: LAWS AND LEGISLATION
Family planning centres, sex therapists and the courts, by I. Freckelton. HEALTHRIGHT. 3:25-28, August 1984.

Fatal hemorrhage from legal abortion in the United States, by D. A. Grimes, et al. SURGERY, GYNECOLOGY AND OBSTET-RICS. 157(5):461-466, November 1983.

Law and family planning, by M. D. Kirby. MEDICAL JOURNAL OF AUSTRALIA. 140(6):356-362, March 17, 1984.

Legislation and teenage sex. BRITISH MEDICAL JOURNAL [CLIN RES]. 287(6408):1826, December 17, 1983.

Moralizing minority/chastity act, by J. Pasternak. GUARDIAN. 36(32):9, May 16, 1984.

Title X and its critics, by J. L. Rosoff, et al. FAMILY PLANNING PERSPECTIVES. 16(3):111-113; 115-116; 119, May-June 1984.

FAMILY PLANNING: MORTALITY AND MORTALITY STATISTICS
The impact of family planning on neonatal mortality, by J. C. Caceres-Baltazar. DISSERTATION ABSTRACTS INTER-NATIONAL: B. 45(6), December 1984.

FAMILY PLANNING: NATURAL
An automatic electronic device (Rite Time) to detect the onset of the infertile period by basal body temperature measurements, by J. P. Royston, et al. BRITISH JOURNAL OF OBSTETRICS AND GYNAECOLOGY. 91(6):565-573, June 1984.

Billings natural family planning method: correlation of subjec-tive signs with cervical mucus quality and ovulation, by J. J. Etchepareborda, et al. CONTRACEPTION. 28(5):475-480, 1983.

Birth control [natural family planning], by R. A. Jonas. MS. 13:54+, August 1984.

Few restrictions in natural family planning [letter], by H. P. Dunn. NEW ZEALAND MEDICAL JOURNAL. 97(760):498, July 25, 1984.

More about natural family planning, by J. Gallagher. AUS-TRALIAN FAMILY PHYSICIAN. 12(11):786-792, November 1983.

Natural family planning, by R. Rodriguez. REVISTA DE ENFERMAGEN. 6(62):12-19, October 1983.

Natural family planning as reflected in contemporary rabbinic response, by G. Ellinson. JEWISH SOCIAL STUDIES. 46:51-60, Winter 1984.

Natural family planning: a comparison of continuers and discontinuers, by K. J. Daly, et al. POPULATION AND ENVIRON-MENT. 6(4):231, Winter 1983.

Natural family planning; interview with Joseph A. Menezes, by T. O'Donnell. REGISTER. 60:1+, April 1, 1984.

Natural family planning (symptothermal method) and objective ovulation parameters— a pilot study, by G. Freundl, et al. GEBURTSHILFE UND FRAUENHEILKUNDE. 44(6):368-374, June 1984.

Natural family planning: a way of life, a way of love, by M. O'Malley. AFER. 25:356-361, December 1983.

Natural family planning in the Philippines, by J. E. Laing. STUDIES IN FAMILY PLANNING. 15:49-61, March-April 1984.

New products [Ovutest 77 Baby Computer (for natural family planning); PMT-eze (for prementrual tension and as a nutritional supplement for women using oral contraceptives); Synphasic (oral contraceptive), by L. Wray. HEALTHRIGHT. 3:35-38, May 1984.

A prospective multicentre trial of the ovulation method of natural family planning. III. Characteristics of the menstrual cycle and of the fertile phase. FERTILITY AND STERILITY. 40(6):773-778, December 1983.

—. IV. The outcome of pregnancy. World Health Organization. FERTILITY AND STERILITY. 41(4):593-598, April 1984.

The role of the clinician in natural family planning, by H. Klaus. JOURNAL OF AMERICAN COLLEGE HEALTH. 32(3):114-120, December 1983.

The shift from natural to controlled fertility: a cross-sectional analysis of ten Indian states, by S. J. Jejeebhoy. STUDIES IN FAMILY PLANNING. 15(4):191-198, July-August 1984.

The statistical evaluation of natural methods of family planning, by T. W. Hilgers. IRNFP. 8:226-264, Fall 1984.

Variations in historical natural fertility patterns and the measurement of fertility control, by P. R. Hinde, et al. JOURNAL OF BIOSOCIAL SCIENCE. 16(3):309-321, July 1984.

FAMILY PLANNING: PSYCHOLOGY AND PSYCHIATRY
The ethics of family planning, by M. F. Fathalla. WORLD HEALTH. June 1984, pp. 27-29.

FAMILY PLANNING: RESEARCH
Chinese family problems: research and trends, by Z. Wei. JOURNAL OF MARRIAGE AND THE FAMILY. 45(4):943-948, November 1983.

A school-, hospital- and university-based adolescent pregnancy prevention program. A cooperative design for service and research, by L. S. Zabin, et al. JOURNAL OF REPRODUCTIVE MEDICINE. 29(6):421-426, June 1984.

Trail blazing . . . in the area of family planning research, by T. Standley, et al. WORLD HEALTH. December 1983, pp. 8-10.

FAMILY PLANNING: RURAL
Fertility status and attitudes in a rural based industrial population in Rajasthan, by A. Narayan, et al. JOURNAL OF

FAMILY WELFARE. 30:30-34, September 1983.

FAMILY PLANNING: STATISTICS
Assessing cohort birth expectations data from the current population survey, 1971-1981, by M. O'Connell, et al. DEMOGRAPHY. 20(3):369, August 1983.

The baby boom and its explanations, by F. D. Bean. SOCIOLOGICAL QUARTERLY. 24:353-366, Summer 1983.

When family planning is necessary, by T. Harford. GUARDIAN. July 18, 1984, p. 23.

Young U. S. women delaying motherhood: 25 percent may remain childless. FAMILY PLANNING PERSPECTIVES. 15:224, September-October 1983.

FAMILY PLANNING: URBAN
Education and family planning in the urban sector, by N. I. Fernandez. HYGIE. 3(2):38-40, June 1984.

Family planning among the urban poor: sexual politics and social policy, by M. Cummings, et al. FAMILY RELATIONS. 32:47-58, January 1983.

FAMILY PLANNING AND COLLEGE STUDENTS
Attitudes of a group of Egyptian medical students towards family planning, by T. el-Mehairy. SOCIAL SCIENCE AND MEDICINE. 19(2):131-134, 1984.

A school-, hospital- and university-based adolescent pregnancy prevention program. A cooperative design for service and research, by L. S. Zabin. JOURNAL OF REPRODUCTIVE MEDICINE. 29(6):421-426, June 1984.

FAMILY PLANNING AND EDUCATION
Instructions on family planning at the ambulatory clinic of Nagasaki University Hospital: the current status of training in pessary use, by H. Hotta, et al. JOSANPU ZASSHI. 37(3): 209-211, March 1983.

Knowledge and attitudes toward sexuality and sex education of

a select group of older people, by M. M. Smith, et al. GERON-
TOLOGY AND GERIATRICS EDUCATION. 3(4):259-269,
Summer 1983.

My interactions with Mrs. Taki Hanyu, by S. Narabayashi.
JOSANPU ZASSHI. 37(3):197-201, March 1983.

Simulation modeling perspectives of the Bangladesh family
planning and female education system, by J. H. Teel, et al.
BEHAVIORAL SCIENCE. 29(3):145-161, July 1984.

Some observations on family planning education in China, by
M. V. Hamburg. HYGIE. 3(2):21-24, June 1984.

FAMILY PLANNING AND NURSES
Action now in family planning: the role of nurse, by A. K.
Malhotra, et al. NURSING JOURNAL OF INDIA. 75(2):27-28,
February 1984.

Developing family planning nurse practitioner protocols, by J.
W. Hawkins, et al. JOGN NURSING. 13(3):167-170, May-June
1984.

Family planning needs of adolescents, by C. Lane, et al. JOGN
NURSING. 13(2 Suppl):61S-65S, March-April 1984.

The family planning nurse: in the family way, part 1, by G. Rands.
NURSING TIMES. 80(13):28-30, March 28-April 3, 1984.

The family planning nurse: the present and future role of the
nurse in family planning, part 2, by A. Cowper. NURSING
TIMES. 80(13):31-33, March 28-April 3, 1984.

Family planning: a nurse's concern, by S. A. Samuel. NURSING
JOURNAL OF INDIA. 75(5):105-106, May 1984.

Medical societies vs. nurse practitioners, by P. Donovan.
FAMILY PLANNING PERSPECTIVES. 15(4):166-171,
July-August 1983.

Planning the family, by M. E. Rankin. NURSING. 2(19):543,
November 1983.

Teenagers and fertility control: legal and ethical issues for
doctors, by V. Wootten. HEALTHRIGHT. 3:6-9, February 1984.

What's new: can't make doctor pay for rearing unplanned child,
by A. Ashman. AMERICAN BAR ASSOCIATION JOURNAL.
70:138-139, September 1984.

FAMILY PLANNING AND PLANNED PARENTHOOD
No way for Planned Parenthood, by A. Singer. ALBERTA RE-
PORT. 11:40, June 25, 1984.

FAMILY PLANNING AND POLITICS
Dispute continues over federal help for world population control,
by J. Frawley. REGISTER. 60:1+, August 12, 1984.

Family planning centres, sex therapists and the courts, by I.
Freckelton. HEALTHRIGHT. 3:25-28, August 1984.

Governor Reagan, welfare reform and AFDC fertility, by D. E.
Keefe. SOCIAL SERVICE REVIEW. 57:234-253, June 1983.

U. N. defends tactics for population control, by F. Pearce. NEW
SCIENTIST. 103:4, August 9, 1984.

FAMILY PLANNING AND RELIGION
Christians and the state policy of family planning: attitudinal
change, by L. Dsilva. JOURNAL OF FAMILY WELFARE.
30:21-29, September 1983.

The ethics of family planning, by M. F. Fathalla. WORLD
HEALTH. June 1984, pp. 27-29.

Pope attacks government family planning methods. OUR
SUNDAY VISITOR. 73:8, June 24, 1984.

Religion and fertility: a replication, by W. D. Mosher. DEMOG-
RAPHY. 21(2):185, May 1984.

Religious preference, religions, participation and sterilization
decisions: findings from the National Survey of Family
Growth, cycle II, by K. W. Eckhardt, et al. REVIEW OF
RELIGIOUS RESEARCH. 25(3):232-246, March 1984.

Societal trends, church beliefs support NFP methods, by L.
Gallahue. HOSPITAL PROGRESS. 64(12):54-56; 60, December
1983.

FAMILY PLANNING AND WOMEN

Children: yes or no, a decision-making program for women, by
J. C. Daniluk, et al. PERSONNEL AND GUIDANCE JOURNAL.
62:240-242, December 1983.

Domestic group, status of women and fertility, by T. Patel.
SOCIAL ACTION. 32:363-379, October-December 1982.

Family planning among a group of coloured women, by A. Roux.
SOUTH AFRICAN MEDICAL JOURNAL. 65(22):898-901,
June 1984.

FAMILY PLANNING AND YOUTH

Adolescent pregnancy program stresses family counseling,
educational services, by B. A. McNeil, e t al. HOSPITAL
PROGRESS. 65(5):12-14; 31, May 1984.

Complementarity of work and fertility among young American
mothers, by F. L. Mott, et al. POPULATION STUDIES. 37(2):
239, July 1983.

Contraceptive continuation among adolescents attending family
planning clinics, by F. F. Furstenberg, Jr., et al. FAMILY
PLANNING PERSPECTIVES. 15(5):211-214; 216-217,
September-October 1983.

An evaluation of an adolescent family planning program, by N.
Ralph, et al. JOURNAL OF ADOLESCENT HEALTH CARE.
4(3):158-162, September 1983.

Family planning needs of adolescents, by C. Lane, et al. JOGN
NURSING. 13(2 Suppl):61S-65S, March-April 1984.

Legislation and teenage sex. BRITISH MEDICAL JOURNAL [CLIN
RES]. 287(6408):1826, December 17, 1983.

A new strategy for preventing unintended teenage childbearing. . .
social and welfare needs of disadvantaged adolescents must
be addressed, by J. G. Dryfoos. FAMILY PLANNING PERSPEC-

TIVES. 16(4):193-195, July-August 1984.

Teenage fertility in developed nations: 1971-1980, by C. F. Westoff, et al. FAMILY PLANNING PERSPECTIVES. 15:105-110, May-June 1983.

Teenagers and fertility control: legal and ethical issues for doctors, by V. Wootten. HEALTHRIGHT. 3:6-9, February 1984.

A theoretical analysis of antecedents of young couples' fertility decisions, by L. J. Beckman, et al. DEMOGRAPHY. 20:519-534, November 1983.

Transferring health and family planning service innovations to the public sector: an experiment in organization development in Bangladesh, by J. F. Phillips, et al. STUDIES IN FAMILY PLANNING. 15(2):62, March-April 1984.

Young U. S. women delaying motherhood: 25 percent may remain childless. FAMILY PLANNING PERSPECTIVES. 15:224, September-October 1983.

FAMILY PLANNING CLINICS
Contraceptive continuation among adolescents attending family planning clinics, by F. F. Furstenberg, Jr., et al. FAMILY PLANNING PERSPECTIVES. 15(5):211-214; 216-217, September-October 1983.

A focused approach to quality of care assessment in family planning, by N. Hirschhorn, et al. AMERICAN JOURNAL OF PUBLIC HEALTH. 74(8):825-829, August 1984.

Life of Mrs. Taki Hanyu, a leader in patient education in the use of pessary application, by K. Nakashige. JOSANPU ZASSHI. 37(3):187-196, March 1983.

Medical societies vs. nurse practitioners, by P. Donovan. FAMILY PLANNING PERSPECTIVES. 15(4):166-171, July-August 1983.

Planning sex: critics suspect the motives at Red Deer's family clinic, by T. Fennell, et al. ALBERTA REPORT. 11:43, March 19, 1984.

Postcoital intervention. A family-planning-clinic experience
of 213 cases, by G. T. Kovacs, et al. MEDICAL JOURNAL OF
AUSTRALIA. 141(7):425-426, September 29, 1984.

The role of the clinician in natural family planning, by H. Klaus.
JOURNAL OF AMERICAN COLLEGE HEALTH. 32:114-120,
December 1983.

The self-sustaining clinic [letter], by L. A. Villadsen. FAMILY
PLANNING PERSPECTIVES. 16(2):100, March-April 1984.

What's new: family planning clinics not required to squeal, by
A. Ashman. AMERICAN BAR ASSOCIATION JOURNAL.
70:140, March 1984.

FAMILY PLANNING COUNSELING
Adolescent pregnancy program stresses family counseling,
educational services, by B. A. McNeil, et al. HOSPITAL
PROGRESS. 65(5):12-14; 31, May 1984.

The family and marital consulting agency, by S. I. Markovich,
et al. SOVETSKOE ZDRAVOOKHRANENIE. (7):46-48, 1983.

FAMILY PLANNING FUNDING
A debate over sovereign rights [U. S. cuts off funds to family
planning agencies that promote abortion], by L. Lopez.
TIME. 124:34, August 20, 1984.

The effects of federal funding cuts on family planning services,
1980-1983, by A. Torres. FAMILY PLANNING PERSPEC-
TIVES. 16(3):134-138, May-June 1984.

The Family Planning Program and cuts in federal spending. 1.
Impact on state management of family planning funds, by
M. T. Orr. FAMILY PLANNING PERSPECTIVES. 15(4):176-
184, July-August 1983.

— . 2. Initial effects on the provision of services, by A. Torres.
FAMILY PLANNING PERSPECTIVES. 15(4):184-191, July-
August 1983.

House reauthorizes family planning funds. CONGRESSIONAL
QUARTERLY WEEKLY REPORT. 42:1438, June 16, 1984.

'Illusory' savings as a result of California's FP copayment system. FAMILY PLANNING PERSPECTIVES. 15(6):281-282, November-December 1983.

U. S. bucks the tide on birth control [decision to halt family planning funds for countries promoting abortion]. U. S. NEWS AND WORLD REPORT. 97:8, August 20, 1984.

U. S. switch on family planning raises fear about economic development: the new limits on use of U. S. funds by international groups that support abortions have buoyed right-to-life groups and worried population experts, by B. Stokes. NATIONAL JOURNAL. 16:1476-1479, August 4, 1984.

FAMILY PLANNING PROGRAMS
A decade of experience. POPULI. 10(1):36, 1983.

The impact of U. S. family planning programs on births, abortions and miscarriages, 1970-1979, by J. D. Forrest. SOCIAL SCIENCE AND MEDICINE. 18(6):461-465, 1984.

FERTILITY AND FERTILITY CONTROL
Coital techniques of fertility control: science or fiction?, by E. Browne. HEALTHRIGHT. 3:27-29, November 1984.

Factors affecting fertility control in India: a cross-sectional study, by K. Srinivasan, et al. POPULATION AND DEVELOPMENT REVIEW. 10:273-296, June 1984.

Fertility control in vas occluded rats and the biochemical effects of ascorbic acid feeding, by J. D. Sharma, et al. EXPERIMENTAL AND CLINICAL ENDOCRINOLOGY. 82(3):337-341, November 1983.

Lactation and fertility regulation, by V. Hull. HEALTHRIGHT. 3:17-21, August 1984.

Male migration, machismo, and conjugal roles: implications for fertility control in a mexican municipio, by R. E. Wiest. JOURNAL OF COMPARATIVE FAMILY STUDIES. 14(2):167-181, Summer 1983.

Marital fertility at older ages in Nepal, Bangladesh and Sri
Lanka, by J. P. Tan. POPULATION STUDIES. 37:433-444,
November 1983.

FERTILITY AND FERTILITY STATISTICS
The challenge of the future, by M. O'Connor. POPULI. 10(4):23-29,
1983.

Community characteristics, women's education, and fertility
in Peru, by M. Tienda. STUDIES IN FAMILY PLANNING.
15(4):162, July-August 1984.

Complementarity of work and fertility among young American
mothers, by F. L. Mott, et al. POPULATION STUDIES. 37(2):
239, July 1983.

Early signs of infertility, by B. Berg. MS. 12:68+, May 1984.

Effect of infant mortality on subsequent fertility of women in
Jordan: a life table analysis, by C. M. Suchindran, et al.
JOURNAL OF BIOSOCIAL SCIENCE. 16:219-230, April 1984.

Evaluation of the Olsen technique for estimating the fertility
response to child mortality, by J. Trussell, et al. DEMOG-
GRAPHY. 20(3):391-405, August 1983.

Fertility and pacification among the Mekranoti of central Brazil,
by D. Werner. HUMAN ECOLOGY. 11(2):227, June 1983.

Fertility and pension programs in LDCs: a model of mutual
reinforcement, by B. Entwisle, et al. ECONOMIC DEVELOP-
MENT AND CULTURAL CHANGE. 32:331-354, January 1984.

Fertility of Indian Tamil concentrations in Sri Lanka, by D. F. S.
Fernando. JOURNAL OF BIOSOCIAL SCIENCE. 15:333-338,
July 1983.

Fertility trends among overseas Indian populations, by A.
Muthiah, et al. POPULATION STUDIES. 37(2):273, July 1983.

Fertilizing ability of spermatozoa of rats treated with STS 557,
by P. K. Warikoo, et al. ARCHIVES OF ANDROLOGY. 11(2):
157-159, October 1983.

Fresh thinking on fertility. POPULI. 10(1):13, 1983.

House reauthorizes family planning funds. CONGRESSIONAL QUARTERLY WEEKLY REPORT. 42:1438, June 16, 1984.

Housing aspirations and fertility, by C. F. Hohm. SOCIOLOGY AND SOCIAL RESEARCH. 68:350-363, April 1984.

Income and other factors influencing fertility in China, by N. Birdsall, et al. POPULATION AND DEVELOPMENT REVIEW. 9:651-675, December 1983.

Infant mortality by socio-economic status for Blacks, Indians, and Whites— a longitudinal analysis of North Carolina, 1968-1977, by F. Bertoli, et al. SOCIOLOGY AND SOCIAL RESEARCH. 68:364-377, April 1984.

Infertility, and how its's treated, by R. W. Miller. FDA CONSUMER. 17(5):7, June 1983.

Modern fertility patterns: contrasts between the United States and Japan, by S. P. Morgan, et al. POPULATION AND DEVELOPMENT REVIEW. 10(1):19, March 1984.

Mortality levels and family fertility goals, by J. Y. Parlange, et al. DEMOGRAPHY. 20(4):535, November 1983.

New data on nuptiality and fertility in China, by J. C. Caldwell, et al. POPULATION AND DEVELOPMENT REVIEW. 10(1):71, March 1984.

Paths to zero population growth, by T. J. Espanshade. FAMILY PLANNING PESPECTIVES. 15:148-149, May-June 1983.

The rapid fertility decline in Guam natives, by S. L. Tung. JOURNAL OF BIOSOCIAL SCIENCE. 16:231-240, April 1984.

The regulation of American fertility: facts and misconceptions, by C. E. Welch, III. INTERNATIONAL JOURNAL OF WOMEN'S STUDIES. 7:273-281, May-June 1984.

Regulation of fertility and child health: a governmental option, by R. F. Mardones. REVISTA MEDICA DE CHILE. 111(5): 544-548, May 1983.

Return of ovulation and fertility in women using norethisterone oenanthate, by K. Fotherby, et al. CONTRACEPTION. 29(5): 447-455, May 1984.

Surprise contraceptive: Canadian zoologist stumbles upon compound to control male fertility, by R. Spence. EQUINOX. 3:16, January-February 1984.

Teenage fertility in developed nations: 1971-1980, by C. F. Westoff, et al. FAMILY PLANNING PERSPECTIVES. 15(3):105, May-June 1983.

Trends and differentials in Moslem fertility, by M. H. Nagi. JOURNAL OF BIOSOCIAL SCIENCE. 16:189-204, April 1984.

HYSTERECTOMY
Abdominal pregnancy following total hysterectomy, by V. K. Arora. INTERNATIONAL SURGERY. 68(3):253-255, July-September 1983.

Hysterectomies in one Canadian province: a new look at risks and benefits, by N. P. Roos. AMERICAN JOURNAL OF PUBLIC HEALTH. 74(1):39, January 1984.

Hysterectomy facilitates proceptive behavior in rats, by H. B. Ahdieh, et al. HORMONES AND BEHAVIOR. 17(1):134-137, March 1983.

Pre-operation indicators and post-hysterectomy outcome, by M. M. Tsoi, et al. BRITISH JOURNAL OF CLINICAL PSYCHOLOGY. 23(2):151-152, May 1984.

Progesterone-induced sequential inhibition of copulatory behavior in hysterectomized rats: relationship to neural cytoplasmic progestin receptors, by H. B. Ahdieh, et al. PHYSIOLOGY AND BEHAVIOR. 31(3):361-365, September 1983.

Reports conflict on link between hysterectomy, prior tubal sterilization. FAMILY PLANNING PERSPECTIVES. 15:229, September-October 1983.

Sterilization at the time of cesarean section: tubal ligation or hysterectomy?, by I. Bukovsky, et al. CONTRACEPTION. 28(4):349-356, October 1983.

Vaginal removal of the ovaries in association with vaginal hysterectomy, by C. V. Capen, et al. JOURNAL OF REPRODUCTIVE MEDICINE. 28(9):589-591, 1983.

MISCARRIAGE
Chorionic biopsy and miscarriage in first trimester [letter], by B. Gustavii. LANCET. 1(8376):562, March 10, 1984.

A common tragedy . . . miscarriage, by J. Moore. COMMUNITY OUTLOOK. June 1984, p. 210.

Doctors 'inoculate' against miscarriages, by J. Chomet. NEW SCIENTIST. 103:6, August 9, 1984.

Fetal loss and work in a waste water treatment plant, by R. W. Mortan, et al. AMERICAN JOURNAL OF PUBLIC HEALTH. 74(5):499-501, May 1984.

Herpesvirus suspect in nearly a third of miscarriages, by G. Morse. SCIENCE NEWS. 125:404, June 30, 1984.

The impact of U. S. family planning programs on births, abortions and miscarriages, 1970-1979, by J. D. Forrest. SOCIAL SCIENCE AND MEDICINE. 18(6):461-465, 1984.

Miscarriage, by P. A. Hillard. PARENTS MAGAZINE. 59(1):72; 75, January 1984.

Miscarriage: a common tragedy, by J. Moore. COMMUNITY OUTLOOK. June 13, 1984, p. 210.

"Miscarriage": a medico-legal analysis, by I. J. Keown. CRIMINAL LAW REPORTER. October 1984, pp. 604-614.

Post-TMI miscarriages may show stress. SCIENCE NEWS. 124:92, August 6, 1983.

Recurrence risk of neural tube defects following a miscarriage,

by H. S. Cuckle. PRENATAL DIAGNOSIS. 3(4):287-289,
October 1983.

Validation of questionnaire reported miscarriage malformation
and birth weight, by G. Axelsson, et al. INTERNATIONAL
JOURNAL OF EPIDEMIOLOGY. 13(1):94-98, March 1984.

Women's reactions to late miscarrage, stillbirth and perinatal
death, by A. Lovell. HEALTH VISITOR. 56(9):325-327,
September 1983.

OVARIECTOMY
Effects of ovariectomy, estrogen treatment and CI-628 on food
intake and body weight in female rats treated neonatally
with gonadal hormones, by T. P. Donohoe, et al. PHYSIOL-
OGY AND BEHAVIOR. 31(3):325-329, September 1983.

SEX AND SEXUALITY
An analysis of self-reported sexual behavior in a sample of
normal males, by A. E. Reading, et al. ARCHIVES OF SEXUAL
BEHAVIOR. 13(1):69-83, February 1984.

Family planning centres, sex therapists and the courts, by I.
Freckelton. HEALTHRIGHT. 3:25-28, August 1984.

Hepatic tumors induced by sex steroids, by E. T. Mays, et al.
SEMINARS IN LIVER DISEASE. 4(2):147-157, May 1984.

Sex advice to the rich nations, by J. Leo. TIME. 123:53, April 16,
1984.

Sex, contraception and parenthood: experience and attitudes
among urban black young men, by S. D. Clark, Jr., et al.
FAMILY PLANNING PERSPECTIVES. 16(2):77-82, March-
April 1984.

Sexual behavior and contraceptive practice at Oxford and Aberdeen Universities, by P. Anderson, et al. JOURNAL OF BIO-
SOCIAL SCIENCE. 16(2):287-290, April 1984.

Social anxiety, sexual behavior, and contraceptive use, by M. R.
Leary. JOURNAL OF PERSONALITY AND SOCIAL PSYCHOL-

OGY. 45(6):1347-1354, December 1983.

The uses of chastity and other paths to sexual pleasures, by G. Greer. MS. 12:53+, April 1984.

STERILIZATION
AID ignores food aid, pays for sterilizations, by J. J. Palmisano. NATIONAL CATHOLIC REPORTER. 20:4, December 23, 1984.

Asymptomatic omental herniation following laparoscopic sterilisation, by D. S. Rajapaksa. CEYLON MEDICAL JOURNAL. 28(1):35-36, March 1983.

Autoantibodies to zona pellucida in tubectomized women, by A. Mhaskar, et al. CONTRACEPTION. 29(1):75-82, January 1984.

Characteristics of women requesting reversal of sterilization, by W. A. Divers, Jr. FERTILITY AND STERILITY. 41(2):233-236, February 1984.

Damages and the 'unwanted child.' BRITISH MEDICAL JOURNAL [CLIN RES]. 288(6412):244-245, January 21, 1984.

Ectopic pregnancy subsequent to sterilization: histologic evaluation and clinical implications, by R. J. Stock, et al. FERTILITY AND STERILITY. 42(2):211-215, August 1984.

The effect of post partum sterilization on manifest anxiety, by R. S. Ammal. INDIAN JOURNAL OF CLINICAL PSYCHOLOGY. 10(2):305-307, September 1983.

The effect of post partum sterilization on the personality dimensions of extraversion-introversion and neutroticism-stability, by R. S. Ammal. INDIAN JOURNAL OF CLINICAL PSYCHOLOGY. 10(2):308-312, September 1983.

Effects of sterilization on menstrual pattern [letter], by K. Kennedy. AMERICAN JOURNAL OF OBSTETRICS AND GYNECOLOGY. 148(6):835, March 15, 1984.

Minilaparotomy under acupuncture analgesia, by P. L. Dias, et al.

JOURNAL OF THE ROYAL SOCIETY OF MEDICINE. 77(4): 295-298, April 1984.

Monitoring sterilization, by B. Hartmann, et al. NATION. 239: 98, August 18-25, 1984.

Pseudocyesis following sterilization: role of the pseudofather, by W. W. Weddington, Jr., et al. PSYCHOSOMATICS. 25(7):563-565, July 1984.

Psychiatric case detection in gynaecological patients, by P. J. Cooper, et al. PSYCHOTHERAPY AND PSYCHOSOMATICS. 40(1-4):246-256, 1983.

The results of epididymal ablation by sclerosing agents in the nonhuman primate, by R. W. Lewis, et al. FERTILITY AND STERILITY. 41(3):465-469, March 1984.

Reversal of female sterilization. Review of 252 microsurgical salpingo-salpingostomies, by E. Owen. MEDICAL JOURNAL OF AUSTRALIA. 141(5):276-280, September 1, 1984.

Risk factors, by C. Dyer. GUARDIAN. April 6, 1984, p. 12.

Sterilization, abortion a way of life, by T. Ackerman. REGISTER. 60:10, August 12, 1984.

What do we know about occupational sterility, abortion, and fetal abnormalities?, by M. Kringelbach, et al. UGESKRIFT FOR LAEGER. 145(43):3348-3351, October 24, 1983.

Sterilization, by W. R. J. JOURNAL OF FAMILY LAW. 20(4):781-784, August 1981-1982.

Sterilization and nidation [letter]. UGESKRIFT FOR LAEGER. 145(47):3676, November 21, 1983.

Sterilization-associated deaths: a global survey, by L. T. Strauss, et al. INTERNATIONAL JOURNAL OF GYNAECOLOGY AND OBSTETRICS. 22(1):67-75, February 1984.

Sterilization at the time of cesarean section: tubal ligation or hysterectomy?, by M. Bukovsky, et al. CONTRACEPTION. 28(4):349-356, 1983.

Sterilization: cross-country chaos, by D. Winn. SUNDAY TIMES. July 15, 1984, p. 36.

Sterilization has little effect on menstrual cycles. AMERICAN FAMILY PHYSICIAN. 29:262, March 1984.

Sterilization of women at a county hospital 1969-1981, by P. E. Bordahl, et al. TIDSSKRIFT FOR DEN NORSKE LAEGE-FORENING. 103(23):1618-1619, August 20, 1983.

Unwanted life. BRITISH MEDICAL JOURNAL [CLIN RES]. 289 (6444):565, September 1, 1984.

Wrongful birth and wrongful conception: the legal and moral issues, by P. Donovan. FAMILY PLANNING PERSPECTIVES. 16(2):64-69, March-April 1984.

AUSTRALIA
Sterilization in Canberra, by D. Lucas. JOURNAL OF BIO-SOCIAL SCIENCE. 16:335, 1984.

CHINA
Sterilization, abortion a way of life, by T. Ackerman. REGISTER. 60:10, August 12, 1984.

GREAT BRITAIN
Voluntary sterilization in North Tynesdie, by K. Carnegie-Smith. JOURNAL OF BIOSOCIAL SCIENCE. 16(2):249-257, April 1984.

HONDURAS
Sterilization in Honduras: assessing the unmet demand, by B. Janowitz, et al. STUDIES IN FAMILY PLANNING. 14(10):252, October 1983.

INDIA
And the poor get sterilized, by B. Hartmann, et al. NATION. 238:798-800, June 30, 1984.

UNITED STATES
Birth-control survey: sterilization tops list in U. S., by S. D. Kash. MS. 12:17, January 1984.

Human sterilization: emerging technologies and reemerging social issues. SCIENCE, TECHNOLOGY AND HUMAN VALUE. 9:8-20, Summer 1984.

Social and clinical correlates of postpartum sterilization in the United States, 1972 and 1980, by W. D. Mosher, et al. PUBLIC HEALTH REPORTS. 99:128-137, March-April 1984.

STERILIZATION: ATTITUDES
Issues in fertility control for mentally retarded female adolescents: II. Parental attitudes toward sterilization, by A. Passer, et al. PEDIATRICS. 73(4):451-454, April 1984.

STERILIZATION: COMPLICATIONS
Ask a lawyer: I had my fallopian tubes tied for sterilization but I still had a baby afterward. Can I sue the doctor?, by L. S. Dranoff. CHATELAINE. 57:28; 32, June 1984.

A new approach to measuring menstrual pattern change after sterilization, by J. A. Fortney, et al. AMERICAN JOURNAL OF OBSTETRICS AND GYNECOLOGY. 147(7):830-836, December 1, 1983.

STERILIZATION: DEVELOPING COUNTRIES
Small families: promoting population stabilization [in developing countries], by J. Jacobsen. TRANSNATIONAL PERSPECTIVES. 9(2):15-18, 1983.

STERILIZATION: FEMALE
Complications of female sterilization: immediate and delayed, by G. R. Huggins, et al. FERTILITY AND STERILITY. 41(3): 337-355, March 1984.

Issues in fertility control for mentally retarded female adolescents: II. Parental attitudes toward sterilization, by A. Passer, et al. PEDIATRICS. 73(4):451-454, April 1984.

Mental health and female sterilization. Report of a WHO collaborative prospective study. JOURNAL OF BIOSOCIAL SCIENCE. 16(1):1-21, January 1984.

Methodologic considerations in studies on female sterilization—a review for clinicans, by I. C. Chi, et al. CONTRACEPTION. 28(5):437-454, November 1983.

Microsurgical reversal of female sterilization, by J. G. Lauritsen. UGESKRIFT FOR LAEGER. 145(51):3976-3979, December 19, 1983.

Psychological consultations in regard to female sterilization and IUD contraception, by Y. W. Zhao. CHUNG HUA SHEN CHING SHEN KO TSA CHIH. 16(3):136-140, June 1983.

Psychological sequelae of female sterilization. LANCET. 2(8395): 144-145, July 21, 1984.

The regrets of sterilised women [letter]. LANCET. 2(8402):578-579, September 8, 1984.

Reversal of female sterilization. Review of 252 microsurgical salpingo-salpingostomies, by E. Owen. MEDICAL JOURNAL OF AUSTRALIA. 141(5):276-280, September 1, 1984.

The reversibility of female sterilization with the use of microsurgery: a report on 102 patients with more than one year of follow-up, by S. R. Henderson. AMERICAN JOURNAL OF OBSTETRICS AND GYNECOLOGY. 149(1):57-65, May 1, 1984.

STERILIZATION: INVOLUNTARY
Forced sterilization, by K. Safford. JUMP CUT. 29:37, February 1984.

Georgia Supreme Court invalidates involuntary sterilization statute, by T. D. Harper. JOURNAL OF THE MEDICAL ASSOCIATION OF GEORGIA. 72(11):795-797, November 1983.

Involuntary sterilizations considered. MENTAL AND PHYSICAL DISABILITY LAW REPORTER. 8(1):27, January-February 1984.

Carrie Buck's daughter [forced eugenic sterilization], by S. J. Gould. NATURAL HISTORY. 93:14-18, July 1984.

Current legal problems of sterilization, by A. Eser, et al. GYNA-KOLOGE. 15(2):62-71, June 1982.

Georgia Supreme Court invalidates involuntary sterilization statute, by T. D. Harper. JOURNAL OF THE MEDICAL ASSOCIATION OF GEORGIA. 72(11):795-797, November 1983.

Human sterilization: emerging technologies and reemerging social issues. SCIENCE, TECHNOLOGY AND HUMAN VALUE. 9:8-20, Summer 1984.

Mental health law— proposed legislation: involuntary sterilization of the mentally incompetent in Illinois. SOUTHERN ILLINOIS UNIVERSITY LAW JOURNAL. 1983:227-245, 1983.

Protection of the mentally retarded individual's right to choose sterilization: the effect of the clear and convincing evidence standard. CAPITAL UNIVERSITY LAW REVIEW. 12:413-438, Fall 1983.

'Wrongful birth' lawsuits raise complex social issues, by C. Cancila. AMERICAN MEDICAL NEWS. 26(38):2; 24, October 14, 1983.

STERILIZATION: MALE
The choice of sterilization: voluntarily childless couples, mothers of one child by choice, and males seeking reversal of vasectomy, by V. J. Callan, et al. JOURNAL OF BIOSOCIAL SCIENCE. 16(2):241-248, April 1984.

STERILIZATION: METHODS
Simple sterilization (methyl cranoacrylate injection), by K. Jenkins. MACLEANS. 97:48b, September 3, 1984.

Vasocllusion sterility induced by ethanol, prostagladin or as-corbic acid in male rats, by M. R. Chinoy, et al. ENDOCRINO-LOGIA EXPERIMENTALIS. 18(1):65-77, March 1984.

Postpartum sterilization and maternal mortality in Paarl
Hospital, by V. P. De Villiers. SOUTH AFRICAN MEDICAL
JOURNAL. 65(2):49-50, January 14, 1984.

STERILIZATION: PSYCHOLOGY AND PSYCHIATRY
Psychological consultations in regard to female sterilization
and IUD contraception, by Y. W. Zhao. CHUNG HUA SHEN
CHING CHING SHEN KO TSA CHIH. 16(3):136-140, June
1983.

Psychological sequelae of sterilisation [letter], by E. Lewis, et al.
LANCET. 2(8398):347, August 11, 1984.

STERILIZATION: RESEARCH
Chemosterilization of male tobacco budworm moths [Lepidop-
tera: Noctuidae); some effects on reproductive physiology,
by M. M. Cyrstal, et al. ANNALS OF THE ENTOMOLOGICAL
SOCIETY OF AMERICA. 75:634-639, November 1982.

Ovulatory function after microsurgical reversal of sterilization
in the rabbit, by A. Pellicer, et al. CLINICAL AND EXPERI-
MENTAL OBSTETRICS AND GYNECOLOGY. 11(1-2):6-10,
1984.

STERILIZATION: TECHNIQUES
Aid to stabilize hinged Strauch clamp during microvasovaso-
tomy, by M. Wosnitzer. UROLOGY. 24(2):168-169, August
1984.

Carbon dioxide laser in tubal microsurgery [letter], by G. M.
Grunert. AMERICAN JOURNAL OF OBSTETRICS AND
GYNECOLOGY. 148(1):117-118, January 1, 1984.

Clinical and histologic evaluation of laser reanastomosis of the
uterine tube, by J. K. Choe, et al. FERTILITY AND STERILITY.
41(5):754-760, May 1984.

Comparison of laparoscopic Falope-Ring and minilaparotomy
sterilization, by P. A. Sherman, et al. OBSTETRICS AND
GYNECOLOGY. 63(1):71-75, January 1984.

Comparison of the operating microscope and loupe for microsurgical tubal anastomosis: a randomized clinical trial, by J. A. Rock, et al. FERTILITY AND STERILITY. 41(2):229-232, February 1984.

Complications in a case of pregnancy interruption by the Aburel method, by S. Grigorov. AKUSHERSTOV I GINEKOLOGIIA. 22(5):406-408, 1983.

Complications in 8509 laparoscopic Falope ring sterilizations performed under local anaesthesia, by R. C. Pattinson, et al. SOUTH AFRICAN MEDICAL JOURNAL. 64(25):975-976, December 10, 1983.

Early readmission following elective laparoscopic sterilization: a brief analysis of a rare event, by I. Chi, et al. AMERICAN JOURNAL OF OBSTETRICS AND GYNECOLOGY. 148(3):322-327, February 1, 1984.

Effect of laparoscopic sterilization and insertion of multiload copper 250 and Progestasert intrauterine devices on serum ferritin levels, by T. H. Goh, et al. CONTRACEPTION. 28(4): 329-336, 1983.

Fallopian tube occlusion with silicone: radiographic appearance, by S. J. Dan, et al. RADIOLOGY. 151(3):603-605, June 1984.

The incidence of intrauterine abnormalities found at hystero-scopy in patients undergoing elective hysteroscopic steriliza-tion, by J. M. Cooper, et al. JOURNAL OF REPRODUCTIVE MEDICINE. 28(10):659-661, October 1983.

Laser-assisted vas anastomosis: a preliminary report, by C. M. Lynne, et al. LASERS IN SURGERY AND MEDICINE. 3(3): 261-263, 1983.

Liability for unsuccessful sterilization?, by O. Gritschneder. GEBURTSHILFE UND FRAUENHEILKUNDE. 43(7):469-471, July 1983.

A low-power magnification technique for the re-anastomosis of the vas— further results in a personal series of 125 patients, by D. Urquhart-Hay. AUSTRALIAN AND NEW ZEALAND

JOURNAL OF SURGERY. 54(1):73-74, February 1984.

Microsurgical tubal anastomosis: a controlled trial in four
Asian centers, by J. A. Rock, et al. MICROSURGERY. 5(2):
95-97, 1984.

Oestrogen deficiency following tubal ligation [letter], by J.
Cattanach. MEDICAL JOURNAL OF AUSTRALIA. 140(5):
309-310, March 3, 1984.

Oviduct occlusion by intraluminal thread and silver clips, by
S. L. Ding. CHINESE MEDICAL JOURNAL. 96(8):604-606,
August 1983.

Probability of requests for desterilization. Prospective study
of 50 cases, by R. Denjean, et al. JOURNAL DE GYNECOLOGIE,
OBSTETRIQUE ET BIOLOGIE DE LA REPRODUCTION. 12(4):
339-343, 1983.

Risk of serum hepatitis following laparoscopic sterilisation
[letter], by S. M. Athale. JOURNAL OF THE INDIAN
MEDICAL ASSOCIATION. 81(7-8):147-148, October 1983.

Risks of sterilization procedures [letter], by J. L. Pfenninger.
JOURNAL OF FAMILY PRACTICE. 18(1):28, January 1984.

Sterilization by colpoceliotomy, by W. Heidenreich. FORT-
SHCRITTE DER MEDIZIN. 101(41):1855-1859, November 3,
1983.

The surgical technic and vaso-vasostomy, by M. Andersen, et al.
UGESKRIFT FOR LAEGER. 145(39):3012-3013, September
26, 1983.

Total ligation syndrome. Does it exist?, by R. C. Strickler.
POSTGRADUATE MEDICINE. 75(1):233; 237, January 1984.

Vasovasostomy: current state of the art, by L. R. Cos, et al.
UROLOGY. 22(6):567-575, December 1983.

STERILIZATION: TUBAL
Animal experiments, morphologic and endocrinologic studies
following various coagulation technics, by H. H. Riedel, et al.

ZENTRALBLATT FUR GYNAEKOLOGIE. 105(24):1568-1584, 1983.

Button-hole technique of tubectomy, by L. N. Garg. JOURNAL OF INDIAN MEDICAL ASSOCIATION. 81(7-8):128-130, October 1983.

Clinical and histological evaluation of laser reanastomosis of the uterine tube, by J. K. Choe, et al. FERTILITY AND STERILITY. 41(5):754-760, May 1984.

Comparison of laparoscopic Falope-Ring and minilaparotomy sterilization, by P. A. Sherman, et al. OBSTETRICS AND GYNECOLOGY. 63(1):71-75, January 1984.

Comparison of three types of tubal sterilisation: the medan experience, by H. Sitompul, et al. CONTRACEPTION. 29(1): 55-63, January 1984.

Complications following postpartum sterilization by bilateral tubal ligation, by C. L. Cook, et al. JOURNAL OF THE KENTUCKY MEDICAL ASSOCIATION. 82(4):171-174, April 1984.

Complications of tubal sterilization [letter], by S. L. Corson. AMERICAN JOURNAL OF OBSTETRICS AND GYNE- COLOGY. 147(6):730-731, November 15, 1983.

Ectopic pregnancy after sterilization [letter], by F. DeStefano, et al. JAMA. 251(11):1432, March 16, 1984.

Endocrine findings in rabbits after sterilization with electro- coagulation, by H. H. Riedel, et al. JOURNAL OF REPRODUC- TIVE MEDICINE. 28(10):665-670, October 1983.

The evolution of tubal sterilization, by J. S. Seiler. OBSTETRIC- AL AND GYNECOLOGICAL SURVEY. 39(4):177-184, April 1984.

Experimental gynecological microsurgery, by S. S. Sorensen, et al. UGESKRIFT FOR LAEGER. 145(51):3984-3986, December 19, 1983.

Female sterilization under laparoscopic observation. Evaluation of two electrosurgical occlusive technics, by L. C. Uribe Ramirez, et al. GINECOLOGIA Y OBSTETRICA DE MEXICO. 50(306):265-271, October 1982.

Female sterilization with silicone tubal rings, by K. Heldaas, et al. TIDSSKRIFT FOR DEN NORSKE LAEGEFORENING. 103(31):2110-2112, November 10, 1983.

Hysteroscopic reversible tubal sterilization, by J. Hamou, et al. ACTA EUROPEA FERTILITY. 15(2):123-129, March-April 1984.

Hysteroscopic tubal occlusion with formed-in-place silicone plugs: a clinical review, by R. M. Houck, et al. OBSTETRICS AND GYNECOLOGY. 62(5):587-591, November 1983.

Immediate sequelae following tubal sterilization. A multicentre study of the ICMR Task Force on Female Sterilization. CONTRACEPTION. 28(4):369-384, October 1983.

The importance and technic of postpartum sterilization, by J. Poradovsky, et al. CESKOSLOVENSKA GYNEKOLOGIE. 48(10):748-751, December 1983.

Insertion of the laparoscopic Trocar without the use of carbon dioxide gas, by S. Pine, et al. CONTRACEPTION. 28(3):233-239, September 1983.

Interval Falope ring sterilization in the Cape Province: experience with 9175 cases over four years, by A. J. Nieuwoudt, et al. SOUTH AFRICAN MEDICAL JOURNAL. 64(25):972-974, December 10, 1983.

Laparoscopic clip sterilization in a free-standing facility: an evaluation of cost and safety, by T. Crist, et al. NORTH CAROLINA MEDICAL JOURNAL. 44(9):546-549, September 1983.

Laparoscopic sterilization during the puerperium employing electrocagulation. A retrospective study of 76 women, by B. Toft, et al. UGESKRIFT FOR LAEGER. 145(48):3731-3733, November 28, 1983.

Late complica et al. ACTA OBSTETRICIA ET GYNECOLOGICA
SCANDINAVICA. 63(2):149-151, 1984.

Late results in fallopian tubes studies on the Bleier clip, by H.
Jung, et al. GEBURTSHILFE UND FRAUENHEILKUNDE.
43(Suppl 1):67-69, June 1983.

Menstrual changes after tubal sterilization, by F. DeStefano, et
al. OBSTETRICS AND GYNECOLOGY. 62(6):673-681, December 1983.

Open forum: preferred method for tubal sterilization. INTER-
NATIONAL JOURNAL OF FERTILITY. 29(1):10-12, 1984.

Pelvic venous changes after tubal sterilization, by M. F. El-
Minawi, et al. JOURNAL OF REPRODUCTIVE MEDICINE.
28(10):641-648, October 1983.

Postpartum sterilization with the Filshie titanium silicon rubber
clip, by V. P. De Villiers, et al. SOUTH AFRICAN MEDICAL
JOURNAL. 64(25):977-978, December 10, 1983.

Povidone-iodine (Betadine) as prophylaxis against wound
infection in abdominal tubal ligation, by A. Khanna, et al.
INDIAN JOURNAL OF MEDICAL SCIENCE. 38(1):1-2, January
1984.

The practice of tubal sterilization: review of a departmental
practice pattern, by N. Gleicher, et al. MT. SINAI JOURNAL
OF MEDICINE. 51(2):157-160, April 1984.

Report of a high pregnancy rate after sterilization with the
Bleier clip, by N. C. Lee, et al. SOUTHERN MEDICAL
JOURNAL. 77(5):601-602, May 1984.

Reports conflict on link between hysterectomy, prior tubal
sterilization. FAMILY PLANNING PERSPECTIVES. 15:229,
September-October 1983.

Request for reversal of tubal sterilization. Survey conducted by
the National College of French Gynecologists and Obstetricians, by J. M. Antoine, et al. JOURNAL DE GYNECOLOGIE,

362

OBSTETRIQUE ET BIOLOGIE DE LA REPRODUCTION. 12(6): 583-591, 1983.

A second look at the Pomeroy method of tubal sterilization, by J. F. Spitaleri. NEW YORK STATE JOURNAL OF MEDICINE. 84(4):157-158, April 1984.

Self perception of women who elect tubal ligation, by G. Coutu-Wakulczyk. INFIRMIERE CANADIENNE. 26(3):26, March 1984.

Tubal lesions after sterilization [letter], by A. McCausland. FERTILITY AND STERILITY. 42(3):493-495, September 1984.

Tubal ligation and mini-laparotomy in an outpatient setting, by F. R. Hurlbutt, et al. HAWAII MEDICAL JOURNAL. 42(7):156-157, July 1983.

Tubal ligations and menstrual cycles, by E. Michaels. CHATE-LAINE. 57:20, June 1984.

Tubal polyps, epithelial inclusions, and endometriosis after tubal sterilization, by J. Donnez, et al. FERTILITY AND STERILITY. 41(4):564-568, April 1984.

Tubal rupture in a sterilized woman, by S, Kruger, et al. UGE-SKRIFT FOR LAEGER. 145(47):3667, November 21, 1983.

Tubal sterilization, by M. Dubois. REVUE MEDICALE DE LIEGE. 39(7):265-266, April 1, 1984.

Tubal sterilization among women of reproductive age, United States, update for 1979-1980, by V. I. Moses, et al. MMWR. 32(3):9SS-14SS, August 1983.

Tubal sterilization using laser coagulation, by P. Bailer. FORT-SHRITTE DER MEDIZIN. 101(43):1977, November 17, 1983.

Tubal sterilization performed in freestanding, ambulatory-care surgical facilities in the United States in 1980, by J. R. Greenspan, et al. JOURNAL OF REPRODUCTIVE MEDICINE. 29(4):237-241, April 1984.

Voluntary female sterilization: psychosocial motivations and effects, by E. Garcia Hassey, et al. GINECOLOGIA Y OBSTET-RICIA DE MEXICO. 50(307):310-305, November 1982.

Voluntary sterilization in North Tyneside, by K. Carnegie-Smith. JOURNAL OF BIOSOCIAL SCIENCE. 16:249-258, April 1984.

STERILIZATION AND CRIMINALS
Practice of using castration as sentence being questioned. CRIMINAL JUSTICE NEWSLETTER. 15(4):3-4, February 15, 1984.

South Carolina rapists given choice: castration or thirty years. CRIME VICTIMS DIGEST. 1(3):6, December 1983.

South Carolina rapists weigh choice: castration or thirty years. CORRECTIONS DIGEST. 14(25):9, November 30, 1983.

Castration for rapists criticized. THE NATIONAL SHERIFF. 36(1):32, February-March 1984.

STERILIZATION AND THE HANDICAPPED
Birth of handicapped child after negligent sterilisation, by D. Brahams. LANCET. 2(8403):649, September 15, 1984.

STERILIZATION AND HOSPITALS
The church and abortion, perception and reality, by P. Zagano. COMMONWEAL. 111:173-175, March 23, 1984.

Why should Catholic hospitals promote abortion, sterilization alternatives? HOSPITAL PROGRESS. 65:67-68, February 1984.

STERILIZATION AND THE MENTALLY RETARDED
Evaluation of mentally retarded persons for sterilization: contributions and limits of psychological consultation, by G. B. Melton, et al. PROFESSIONAL PSYCHOLOGY: RESEARCH AND PRACTICE. 15(1):34-48, February 1984.

Exclusive juvenile jurisdiction to authorize sterilization of incompetent minors. INDIANA LAW REVIEW. 16:835-860, 1983.

Issues in fertility control for mentally retarded female adolescents: II. Parental attitudes toward sterilization, by A. Passer, et al. PEDIATRICS. 73(4):451-454, April 1984.

Mental health law— proposed legislation: involuntary sterilization of the mentally incompetent in Illinois. SOUTHERN ILLINOIS UNIVERSITY LAW JOURNAL. 1983:227-245, 1983.

Mental illness— sterilization— due process. THE FAMILY LAW REPORTER: COURT OPINIONS. 9(49):2742, October 18, 1983.

Non-therapeutic sterilization of mentally retarded patients: yes in certain cases, under certain conditions, by A. Cole. UNION MEDICALE DU CANADA. 112(8):737-740, August 1983.

Procreation: a choice for the mentally retarded. WASHBURN LAW JOURNAL. 23:359-378, Winter 1984.

Protection of the mentally retarded individual's right to choose sterilization: the effect of the clear and convincing evidence standard. CAPITAL UNIVERSITY LAW REVIEW. 12:413-438, Fall 1983.

Sterilization of the mentally retarded. The rules change but the results remain the same, by R. M. Soskin. MEDICINE AND LAW. 2(3):267-276, 1983.

STERILIZATION AND PARENTAL CONSENT
Issues in fertility control for mentally retarded female adolescents: II. Parental attitudes toward sterilization, by A. Passer, et al. PEDIATRICS. 73(4):451-454, April 1984.

STERILIZATION AND PHYSICIANS
Ask a lawyer: I had my fallopian tubes tied for sterilization but I still had a baby afterward. Can I sue the doctor?, by L. S. Dranoff. CHATELAINE. 57:28; 32, June 1984.

The surgical solution: the writings of activist physicians in the early days of eugenical sterilization, by P. Reilly. PERSPECTIVES IN BIOLOGY AND MEDICINA. 26:637-656, Summer 1983.

Religious preference, religious participation, and sterilization decisions: findings from the National Survey of Family Growth, cycle 2, by K. W. Eckhardt, et al. REVIEW OF RELIGIOUS RESEARCH. 25:232-246, March 1984.

Vatican orders hospitals to stop tuballigations. OUR SUNDAY VISITOR. 72:8, December 11, 1983.

STERILIZATION AND RESEARCH
Why should Catholic hospitals promote abortion, sterilization alternatives? HOSPITAL PROGRESS. 65(2):67-68, February 1984.

STERILIZATION AND YOUTH
Exclusive juvenile jurisdiction to authorize sterilization of incompetent minors. INDIANA LAW REVIEW. 16:835-860, 1983.

Issues in fertility control for mentally retarded female adolescents: II. Parental attitudes toward sterilization, by A. Passer, et al. PEDIATRICS. 73(4):451-454, April 1984.

STERILIZATION FUNDING
Public funding of contraceptive, sterilization and abortion services, 1982, by B. Nestor, et al. FAMILY PLANNING PERSPECTIVES. 16(3):128-133, May-June 1984.

VASECTOMY
Cardiovascular disease and vasectomy. AMERICAN FAMILY PHYSICIAN. 28:304, October 1984.

Cardiovascular disease and vasectomy: findings from two epidemiologic studies, by M. J. Goldacre, et al. NEW ENGLAND JOURNAL OF MEDICINE. 308:805-808, April 7, 1983.

Counseling the patient for vasectomy, by A. E. Kilgore, Jr. AUAA J. 3(1):26, July-September 1982.

Decision for vasectomy— a case study, by S. R. Grover. JOURNAL OF FAMILY WELFARE. 30:49-55, December 1983.

Epithelial changes of the vas deferens after vasectomy and vasovasostomy in dogs, by N. Wright, et al. SCANNING ELECTRON MICROSCOPY. 1983(3):1435-1440, 1983.

Impairment of vas sympathetic nervous system and contractility following vasectomy in rat, by K. C. Kanwar, et al. INDIAN JOURNAL OF EXPERIMENTAL BIOLOGY. 21(11):585-586, 1983.

Knowledge, attitudes, and practice regarding vasectomy among residents of Hamilton County, Ohio, 1980, by C. A. Huether, et al. AMERICAN JOURNAL OF PUBLIC HEALTH. 74(1): 79-82, January 1984.

Long-term effect of vasectomy on coronary heart disease, by E. B. Perrin, et al. AMERICAN JOURNAL OF PUBLIC HEALTH. 74:128-132, February 1984.

The long-term effects of vasectomy on sexual behaviour, by P. L. Dias. ACTA PSYCHIATRICA SCANDINAVICA. 67(5):333-338, May 1983.

Long-term effects of vasectomy. 1. Biochemical parameters, by Z. Shikary, et al. CONTRACEPTION. 28(5):423-436, 1983.

Long-term vasectomy shows no association with coronary heart disease. JAMA. 252:1005, August 24, 1984.

Major study dispels fear of possible ahrm in vasectomy, by J. E. Brody. NEW YORK TIMES. November 15, 1983, p. C1.

Study of impotent men raises a question about vasectomy, by S. Stanik, et al. AMERICAN FAMILY PHYSICIAN. 28:180, August 1983.

Surgical and chemical vasectomy in the cat, by M. H. Pineda, et al. AMERICAN JOURNAL OF VETERINARY RESEARCH. 45(2):291-300, February 1984.

Vasectomies and health. DISCOVER. 5:11, January 1984.

Vasectomy and health: results from a large cohort study, by

F. J. Massey, Jr., et al. JAMA. 252:1023-1029, August 24, 1984.

Vasectomy and nonfatal myocardial infarction: continued observation indicates no elevation of risk, by A. M. Walker, et al. JOURNAL OF UROLOGY. 130(5):936-937, 1983.

Vasectomy failure using an open-ended technique, by M. Goldstein. FERTILITY AND STERILITY. 40(5):699-700, November 1983.

Vasectomy for contraception, by J. C. Rageth, et al. SCHWEIZERISCHE MEDIZINISCHE WOCHENSCHRIFT. 113(34):1191-1198, August 27, 1983.

Vasectomy/heart disease link questioned. RN. 46:19, September 1983.

Vasectomy in the framework of contraception, by H. Stamm, et al. GYNAEKOLFOGISCHE RUNDSCHAU. 24(2):85-97, 1984.

Vasectomy— safe and simple. POPULATION REPORTS. 11(5): D61, December 1983.

Vasectomy study. AMERICAN FAMILY PHYSICIAN. 29:383, January 1984.

Vasectomy— the unpopular choice, by J. C. Horn. PSYCHOLOGY TODAY. 18:17, June 1984.

VASOVASOSTOMY
The choice of sterilization: voluntarily childless couples, mothers of one child by choice, and males seeking reversal of vasectomy, by V. J. Callan, et al. JOURNAL OF BIOSOCIAL SCIENCE. 16(2):241-248, April 1984.

Experience with microsurgical two-layer vasovasostomy, by Y. Hirao, et al. HINYOKIKA KIYO. 29(4):385-393, April 1983.

Immunologic considerations before and after vasovasostomy, by E. F. Fuchs, et al. FERTILITY AND STERILITY. 40(4):497-499, October 1983.

Microsurgery for vasectomy reversal and vasoepididymostomy,

by S. J. Silber. UROLOGY. 23(5):505-524, May 1984.

Relationship of gross appearance of vas fluid during vasovasostomy to sperm quality, obstructive interval and sperm granuloma, by I. D. Sharlip, et al. JOURNAL OF UROLOGY. 131(4):681-683, April 1984.

Vasectomy reversal [letter]. MEDICAL JOURNAL OF AUSTRALIA. 140(11):681, May 26, 1984.

Vasectomy reversal. Review of 475 microsurgical vasovastomies, by E. Owen, et al. MEDICAL JOURNAL OF AUSTRALIA. 140(7):398-400, March 31, 1984.

Vasovasostomy in rabbits after vasectomy or vas occlusion by tantalum clip, by N. K. Lohiya, et al. JOURNAL OF REPRODUCTION AND FERTILITY. 71(1):243-248, May 1984.

Vasovasostomy: what to tell the patient who wants a vasectomy reversal, by D. T. Vetrosky, et al. PHYSICIAN ASSISTANT. 8(5):130; 132; 134+, May 1984.

AUTHOR INDEX

Gallahue, L. 132
Galliani, G. 39
Gandhi, M. 110
Garcia, A. L. 100
Garcia-De La Torre, I. 111
Garcier, F. 54
Gardner, M. J. 52
Garg, L. N. 22-23
Garg, S. K. 129
Garrison, 38
Gaspard, U. J. 28, 101, 105
Gates, D. 21
Gavin, W. F. 34
Geis, B. D. 109-110
Gellén, J. 22
Georgieva, V. 58
Gerais, A. S. 32
Gerasimovich, G. I. 56
Gerhard, I. 110
Gibbons, M. 116
Gibson, R. 97
Giges, N. 53
Gilchrist, L. D. 39, 140
Gillespie, L. 44
Gimes, R. 112
Gjorup, T. 30
Glantz, L. H. 82
Gleicher, N. 109
Godo, G. 61
Goffman, T. E. 143
Goh, T. H. 48
Gold, D. 75
Goldacre, M. J. 24
Goldenberg, R. L. 149
Goldhaber, S. Z. 105
Goldkamp, D. 79, 114, 126
Goldsmith, M. F. 107
Goldstein, M. S. 6, 40, 151
Goldstein, S. R. 137
Goldzieher, J. W. 68
Gollub, E. 29
Gombe, S. 123
Gookin, K. S. 33
Gordon, E. M. 75
Gordon, P. H. 121
Göretzlehner, G. 68
Gorins, A. 24

Gormley, M. J. 137
Gould, D. 87
Gould, K. H. 21
Gould, S. J. 24
Granberg, D. 8
Grant, E. 23
Grassler, W. 89
Green, W. 102
Greenspan, J. R. 145
Greer, G. 149
Greer, J. G. 116
Grice, G. C. 11
Grigorov, S. 33
Grimes, D. A. 60, 70, 81, 112
Grimmer, S. F. 48
Grisez, G. G. 41
Gritschneder, O. 82
Groll, M. 53
Grover, S. R. 42
Grunert, G. M. 24
Grzeniewski, L. 125
Gubhaju, B. 61
Gupta, I. 117
Gustavii, B. 29

Habermann, P. 46
Hagenfeldt, K. 44
Hagstad, A. 52
Hamburg, M. V. 133
Hamilton, J. 130
Hammerslough, C. R. 27
Hammond, G. L. 129
Hamou, J. 70
Hankins, G. D. 45
Hanski, W. 67
Hanssen, C. 24-25
Hanyu, T. 141
Hardie, L. 101
Hardy, E. E. 149
Harger, J. H. 55
Harper, T. D. 64
Harriman, L. 59
Harrison, F. 146
Hart, J. 8
Hartmann, B. 18
Harvey, P. D. 12

Haseltine, F. P. 149
Hassold, T. 102
Hatch, M. 102
Havranek, F. 12, 89
Hawkins, J. W. 44
Hayford, A. 14, 104
Hays, Charlotte, 24
Healy, J. B. 14
Healey, J. M. 8
Hebert, F. 93
Hecht, F. 14, 40
Heeren, H. J. 114
Heidam, L. Z. 133
Heidenreich, W. 135
Heinrich, J. F. 73
Heisterberg, L. 88
Heldaas, K. 60-61
Helmrich, S. P. 80
Hendershot, G. E. 31, 60, 86
Henderson, B. E. 66-67
Henderson, S. R. 123
Hennekens, C. H. 24
Henry, A. 43, 156
Henry, L. 132
Henry, N. F. 132
Henshaw, S. K. 10, 86, 96
Hentoff, N. 29
Herchak, G. 45
Hern, W. M. 128
Herold, E. S. 86
Herrmann, W. 51
Hertz, J. B. 44, 129-130
Hertz, R. 117
Hettiarachchy, N. S. 49
Hickler, L. 124
Higgins, J. J. 118
Higgins, J. 114
Higgins, K. 85
Higgs, R. 85
Hiilesmaa, V. K. 128-129
Hilgers, T. W. 135
Hill, M. F. 140
Hillard, P. A. 89
Hinde, P. R. 150
Hines, M. 111
Hirano, K. 96
Hirao, Y. 56

Hirschhorn, K. 64
Hirschhorn, N. 63
Hislop, T. G. 98
Hitchcock, J. F. 28
Ho, A. 90
Hobcraft, J. 28
Hodge, K. 139
Hofmann, A. D. 36
Hogue, C. J. 119
Hohm, C. F. 68
Holden, C. 113, 114, 155
Holder, L. 126
Holmes, P. 59
Holzgreve, W. 156
Homonnai, Z. T. 104
Hoodbhoy, N. 9
Hook, J. 7
Hopflinger, F. 36
Horan, F. 10
Horn, C. 68
Horn, J. C. 151
Horowitz, I. L. 133
Hosken, F. D. 41
Hotta, H. 76
Houck, R. M. 70
Hsieh, C. C. 97
Huang, N. H. 10
Huang, S. C. 127
Hubbard, B. J. 107
Hubbard, H. J. 122
Huether, C. A. 79-80
Huffmann, S. L. 43-44
Huggins, G. R. 33
Hughes, G. R. 142
Huisjes, H. J. 25
Huisveld, I. A. 48
Hull, R. G. 15
Hull, V. J. 122
Hull, V. 80
Hulme, H. 141
Humble, C. G. 106
Hunt, G. W. 97
Hunter, N. 137
Hurlbutt, F. R. 144-145
Hutapea, H. 11
Hyde, H. J. 6, 69